Getting Started with SIOP®

Pearson partners with hundreds of school districts like yours to help educators learn the SIOP® Model, implement it in their classrooms, build capacity throughout the district, and close the achievement gap with English learners and struggling students.

Our proven professional development includes everything your district needs to get started with the SIOP® Model and get results in alignment with your district's objectives and resources.

We provide your teachers and administrators with the training and support needed to learn and implement the SIOP® Model successfully. The first step is for all district and school leaders to learn about the SIOP® Model. The next step is to provide teachers with professional development in implementing the SIOP® Model. Continued support inside the classroom is available with our SIOP® Lesson Coaching and Modeling services.

Books in the SIOP® Model Series

Trusted by more than 600,000 educators, this ground-breaking series is a must-have for anyone working with English learners and with ALL students in need of an empirically-based instructional model to improve student achievement and get our students college and career ready. Teachers, professional development coordinators, coaches, and administrators now have access to a wealth of indispensable resources that will help them effectively implement the SIOP® Model in any classroom.

The SIOP® Model Series will help you build a sustainable sheltered instruction model to help all students succeed and meet federal and AYP requirements. The SIOP® Model Series is intended for mainstream classrooms, and supports progress in language skills and content knowledge for all students.

This series of books helps teachers plan and deliver lessons while keeping student language needs in mind.
Language is the vehicle for learning, so students acquire academic knowledge as they develop English language proficiency.

"After only one year of SIOP® training, students achieved measurable gains on the Missouri Assessment Program (MAP). From 2006 to 2007, our teachers went through the first four components of the SIOP® Model. When our state test scores came back, it confirmed our teachers' belief that this is a really good process that's making a difference in students' lives."

- Ronald Tucker; Principal, Bayless Junior High; Bayless, Missouri

ALWAYS LEARNING   PEARSON

SIOP® support that's right for your district, only from Pearson

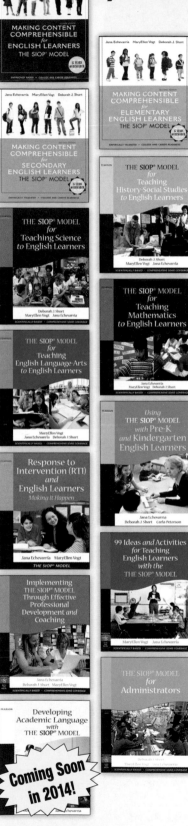

Making Content Comprehensible for English Learners:
The SIOP® Model, 4/e (with PDToolkit)
ISBN: 9780132689724 • ©2013 • 288 pp.

Making Content Comprehensible for Elementary English Learners:
The SIOP® Model, 2/e (with PDToolkit)
ISBN: 9780133362602 • ©2014 • 368 pp.

Making Content Comprehensible for Secondary English Learners:
The SIOP® Model, 2/e (with PDToolkit)
ISBN: 9780133362770 • ©2014 • 368 pp.

The SIOP® Model for Teaching History–Social Studies to English Learners
ISBN: 9780205627615 • ©2011 • 240 pp.

The SIOP® Model for Teaching Science to English Learners
ISBN: 9780205627592 • ©2011 • 240 pp.

The SIOP® Model for Teaching Mathematics to English Learners
ISBN: 9780205627585 • ©2010 • 192 pp.

The SIOP® Model for Teaching English Language-Arts to English Learners
ISBN: 9780205627608 • ©2010 • 216 pp.

Using The SIOP® Model with Pre-K and Kindergarten English Learners
ISBN: 9780137085231 • ©2012 • 144 pp.

Response to Intervention (RTI) and English Learners: Making it Happen
ISBN: 9780137048908 • ©2011 • 168 pp.

99 Ideas and Activities for Teaching English Learners with The SIOP® Model
ISBN: 9780205521067 • ©2008 • 208 pp.

Implementing The SIOP® Model Through Effective
Professional Development and Coaching
ISBN: 9780205533336 • ©2008 • 208 pp.

The SIOP® Model for Administrators
ISBN: 9780205521098 • ©2008 • 120 pp.

Schools and districts save 25%! To place your order, visit k12oasis.pearson.com
Individuals order online and receive free shipping at www.allynbaconmerrill.com
To learn more, call 1-800-348-4474, option 2
Find your Pearson sales representative: www.allynbaconmerrill.com/store/sales.aspx

ALWAYS LEARNING   PEARSON

Full Suite of SIOP® Professional Development Services

SIOP Services for Teachers

SIOP® Training for Teachers
This training gives educators an in-depth understanding of the components of the SIOP® Model and strategies to implement it in their schools and classrooms. We also offer SIOP® Training for Elementary Teachers and SIOP® Training for Secondary Teachers.

Implementation options: 3 days face-to-face, facilitated Virtual Institute, or self-paced Online Workshop.

SIOP® for Mathematics Teachers
This training gives educators an in-depth understanding of the components of the SIOP® Model for use in mathematics classrooms and strategies to implement it in their schools and classrooms. (3 days)

SIOP® Component Enrichment (8 Components)
This training helps educators deepen their understanding of the features of each component of the SIOP® Model. Prerequisite: SIOP® Training for Teachers.

Implementation options: 1 day face-to-face, or a self-paced Online Workshop.

SIOP® Mathematics Component Enrichment
Each one-day session helps educators build a deeper understanding of three SIOP® components for use in mathematics classrooms. Prerequisite: SIOP® Training for Teachers.

SIOP® English/Language Arts Component Enrichment
Each one-day session helps educators build a deeper understanding of three SIOP® components for use in English/Language Arts classrooms. Prerequisite: SIOP® Training for Teachers. (1 day)

SIOP® Lesson Coaching and Modeling
This job-embedded professional development supports teachers in planning, delivering, and observing lessons using the SIOP® Model. (5 days)

SIOP® Observation and Feedback
This training includes a SIOP® consultant observing 4 teachers per day and completing the SIOP® protocol to provide feedback and coaching. Prerequisite: SIOP® Training for Teachers. (1 day)

For more information about Virtual Institutes, please contact your
Pearson sales representative at **www.allynbaconmerrill.com/store/sales.aspx**

Full Suite of SIOP® Professional Development Services

SIOP Services for Leaders and Coaches

SIOP® Training for Administrators

Administrators learn about the SIOP® Model, how to support teachers using the Model, and how SIOP can have a positive impact on teaching all students, especially English learners.

 Implementation options: 1 day face-to-face, or facilitated Virtual Institute.

SIOP® Coaching and Implementation

This training helps districts develop effective SIOP® coaches and learn to successfully use the SIOP® Model in coaching sessions to improve classroom instruction. (2 days)

SIOP® Coaching and Observation

This training helps SIOP® coaches become effective by developing skills to support their SIOP® delivery and instruction. (2 days) Prerequisite: SIOP® Coaching and Implementation

Response to Intervention for English Learners

Coaches and Leaders will understand specific considerations, interventions, and instruction for English learners (ELs) in the RTI process.

Implementation options: 3 days face-to-face, or facilitated Virtual Institute.

SIOP® Inter-rater Reliability

Administrators and coaches will learn how to use the observation protocol to establish common standards of effective classroom lessons and rate the quality of instruction and the effectiveness of SIOP® implementation across the school or district. (2 days)

Pearson School Achievement Services is now an approved IACET provider.

Let's discuss what a SIOP® implementation plan might look like for your school or district.

f **t** siop.pearson.com   www.PearsonPD.com/SIOP | 1.877.637.1604 | info@PearsonPD.com

ALWAYS LEARNING   PEARSON

second edition

Making Content Comprehensible for Elementary English Learners: The SIOP® Model

JANA ECHEVARRÍA

California State University, Long Beach

MARYELLEN VOGT

California State University, Long Beach

DEBORAH J. SHORT

Academic Language Research & Training, Arlington, VA

PEARSON

Boston   Columbus   Indianapolis   New York   San Francisco   Upper Saddle River
Amsterdam   Cape Town   Dubai   London   Madrid   Milan   Munich   Paris   Montreal   Toronto
Delhi   Mexico City   São Paulo   Sydney   Hong Kong   Seoul   Singapore   Taipei   Tokyo

Vice President, Editor-in-Chief: Aurora Martínez Ramos
Associate Sponsoring Editor: Barbara Strickland
Editorial Assistant: Katherine Wiley
Senior Marketing Manager: Christine Gatchell
Senior Production Editor: Janet Domingo
Editorial Production Service: Cenveo® Publisher Services
Manufacturing Buyer: Megan Cochran
Electronic Composition: Cenveo® Publisher Services
Interior Design: Cenveo® Publisher Services
Cover Designer: Jennifer Hart

Credits and acknowledgments borrowed from other sources and reproduced, with permission, in this textbook appear on the appropriate page within the text.

Many of the designations by manufacturers and sellers to distinguish their products are claimed as trademarks. Where those designations appear in this book, and the publisher was aware of a trademark claim, the designations have been printed in initial caps or all caps.

Photo Credits: Cover: Apollofoto/Shutterstock, Stockyimages/Shutterstock, Rob Marmion/Shutterstock, Kalmatsuy Tatyana/Shutterstock, Andresr/Shutterstock, Tetra Images/Corbis; Insert: Stevecoleimages/ iStockphoto, Ryan McVay/Photodisc/Getty Images, Monkeybusinessimages/iStockphoto, Chris Schmidt/ iStockphoto; p. xxi, Courtesy of Jana Echevarria, Courtesy of MaryEllen Vogt, Courtesy of Deborah J. Short; p. 2, Hill Street Studios/Blend Images/Alamy; p. 27, Annie Fuller/Pearson Education; p. 65, Monkey Business/Fotolia; p. 96, Michael Austen/Alamy; p. 116, Corbis Flirt/Alamy; p. 144, Ron Nickel/ Design Pics Inc./Alamy; p. 170, Creative Imaging Photography/Alamy; p. 191, Erik Isakson/Tetra Images/ Alamy; p. 210, Christopher Futcher/iStockphoto; p. 238, Comstock/Jupiter Images; p. 260, Bob Daemmrich/Alamy; p. 279, Ariel Skelley/Blend Images/Alamy.

10 9 8 7 6 5 4 3 2 1

ISBN 10: 0-13-336260-4
ISBN 13: 978-0-13-336260-2

For my husband, Casey Vose, for his generosity, support, and love.
JE

To my children and grandchildren: Scott, Kevin, Jeff, Karlin,
Kyndal, Kameron, True, Arik, and Emerson, for their inspiration.
MEV

In memory of my dad, John M. Short, who taught me to love teaching.
DJS

Contents

Preface and Acknowledgments   xi

1 Introducing the SIOP® Model   1

Content and Language Objectives   1
Background on English Learners   3
   Demographic Trends   3
   Diverse Characteristics   4
   Achievement Gaps   7
School Reform, Standards, and Accountability   9
Academic Language and Literacy   10
   Relationship to Second Language Learning   11
   Role in Schooling   11
   Research on Academic Language and Literacy   12
Effective Instructional Practice for English Learners: The SIOP® Model   14
   Content-based ESL and Sheltered Content Instruction   15
   Research and Development of the Sheltered Instruction Observation Protocol (SIOP®) Model   17
   Effective SIOP® Model Instruction   19
Implementing the SIOP® Model   23
Summary   23
Discussion Questions   24

2 Lesson Preparation   26

Content and Language Objectives   26
Background   27
SIOP® Feature 1: Content Objectives Clearly Defined, Displayed, and Reviewed with Students   28
SIOP® Feature 2: Language Objectives Clearly Defined, Displayed, and Reviewed with Students   30
Writing Content and Language Objectives   33
SIOP® Feature 3: Content Concepts Appropriate for Age and Educational Background   40
SIOP® Feature 4: Supplementary Materials Used to a High Degree   41
SIOP® Feature 5: Adaptation of Content to All Levels of Student Proficiency   43
SIOP® Feature 6: Meaningful Activities That Integrate Lesson Concepts with Language Practice Opportunities   45
Teaching Ideas for Lesson Preparation   46
Differentiating Ideas for Multi-level Classes   49

Rating Lessons with the SIOP® Protocol   51

The Lesson   51

    The Gold Rush (Fourth Grade)   51

Teaching Scenarios   52

Discussion of Lessons   57

Summary   62

Discussion Questions   63

3   Building Background   64

Content and Language Objectives   64

Background   65

SIOP® Feature 7: Concepts Explicitly Linked to Students' Background Experiences   66

    Something to Think About   68

SIOP® Feature 8: Links Explicitly Made between Past Learning and New Concepts   68

SIOP® Feature 9: Key Vocabulary Emphasized   69

    Academic Vocabulary   69

    One, Two, and Three Tier Words   72

    Word Consciousness   74

    Teaching Academic Vocabulary   75

Teaching Ideas for Building Background   76

Differentiating Ideas for Multi-level Classes   84

The Lesson   84

    Short Story: *Two Were Left* (Sixth Grade)   84

Teaching Scenarios   85

Discussion of Lessons   90

Summary   93

Discussion Questions   94

4   Comprehensible Input   95

Content and Language Objectives   95

Background   97

SIOP® Feature 10: Speech Appropriate for Students' Proficiency Levels   97

SIOP® Feature 11: Clear Explanation of Academic Tasks   99

SIOP® Feature 12: A Variety of Techniques Used to Make Content Concepts Clear   101

Teaching Ideas for Comprehensible Input   104

Differentiating Ideas for Multi-level Classes   104

The Lesson   105

    Economics: Natural Resources and Products (Third Grade)   105

Teaching Scenarios   106

Discussion of Lessons   110

Summary   113
Discussion Questions   113

5 Strategies   115

Content and Language Objectives   115
Background   116
SIOP® Feature 13: Ample Opportunities Provided for Students to Use Learning Strategies   117
    Things to Remember about Teaching Learning Strategies   119
SIOP® Feature 14: Scaffolding Techniques Consistently Used, Assisting and Supporting Student Understanding   120
    Three Types of Scaffolding   121
SIOP® Feature 15: A Variety of Questions or Tasks That Promote Higher-Order Thinking Skills   124
Teaching Ideas for Strategies   126
Differentiating Ideas for Multi-level Classes   129
The Lesson   130
    Saving Our Planet (Fifth Grade)   131
Teaching Scenarios   131
Discussion of Lessons   138
Summary   141
Discussion Questions   141

6 Interaction   143

Content and Language Objectives   143
Background   145
    Mainstream Lesson   146
    SIOP® Model Lesson   147
SIOP® Feature 16: Frequent Opportunities for Interaction and Discussion   149
    Oral Language Development   149
SIOP® Feature 17: Grouping Configurations Support Language and Content Objectives of the Lesson   153
SIOP® Feature 18: Sufficient Wait Time for Student Responses Consistently Provided   156
SIOP® Feature 19: Ample Opportunity for Students to Clarify Key Concepts in L1   157
Teaching Ideas for Interaction   157
Differentiating Ideas for Multi-level Classes   159
The Lesson   160
    Addition and Subtraction (First Grade)   160
Teaching Scenarios   161
Discussion of Lessons   164
Summary   167
Discussion Questions   167

7 Practice & Application 169

Content and Language Objectives 169

Background 170

SIOP® Feature 20: Hands-On Materials and/or Manipulatives Provided for Students to Practice Using New Content Knowledge 172

SIOP® Feature 21: Activities Provided for Students to Apply Content and Language Knowledge 173

SIOP® Feature 22: Activities Integrate All Language Skills 174

Teaching Ideas for Practice & Application 176

Differentiating Ideas for Multi-level Classes 177

The Lesson 179

   Weather (Second Grade) 179

Teaching Scenarios 179

Discussion of Lessons 185

Summary 188

Discussion Questions 188

8 Lesson Delivery 190

Content and Language Objectives 190

Background 191

SIOP® Feature 23: Content Objectives Clearly Supported by Lesson Delivery 191

SIOP® Feature 24: Language Objectives Clearly Supported by Lesson Delivery 192

   Meeting Content and Language Objectives 192

SIOP® Feature 25: Students Engaged Approximately 90% to 100% of the Period 193

SIOP® Feature 26: Pacing of the Lesson Appropriate to Students' Ability Levels 195

The Relationship Between Lesson Preparation and Lesson Delivery 197

Teaching Ideas for Lesson Delivery 198

Differentiating Ideas for Multi-level Classes 199

The Lesson 200

   The Gold Rush (Fourth Grade) 200

Teaching Scenarios 200

Discussion of Lessons 204

Summary 207

Discussion Questions 208

9 Review & Assessment 209

Content and Language Objectives 209

Background 210

   Classroom Context and the Review & Assessment Component 211

   Formative and Summative Assessment 212

Informal Assessment   212

Formal Assessment   213

SIOP® Feature 27: Comprehensive Review of Key Vocabulary   213

SIOP® Feature 28: Comprehensive Review of Key Content Concepts   215

SIOP® Feature 29: Regular Feedback Provided to Students on Their Output   216

SIOP® Feature 30: Assessment of Student Comprehension and Learning
of All Lesson Objectives throughout the Lesson   218

Teaching Ideas for Review & Assessment   219

Differentiating Ideas for Multi-level Classes   223

The Lesson   224

Measurement and Geometry: Concepts of shorter/taller; lighter/heavier;
holds less/holds more (Kindergarten)   224

Teaching Scenarios   225

Discussion of Lessons   231

Summary   235

Discussion Questions   235

10 Issues of Reading, RTI, and Special Education for English Learners   237

Content and Language Objectives   237

Issues of Reading Development and Assessment   238

Estimating Students' Reading Levels   241

English Learners and the Common Core State Standards for Reading, Writing, Listening,
and Speaking   244

Assisting Struggling Learners: Response to Intervention   246

Issues Related to Special Education   248

Special Education Services: When Are They Appropriate?   251

Search for Intervention Rather Than Disability   254

Teaching Ideas for Students with Special Needs   255

Summary   256

Discussion Questions   257

11 Effective Use of the SIOP® Protocol   259

Content and Language Objectives   259

Best Practice in Using the SIOP® Protocol   260

Scoring and Interpreting the SIOP® Protocol   261

Assigning Scores   262

Not Applicable (NA) Category   263

Calculating Scores   264

Sample Lesson   265

Using SIOP® Scores and Comments   268

Reliability and Validity of the SIOP®   277

Summary   277

Discussion Questions   277

12 Frequently Asked Questions: Getting Started with the SIOP® Model   278

Content and Language Objectives   278

General SIOP Questions   279

Questions about Getting Started with the SIOP® Model in the Classroom   280

Questions about Schoolwide Implementation of the SIOP® Model   282

Appendix A   The Sheltered Instruction Observation Protocol (SIOP®)   286

Appendix B   Lesson Plans   294

Appendix C   Research on the Sheltered Instruction Observation Protocol (SIOP®) Model   300

Appendix D   SIOP® Professional Development Resources   306

Glossary   309

References   315

Index   335

Welcome to the SIOP Model! This book has been designed especially for you as an elementary school educator, and we hope that it will soon be marked up and stuffed with sticky notes, and that it will become a valuable resource to you as you strive to become a high-implementing SIOP teacher. As you read, you will find K–6 lesson plans, teaching ideas, and many effective activities for working with children who are English learners. Our recent research confirms that the SIOP Model makes a positive difference academically for all students, so what works well for English learners will work equally well with your other students.

For those of you who teach pre-K or kindergarten, you also might wish to read *Using the SIOP® Model with Pre-K and Kindergarten English Learners* (Echevarría, Short, & Peterson, 2012). It was written specifically for those of you who are early childhood educators, and you'll find many more helpful suggestions, lessons plans, and activities in this book.

If you or your colleagues have read the K–12 text, *Making Content Comprehensible for English Learners: The SIOP® Model* (4th edition, 2013), you will note that this SIOP text for elementary educators and the SIOP text for secondary educators are parallel to the K–12 SIOP book. This is intentional so that educators can select the book that is most appropriate for the students they teach. Having the parallel texts also provides district SIOP leaders and university professors with the opportunity to work with teachers across grade levels while using all three books, since the essential information about teaching with the SIOP Model is consistent from book to book (4th edition of *Making Content Comprehensible* and 2nd editions of elementary and secondary SIOP texts). What differs in the books are the SIOP lesson plans and many of the teaching ideas that are targeted for the specific grade level(s) of students.

It is hard to believe that over 15 years have passed since we first began our journey with the SIOP Model. In the beginning, it would have been difficult to fathom that at this time, the SIOP Model would be implemented in districts throughout all 50 states in the United States, and in dozens of countries. Whether you are already familiar with the SIOP Model or are just now learning about the SIOP, we hope that you will find this second edition to be informative, helpful, and, most important, beneficial to the English learners and other students with whom you work. When we began our research, we recognized the need for a comprehensive, well-articulated model of instruction for preparing teachers to work with English learners. From this need, the Sheltered Instruction Observation Protocol (SIOP®) was created. Now, with the widespread use of the SIOP Model throughout the country—and in numerous countries around the world—we have since written 12 additional books on topics related to SIOP implementation. (See Appendix D.)

Our work on the SIOP Model began with reviewing the literature and examining district-produced guidelines for English learners to find agreement on a definition of sheltered instruction, also known as SDAIE (Specially Designed Academic Instruction in English) in some regions. A preliminary observation protocol was drafted and field-tested with sheltered teachers. A research project through the Center for Research on Education, Diversity, & Excellence (CREDE) enabled us to engage in an intensive refinement process and to use the SIOP Model in a sustained professional development effort with teachers on both the East and West Coasts. Through this process of classroom observation, coaching, discussion, and reflection, the instrument was refined and changed, and eventually it evolved into the Sheltered Instruction Observation Protocol, or as it has come to be known, the SIOP® (pronounced sī-ŏp). The SIOP operationalizes sheltered instruction by offering teachers a model for lesson planning and implementation that provides English learners with access to grade-level content standards. By providing this access, we help prepare students for life after high school as well, in colleges or careers.

Although over the years a number of approaches to teaching English learners have emerged, at present, the SIOP remains the only research-validated model of sheltered instruction. In fact, because of its applicability across content areas, the national Center for Research on the Educational Achievement and Teaching of English Language Learners (CREATE) used the SIOP Model as a framework for comprehensive schoolwide intervention in its research aimed to improve the achievement of English learners in middle school. The SIOP Model is now being implemented at all levels of education from pre-K to community colleges and universities. It is used in sheltered content classes, dual language programs, content-based ESL classes, special education, and general education classrooms.

Since the first edition of this book was published, we have continued to develop and refine the SIOP Model, but we have not changed the eight components and 30 features. They have withstood the test of time. In our work with thousands of teachers and administrators throughout the country, our own understanding of effective sheltered instruction and the needs of English learners has grown substantially. We believe, and our research confirms, that when teachers consistently and systematically implement the SIOP Model's 30 features in lessons for English learners and English speakers alike, the result is high-quality, effective instruction and improvement of student achievement.

As the authors of this book, we have approached our teaching, writing, and research from different and complementary fields. Jana Echevarría's research and publications have focused on issues in the education of English learners, and on English learners with special education needs, as well as on professional development for regular and special education teachers. MaryEllen Vogt's publications focus primarily on improving reading instruction, including improving comprehension in the content areas, content literacy for English learners, and teacher change and development. Deborah Short is a researcher and former sheltered instruction teacher with expertise in second-language development, academic literacy, methods for integrating language and content instruction, materials development, and teacher change.

The strength of our collaboration is that we approach the issue of educating English learners from different perspectives. In writing this second edition of *Making Content Comprehensible for Elementary English Learners: The SIOP® Model*, we each provided a slightly different lens through which to view and discuss instructional situations. But our varied experiences have led us to the same conclusion: Educators need a resource for planning and implementing high-quality lessons for English learners and other students—lessons that will prepare students eventually for college and careers—and the SIOP Model is fulfilling this need.

What's New in This Edition

In this second edition, we have made substantial changes to the book while maintaining its easy-to-use format. We have added a number of features based on the feedback we have received from educators who use the SIOP Model. Also, a new chapter has been added that addresses how to get started implementing the SIOP Model based on frequently asked questions. Specifically, the changes to chapters include:

Chapter 1 Introducing the SIOP® Model

- Updated demographics and research throughout
- Revised discussion of English learners' backgrounds and academic performance
- Updated discussion of current educational trends, including the Common Core State Standards
- Up-to-date discussion of academic language
- Revised discussion of English learners' backgrounds and academic performance, including a new figure on their diverse characteristics
- Reorganization of the chapter
- Revised discussion questions

Chapter 2 Lesson Preparation

- Updated research throughout
- Revised sections discussing content and language objectives
- New figures related to Lesson Preparation
- New section: Teaching Ideas for Lesson Preparation
- New section: Differentiating Ideas for Multi-level Classes
- Revised discussion questions

Chapter 3 Building Background

- Substantive discussion of three categories of academic vocabulary
- New section: Teaching Ideas for Building Background
- New section: Differentiating Ideas for Multi-level Classes
- New Teaching Scenarios: Grade 6 elementary literature lesson with SIOP ratings and discussion
- Revised discussion questions

Chapter 4 Comprehensible Input

- Updated research throughout
- Revised discussion of the features including a new figure illustrating Feature #11
- New section: Teaching Ideas for Comprehensible Input
- New section: Differentiating Ideas for Multi-level Classes

- New Teaching Scenarios: Grade 3 elementary economics lesson with SIOP ratings and discussion
- Revised discussion questions

Chapter 5 Strategies

- Updated description of strategic processing
- Reorganized classification of learning strategies
- New model of scaffolding: Gradual Increase of Student Independence
- New comparison of Webb's Depth of Knowledge and Anderson & Krathwold's revised taxonomy (from Bloom's original taxonomy)
- New section: Teaching Ideas for Strategies
- New section: Differentiating Ideas for Multi-level Classes
- Revised discussion questions

Chapter 6 Interaction

- Updated research throughout
- Revised discussion of the features including examples of the Common Core State Standards
- New section: Teaching Ideas for Interaction
- New section: Differentiating Ideas for Multi-level Classes
- Teaching Scenarios: Grade 1 math lesson with SIOP ratings and discussion
- Revised discussion questions

Chapter 7 Practice & Application

- Updated research throughout
- New section: Teaching Ideas for Practice & Application
- New section: Differentiating Ideas for Multi-level Classes
- Revised Teaching Scenario: Grade 2 classrooms include newcomer students
- Revised discussion questions

Chapter 8 Lesson Delivery

- Revised chapter objectives
- Updated research throughout
- New section and figure: The Relationship between Lesson Preparation and Lesson Delivery
- New figure: Amount of Academic Learning Time in Typical Instruction and SIOP® Instruction
- New section: Teaching Ideas for Lesson Delivery
- New section: Differentiating Ideas for Multi-level Classes
- Revised discussion questions

Chapter 9 Review & Assessment

- New discussion exploring the relationship between classroom context and assessment
- New questions to consider during progress monitoring students' reading development
- Expanded discussion on issues related to the formal and informal assessment of English learners
- New section: Teaching Ideas for Review & Assessment
- New section: Differentiating Ideas for Multi-level Classes
- Revised discussion questions

Chapter 10 Issues of Reading, RTI, and Special Education for English Learners

- New section: Discussion of Response to Intervention (RTI) for English learners and struggling students
- Updated discussion of reading and assessment issues for English learners
- Revised, comprehensive section on English learners and special education
- Updated research throughout
- New section: Teaching Ideas for Special Education
- Revised discussion questions

Chapter 11 Effective Use of the SIOP® Protocol

- Updated and revised discussion of best practices in using the SIOP protocol and the use of SIOP scores
- New section: Ideas for Using the SIOP® Protocol
- Revised discussion questions

Chapter 12 Frequently Asked Questions: Getting Started with the SIOP® Model (New for this edition)

- Frequently asked general questions about the SIOP Model
- Frequently asked questions about getting started with the SIOP Model in the classroom
- Frequently asked questions about schoolwide implementation of the SIOP Model

Appendix C

- Updated discussion of SIOP research

Appendix D (New for this edition)

- List of resources for further information, including books, journal articles, book chapters, and downloadable research briefs
- Web site with information about SIOP Model professional development, http://siop.pearson.com

Highlights in the Book

- **Content and language objectives.** One of the most important aspects of the SIOP Model is the inclusion of both content and language objectives for each and every lesson. Many teachers have found writing these objectives to be challenging, even as they acknowledge their importance both for their own planning and for their students' understanding of the lesson's content goals and language focus. Therefore, you will find an expanded section in Chapter 2 (Lesson Preparation) that provides specific guidance for writing a range of content and language objectives, along with recommendations for how to effectively present them orally and in writing to students.

- **Discussion of the eight components and 30 features of the SIOP.** Each chapter begins with discussion of a component of the SIOP and its various features. For example, the discussion of lesson planning and preparation is found in the first half of Chapter 2. As you read about each feature in this section, think about how it would "look" in an actual classroom setting and how teachers might use this information to plan and prepare effective sheltered lessons.

- **Teaching scenarios.** The second half of each component chapter includes teaching scenarios. In these vignettes, three elementary teachers, who are teaching the same grade level and content, attempt to include the focal SIOP features, but with varying degrees of success. At the end of each teaching scenario, you will have the opportunity to use that component section of the SIOP to rate the effectiveness of the lesson in implementing these particular SIOP features. For example, as you read the teaching scenarios in Chapter 2, think about how well the three elementary teachers included the features of the Lesson Preparation component in their planning and preparation. Note that the illustrated lessons throughout the book range from kindergarten to grade 6, and they cover a variety of content areas and student language proficiency levels. Several address the Common Core State Standards.

- **Discussion of the three teaching scenarios.** Following the description of the three teachers' lessons, you will be able to see how we have rated the lessons for their inclusion of the SIOP features of effective sheltered instruction. We provide detailed explanations for the ratings and encourage you to discuss these with others in order to develop a high degree of inter-rater reliability.

- **Teaching ideas.** In a new section in each chapter, you will find a variety of ideas and activities for implementing the eight components of the SIOP Model. All of the ideas and activities are appropriate for children in elementary classrooms. Some are for very young children, and these are identified as such. Some activities may be familiar because you use them in your own classroom. We hope you'll be motivated to try the others because they represent best practice—those ideas and activities that are included have been found to be especially effective for English learners and struggling learners.

- **Differentiating Ideas for Multi-level Classes.** In this new section found in Chapters 2–9, we show ways to differentiate instruction for elementary students with various levels of language proficiency and academic skills.

- **Summary.** Each chapter has easy-to-read bulleted information that highlights the chapter's key points.

- **Discussion questions.** Based upon input from educators who have used this book, we have revised some of the discussion questions found at the end of each chapter to better reflect actual classroom practice with the SIOP Model. We hope these questions will promote thinking about your own practice, conversations during professional development, and opportunities for portfolio reflection for preservice university and inservice courses.

- **The SIOP protocol.** In Appendix A, you will find both an extended version of the SIOP protocol and a two-page abbreviated protocol. The eight components and 30 features of the SIOP Model are identical in both instruments and they are included as options for your personal use.

- **SIOP lesson plans.** We have been asked frequently for assistance with lesson planning for the SIOP Model. In this edition, we have included four different lesson plan formats for lesson plans (see Appendix B); we hope you will find one that is useful for you. In Chapters 2 and 5, you will also find complete plans for two of the lessons featured in the chapter scenarios (for Ms. Chen and Miss Abbas). These lesson plans are written with different formats, grade levels, and subject areas. (For additional sample lesson plans and sample units, see Echevarría, Vogt, & Short, 2010c; Short, Vogt, & Echevarría, 2011a, 2011b; Vogt & Echevarría, 2008; and Vogt, Echevarría, & Short, 2010.)

- **Discussion of reading and assessment issues, and special education for English learners.** In our work with the SIOP Institutes and in district trainings, we have heard many educators ask questions about English learners who have reading or learning problems and are struggling academically because of them. Based on the published report of the National Literacy Panel on Language-Minority Children and Youth (August & Shanahan, 2006), and the Response to Intervention (RTI) initiative, we have updated Chapter 10 with information and recommendations that we hope you will find helpful in SIOP Model program design and implementation for students with special needs. (More detailed information can be found in Echevarría & Vogt, 2011.)

- **SIOP Model research.** In Appendix C, you will find an overview of the findings from the original SIOP Model research as well as a discussion of the findings of several national research studies on the SIOP Model. If you are involved in a research study in your school, district, state, or university and have findings that contribute to the research literature on the SIOP Model, we would greatly appreciate hearing about them.

Accompanying *Making Content Comprehensible for Elementary English Learners: The SIOP® Model*, Second Edition, is an online resource site with media tools that, together with the text, provide you with the tools you need to implement the SIOP Model.

The PDToolkit for SIOP is available free for 12 months after you use the code that comes with this book. After that, you can purchase access for an additional 12 months. Be sure to explore and download the resources available at the website.

Currently the following resources are available:

- Information About the Authors
- SIOP Research
- SIOP Resources

- SIOP Lesson Plans and Activities
- SIOP Videos (*Note:* These video segments were filmed in classrooms with real teachers and students. They have been edited for brevity so you will not see all SIOP features in every video. The teachers who agreed to share their SIOP lessons represent a range of teacher implementation from experienced, high implementers to teachers just learning the model. We hope you will find the videos informative and helpful as you implement the SIOP Model in your classroom.)

To learn more, please visit: http://pdtoolkit.pearson.com.

Overview of the Chapters

The following section briefly describes each of the chapters in this new edition.

- The first chapter in the book introduces you to the pressing educational needs of English learners and to the SIOP Model of sheltered instruction. Issues related to English learner diversity, school reform accountability, the Common Core State Standards, No Child Left Behind, and academic language are also discussed.
- In Chapters 2 through 9, we explain the SIOP Model in detail, drawing from educational theory, research, and practice to describe each component and feature. Teaching scenarios drawn from elementary classroom lessons of sheltered instruction teachers follow. The features of the SIOP Model that pertain to each chapter are included for the lesson descriptions in the teaching scenarios. After you read about each of the teachers' lessons, use the SIOP protocol to rate on the 4 to 0 rubric the degree to which the features are present. The classroom scenarios reflect a different grade level and content area in each chapter and are linked to core curriculum objectives. All the elementary classrooms include English learners, and many also include native English speakers. Some have newly arrived English learners, known as newcomers.
- In Chapter 10, we discuss the special needs of English learners who have reading problems and/or learning disabilities. You may wish to read this chapter before you delve into the SIOP Model, especially if you have had little experience teaching English learners. It will assist you in situating the SIOP Model in "real" classrooms with English learners who have a wide variety of academic and literacy abilities and needs.
- Chapter 11 provides a discussion of scoring and interpreting the SIOP protocol, explaining how the instrument can be used holistically to measure teacher fidelity to the Model and strategically to guide the teacher in planning lessons for one or more targeted SIOP components. A full lesson from one research classroom is described and rated, revealing areas of strength and areas for improvement that can guide the teacher in future planning and teaching.
- Chapter 12, new to this second edition, provides ideas and recommendations for implementing the SIOP Model in the classroom, and in schools and districts. Frequently asked questions are included to guide you as you begin working with SIOP.
- In the Appendices, you will find the Sheltered Instruction Observation Protocol (SIOP®), both the comprehensive and the abbreviated versions. You will also

find four lesson planning formats to guide your lesson design and implementation. Further, we have included an appendix that details SIOP research to date and another that lists a variety of resources including additional SIOP Model books, research articles, book chapters, and research briefs. The book concludes with a Glossary of terms related to the instruction of English learners.

CourseSmart eBook and Other eBook Options Available

CourseSmart is an exciting new choice for purchasing this book. As an alternative to purchasing the printed book, you may purchase an electronic version of the same content via CourseSmart for reading on PC or Mac, as well as Android devices, iPad, iPhone, and iPod Touch with CourseSmart Apps. With a CourseSmart eBook, readers can search the text, make notes online, and bookmark important passages for later review. For more information or to purchase access to the CourseSmart eBook, visit http://www.coursesmart.com. Also look for availability of this book on a number of other eBook devices and platforms.

Acknowledgments

Many educators throughout the United States have contributed to this book through their work as SIOP teachers, bilingual specialists, curriculum coordinators, school and district administrators, and professional developers. We thank them for their insights and critical analyses of the SIOP Model and protocol. Further, we appreciate the contributions of those who have participated in the SIOP Institutes and professional development throughout the country (for more information, see http://siop.pearson.com/). At each of these Institutes and trainings, we gain new understanding about our work from those who participate in them.

We also thank the many teachers and administrators in whose schools we have conducted research on the SIOP Model, both past and present. Their willingness to let us observe and discuss their teaching of English learners has enhanced our understandings and validated our work. The contributions of these fine educators to the ongoing development of the SIOP Model are many, and we are grateful for their continued interest and encouragement. Our colleagues and fellow researchers on these projects deserve our gratitude as well.

We found the comments and suggestions from our reviewers to be of great help and we thank them: Ramona Morin Aguilar, Texas A&M University–Commerce; Rebecca L. Canges, Metropolitan State University of Denver–Auraria Campus; and Daniel DeLaO, Lew Wallace Elementary, Albuquerque, New Mexico. We also appreciate the ongoing support, assistance, and patience of our Pearson team, including Kathy Smith, our project manager, and our phenomenal editor in chief, Aurora Martínez Ramos.

The original SIOP work was supported under the Education Research and Development Program, PR/Award No. R306A60001, the Center for Research on Education, Diversity & Excellence (CREDE), as administered by the former Office of Educational Research and Improvement, now the Institute of Education Sciences

(IES), National Institute on the Education of At-Risk Students (NIEARS), and U.S. Department of Education (ED). The contents, findings, and opinions expressed here are those of the authors and do not necessarily represent the positions or policies of IES, NIEARS, or ED. Additional SIOP research has been supported by the Carnegie Corporation of New York, the Rockefeller Foundation, and the U.S. Department of Education, Institute of Education Sciences, under the CREATE research center.

Finally, we express appreciation to our families, whose ongoing support has enabled us to pursue our professional interests.

je   mev   djs

JANA ECHEVARRÍA, Ph.D., is Professor Emerita of Education at California State University, Long Beach where she was selected as Outstanding Professor. She has taught in elementary, middle, and high school in general education, special education, ESL, and bilingual programs. She has lived in Taiwan, Spain, and Mexico. Her UCLA doctorate earned her an award from the National Association for Bilingual Education's Outstanding Dissertations Competition and subsequent research and publications focus on effective instruction for English learners, including those with learning disabilities. She has presented her research across the U.S. and internationally including Oxford University (England), Wits University (South Africa), Harvard University (U.S.), South East Europe University (Macedonia), and University of Barcelona (Spain). Publications include the popular SIOP book series and over 50 books, book chapters and journal articles.

MARYELLEN VOGT, Ed.D., is Professor Emerita of Education at California State University, Long Beach. Dr. Vogt has been a classroom teacher, reading specialist, special education teacher, curriculum coordinator, and university teacher educator. She received her doctorate from the University of California, Berkeley, and is a co-author of 16 books, including *Reading Specialists and Literacy Coaches in the Real World* (3rd ed.) (Allyn & Bacon, 2011), and the SIOP® book series. Her research interests include improving comprehension in the content areas, teacher change and development, and content literacy for English learners. She has provided professional development for teachers and administrators in all 50 states and in nine countries. Dr. Vogt received her university's Distinguished Faculty Teaching Award, and is a Past President of the International Reading Association.

DEBORAH J. SHORT, Ph.D., directs Academic Language Research & Training and provides professional development on sheltered instruction and academic literacy worldwide. Formerly she was a Division Director at the Center for Applied Linguistics, Washington, DC, where she directed quasi-experimental and experimental studies on English learners funded by the Carnegie Corporation of New York, Rockefeller Foundation, and U.S. Department of Education, among others. Her publications include journal articles, the SIOP® Model book series, and several ESL textbook series for National Geographic/Cengage. She taught English as a second/foreign language in New York, California, Virginia, and the Democratic Republic of the Congo.

CHAPTER 1

Introducing the SIOP® Model

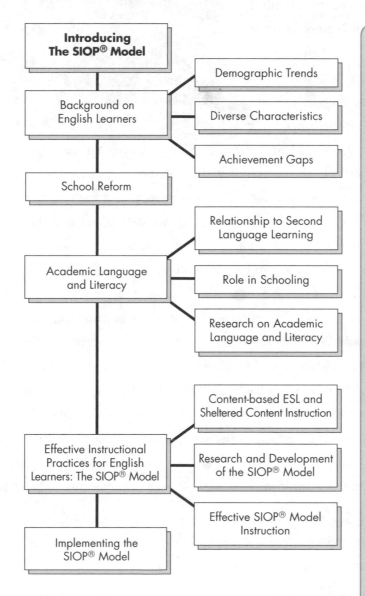

Introducing
The SIOP® Model

Background on
English Learners
- Demographic Trends
- Diverse Characteristics
- Achievement Gaps

School Reform

Academic Language
and Literacy
- Relationship to Second
Language Learning
- Role in Schooling
- Research on Academic
Language and Literacy

Effective Instructional
Practices for English
Learners: The SIOP® Model
- Content-based ESL and
Sheltered Content Instruction
- Research and Development
of the SIOP® Model
- Effective SIOP® Model
Instruction

Implementing the
SIOP® Model

After reading, discussing, and engaging in activities related to this chapter, you will be able to meet the following content and language objectives.

Content Objectives

List characteristics of English learners that may influence their success in school.

Distinguish between content-based ESL and sheltered instruction.

Explain the research supporting the SIOP Model.

Language Objectives

Discuss the benefits and challenges of school reform and their effects on English learners.

Develop a lexicon related to the SIOP Model.

Compare your typical instruction with SIOP instruction.

"Hola prima," called Graciela to her cousin, Jocelyn, on the playground. "¡Ayúdame con mi tarea!" Graciela asked her cousin for help with a homework assignment. "Cúal es el problema?" replied Jocelyn. Graciela went on to explain that she had to write a paper about recycling. She had to write an action plan, but she didn't know what an action plan was.

The two girls are cousins from Central America who entered fourth grade in Bray Elementary School together seven months earlier. They were placed in different classes in this suburban setting, but because the fourth-grade science teachers all did the same project, Jocelyn knew how to help her cousin. She explained that they had already started to work on that project. They had looked through the trash can in the lunchroom and found many things that could be recycled. They were creating a bulletin board with vocabulary and pictures about recycling. They had watched two videos, one about neighborhood families recycling and one about a recycling plant. They were going to make paper the next day. "We have to make a poster with our partner telling why it is important to recycle," Jocelyn told her cousin. "We made a list in class of reasons, and I decided to try to stop pollution in the sea. Ms. Sylvan showed us two posters from last year's class. Then she bookmarked some Web sites for me to look at. Some of them are in Spanish and you can listen to people talking about pollution and recycling. What did you do in class?"

Graciela explained that one day the teacher had talked to them for a long time about what recycling is and why it is important. "She told us to take notes when she talked, but it was hard. She talked too fast and she didn't write anything on the board. Then we read a few pages in our science textbook and answered questions yesterday. Today she gave us this sheet and told us to start writing our ideas." Graciela showed her cousin the assignment:

> Think of a recycling project. What needs to be improved in your school or town? Write an action plan proposing that the school board or the town council take steps to alleviate the problem or introduce a new program.

Jocelyn shook her head slowly as she looked at the paper. "I know what we can do. Let's go ask Ms. Sylvan. She just came out of the cafeteria." ●

Graciela and Jocelyn have experienced different teaching styles in their fourth-grade classrooms. Graciela's teacher uses a teacher-directed approach with an emphasis on mini-lectures and textbook reading. She provides little scaffolding for her English learners—indeed, little scaffolding for any of her students. Recycling, a topic that lends itself easily to visuals and other realia, hands-on materials, field trips, and more, is not brought alive in her classroom. Nor was a model for the action plan presented. Ms. Sylvan, on the other hand, provides a range of activities that help children understand the concept of recycling and see its application in their everyday lives. Her lessons built background and vocabulary for the fourth-graders and gave them hands-on experiences. She tapped into the students' different learning modes and supported her English learners with access to Web sites in their native language.[1] Her lessons reveal a great deal of preparation that will lead to the success of all her students.

Jocelyn is luckier than a number of English learners. She has a teacher who provides effective instruction as she learns content through English, a new language. If more teachers learn the techniques that Ms. Sylvan uses, then many more English learners will have a chance to develop academic literacy in English and be successful in elementary school. But it will take significant effort on the part of schools, districts, and universities to make this happen for Graciela and other students like her.

Background on English Learners

Demographic Trends

Graciela is one of many English learners in our schools. In fact, she represents the fastest growing group of students. During the decade from 1998–99 to 2008–09, the English learner population in pre-K–12 schools increased 51%, but the total pre-K–12 population, which includes these students, grew only 7.2%. In 2008–09, 11% of the students in U.S. schools were English learners, equaling over 5.3 million students out of a total enrollment of close to 49.5 million. At the current rate of growth, the English learner population in U.S. schools is projected to be 8 million in 2019–20 (NCELA, 2011).

However, it is important to recognize that the reported numbers refer to the identified English learners currently in language support programs or still being monitored. The number would be much higher if we added in the students who have passed their proficiency tests but are still struggling with *academic* English, the language used to read, write, listen, and speak in content classes to perform academic tasks and demonstrate knowledge of the subject standards.

The rise in English learners conforms to the increase in the immigrant population in the United States. The results of the 2010 American Community Survey estimated that 13% of the population was foreign born and 21% spoke a language

---

[1]For more information about a unit on recycling designed for classes with English learners, see Syvanen, 2000.

other than English. Of these 21% who were age 5 or older, 42% reported not speaking English very well (the U.S. Census Bureau's classification of limited English proficiency) (U.S. Census Bureau, 2012). Children age 5–17 make up about 19% of the U.S. population, and within this group, 23% are reported as not speaking English very well.[2] One in four children under the age of 18 live in immigrant families (Migration Policy Institute, 2012). Furthermore, over 75% of English learners in our elementary schools were born in the United States; that is, they are second- or third-generation immigrants (Fix & McHugh, 2009).

The states with the highest numbers of limited English proficient individuals in 2010 were California, Texas, New York, Florida, Illinois, and New Jersey. These six states account for 67% of the limited English population in the United States. The top six states with the highest growth in limited English proficient individuals from 1990 to 2010 were not the same; these new destination states were Nevada, North Carolina, Georgia, Arkansas, Tennessee, and Nebraska (Pandya, Batalova, & McHugh, 2011).

The distribution picture is a little different when we consider the English learners in our pre-K–12 schools. The states with the highest numbers of English learners are California, Arizona, Texas, Colorado, New York, Florida, Illinois, and North Carolina. The states that have experienced the most growth in pre-K–12 English learner enrollment (more than 200% change) from 1999–2000 to 2009–10 are Illinois, Kentucky, Virginia, Delaware, South Carolina, and Mississippi (NCELA, 2011). Another consideration is the linguistic isolation our English learners experience. Many of them are in linguistically segregated schools. More than half of the elementary and secondary English learners were in schools where more than 30% of the student population was identified as limited English proficient (Batalova, Fix, & Murray, 2007).

Changes in the geographic distribution of English learners to these new destination states present many challenges to the numerous districts that have not served these students before. Academic programs are not well established; sheltered curricula and appropriate resources are not readily available; and, most important, many teachers are not trained to meet the needs of these second language learners.

Diverse Characteristics

In order to develop the best educational programs for English learners, we need to understand their diverse backgrounds. These learners bring a wide variety of educational and cultural experiences to the classroom as well as considerable linguistic differences, and these characteristics have implications for instruction, assessment, and program design. When we know students' backgrounds and abilities in their native language, we can incorporate effective techniques and materials in our instructional practices.

All English learners in elementary schools are not alike. They enter U.S. schools with a wide range of language proficiencies (both in English and in their native lan-

---

[2]Calculations for children age 5–17 not speaking English very well are based on data found at http://factfinder2.census.gov/faces/tableservices/jsf/pages/productview.xhtml?pid=ACS_10_1YR_C16004&prodType=table (retrieved July 8, 2012).

guages) and much divergence in their subject matter knowledge. In addition to the limited English proficiency and the approximately 180 native languages among the students, we also find diversity in their educational backgrounds, expectations of schooling, socioeconomic status, age of arrival, personal experiences while coming to and living in the United States, and parents' education levels and proficiency in English. Some English learners are newcomers (i.e., new arrivals to the United States), some have lived in the United States for several years, and some are native born. Figure 1.1 shows some background factors that should be considered when planning programs and instruction so English learners can succeed in school.

- Some immigrant English learners had strong academic backgrounds before coming to the United States. Some are at or above equivalent grade levels in certain subjects—math and science, for example. They are literate in their native

---

FIGURE 1.1 Diverse Characteristics of English Learners

English Knowledge

- Exposure to English
- Familiarity with Roman alphabet and numbers
- Proficiency in spoken English
- Proficiency in written English
- English being learned as a third or fourth language

First Language (L1) Knowledge

- Proficiency in spoken L1
- Literacy in the first language

Educational Background

- On-grade level schooling in home country
- On-grade level schooling in U.S. schools (in L1 or English)
- Partial schooling in L1
- No schooling in L1
- Partial schooling in English
- No schooling in English
- Long-term English learner

Sociocultural, Emotional, and Economic Factors

- Poverty level
- Mobility
- Exposure to trauma, violence, abuse, and other serious stressors
- Refugee or asylee status
- Parents' educational background

Other Educational Categories

- Special education
- Tier 2 or Tier 3 (Response to Intervention)
- Migrant
- Reclassified English learner
- Gifted and talented

---

language and may have started studying a second language. Much of what these learners need is English language development so that as they become more proficient in English, they can transfer the knowledge they learned in their native country's schools to the courses they are taking in the United States. A few subjects not previously studied, such as social studies, may require special attention. These students have a strong likelihood of achieving educational success if they receive appropriate English language and content instruction in their U.S. schools.

- Some other immigrant students had very limited formal schooling—perhaps due to war in their native countries or the remote, rural location of their homes. These students have little or no literacy in their native language, and they may not have had such schooling experiences as sitting at desks all day, changing classrooms for art or music, or taking high-stakes tests. They have significant gaps in their educational backgrounds, lack knowledge in specific subject areas, and need time to become accustomed to school routines and expectations. These English learners with limited formal schooling and below-grade-level literacy are most at risk for educational failure.

- There are also English learners who have grown up in the United States but who speak a language other than English at home. Some students in this group are literate in their home language, such as Mandarin, Arabic, or Spanish, and will add English to their knowledge base in school. If they receive appropriate English language and content instruction, they too are likely to be academically successful.

- Some other native-born English learners who do not speak English at home have not mastered either English or their native language. There is a growing number of English learners in this group who continue to lack proficiency in English even after five, six, or more years in U.S. schools. These students are referred to as *long-term English learners* (Menken & Kleyn, 2010). They typically have oral proficiency in English, but lack English reading and writing skills in the content areas. They struggle academically (Flores, Batalova, & Fix, 2012; Olsen, 2010).

Sociocultural, emotional, and economic factors also influence English learners' educational attainment (Dianda, 2008). Poorer students, in general, are less academically successful (Glick & White, 2004). Undocumented status affects socioeconomic and postsecondary educational opportunities. Mobility can impinge on school success: Students who had moved were twice as likely not to complete high school as those who had not faced such transitions (Glick & White, 2004). Refugee students who experienced significant trauma during journeys to refugee camps or to the United States may struggle in school. The parents' level of education also influences their children's success. Parents with more schooling are typically more literate and have more knowledge to share with their children, whether through informal conversations or while helping with homework.

Some students are dually identified, which has implications for educational services. Besides being English learners, some students have learning disabilities or other special education needs. Unfortunately, English learners tend to be over- or underrepresented in special education because a number of districts struggle to distinguish between a delay in developing second language proficiency and a learning disability. Even when students are appropriately identified, districts have difficulty providing effective services to bilingual special education students. Others, such as English learners and redesignated English learners who score poorly on reading assessments, may need additional services to improve their reading achievement, such as Tier 2 or Tier 3 in a Response to Intervention (RTI) program. While we believe that the SIOP Model we present in this book is the best option for Tier 1 instruction and may help avoid Tier 2 and 3 placements (see Echevarría & Vogt, 2011), not all schools utilize SIOP instruction. Other students are migrant English learners who may move from school to school in the same year, jeopardizing their learning with absences and potentially incompatible curricula across districts or states.

Achievement Gaps

While the number of students with limited proficiency in English has grown exponentially across the United States, their level of academic achievement has lagged significantly behind that of their language-majority peers. There exists growing evidence that most schools are not meeting the challenge of educating these students well. Consider the following statistics:

- On the National Assessment for Educational Progress (NAEP) exams for reading in 2011, English learners performed poorly at fourth grade (National Center for Education Statistics [NCES], 2012b).
  - The achievement gap between the average scores of non-English learners and English learners was 37 points, similar to the gap for the 2009 and 2007 administrations of the test.
  - Sixty-nine percent of the fourth-grade English learners performed Below Basic, but only 28% of the non-English learners did. Only 7% of English learners scored as Proficient in Reading, and none as Advanced, while 37% of non-English learners were Proficient and 9% were Advanced.
- The pattern on the 2011 NAEP mathematics assessment was not much different for fourth graders (NCES, 2012a).
  - The achievement gap between the average scores of non-English learners and English learners was 24 points, similar to the gap for the 2009 and 2007 administrations of the test.
  - Forty-one percent of the fourth-grade English learners performed Below Basic, but only 15% of the non-English learners did. Further, only 15% of English learners performed at Proficient or Advanced levels, while 51% of non-English learners reached those higher levels.
- Spanish-speaking students enter kindergarten with a gap in language and math skills compared to English-only students. In some states, this gap widens as students progress to fifth grade (Rumberger, 2007); in others, it narrows, but non-English speakers do not come close to catching up (Reardon & Galindo, 2009).

- A five-year, statewide evaluation study found that English learners with 10 years of schooling in California had less than a 40% chance of meeting the criteria to be redesignated as fluent English proficient (Parish et al., 2006). They pass the English language proficiency test, but do not pass the state content achievement tests.

- Since the No Child Left Behind (NCLB) Act was implemented in 2001, there has been an increase in the number of high school English learners not receiving a diploma. Some failed high-stakes tests despite fulfilling all other graduation requirements (Alliance for Excellent Education, 2010; Biancarosa & Snow, 2004; Human Resources Research Organization, 2010, reported in Dietz, 2010; Kober et al., 2006; McNeil et al., 2008).

- English learners are more likely to drop out than other student groups (Dianda, 2008; New York City Department of Education, 2011; Rumberger, 2011).

The lack of success in educating linguistically and culturally diverse students is problematic because federal and state governments expect *all* students to meet high standards, and they have adjusted national and state assessments as well as state graduation requirements to reflect new levels of achievement and to accommodate requirements of the No Child Left Behind Act (2001). However, we test students before they are proficient in English. We should not be surprised if they don't score at the proficient level because by definition they are *not* proficient if they are classified as English learners.

Apart from the testing issues, English learners also have difficulty in school when program designs, instructional goals, and human and material resources do not match these students' needs. The number of English learners has increased without a comparable increase in ESL or bilingual certified teachers. Despite the demographic trends, only six states require specific coursework for all teacher candidates on topics like ESL methods and second language acquisition: Alaska, Arizona, California, Florida, Pennsylvania, and New York (National Comprehensive Center on Teacher Quality, 2009). As a result, most mainstream teachers are underprepared to serve ELs when they exit their preservice institutions (McGraner & Saenz, 2009). Curricula that develop subject area knowledge in conjunction with academic English are lacking, too. State policies limit the number of years that students have access to language support services; in fact, in Massachusetts, Arizona, and California, the goal is to move students into regular classrooms after one year, even though research strongly shows that students need more time with specialized language support (Saunders & Goldenberg, 2010).

We know that conversational fluency develops inside and outside of the classroom and can be attained in one to three years (Thomas & Collier, 2002). However, the language that is critical for educational success—academic language (Cummins, 2000)—is more complex and develops more slowly and systematically in academic settings. It may take students from four to seven years of study, depending on individual and sociocultural factors, before they are proficient in academic English (Collier, 1987; Hakuta, Butler, & Witt, 2000; Lindholm-Leary & Borsato, 2006; Thomas & Collier, 2002).

When policies and programs that complement the research on second language acquisition are in place, we see more positive outcomes. For example, analyses from

New York City and the states of New Jersey, Washington, and California reveal that former English learners outperformed students as a whole on state tests, exit exams, and graduation rates (DeLeeuw, 2008; New York City Department of Education, 2004; State of New Jersey Department of Education, 2006; Sullivan et al., 2005). The results of these studies indicate that when English learners are given time to develop academic English proficiency in their programs and are exited (and redesignated) with criteria that measure their ability to be successful in mainstream classes, they perform, on average, as well as or better than the state average on achievement measures.

School Reform, Standards, and Accountability

Unfortunately, we do not yet have strong, research-based policies and programs in place nationwide for English learners; yet the pressure for academic success is high. The No Child Left Behind (NCLB) Act of 2001 holds schools accountable for the success of all of their students, and each state has standards for mathematics, reading, language arts, English language development, and science; all states implement high-stakes tests based on these standards.

NCLB has had positive and negative impacts on educational programs (Dianda, 2008). On the positive side, the education of English learners is part of school improvement conversations. More attention is paid to providing better educational opportunities for the learners and monitoring their language proficiency growth and academic progress. More funding is available to help teachers strengthen their instruction so students develop academic literacy skills and can access core content. More schools analyze assessment data to determine the progress of their efforts and adjust programs, instruction, and resources as indicated. Some states have allocated additional resources for English learner programs, such as grants for specialized services for newcomers and students with interrupted educational backgrounds (Short & Boyson, 2012).

Negative effects of NCLB include penalties to schools and older students. Schools have been labeled "low performing" or "needs improvement" if their subpopulation of English learners does not attain testing achievement targets set for native English speakers on tests that have not been designed or normed for English learners (Abedi, 2002). After three subsequent years of such labels, many schools face corrective action. Teachers report pressure to "teach to the test," which reduces their implementation of creative lessons, project-based learning, and interdisciplinary units (Short & Boyson, 2012).

Although more money is available for professional development, it is not always well spent. Numerous studies have shown that sustained, job-embedded, and research-based professional development is needed if comprehensive school reform is to become a reality, but one-shot workshops and disconnected interventions continue (Alliance for Excellent Education, 2011a; Calderón & Minaya-Rowe, 2011; Darling-Hammond & Richardson, 2009; Wei et al., 2009). Further, Ballantyne, Sanderman, and Levy (2008) report that only 26% of mainstream teachers with ELs in their classrooms have had professional development related to instructional practices for these learners.

Additional standards-based reforms are taking place. As of the 2012–13 school year, 46 states have adopted a common set of K–12 English language arts and mathematics standards, called the Common Core State Standards (NGA & CCSSO, 2010a, 2010b). Educators in these states are working on implementation activities such as modifying their current curriculum frameworks to ensure the required standards are included, and the U.S. Department of Education (USED) is requiring participating states to revise their NCLB assessments. On the one hand, these national standards are appealing because they place an emphasis on college and career readiness. If implemented as envisioned, high school graduates will be autonomous learners who effectively seek out and use resources to assist them in daily life, in academic pursuits, and in their jobs. On the other hand, the standards may be problematic for English learners. The developers decided not to address English learners' second language development needs in the standards. For instance, although there are standards related to foundations of literacy in grades K–5 (e.g., standards related to phonics), there are none in grades 6–12. This oversight ignores the needs of adolescent English learners such as newly arrived immigrant students who are not literate when they enter secondary school. It remains to be seen if and how states will accommodate the language development needs of English learners as they implement the Common Core. (See www.corestandards.org/assets/application-for-english-learners .pdf for more information.)[3]

Academic Language and Literacy

PD **TOOLKIT**™ **for SIOP**®

Click on Videos, then search for "Strategies to Develop Academic Language" to hear teachers discuss ways to encourage students to use academic language in class.

The foundation of school success is academic language and literacy in English. Age-appropriate knowledge of the English language is a prerequisite in the attainment of content standards. We learn primarily through language, and use language to express our understanding. As Lemke (1988, p. 81) explained,

> [E]ducators have begun to realize that the mastery of academic subjects is the mastery of their specialized patterns of language use, and that language is the dominant medium through which these subjects are taught and students' mastery of them tested.

Simply put, for English learners to have access to core content, they need academic language and literacy skills.

Educators and researchers in the field of second language acquisition and literacy have defined academic language or academic literacy in a number of ways. Most definitions incorporate reading, writing, listening, and speaking skills as part of academic language and refer to a specialized academic register of the formal written and spoken code. Although there is not yet a single agreed-upon definition, each one considers how language is used in school to acquire new knowledge and

---

[3]A similar effort is taking place for science. At the time of this writing, 26 states led by Achieve, with support from science professional organizations, drafted Next Generation Science Standards for K–12 students and solicited public feedback. These standards are expected to be released in Spring 2013. (See www.nextgenscience.org for more details and updates.)

foster success on academic tasks (Anstrom et al., 2010; Bailey, 2007; Gibbons, 2002; Schleppegrell, 2004; Short, 2002). Without proficient oral and written English language skills, students are hard pressed to learn and demonstrate their knowledge of mathematical reasoning, science skills, historical perspectives, and other academic concepts.

Relationship to Second Language Learning

Academic language is used by all students in school settings, both native English speakers and English learners alike. However, this type of language use is particularly challenging for English learners who are beginning to acquire English at the same time that school tasks require a high level of English usage. Participation in informal conversation demands less from an individual than joining in an academic discussion (Cummins, 2000). While the distinction is not truly dichotomous, it is widely accepted that the language skills required for informal conversation differ from those required for academic processes such as summarizing information, evaluating perspectives, and drawing conclusions. Certainly, one may converse in a cognitively demanding way—such as debating a current event that requires significant knowledge of both sides of the topic—but that is not the typical social conversation. The distinction becomes clearer when we recognize that students have the ability to converse in English without needing strong academic language skills. English learners appear to speak English well in hallways, on playing fields, and in small talk before a lesson begins, but they struggle to use English well in classroom assignments or on tests. This situation occurs because they have not yet acquired a high level of academic language, which is cognitively demanding and highly decontextualized (Cummins, 1984).

Role in Schooling

The relationship between literacy proficiency and academic achievement grows stronger as grade levels rise—regardless of individual student characteristics. In secondary school classes, language use becomes more complex and more content area specific (Biancarosa & Snow, 2004). English learners must develop literacy skills for each content area *in* their second language as they simultaneously learn, comprehend, and apply content area concepts *through* their second language (Garcia & Godina, 2004; Short & Fitzsimmons, 2007).

Specifically, English learners must master academic English, which includes semantic and syntactic knowledge along with functional language use. Using English, students, for example, must be able to

- read and understand the expository prose in textbooks and reference materials,
- write persuasively,
- argue points of view,
- take notes from teacher lectures or Internet sites, and
- articulate their thinking processes—make hypotheses and predictions, express analyses, draw conclusions, and so forth.

In content classes, English learners must pull together their emerging knowledge of the English language with the content knowledge they are studying in order to complete the academic tasks. They must also learn *how* to do these tasks—generate the format of an outline, negotiate roles in cooperative learning groups, interpret charts and maps, and such. These three knowledge bases—knowledge of English, knowledge of the content topic, and knowledge of how the tasks are to be accomplished—constitute the major components of academic literacy (Short, 2002).

There is some general agreement about how best to teach academic language to English learners, including some targeted focus on the lexical, semantic, and discourse levels of the language as they are applied in school settings (Saunders & Goldenberg, 2010). Brown and Ryoo (2008) found that elementary students who learn science content through everyday vernacular before learning the scientific language assimilate the content better. Researchers such as Bailey and Butler (2007) found that there is content-specific language (e.g., technical terms like *latitude* and *longitude*, phrases like "We hypothesize that . . .") and general academic language (e.g., cross-curricular words like *effect, cause, however*) that are used across subject areas. Similarly, there are general academic tasks that one needs to know how to do to be academically proficient (e.g., create a timeline, structure an argument) and more specific subject assignments (e.g., explain steps to the solution of a math word problem). Teachers and curricula should pay attention to this full range of academic language. As a result, the enhancement of English learners' academic language skills should enable them to perform better on assessments. This conclusion is bolstered by an older study: Snow et al. (1991) found that performance on highly decontextualized (i.e., school-like) tasks, such as providing a formal definition of words, predicted academic performance, whereas performance on highly contextualized tasks, such as face-to-face communication, did not.

The emphasis on teaching academic language is also reflected in the national ESL standards (Teachers of English to Speakers of Other Languages, 2006). Four of the five *Pre-K–12 English Language Proficiency Standards* specifically address the academic language of the core subject areas. Standards 2, 3, 4, and 5 state: "English language learners communicate information, ideas, and concepts necessary for academic success in the area of _____ [language arts (#2), mathematics (#3), science (#4), and social studies (#5)]." By 2012, 31 states and the District of Columbia had adopted English language proficiency standards (ELP) similar to TESOL's, known as the WIDA (World-Class Instructional Design and Assessment) standards. Twenty-eight of these entities use the companion English language proficiency test, *ACCESS for ELLs*® (ACCESS: Assessing Comprehension and Communication in English State to State for English Language Learners), to guide and measure annual gains in English language proficiency (WIDA, 2005–11).

Research on Academic Language and Literacy

Findings from two major syntheses of the research on academic literacy and the education of English learners are useful to keep in mind as we plan instruction and programs for English learners. The National Literacy Panel on Language-Minority Children and Youth (NLP) (August & Shanahan, 2006) analyzed and synthesized the research on these learners with regard to English literacy attainment. Many of

FIGURE 1.2 Research Findings from the National Literacy Panel on Language-Minority Children and Youth

1. English language learners (ELLs) benefit from instruction in the key components of reading as defined by the National Reading Panel (NICHD, 2000) as phonemic awareness, phonics, fluency, vocabulary, and text comprehension.

2. Instruction in these five components is necessary but not sufficient to teach ELLs to read and write proficiently in English. Oral language proficiency is needed also, so ELLs need instruction in this area.

3. Oral proficiency and literacy in the student's native language (L1) will facilitate development of literacy in English, but literacy in English can also be developed without proficiency in the L1.

4. Individual student characteristics play a significant role in English literacy development.

5. Home language experiences can contribute to English literacy achievement, but on the whole, the research on the influence of sociocultural factors is limited.

August & Shanahan, 2006, pp. 5-6

the studies that the 13-member expert panel examined looked at the reading and writing skills needed for successful schooling. The panel considered second language literacy development, cross-linguistic influences and transfer, sociocultural contexts, instruction and professional development, and student assessment. Figure 1.2 summarizes the findings of the NLP that appeared in the executive summary (August & Shanahan, 2006).

The second major review was conducted by researchers from the former National Center for Research on Education, Diversity & Excellence (CREDE). Their focus was on oral language development, literacy development (from instructional and cross-linguistic perspectives), and academic achievement. Both syntheses led to similar findings.

Following are some of the findings that are closely related to the topics in this book:

- Processes of second language (L2) literacy development are influenced by a number of variables that interact with each other in complex ways (e.g., first language [L1] literacy, second language [L2] oralcy, socioeconomic status, and more).

- Certain L1 skills and abilities transfer to English literacy: phonemic awareness, comprehension and language learning strategies, and L1 and L2 oral knowledge.

- Teaching the five major components of reading (NICHD, 2000) to English learners is necessary but not sufficient for developing academic literacy. English learners need to develop oral language proficiency as well.

- Oralcy and literacy can develop simultaneously.

- Academic literacy in the native language facilitates the development of academic literacy in English.

- High-quality instruction for English learners is similar to high-quality instruction for other, English-speaking students, but English learners need instructional accommodations and support to fully develop their English skills.

- English learners need enhanced, explicit vocabulary development.

These findings have formed the foundation of a recent book that offers applications for classrooms with English learners, *Improving Education for English Learners: Research-based Approaches* (California Department of Education, 2010). More information on these findings and their implications for developing academic literacy can be found in August and Shanahan (2006), Cloud, Genesee, and Hamayan (2009), Freeman and Freeman (2009), Genesee et al. (2006), Goldenberg (2006), and Short and Fitzsimmons (2007).

Effective Instructional Practice for English Learners: The SIOP® Model

One positive outcome of the student performance measures put into place in response to the NCLB legislation is that schools have started to focus on the development of academic language and literacy skills in students who struggle academically, including English learners. Schools have sought to improve the educational programs, instructional practices, and the curricula and materials being offered to these students. Opportunities for ongoing professional development are moving teachers in the right direction. However, we have a long way to go, as the data and research findings about the poor performance of English learners on accountability measures presented in this chapter reveal.

This book, *Making Content Comprehensible for Elementary English Learners: The SIOP® Model*, offers a solution to one aspect of school reform needed for English learners' acquisition of English and academic achievement, namely classroom instruction. It introduces a research-based model of sheltered instruction, provides teaching ideas for each of the model's eight components, suggests ways to differentiate instruction in multi-level classrooms, and demonstrates through lesson scenarios how the model can be implemented across grades and subject areas. The model provides guidance for the best practices for English learners, grounded in more than two decades of classroom-based research, the experiences of competent teachers, and findings from the professional literature. It has been used successfully in both language and content classrooms, and with this approach, teachers can help English learners attain the skills and knowledge associated with college and career readiness.

In addition, the SIOP Model has been used widely in classrooms that have a mix of English learners and English-speaking students. For many years, school district personnel around the United States have reported anecdotally that English speakers and English learners alike benefit when teachers use the SIOP Model in their classes, and they point to increased student achievement data to substantiate their reports. However, these were not controlled research studies. Recently, though, research studies have shown that all students in SIOP classes performed better than comparison or control groups (Echevarría, Richards-Tutor, Canges, & Francis, 2011; Echevarría, Richards-Tutor, Chinn, & Ratleff, 2011). These findings indicate that English-speaking students are not disadvantaged when they are in SIOP classes with English learners and that they also benefit from SIOP practices.

FIGURE 1.3 Goals of Content-based ESL/ELD and Sheltered Content Instruction

Content-based ESL/ELD	Primary goal	Academic English language development, meeting ELP standards, addressing some ELA standards
	Secondary goal	Introduction to content topics, vocabulary, reading and writing genres, classroom tasks
	Student grouping	English learners
	Teacher	ESL certification
Sheltered Content	Primary goal	Grade-level, standards-based content knowledge of specific subject
	Secondary goal	Academic language development as pertains to each specific content area
	Student grouping	All English learners or English learners mixed with non-English learners and/or former English learners
	Teacher	Content certification, ESL or bilingual endorsed or certified, or trained in sheltered techniques

Source: Adapted from Echevarria & Short, 2010, p. 259. Reprinted with permission from California Department of Education, CDE Press, 1430 N. Street, Suite 3705, Sacramento, CA 95814.

Content-based ESL and Sheltered Content Instruction

PD TOOLKIT™ for SIOP®

Click on Videos, then search for "Sheltered Instruction" to listen to an explanation of how SIOP® is "good teaching plus" (content and language taught concurrently).

Currently, in the United States, content-based English as a second language (ESL) and sheltered instruction are acknowledged methods for developing academic English and providing English learners access to core content coursework in grades K–12. Ideally, these two approaches work in tandem: one, with a primary focus on academic (and where needed, social) language development; the other, on content standards and topics. In the ESL classes, the curricula are tied to the state standards for English language proficiency, the students are all English learners, and the teacher is ESL or bilingual certified. In sheltered content instruction classes, the curricula are tied to the state subject area standards, such as the Common Core, and the students may be all English learners or mixed with native English speakers. The teachers have elementary or secondary content certification plus an endorsement or certification in ESL or bilingual education (see Figure 1.3).

In content-based ESL, material from multiple subject areas is often presented through thematic or interdisciplinary units. For example, in a first-grade classroom, one theme might be "Life on a Farm." While students learn such language-related elements as names of animals, adjectives, how to ask and answer questions, and the present continuous tense, they also solve addition and subtraction problems, read poems and sing songs about farm animals, and discuss the food chain, thus exploring objectives from mathematics, language arts, music, and science. Some young English learners may share stories from their families about living on farms in their countries of origin.

For the fifth-grade classroom, a theme such as "the marketplace" might be selected, and lessons could include objectives drawn from economics, science, geography, social studies, and mathematics. Students with less proficiency might create maps showing how goods move from farms and manufacturing plants to city markets, and design a brochure to sell a good or service. Advanced students might learn to use reference materials and computers to conduct research to learn about the supply and demand of certain goods or to develop a business plan for a good or service they would like to sell. They might study persuasive language to advertise their good or service. English learners may contribute valuable insights to this topic because some have lived in places where their parents or neighbors moved goods to market. Some may have experienced the effects of adverse weather on the production of foodstuffs or the effects of poor infrastructure on the transportation of goods.

In general, content-based ESL/ELD teachers seek to develop the students' English language proficiency by incorporating information from the subject areas that students are likely to study or from courses they may have missed if they are new immigrants. Whatever subject matter is included, for effective content-based ESL instruction to occur, teachers need to provide practice in academic skills and tasks common to regular, grade-level classes (Mohan, Leung, & Davison, 2001; Short, 2002).

In sheltered content classes, teachers deliver grade-level objectives for the different subject areas to English learners through modified instruction that makes the information comprehensible to the students while promoting their academic English development. In elementary schools, sheltered instruction is generally taught by classroom teachers rather than ESL specialists and can be offered to students of all levels of English proficiency. A goal is to teach content to students learning English through a developmental language approach.

Effective sheltered instruction is *not* simply a set of additional or replacement instructional techniques that teachers implement in their classrooms. Instead, it draws from and complements methods advocated for both second language and mainstream classrooms. For example, some techniques include cooperative learning, connections to student experiences, culturally responsive activities, targeted vocabulary development, slower speech and fewer idiomatic expressions for less proficient students, use of visuals and demonstrations, and use of adapted text and supplementary materials (Short & Echevarría, 2004).

In the 1990s, there was a great deal of variability in both the design of sheltered instruction courses and the delivery of sheltered lessons, even among trained teachers and within the same schools (August & Hakuta, 1997; Echevarría & Short, 2010). Some schools, for instance, offered only sheltered courses in one subject area, but not in other core areas. It was our experience as well that one sheltered classroom did not look like the next in terms of each teacher's instructional language; the tasks the students were to accomplish; the degree of interaction that occurred between teacher and student, student and student, and student and text; the amount of class time devoted to language development versus content knowledge; the learning strategies taught to and used by the students; the availability of appropriate materials;

and more. In sum, there was no model for teachers to follow and few systematic and sustained forms of professional development.

This situation was the impetus for our research: to develop a valid, reliable, and effective model of sheltered instruction.

Research and Development of the Sheltered Instruction Observation Protocol (SIOP®) Model

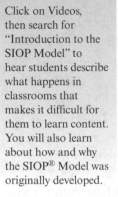

PD TOOLKIT™ for SIOP®

Click on Videos, then search for "Introduction to the SIOP Model" to hear students describe what happens in classrooms that makes it difficult for them to learn content. You will also learn about how and why the SIOP® Model was originally developed.

We developed the Sheltered Instruction Observation Protocol (SIOP®) Model as an approach for teachers to integrate content and language instruction for students learning through a new language. Teachers would employ techniques that make the content concepts accessible and also develop the students' skills in the new language. We have been fortunate in securing funding and the participation of many schools and teachers since 1996 to research, develop, and refine the SIOP Model. Details of the SIOP Model research studies can be found in Appendix C of this book and in Short, Echevarría, and Richards-Tutor (2011). We present a brief overview here.

The first version of the Sheltered Instruction Observation Protocol (SIOP) was drafted in the early 1990s. We used it exclusively as a research and supervisory tool to determine if observed teachers incorporated key sheltered techniques consistently in their lessons. This early draft, like subsequent ones, pulled together findings and recommendations from the research literature with our professional experiences and those of our collaborating teachers on effective classroom-based practices.

The protocol evolved into a lesson planning and delivery approach, known as the SIOP Model (Echevarría, Vogt, & Short, 2000), through a seven-year research study, "The Effects of Sheltered Instruction on the Achievement of Limited English Proficient Students," sponsored by the Center for Research on Education, Diversity & Excellence (CREDE) and funded by the U.S. Department of Education. The study began in 1996 and involved collaborating middle school teachers who worked with the researchers to refine the features of the original protocol: distinguishing between effective strategies for beginner, intermediate, and advanced English learners; determining "critical" versus "unique" sheltered teaching strategies; and making the SIOP more user friendly. A substudy confirmed the SIOP to be a valid and reliable measure of sheltered instruction (Guarino et al., 2001).

Specifically, the SIOP is composed of 30 features grouped into eight main components:

- The features under *Lesson Preparation* initiate the lesson planning process, so teachers include content and language objectives, use supplementary materials, and create meaningful activities.
- *Building Background* focuses on making connections with students' background experiences and prior learning, and developing their academic vocabulary.
- *Comprehensible Input* considers how teachers should adjust their speech, model academic tasks, and use multimodal techniques to enhance comprehension.
- The *Strategies* component emphasizes teaching learning strategies to students, scaffolding instruction, and promoting higher-order thinking skills.

- *Interaction* prompts teachers to encourage students to elaborate their speech and to group students appropriately for language and content development.
- *Practice & Application* provides activities to practice and extend language and content learning.
- *Lesson Delivery* ensures teachers present a lesson that meets the planned objectives and promotes student engagement.
- The *Review & Assessment* component reminds teachers to review the key language and content concepts, assess student learning, and provide specific academic feedback to students on their output.

You will read about each component and its features in subsequent chapters of this book. During four years of field testing, we analyzed teacher implementation and student effects. This CREDE research showed that English learners whose teachers were trained in implementing the SIOP Model performed statistically significantly better on an academic writing assessment than a comparison group of English learners whose teachers had no exposure to the model (Echevarría, Short, & Powers, 2006).

From 1999 to 2002, we field tested and refined the SIOP Model's professional development program, which includes professional development institutes, videotapes of exemplary SIOP teachers (Hudec & Short, 2002a, 2002b), facilitator's guides (Echevarría & Vogt, 2008; Short, Hudec, & Echevarría, 2002), and other training materials.

We continued to test and refine the SIOP Model in several later studies. From 2004–07, we replicated and scaled up the SIOP research in a quasi-experimental study in two districts at the middle and high school levels. The treatment teachers participated in the professional development program with summer institutes, follow-up workshops, and on-site coaching. Students with SIOP-trained teachers made statistically significant gains in their average mean scores for oral language, writing, and total proficiency on the state assessment of English language proficiency, compared to the comparison group of English learners (Short, Fidelman, & Louguit, 2012).

From 2005–12, we participated in the Center for Research on the Educational Achievement and Teaching of English Language Learners (CREATE), looking first at the SIOP Model in middle school science classrooms (Himmel, Short, Richards, & Echevarría, 2009) and later at the SIOP Model as the professional development framework for a schoolwide intervention (Echevarria, Short, Richards-Tutor, & Himmel, in press). The results from the Year 2 experimental study showed that students who had teachers who implemented the SIOP Model with greater fidelity performed better than those who did not implement the SIOP Model to a high degree (Echevarría, Richards-Tutor, Chinn, & Ratleff, 2011).

During the past decade, a number of school districts have also conducted program evaluations on their implementation of the model. A number of these can be reviewed in *Implementing the SIOP® Model Through Effective Professional Development and Coaching* (Echevarría, Short, & Vogt, 2008). In addition, other researchers have studied SIOP Model professional development programs (Batt, 2010; McIntyre et al., 2010).

FIGURE 1.4 SIOP® Terminology

SIOP® Model — the lesson planning and delivery system
SIOP® protocol — the instrument used to observe, rate, and provide feedback on lessons

---

A note about terminology is helpful before you read further. The SIOP term now refers to both the observation instrument for rating the fidelity of lessons to the model (as shown in Appendix A) and the instructional model for lesson planning and delivery that we explain in detail in the following chapters. Figure 1.4 shows the terminology we will be using in this book to distinguish between these two uses. In addition, we will use SIOP as a modifier to describe teachers implementing the model (SIOP teachers) and lessons incorporating the 30 features (SIOP lessons).

Effective SIOP® Model Instruction

As you continue to read this book, you will explore the components and features of the SIOP Model in detail and have the opportunity to try out numerous techniques for SIOP lessons. You will see that the SIOP Model shares many features recommended for high-quality instruction for all students, such as cooperative learning, strategies for reading comprehension, writers' workshop, and differentiated instruction. However, the SIOP Model adds key features for the academic success of these learners, such as the inclusion of language objectives in every content lesson, the development of background knowledge, the acquisition of content-related vocabulary, and the emphasis on academic literacy practice.

Here we briefly describe the instructional practices that effective SIOP teachers use. You can compare your typical instruction with that of SIOP teachers, and you might find that you are already on the path to becoming a skillful SIOP teacher yourself!

In effective SIOP lessons, language and content objectives are systematically woven into the curriculum of one particular subject area, such as fourth-grade language arts, U.S. history, algebra, or life science, or in one ESL level, such as beginner, intermediate, or advanced. Teachers must develop the students' academic language proficiency consistently and regularly as part of the lessons and units they plan and deliver (Echevarría & Graves, 2007; Short, 2002).

- Classroom teachers generally present the regular, grade-level subject curriculum to the students through modified instruction in English, although some special curricula may be designed for students who have significant gaps in their educational backgrounds or very low literacy skills.

- Classroom teachers identify how language is used in the different subjects and give students explicit instruction and practice with it.

- ESL teachers advance students' English language development with curricula addressing language proficiency standards, but incorporating the types of texts, vocabulary, and tasks used in core subjects to prepare the students for success in the regular, English-medium classroom.

Accomplished SIOP teachers determine students' baseline understandings in their subject area and move them forward, both in their content knowledge and in their language skills through a variety of techniques.

- SIOP teachers provide rigorous instruction aligned with state content and language standards, such as the Common Core and WIDA.

- SIOP teachers make specific connections between the content being taught and students' experiences and prior knowledge, and they focus on expanding the children's vocabulary base.

- They modulate the level of English they use and the texts and other materials used with and among students.

- They make the content comprehensible through techniques such as the use of visual aids, modeling, demonstrations, graphic organizers, vocabulary previews, adapted texts, cooperative learning, peer tutoring, and native language support.

- SIOP teachers help English learners articulate their emerging understandings of the content both orally and in writing, often with sentence starters and language frame scaffolds.

- Besides increasing students' declarative knowledge (i.e., factual information), SIOP teachers highlight and model procedural knowledge (e.g., how to accomplish an academic task like solving a two-step math problem or conducting research on the Internet) along with study skills and learning strategies (e.g., note-taking and self-monitoring comprehension when reading).

In effective SIOP lessons, there is a high level of student engagement and interaction with the teacher, with other students, and with text, which leads to elaborated discourse and critical thinking.

- Student language learning is promoted through social interaction and contextualized communication as teachers guide students to construct meaning and understand complex concepts from texts and classroom discourse (Vygotsky, 1978).

- Students are explicitly taught functional language skills, such as how to negotiate meaning, confirm information, describe, compare, and persuade.

- Teachers introduce English learners to the classroom discourse community and demonstrate skills such as taking turns in a conversation and interrupting politely to ask for clarification.

- Through instructional conversations (Goldenberg, 1992–93) and meaningful activities, students practice and apply their new language and content knowledge.

Not all teaching is about the techniques in a lesson. SIOP teachers also consider their students' affective needs, cultural backgrounds, and learning styles. They strive to create a nonthreatening environment where students feel comfortable taking risks with language.

- SIOP teachers engage in culturally responsive teaching and build on the students' potentially different ways of learning, behaving, and using language (Bartolome, 1994).

- They socialize English learners to the implicit classroom culture, including appropriate behaviors and communication patterns.
- They plan activities that tap into the auditory, visual, and kinesthetic preferences of the students and consider their multiple intelligences as well (Gardner, 1993).
- SIOP teachers reach out to the families of English learners and orient them to the expectations of schooling in the United States and seek to determine the funds of knowledge in the children's households.

The SIOP Model is also distinguished by use of supplementary materials that support the academic text. The purpose of these materials is to enhance student understanding of key topics, issues, and details in the content concepts being taught through means other than teacher lecture or dense textbook prose.

- To present key topics or reinforce information, SIOP teachers find related reading texts (e.g., trade books, leveled readers), graphics and other illustrations, models and other realia, multimedia and computer-based resources, adapted text, and the like.
- SIOP teachers use supplementary materials to make information accessible to children with mixed proficiency levels of English. For example, some students in a mixed class may be able to use the textbook, while others may need an adapted text.

When advances in technology are used effectively in the classroom, English learners can reap many benefits. Digital content is motivating for students, allows for a personalized learning experience, is multimodal, and can give students experience with meaningful and authentic tasks (Lemke & Coughlin, 2009).

- Technology such as interactive whiteboards with links to the Internet, visual displays, audio options, and more offer a wealth of resources to support English learners' acquisition of new information and of academic English.
- Technology and digital learning "specifically provide the opportunity for increased equity and access; improved effectiveness and productivity of teachers and administrators; and improved student achievement and outcomes" (Alliance for Excellent Education, 2011b, p. 2).
- SIOP teachers give students opportunities to use the technology for multiple purposes, such as access to information presented in the students' native language, cyber-group learning interactions such as simulations and virtual field trips, self-paced research, and writing and editing tools.

Depending on the students' proficiency levels, SIOP teachers offer multiple pathways for children to demonstrate their understanding of the content. In this way, teachers can receive a more accurate picture of most English learners' content knowledge and skills through an assortment of assessment measures than they could through one standardized test. Otherwise, a student may be perceived as lacking mastery of content when actually he or she is following the normal pace of the second language acquisition process (Abedi & Lord, 2001; Solano-Flores & Trumbull, 2003).

- SIOP teachers plan pictorial, hands-on, or performance-based assessments for individual students; group tasks or projects; oral reports; written assignments; and portfolios, along with more traditional measures such as paper-and-pencil tests and quizzes to check student comprehension and language growth.

- Teachers use rubrics to measure student performance on a scale leading to mastery, and they share those rubrics with students in advance.

- Teachers dedicate some time to teaching students how to read and understand standardized test questions, pointing out the use of specific verbs or synonyms in the question stems and possible responses (Bailey & Butler, 2007; Kilgo, no date).

It is important to recognize that the SIOP Model does not require teachers to discard their favored techniques or to add copious new elements to a lesson. Rather, this model of sheltered instruction brings together *what* to teach by providing a framework for *how* to teach it. It acts as an umbrella, allowing teachers the flexibility to choose techniques they know work well with their particular group of students (see Figure 1.5). It reminds teachers to pay attention to the language development needs of their students and to select and organize techniques that facilitate the integration of district- or state-level standards for ESL and for specific content areas.

FIGURE 1.5 The SIOP® Model Framework for Organizing Best Practices

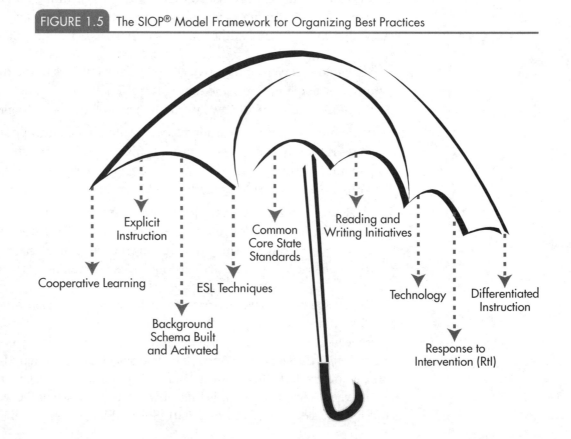

Implementing the SIOP® Model

The goal of this book is to prepare teachers to teach content effectively to English learners as they develop their students' academic English ability. The SIOP Model may be used as part of a program for preservice and inservice professional development, as a lesson planner for sheltered content and content-based ESL lessons, and as a training resource for university faculty. Research shows that professional development approaches that improve teaching include the following: sustained, intensive development with modeling, coaching, and problem solving; collaborative endeavors for educators to share knowledge; experiential opportunities that engage teachers in actual teaching, assessment, and observation; and development grounded in research but also drawing from teacher experience and inquiry, connected to the teachers' classes, students, and subjects taught (Borko, 2004; Darling-Hammond & Richardson, 2009). In our research studies, we found that SIOP implementation does not happen quickly. Teachers may take one to two years before they implement the model consistently to a high degree, and coaching helps get them to that level (Short, Fidelman, & Louguit, 2012). McIntyre and colleagues (2010) suggest that teachers' proficiency in implementing the model may depend on their background teaching experiences and the design of their professional development.

Effective implementation of the SIOP Model is one key to improving the academic success of English learners. Preservice teachers need to learn the model to develop a strong foundation in best practice for integrating language and content in classes with English learners. Practicing teachers need the model to strengthen their lesson planning and delivery and to provide students with more consistent instruction that meets language and content standards. Site-based supervisors and administrators use the model to train and coach teachers and systematize classroom observations. Teacher education faculty also present the SIOP Model in their methods courses and use it in student teacher supervision.

Any program in which students are learning content through a nonnative language could use the SIOP Model effectively. It may be an ESL program (with pullout or self-contained classes), a late-exit bilingual program, a dual language/two-way bilingual program, a newcomer program, a sheltered program, or even a foreign language immersion program. The model has been designed for flexibility and tested in a wide range of classroom situations: with students who have strong academic backgrounds and those who have had limited formal schooling; with students who are recent arrivals and those who have been in U.S. schools for several years; and with students at beginning levels of English proficiency and those at advanced levels. For students studying in content-based ESL or bilingual courses, SIOP instruction often provides the bridge to the general education program. More discussion of getting started with the SIOP Model is found in Chapter 12.

PD **TOOLKIT™ for SIOP®**

Click on Videos, then search for "If the SIOP Model is intended for content teachers, where does this leave the ESL teacher?" to hear about ESL teachers using the SIOP Model.

Summary

As you reflect on this chapter and the impact of the SIOP Model on elementary school English learners' content and academic language learning, consider the following main points:

- Students who are learning English as an additional language are the fastest-growing segment of the school-age population in the United States, and almost all candidates in teacher education programs will have linguistically and culturally diverse students in their classes during their teaching careers. However, many of these future teachers—as well as most practicing teachers—are not well prepared to instruct these learners.

- School reform efforts, standards, and increased state accountability measures put pressure on schools and districts to improve their educational opportunities and practices with English learners. This pressure has had both positive and negative outcomes. Teachers can use the SIOP Model to help students meet Common Core standards and prepare English learners for college and careers.

- The SIOP Model has a strong, empirical research base. It has been tested across multiple subject areas and grade levels. The research evidence shows that the SIOP Model can improve the academic literacy of English learners.

- The SIOP Model does not mandate cookie-cutter instruction, but it provides a framework for well-prepared and well-delivered lessons for any subject area. As SIOP teachers design their lessons, they have room for creativity. Nonetheless, critical instructional features must be attended to in order for teachers to respond appropriately to the unique academic and language development needs of English learners.

- The model is operationalized in the SIOP protocol, which can be used to rate lessons and measure the level of SIOP implementation.

- Our research shows that both language and content teachers can implement the SIOP Model fully to good effect. The model is best suited for content-based ESL and sheltered content classes that are part of a program of studies for English learners, and for English-medium classrooms with English learners and struggling readers. Together, these classes can be a promising combination when implemented schoolwide.

- We need students like Graciela and Jocelyn to be successful in school and beyond. In the long run, such success will benefit the communities in which these students live and the national economy as a whole.

Discussion Questions

1. In reflecting on the content and language objectives at the beginning of the chapter, are you able to:
   a. List characteristics of English learners that may influence their success in school?
   b. Distinguish between content-based ESL and sheltered instruction?
   c. Explain the research supporting the SIOP Model?
   d. Discuss the benefits and challenges of school reform and their effects on English learners?
   e. Develop a lexicon related to the SIOP Model?
   f. Compare your typical instruction with SIOP instruction?

2. Consider one elementary school class of English learners. Identify the individual and sociocultural factors that may influence the educational success of these students. In what ways might instruction using the SIOP Model help them?

3. How would you characterize the type(s) of instruction offered to English learners in your school or schools you know: traditional ESL, content-based ESL, sheltered content, bilingual content, traditional content? Provide evidence of your characterization in terms of curricula and instruction. Are the ELs successful when they exit English language support programs and are placed in regular classrooms without support, either in the upper elementary grades or in middle school? Explain.

4. Many elementary classroom teachers using sheltered instruction, whether they had special training in a subject area or in second language acquisition, fail to take advantage of the language learning opportunities for children in sheltered content classes. Why do you think this is so? Offer two concrete suggestions for these teachers to enhance their students' academic language development.

5. Look at one of your own lesson plans. Which characteristics of the SIOP Model do you already incorporate? Consider the components and features of the model as found in Appendix A.

CHAPTER 2

Lesson Preparation

After reading, discussing, and engaging in activities related to this chapter, you will be able to meet the following content and language objectives.

Content Objectives

Identify content objectives for English learners that are aligned to state, local, or national standards.

Incorporate supplementary materials suitable for English learners in a lesson plan.

Select from a variety of techniques for adapting content to the students' proficiency and cognitive levels.

Language Objectives

Write language and content objectives.

Discuss advantages for writing both language and content objectives for a lesson and sharing the objectives with students.

Explain the importance of meaningful academic activities for English learners.

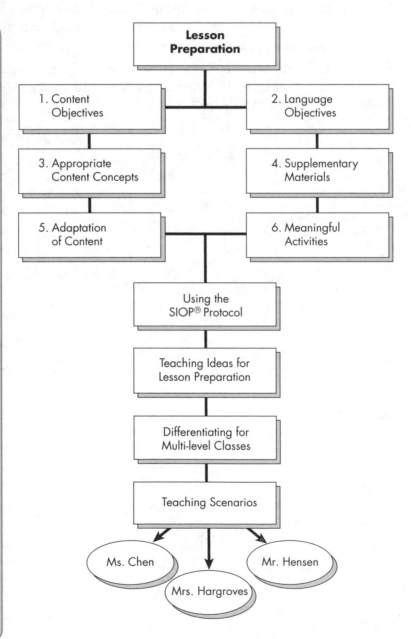

In this and subsequent chapters, we explain each SIOP (Sheltered Instruction Observation Protocol) Model component and its features. Each chapter begins with an explanation of the component, offers classroom activities, and then describes how three different teachers teach the same lesson. The lesson scenarios throughout the book are about varied topics and are for different grade levels.

This chapter introduces the first component of the SIOP Model, Lesson Preparation. We present background information and the rationale for each of the six features in this component, list some teaching ideas for this component and for differentiating instruction in multi-level classrooms, and demonstrate through the teaching scenarios how the model can be implemented. As you read the scenarios, think about the SIOP features that have been explained in the chapter, and try to rate the lessons according to their best practice. Reflect on how effectively each teacher is meeting the needs of English learners in relation to each feature. At the conclusion of the teaching scenarios, we discuss our assessment of the teachers' efforts to provide SIOP instruction, and we invite you to compare your appraisal to ours. ●

Background

As we all know, lesson planning is critical to both a student's and a teacher's success. For maximum learning to occur, planning must produce lessons that target specific learning goals, enable students to make connections between their own knowledge and experiences and the new information being taught, give students practice using and applying the new information, and assess student learning to determine whether to move on or reteach the material. With careful planning, we make learning meaningful and relevant by including appropriate motivating materials and activities that foster real-life application of concepts studied.

Traditionally, to meet the needs of students who struggled with grade-level reading materials, texts have been rewritten according to readability formulae or lexile levels (Gray & Leary, 1935; Stenner & Burdick, 1997). The adapted texts included controlled vocabulary and a limited number of concepts, resulting in the omission of critical pieces of information. We have learned that if students' exposure to content concepts is limited by vocabulary-controlled materials, the amount of information they learn over time is considerably less than that of their peers who use grade-level texts. The result is that the "rich get richer and the poor get poorer" (Stanovich, 1986). That is, instead of closing the gap between native English speakers and English learners, the learning gap is increased, and eventually it becomes nearly impossible to close. Therefore, it is imperative that we plan lessons that are not negatively biased against students acquiring English and that include age-appropriate content and materials. However, our lessons must provide appropriate scaffolds so our students can meet the rigor of new standards, such as the Common Core, over time and be prepared for college and careers.

This component, Lesson Preparation, is therefore very important to the SIOP Model. If properly prepared, a lesson will include most of the SIOP features in advance. It is then up to the teachers and class to accomplish them as the lesson unfolds. However, when planning, teachers have asked how they can meet all 30 features in a given period. We explain that a SIOP lesson may be single day or multi-day in length. Over the course of several days, all 30 features should be met. See Vogt and Echevarría (2008, pp. 18–19) for a SIOP lesson planning flow chart.

As you learn the model, we strongly encourage you to write out lessons in detail. We suggest you use the SIOP protocol as a checklist to ensure all of the features are incorporated. You may want to try one or more of the lesson plan templates we have included in Appendix B or the templates in Chapter 7 of *Implementing the SIOP® Model Through Effective Professional Development and Coaching* (Echevarría, Short, & Vogt, 2008). All of these templates have been used successfully in classrooms. In addition, sample lesson plans and units can be found in the SIOP content books for English-language arts, mathematics, science, and history and social studies (Echevarría, Vogt, & Short, 2010c; Short, Vogt, & Echevarría, 2011a, 2011b; Vogt, Echevarría, & Short, 2010).

"How do I start implementing SIOP lessons?" is a frequent question from teachers new to the SIOP Model. We suggest that

- elementary school teachers begin with one subject area, and
- secondary school teachers begin with one course.

It is better to begin on a small scale so you do not have to write multiple SIOP lessons each day while you are learning the model. In some cases, teachers learn the SIOP Model over time, component by component, and they build their lesson planning skills in the same way. Once you have internalized the model, you may write less detailed lesson plans, and you will probably find that writing SIOP lessons across subject areas or courses is easier.

PD TOOLKIT™ for SIOP®

Click on SIOP® Lesson Plans & Activities, then visit the SIOP® Lesson Plan Templates and the Sample SIOP® Lesson Plans.

SIOP® FEATURE 1:

Content Objectives Clearly Defined, Displayed, and Reviewed with Students

In effective instruction, concrete content objectives that identify what students should know and be able to do must guide teaching and learning. When planning content objectives, keep the following principles in mind:

FIGURE 2.1 How to Start an Objective

Students will be able to (SWBAT) _____

Students will (SW) _____

We will _____

Today I will _____

The learner will _____

Our job is to _____

- Plan objectives that support school, district, or state content standards and learning outcomes. The Common Core State Standards for English language arts and mathematics are a source of content objectives, and well-implemented SIOP instruction can help students meet them.

- Write lesson-level objectives (something that can be taught and learned in one lesson or two) and use student-friendly language that suits the age and proficiency levels in the class. Content objectives and state standards are frequently complex and not written in a manner that is accessible to English learners or students in primary grades. Often standards are too generic or broad—such as "Apply and extend previous understandings of multiplication and division to multiply and divide fractions" from the Common Core grade 5 math standards (p. 36)—to be useful as a single lesson's learning goal.

(© Copyright 2010. National Governors Association Center for Best Practices and Council of Chief State School Officers. All rights reserved.)

- Write objectives in terms of student learning, not as an agenda item. See Figure 2.1 for several ways that teachers in our research studies have started their objectives. You will note that all focus on the student.

- Limit the number of content objectives to only one or two per lesson to reduce the complexity of the learning task and to ensure that instruction can meet the objectives.

- Share objectives with the children, orally and in writing. Typically teachers do not consistently present objectives to students. As a result, students do not know what they are supposed to learn each day. SIOP teachers tell students the objectives for every lesson.

- Plan lessons so you provide some explicit instruction and practice opportunities related to each objective.

- Review the objectives at the end of the lesson to determine if students have mastered them. Use that assessment when deciding whether to move to the next topic or spend some time reteaching.

We know from our research studies and professional development experiences that presenting objectives each day can be challenging for teachers. But the effort is worth it. One of the sheltered teachers who was learning the SIOP Model reported her growing awareness of the importance of clearly stated content objectives that are displayed for English learners:

> *The objectives are still going on in my class. They're on the board every day and the students are getting used to seeing them, reading them out loud, and evaluating whether or not we achieved them at the end of each class. I still have questions about the wording and what's a good objective . . . but that will come with time and more discussion and study. I just wanted to say that defining the objectives each day definitely brings more focus to my planning and thinking, and it helps bring order to my classroom procedures. So far, it has not been too burdensome and the habit is definitely forming.*

Content-based ESL teachers sometimes need assistance in identifying appropriate content objectives to add to their lessons. They may feel unprepared for in-depth instruction on a content topic, they may not know the key concepts that should be taught, and they may not know what types of activities usually support the topic. For these reasons, we advocate that content and language teachers collaborate closely as they prepare lessons and help their students meet language and content goals.

The bottom line for English learners is that content objectives need to be written in terms of what students will learn or do; they should be stated simply, orally and in writing, and tied to specific grade-level content standards.

Examples of content objectives and language objectives, discussed below, can be found throughout each chapter in this book, in *99 Ideas and Activities for Teaching English Learners with the SIOP® Model* (Vogt & Echevarría, 2008), in *Helping English Language Learners Succeed in Pre-K-Elementary Schools* (Lacina, Levine, & Sowa, 2006), in lesson plans presented in *Science for English Language Learners* (Fathman & Crowther, 2006), and in the SIOP content books mentioned above.

SIOP® FEATURE 2:

Language Objectives Clearly Defined, Displayed, and Reviewed with Students

PD TOOLKIT™ for SIOP®

Click on Videos, then search for "Incorporating Language Objectives" to see an example of adding language objectives to regular lessons.

While carefully planning and delivering content objectives, SIOP teachers must also incorporate into their lesson plans objectives that support students' academic language development, and ESL teachers may have to build social language skills too (Gersten et al., 2007; Saunders & Goldenberg, 2010). The same principles we discuss above for content objectives also should apply to planning language objectives. Language objectives should be stated clearly and simply, and students should be informed of them, both orally and in writing. They should be limited in number for a given lesson and reviewed at the end. The objectives should be drawn from the state English language proficiency standards and English language arts standards. Most importantly, the objectives should represent an aspect of academic English that students need to learn or master.

Although incorporating language objectives in all content lessons is a hallmark of the SIOP Model, we recognize that many content teachers are not used to thinking about the language demands of their subject. What we propose in the SIOP Model calls for a new perspective on your subject area. It is not sufficient to only have a deep understanding of topics in your content area; rather, an effective teacher also needs to know how language is used in the content area in order to convey information (orally or in text) and to use and apply that information (through class reading, writing, and discussion activities). It also requires you to know your students' proficiency levels so the language objectives can be targeted to what they need to learn about the academic language of history, science, mathematics, or other subjects, but not be at a level too high for their current understanding.

Because it may be a new way of thinking for you, here are some points to keep in mind from research on second language acquisition:

- When considering which language objectives to include in a lesson and how to write them, it is important to keep in mind that acquiring a second language is a process. As such, language objectives may cover a range from process-oriented to performance-oriented statements over time so that students have a chance to explore, and then practice, before demonstrating mastery of an objective. The following objectives from a SIOP language arts class show the progression of objectives that might be taught over several days:

  Students will be able to

  1. Recognize similes in text (Day 1)

  2. Discuss the functions of similes (Days 1–2)

  3. Write three similes (Day 2)

  4. Write a paragraph that describes a setting using similes (Days 3–4)

  For the first lesson (Day 1), students learn to recognize similes in text, perhaps by focusing on the key words *like* and *as*, and the class discusses the purpose of similes. After that (Day 2), they might discuss reasons why authors use similes and then generate their own similes in decontextualized sentences. On Day 3 they describe a setting using similes and turn that description into a paragraph, an authentic purpose. On Day 4 the teacher might have students edit their paragraphs and then share some aloud.

  Figure 2.2 displays possible verbs for objective statements that reflect this process-to-performance continuum.

FIGURE 2.2   Process-to-Performance Verbs

Process-Oriented -------> ------> ------> Performance-Oriented		
Explore	Define	
Listen to	Draft	
Recognize		Write
Discuss in small groups		Give an oral presentation
		Edit

- It is important to distinguish between receptive and productive language skills. English learners tend to develop receptive skills (listening and reading) faster than productive skills (speaking and writing), but all the skills should be worked on in a unified manner. Students don't have to learn to speak, for instance, before they learn to read and write (August & Shanahan, 2006; Saunders & Goldenberg, 2010).

- We cannot ignore oral language practice and focus our objectives only on reading and writing. We know from research (Goldenberg, 2008; Guthrie & Ozgungor, 2002) that the absence of planned speaking practice—be it formal or informal—by English learners in content classrooms is detrimental to their development of academic English. Gibbons (2003) argues that skillful teachers should take advantage of oral interaction to move children from informal, everyday explanations of a content topic (e.g., a scientific process) to the more specialized academic register of the formal written and spoken code.

- A focus on function and form is necessary to move students to advanced levels of academic English and full proficiency, which also set students up to be college and career ready. The ESL and English language arts teachers play important roles in making this happen, but content teachers should not let students coast in class. If some English learners are ready to produce more sophisticated language (e.g., during an oral presentation on a country studied, or in a science fair project), they should be challenged to do so. Schleppegrell and colleagues (Schleppegrell, 2004; Schleppegrell, Achugar, & Orteíza, 2004) have conducted linguistic analyses of the lexical and grammatical forms that construe meaning in written and spoken school discourse and have identified implications for instruction. SIOP teachers might make the development of specialized grammar and lexical forms part of their scope and sequence of language objectives (Dutro & Kinsella, 2010; Ellis, 2006; Hinkel 2006).

- The more exposure students have to academic language and the more time they spend using it, the faster they will develop language proficiency (Echevarría & Graves, 2010; Saunders & Goldenberg, 2010). If the ESL teacher is the only educator who works on language development with an English learner during the school day, less progress will be made than if all the teachers on the English learner's schedule attend to language development and practice (Snow & Katz, 2010).

- It is important to assess the language objectives to determine if students are making progress toward mastery. You can plan for multi-level responses from the students according to their proficiency in English. For example, use group response techniques (e.g., thumbs-up/thumbs-down) for students who are in the early stages of English language development. For students who are more proficient English speakers, incorporate activities that involve partner work and small group assignments so that English learners can practice their English in a less threatening setting. Accept approximations and multiple-word responses rather than complete sentences from children at early stages of English development. However, it is also appropriate to require English learners with more proficiency to give answers in one or two complete sentences. This practice develops language skills because it requires students to move beyond what may be their comfort zone in using English. You will find this topic discussed in more detail in Chapter 9.

You also need to know about sources of language objectives. The first place to start is the state English language proficiency (ELP) standards. Second, as we mentioned in Chapter 1, look at the WIDA standards. The WIDA consortium has compiled a list of "Can Do" descriptors that can help teachers identify the kind of language tasks students should be able to perform according to five differing levels of English proficiency and different grade-level clusters. (To view these descriptors, go to http://www.wida.us/standards/CAN_DOs/)

Individual state and Common Core English language arts standards are other resources. Some states also have content area standards that include a strand focused on communication. Ideas for objectives will be found in all of these official documents as well as in local district curricula and instructional materials. By reviewing the course textbook and other materials, you can see if there are language skills and academic vocabulary that students need to develop in order to comprehend the information.

One critically important source for successful SIOP lesson implementation is your colleagues. If you are a content or grade-level classroom teacher, pair up with an ESL or bilingual teacher. Tap his or her expertise for language topics and knowledge of the English learners' academic language needs. If you are an ESL teacher, you have a plethora of language objectives at your disposal. You need to partner with one or more content teachers to identify content objectives and lesson tasks that the English learners need assistance with and align them to your language objectives. You may want to focus on thematic units to cover a variety of content topics or focus on one subject area per quarter. (See Lacina, Levine, and Sowa, 2006, for examples of collaboration between elementary ESL and classroom teachers.)

Writing Content and Language Objectives

PD **TOOLKIT™ for SIOP®**

Click on Videos, then search for "Objectives" to hear a discussion on the importance of including content and language objectives in lessons.

All the content and language objectives should evolve from the lesson topic and be part of the instructional plan. After a teacher writes content and language objectives, posts them, and discusses them with the students at the start of class, at some point in the lesson explicit instruction must be provided on these objectives. Students would then have practice opportunities aligned to the objectives and be assessed on their progress toward meeting them at the close of the lesson. In other words, each objective is what we want the students to learn, and each needs explicit attention. An objective is not a by-product of an activity but the foundation of one.

Remember: Writing an agenda or list of activities on the board is not the same as writing the content and language objectives!

Content objectives, as mentioned earlier, are usually drawn from the state subject area standards. Consider this standard of learning from Virginia: "Students will investigate and understand the basic needs and life processes of plants and animals." It is too broad to be addressed in one lesson, but it is written in a straightforward manner. Surprisingly, however, it is an objective for kindergarten. Posting this objective word for word in the kindergarten classroom would not be helpful for your students. How might you revise it to present to five- and six-year-olds? You might write the following on a lesson plan: "Students will identify parts of a tree and their functions"; but for the students you might post a tree picture and write on the board, "Identify parts of a tree. Tell what the parts do." When you explain it, you might elaborate, "Today you will learn about parts of a tree (point to the tree picture). You will be able to identify the parts (point to the different parts) and tell what the parts do (explain that leaves make food for the tree)."

After you have rewritten the state standard as an appropriate content objective for the kindergartners, you will need to plan the lesson and determine a language objective. One teacher we worked with combined the science lesson with a reading of *The Giving Tree* (Silverstein, 1964). For his language objective, he decided on "Students will listen to *The Giving Tree* and act out the story miming vocabulary words (trunk, branch, leaf)." He explained to the students that they would listen to a story, look at the pictures, name the parts of the tree, and then act out parts of the tree when he read the story again. In this lesson he would therefore reinforce the skill of listening for specific information and have students physically demonstrate their understanding of vocabulary terms.

Language objectives should be planned to meet learning goals and prepare students for the type of academic language they need to understand the content and perform the activities in the lesson. But the activities alone are not language objectives, although they could provide language practice. In some lessons, language objectives may focus on developing students' vocabulary, introducing new words and concepts, or teaching word structure to help English learners discern the meaning of new words. Other lessons may lend themselves to practice with reading comprehension skills or the writing process. Sometimes objectives will highlight functional language use, such as how to request information, justify opinions, negotiate meaning, provide detailed explanations, and so forth. Higher-order thinking skills, such as articulating predictions or hypotheses, stating conclusions, summarizing information, and making comparisons, can be tied to language objectives, too. Sometimes specific grammar points can be taught as well; for example, learning about capitalization when studying famous historical events and persons.

A colleague of ours, Amy Washam, who is a very experienced SIOP professional developer, uses some effective techniques to help teachers conceptualize academic language in their lesson planning process:

> First, I ask teachers what they would need in order to learn another language fluently enough to attend a graduate course in a country where that language is spoken. Teachers brainstorm ideas, which often include a tutor, a specialized glossary of key terms in the course, extra time spent in the country before the class starts practicing the language, and language learning programs on tape that they can listen to over and over.

I tell them that what they listed—modeling, repetition, feedback, practice speaking the language—are all good language activities for their English learners. But they also need to have a language target for each activity.

So next I ask teachers to think of an English learner they have worked with recently and write down all of the reasons this student is not considered English proficient in their class. Common reasons cited are poor reading comprehension, technical difficulties in writing, problems with English pronunciation, and limited background knowledge which results in limited academic vocabulary.

My response at this point is "The reasons you listed for your student not being classified as English proficient are your language objectives. You can have language objectives for reading comprehension, academic vocabulary development, grammar, and even pronunciation." I then push them to think about their planning and ask, "Is it more important for this student to work on the content standards in their classes or the list of skills that you say this student does not possess yet in English?"

Now they typically say both are important. So we move to the next step: I ask them to respond to these questions:

1. What language will students need to know and use to accomplish this lesson's content objectives?

2. How can I move my students' English language knowledge forward in this lesson?

We suggest you consider the following four categories as the starting point for generating language objectives. Think about how language will be used in your lesson: in your speech, in class discussion, in the reading assignments, in writing tasks, and in the lesson activities. Then, given the content topic and an understanding of the students' level of academic language acquisition, write an objective that complements the topic and that you will explicitly address in the lesson.

- **Academic Vocabulary.** Key words needed to discuss, read, or write about the topic of the lesson (e.g., names of important people, places, and events; scientific and mathematical terms; social studies or health concepts) can be the focus of language objectives. Vocabulary for a lesson can be drawn from three subcategories, which are described in detail in Chapter 3:

  - *Content vocabulary:* These key words and technical terms are subject specific. They are often the highlighted words in textbooks. Students need them to understand lesson concepts, but they are generally low-frequency words (i.e., not regularly used outside of the classroom), particularly those in secondary school courses. (Ask yourself: When was the last time you used *magma* in conversation?)

  - *General academic vocabulary:* These words include cross-curricular academic terms (e.g., *circumstances, impact, observe*), transition words and logical connectors (e.g., *however, because, next*), and language function words (e.g., *compare, persuade*). This category includes medium and high-frequency words that are used in academic and social conversations.

  - *Word parts:* This category refers to roots, prefixes, and suffixes. Attention to the structure of words can help expand a child's vocabulary knowledge considerably. For example, if a child knows that *vis* is the root meaning "to see," she can begin to guess the meaning of words like *vision, visual, invisible,* and *visualize.*

● **Language Skills and Functions.** This category reflects the ways students use language in the lesson.

   ◆ Students are expected to read, write, listen, and speak, but how well they do so varies. English learners need some direct instruction in these language skills, along with opportunities to practice. The skills taught need to link to the topic of the lesson. In a language arts class, for example, will students need to read and find key details in the text to cite as evidence? In social studies, will they need to listen to an audio recording of a speech by an historical figure? In science class, will they have to record their observations during an experiment?

   ◆ Any lesson may also call for students to use language for a specific purpose—to describe, compare, or predict, for example. English learners need instruction here as well, particularly in ways to articulate their descriptions or comparisons or predictions.

● **Language Structures or Grammar.** Teachers can pay attention to the language structures in the written or spoken discourse of their class and teach students the structures that are widely used. For example, students might be struggling with a text that includes the passive voice, imperatives, or if-then sentences. If so, the teacher may teach students how to interpret these sentences. If you are a content teacher, we are not asking you to become a grammar expert, but we do want you to be aware of the syntax used in your subject area. If you are an ESL teacher, this category might offer the opportunity to teach some grammar that will really advance the students' language proficiency.

● **Language Learning Strategies.** This category provides a way for teachers to give students resources to learn on their own. Strategies to be taught may include

   ◆ corrective strategies (e.g., reread confusing text),

   ◆ self-monitoring strategies (e.g., make and confirm predictions),

   ◆ prereading strategies (e.g., preview headings, relate to personal experience), or

   ◆ language practice strategies (e.g., repeat or rehearse phrases, imitate a native speaker).

Teaching students with Latin-based native languages to consider cognates when they see new academic terms is a very powerful strategy as well. More discussion on strategies is found in Chapter 5.

In Figure 2.3, we show how language objectives might be written for these four categories. One column shows language objectives for a first-grade science class. Another column shows language objectives for third-grade math lessons on geometric shapes. These objectives are illustrative and would not all be placed in one lesson; they could be used over a series of lessons. Note that it is important to include a variety of language objectives over the course of one week. Many teachers feel comfortable teaching vocabulary as their language objective. This is a good first

FIGURE 2.3 Categories and Examples for Developing Language Objectives

Type of Language Objective	Grade 1 Science Example	Grade 3 Math Example
Academic Vocabulary ↓	Students will be able to use key words like *feathers, scales, fur*, and adjectives of size and color to describe animals.	Students will be able to define the terms *square, rectangle, rhombus, trapezoid*, and *parallelogram* orally and in writing.
What it means instructionally	Teacher reminds students of key terms and definitions and models how to use them to describe animals.	Teacher teaches (or reminds) students how to define a term: state attributes, give an example, draw a picture, or use in a sentence.
Language Skills and Functions ↓	Students will be able to compare features of animals.	Students will be able to listen to teacher descriptions in order to draw different types of parallelograms.
What it means instructionally	Teacher teaches comparative language frames, such as "Both ___ and ___ have." and "___ and ___ are alike/different because ___."	Teacher teaches a listening comprehension skill—paying attention to key words—and asks students to draw the shapes or construct them on a geoboard.
Language Structures or Grammar ↓	Students will be able to use singular and plural nouns with correct forms of present tense irregular verbs.	Students will be able to use comparative phrases, such as greater than, larger than, smaller than, less than, and equal to orally and in writing when comparing geometric figures and angles.
What it means instructionally	Teacher introduces (or reviews) the difference between singular and plural nouns (using animal examples) and explains how to match a noun to present tense irregular verb forms (e.g., is/are, has/have).	Teacher introduces (or reviews) these comparative phrases and also shows the corresponding mathematical symbols (i.e., >, <, and =).
Language Learning Strategies ↓	Students will be able to monitor subject-verb agreement in sentences they write.	Students will be able to visualize and relate the geometric shapes to their lives.
What it means instructionally	Teacher models writing a sentence about one animal (e.g., The bird has feathers.) and another about two (e.g., The snakes are brown.). He shows students how to check a sentence for subject-verb agreement.	Teacher explains how to visualize and make a personal connection and how to articulate the mental image, perhaps through a think-aloud.

Writing Content and Language Objectives

step, but it is not the complete picture of the language development our English learners need to be successful in school and beyond.

Sometimes the language and content objectives may be closely linked as in the following upper elementary math lesson:

- Students will solve word problems using a two-step process.
- Students will write a word problem for a classmate to solve requiring a two-step process.

The first statement is the content objective. It focuses on a mathematical procedure. The second is the language objective, wherein students practice mathematical writing skills.

At other times, the language objective might extend the content knowledge, as in this upper elementary geography lesson:

- Students will be able to (SWBAT) identify specific landforms on a map of South America.
- SWBAT present an oral report about one landform and its influence on economic development.

In this lesson, learning to read a map is likely to be easier for the students than learning to give an oral presentation. The teacher may have to explain the key of a map, but finding the landforms (assuming they had been taught in a prior lesson) would not be too time consuming. However, guiding students in giving oral presentations will take more effort. Besides providing time for students to research a landform and cull the information into a set of facts to present, the teacher must help students with articulating their information orally and adding nonlinguistic aspects of the presentation such as eye contact and intonation.

For language arts and reading teachers, teasing apart language and content objectives can be tricky. Certain curriculum concepts like *plot* and *setting* are clearly ingredients for language arts content objectives, but some potential objectives like "produce writing that conveys a clear point of view and maintains a consistent tone" could be either a language or a content objective. We encourage language arts and reading teachers to nonetheless consistently identify a content and a language objective for each lesson, even if some might be placed in either category. Because we are aiming for whole-school implementation of the SIOP Model, having students recognize and expect both types of objectives across all their classes is a valuable goal.

The following objectives are from a fifth-grade language arts class. Either could be the content objective or the language objective. We might label the first as the language objective because learning to use descriptive adjectives is a skill applicable across content areas. The second, focusing on characterization, falls neatly into the language arts curriculum.

- Students will use descriptive adjectives to write sentences about the characters.
- Students will compare traits of two characters in a story.

As you write your objectives, keep the verbs in Figure 2.4 in mind. Although the verbs are not exclusive to one type or another, they are more common to the

FIGURE 2.4 Sample Verbs for Writing Content and Language Objectives

Verbs for Content Objectives	Verbs for Language Objectives
Identify	Listen for
Solve	Retell
Investigate	Define
Distinguish	Find the main idea
Hypothesize	Compare
Create	Summarize
Select	Rehearse
Draw conclusions about	Persuade
Determine	Write
Find	Draft
Calculate	Defend a position on
Observe	Describe

category presented. Over time, add to this list to further distinguish between the content and language goals of your lesson. Also be sure to use active verbs; avoid *learn, know,* and *understand*.

Note that even if you have students with mixed levels of English proficiency in class, we do not suggest you write different language objectives per proficiency level. Instead, write an objective that all students should attain based on the content concepts in the lesson, but adjust the intended outcomes to match the students' ability levels. Some students may master the objective by the end of the lesson; others will be at some point on a path toward mastery.

After you have written your content and language objectives, we suggest you refer to this checklist to evaluate them:

_____ The objectives are aligned to state or district standards.

_____ The objectives are observable.

_____ The objectives are written and will be stated simply, in language the students can understand.

_____ The objectives are written in terms of student learning.

_____ The content objective is related to the key concept of the lesson.

_____ The language objective promotes student academic language growth (i.e., it is not something most students already do well).

_____ The language objective connects clearly with the lesson topic or lesson activities.

_____ The objectives are measurable. I have a plan for assessing student progress on meeting these objectives during the lesson.

SIOP® FEATURE 3:

Content Concepts Appropriate for Age and Educational Background Level of Students

SIOP teachers must carefully consider the content concepts they wish to teach, and use district curriculum guidelines and grade-level content standards as guides. In SIOP classrooms, this entails ensuring that although materials may be adapted to meet the needs of English learners, the content is not diminished. When planning lessons around content concepts, consider the following:

- the students' first language literacy,
- their English language proficiency,
- their schooling backgrounds and academic preparation for grade-level work,
- their background knowledge of the topic,
- the cultural and age appropriateness of instructional materials, and
- the difficulty level of any text or other material to be read.

Our goal as SIOP teachers is to provide the grade-level curriculum to our English learners. By employing the type of techniques we propose in the SIOP Model, teachers skillfully make that content comprehensible to the children. Sometimes we adapt the materials being read or the materials used to accomplish a task. The following considerations are worth keeping in mind.

- In general, it is inappropriate to use the curriculum materials and books from much earlier grades. Students in high school who are developing literacy for the first time should not be reading about "doggies and birdies," for example. Likewise, upper elementary children deserve books with age-appropriate illustrations. Other materials should be found, and if necessary, the teacher should provide the scaffolding needed to understand the content concepts and complex text.

- In some cases, students with major gaps in their educational backgrounds may be placed in newcomer programs or specialized classes that pull objectives and content concepts from earlier grades in order to provide the foundational knowledge the students need to perform grade-level work successfully and catch up to their classmates (Short & Boyson, 2012). Ideally, specialized courses would be developed to accelerate the learning of students with limited formal schooling, such as FAST Math developed by Fairfax County (VA) Public Schools (Helman & Buchanan, 1993), which can help students gain several years' worth of mathematics instruction in one subject area in six months or one year.

- We should also be mindful of concepts our upper elementary and secondary English learners may have already learned through their life experiences or prior schooling. Sometimes, an illustration or demonstration can help students recall a concept and then the teacher can help them learn new English words to describe the concept and add to their understanding of it. As Torgesen and colleagues (2007) point out, "ELLs who already know and understand a concept in their first language have a far simpler task to develop language for the concept in English than do students who lack knowledge of the concept in either language" (p. 92).

- To help students make connections to the content topics, reflect on the amount of background knowledge needed to learn and apply the concepts, and plan ways to build or activate students' prior knowledge related to them. For example, fourth-grade students typically learn about magnetism, yet some adolescent English learners may not have studied this concept. Rather than diminish the content, use what prior knowledge students do have, perhaps about attraction, and then explicitly build background on magnetism as a foundation for the lesson.

- Another way to build background for a small group of learners so they are ready for the content concepts is through a small group minilesson that precedes the regular whole-class lesson (Rance-Roney, 2010; Vogt, 2000). This minilesson provides a "jump-start" by reviewing key background concepts, introducing vocabulary, leading a picture or text "walk" through the reading material, engaging in simulations or role-plays, or participating in hands-on experiential activities. The jump-start minilesson develops context and gives access to children who may lack appropriate background knowledge or experience with the grade-level content concepts. In heterogeneous classes in which English learners study with native English speakers, peer tutors can be used to teach some of the requisite background information as well. Another option, where available, is to provide the minilesson in the students' native language.

- In schools where an ESL teacher and a classroom teacher work collaboratively with the same group of students, the ESL teacher can offer lessons that build background and vocabulary before the English learners study the topic in their regular class.

SIOP® FEATURE 4:

Supplementary Materials Used to a High Degree, Making the Lesson Clear and Meaningful

Information that is embedded in context allows English learners to understand and complete more cognitively demanding tasks. Effective SIOP instruction involves the use of many supplementary materials that support the core curriculum and contextualize learning. This is especially important for children who do not have grade-level academic backgrounds and/or who have language and learning difficulties. Because lectures and pencil-and-paper activities centered on a text are often difficult for these students, remember to plan for supplementary materials that will enhance meaning and clarify confusing concepts, making lessons more relevant.

A variety of supplementary materials also support different learning styles and multiple intelligences because information and concepts are presented in a multifaceted

PD TOOLKIT™ for SIOP®

Click on Videos, then search for "Supplementary Materials" to see a first grade class use supplementary materials.

manner. Students can see, hear, feel, perform, create, and participate in order to make connections and construct relevant meanings. The use of technology (e.g., interactive whiteboards) and multimedia can enhance student understanding and engagement with the content topics and related language practice opportunities. Supplementary materials provide a real-life context and enable students to bridge prior experiences with new learning. To the extent possible, choose materials that are culturally responsive to student backgrounds (Nieto & Bode, 2008).

Examples of supplementary materials and resources that can be used to create context and support content concepts include the following:

- **Hands-on Manipulatives:** These can include anything from counter chips for math to microscopes for science to interactive maps for social studies. Manipulating objects physically can reduce the language load of an activity; beginning-level students in particular can still participate and demonstrate their understanding.

- **Realia:** These are real-life objects that enable students to make connections to their own lives. Examples include play money (coins and bills) for a unit on money; historical realia such as photos, recordings, and clothing from the Great Depression; or nutrition labels on food products for a health unit.

- **Pictures and Visuals:** Photographs and illustrations are available that depict nearly any object, process, or setting. Web sites, magazines, commercial photos, and hand drawings can provide visual support for a wide variety of content and vocabulary concepts and can build background knowledge. Models, graphs, charts, timelines, maps, props, and bulletin board displays also convey information. Many teachers now have electronic document viewers that they use to display book pages, photos, and more to the class. Many teachers also use PowerPoint slides and interactive whiteboards. Students with diverse abilities often have difficulty processing an inordinate amount of auditory information and so instruction that is supported with visual clues is more beneficial to them.

- **Multimedia:** A wide variety of multimedia materials are available to enhance teaching and learning. These range from simple tape recordings to videos, DVDs, interactive CD-ROMs, podcasts, and an increasing number of resources available on the Internet. Brief video clips at www.discoveryeducation.com, www.pbs.com, and www.nationalgeographic.com are effective tools. For some children and tasks, media in the students' native language may be a valuable source of information, with audio links as well as written text. It is important to preview Web sites for appropriateness and readability, especially when using them with beginning and intermediate-level students.

- **Demonstrations:** Demonstrations provide visual support and modeling for English learners. If you have a lesson task that includes supplementary materials, then you can scaffold information by carefully planning demonstrations that model how to use the materials and follow directions. Children can then practice these steps in groups or alone, with you or other experienced individuals nearby to assist as needed.

- **Related Literature:** A wide variety of fiction and nonfiction texts can be included to support content teaching. Many elementary classroom teachers create class libraries with trade books and leveled readers on key topics. Some teachers ask librarians to set aside books on related topics as well.[1] Students can read these as supplements to the textbook. They offer a motivating way to look at a topic in more depth. Class libraries can promote more independent reading among students, which is valuable for vocabulary development and reading comprehension practice.

- **Hi-lo Readers and Thematic Sets:** Some publishers offer classic literature as well as fiction and nonfiction selections in a hi-lo format. The stories are of high interest but lower readability levels and tend to include many visuals and a glossary. Some books are grouped into thematic sets (e.g., Civil Rights Leaders Around the World) and can accompany different content area courses. The books in each set are written at different reading levels (e.g., one below-level book, two on-level books, one above-level book). They are useful for classes that have students with multiple proficiency levels in English.

- **Chapter Summaries:** Some textbook publishers provided one-page summaries of each chapter. These overviews present the key ideas. The summaries are often available in Spanish and sometimes in other languages as well. They can be used to preview the topic or to review it afterward.

- **Adapted Text:** A type of supplementary reading material that can be very effective for English learners, as well as struggling readers, is adapted text. Without significantly diminishing the content concepts, a piece of text (usually from a grade-level textbook or a primary source document) is adapted to reduce the reading level demands. Complicated, lengthy sentences with specialized terminology are rewritten in smaller chunks. Definitions are given for difficult vocabulary in context. Please note that we are not advocating "dumbing down" the textbook, an approach that in the past yielded easy-to-read materials with virtually no content concepts left intact. Rather, we suggest that the major concepts be retained, but the reading level demands of the text be aligned to the children's abilities.

SIOP® FEATURE 5:

Adaptation of Content to All Levels of Student Proficiency

In many schools, teachers are required to use textbooks that are too difficult for English learners to read. We have previously mentioned the problem of "watering down" text to the point where all students can read it; content concepts are frequently lost when the text is adapted in this way. We also know English learners cannot be expected to learn all content information by listening to lectures.

Therefore, we must find ways to make the text and other resource materials accessible for all students, adapting them so that the content concepts are left intact.

---

[1]See Short, Cloud, Morris, and Motta (2012) to learn about a project organizing library books by lesson topic and English proficiency level and creating bookmarks for book sets.

Several ways of doing this have been recommended for students who have reading difficulties (Readance, Bean, & Baldwin, 2001; Ruddell, 2007; Vacca, Vacca, & Mraz, 2010), and they work equally well for English learners. These approaches can be used throughout a lesson, as a prereading instructional strategy, as an aid during reading, and as a postreading method for organizing newly learned information.

Native language supports can help with adapting the content, too. If some students are literate in their native language, texts written in that language may be used to supplement a textbook or clarify key concepts. Students may conduct research using native language materials and share the information with classmates in English. Increasingly, the Internet offers native language Web sites, especially for the more commonly taught languages, and authentic materials such as newspapers can be found online. For students who are not literate in their native language but have oral skills, native language broadcasts, podcasts, audio books, and access to knowledgeable adults who speak their language may be additional sources of information.

Suggestions for adapting text to make it more accessible include the following:

- **Summarizing the text to focus on the key points of information:** This approach can help focus the learning on key historical events, steps for solving a math problem, or understanding the plot in a story. The new text might be written as an outline, a list of bulleted points, or a graphic organizer like a flow chart.
- **Elaborating the text to add information:** This approach may make a text longer, but the adapter can embed definitions of difficult words or provide more background information.

Although time consuming, rewriting text is an effective modification of curricular materials because information is organized in small sequential steps, or logical chunks of information. Short, simpler sentences are rewritten from long, complex, dense ones. An example of a complex sentence from a science text follows: "Electrons have negative electric charges and orbit around the core, nucleus, of an atom." A simple adaptation of this sentence is, "Electrons have negative charges. They orbit around the core of the atom. The core is called the nucleus."

Ideally, rewritten paragraphs should include a topic sentence with several sentences providing supporting details. Maintaining a consistent format promotes easier reading for information-seeking purposes. All sentences included in the rewritten text should be direct and relevant to the subject. In the following example, a paragraph of original text is taken from an anthology theme in a reading series (Cooper et al., 2003). This passage was excerpted from a piece of nonfiction literature, *Into the Mummy's Tomb*, written by Nicholas Reeves.

Original text: "Tutankhamen's mummy bore a magnificent mask of burnished gold, which covered its face and shoulders. Its head cloth was inlaid with blue glass. The vulture and cobra on its forehead, ready to spit fire at the pharaoh's enemies, were of solid gold" (p. 237).

We have rewritten the original text as follows:

Adapted text: "King Tutankhamen's mummy wore a magnificent mask, made of very shiny gold. It covered the face and shoulders of the body. The part of the mask over the forehead looked like a gold head cloth. Blue glass was sewed into the head cloth. Shapes of a vulture (a type of bird) and a cobra (a type of snake) were above the eyes on the mask. They were made of solid gold. They looked like they could attack King Tut's enemies."

As you compare the texts, you see some thought was involved in the rewrite. Some words, like "magnificent," are Latin cognates and should be kept if you have students who speak a language like Spanish or Portuguese. Some patterns and expressions are repeated, such as "made of," because once children figure them out, they can read more fluently the next time they encounter them. Here are some guiding principles to keep in mind when rewriting text:

- Decide what students need to learn from the text.
- Focus on concrete concepts first, then abstract.
- Reduce nonessential details.
- Relate new information to students' experiences (e.g., include a familiar analogy).
- Use visual representations—maps, charts, timelines, outlines.
- Simplify vocabulary, but keep key concepts and technical terms.
- Elaborate to explain concepts if necessary.
- Check word choice and sentence order (e.g., for a question, begin with the question word; for an if-then statement, begin with the if clause).

Obviously, adapting text like this takes time, and it is not easy to do. Note here that the adapted version is slightly longer than the original, which often happens when definitions are included. If you have a large number of English learners in your classroom, adapted text can be very beneficial, and it is worth the time and effort to provide students with more accessible material. Be sure to have a colleague read the adapted text to make sure it clarifies rather than confuses the content.

SIOP® FEATURE 6:

Meaningful Activities That Integrate Lesson Concepts with Language Practice Opportunities for Reading, Writing, Listening, and/or Speaking

To the extent possible, lesson activities should be planned to promote language development in all skills while English learners are mastering content objectives. We want to provide oral and written language practice that is relevant to the lesson concepts, but remember that activities that generate language practice are not language objectives. Language objectives require explicit instruction, for example, about a language skill or structure needed to accomplish the activities.

Children are more successful when they are able to make connections between what they know and what they are learning by relating classroom experiences to their own lives. These meaningful experiences are often described as "authentic," because they represent a reality for students. That is, classroom experiences mirror what actually occurs in the learner's world. Authentic, meaningful experiences are especially important for English learners because they are learning to attach labels and terms to things already familiar to them. Their learning becomes situated rather than abstract when they are provided with the opportunity to actually experience what they are being taught.

Too often, however, English learners have been assigned activities that are not meaningful and are unrelated to the content and activities pursued by the other English proficient students in their classes. It is essential that content standards that apply to students with English proficiency also apply to English learners, and that the planned activities reflect and support these standards.

Consider a class of fifth-grade students studying insects—butterflies in particular. While the rest of the class learns the scientific names and habitats of various kinds of butterflies, the teacher has the English learners color and cut out pictures of butterflies to make a butterfly mobile. This activity is neither authentic nor is it relevant for these students. In this instance, the teacher obviously has not provided meaningful activities that support the grade-level science content standards.

As you continue to read this chapter and the remaining ones, you will find a host of teaching ideas for meaningful activities that integrate the concepts with language practice. The resources listed in Appendix D provide many more as well.

Teaching Ideas for Lesson Preparation

- **Presenting Objectives to the Class.** Effective SIOP teachers do more than just go through the motions by writing the objectives on the board and reading them quickly to the class. Getting the students involved in thinking about the objectives provides a teaching opportunity that should not be squandered. Here are some ways to make the presentation of objectives more productive. Other ideas can be found in Echevarría, Vogt, and Short (2010c, p. 21).

  - Ask students to pick out important words from the objective and highlight them—for example, the verbs and nouns.

  - Ask students to paraphrase the objectives with a partner, each taking a turn, using the frame: "We are going to learn."

  - Present the objective and then do a Think-Pair-Share, asking students to predict some of the things they think they will be doing for the lesson that day.

- **Number 1, 2, 3 for Self-Assessment of Objectives** (Short, Vogt, & Echevarría, 2011a, p. 71; Vogt & Echevarría, 2008, p. 179). In this activity, students are asked to diagnose their knowledge about a topic and then take some responsibility for learning new information during the lesson. At the beginning of the lesson, display the objectives and ask students to rate themselves on how well they understand each one. You may read each aloud and have children show with their fingers which of the following ratings fit:

  1. I understand this concept.

  2. It looks familiar, or I have studied something like this before.

  3. I don't know this.

At the end of the lesson, return to the objectives and ask students to rate again, "How well did you meet the objective today?"

1. I can teach the concept to someone else.

2. I understand most of it, but not everything.

3. I don't understand completely. I need more time/practice/examples.

- **Jigsaw Text Reading** (Aronson et al., 1977). Originally designed as a cooperative learning activity for all students, Jigsaw works well with English learners when there is a difficult-to-read text.

    1. Form cooperative learning "home" groups and then have one or two members from each come together to form a new group of "experts."

    2. Assign each new "expert" group a different section of the text to be read. This group either reads the text orally taking turns, or partners read to each other, or group members read the text silently.

    3. Following the reading, each "expert" group reviews and discusses what was read, determining the essential information and key vocabulary. You may have a worksheet for them to complete to record key information.

    4. Check carefully with each "expert" group to make sure all members understand the material they have read.

    5. After you are confident that the "experts" know their assigned information, they return to their "home" groups and teach fellow group members what they learned.

    This process scaffolds the learning of English learners because in both groups they are working with others to understand the text. Some classmates may have more background information on the topic. Text can be read with other students, reducing the demands of tackling lengthy sections alone. Depending on English proficiency, English learners may join an "expert" group individually or with a partner. It is important that you form the "expert" groups rather than letting the students choose their own group members.

- **Graphic Organizers.** These schematic diagrams are ubiquitous in today's classrooms, but that does not reduce their value. When preparing a lesson, teachers should think about possible graphic organizers that can provide conceptual clarity for information that is difficult to grasp. They help students identify key content concepts and make relationships among them (McLaughlin & Allen, 2009). Graphic organizers also provide students with visual clues they can use to supplement written or spoken words that may be hard to understand.

    - When used *before reading*, graphic organizers can build background for complex or dense text.

    - When used *concurrently with reading*, they focus students' attention and act as a guide to the information. They help students make connections (e.g., a Venn diagram helps children make comparisons), take notes, and understand the text structure (e.g., a timeline informs students the text will be organized chronologically).

    - When used *after reading*, graphic organizers can be used to record key content information or personal understandings and responses (Buehl, 2009).

Graphic organizers include story or text structure charts, Venn diagrams, story or text maps, timelines, discussion webs, word webs, thinking maps, and flow charts. Vogt and Echevarría (2008) include a number of templates for these graphic organizers.

- **Outlines.** Teacher-prepared outlines equip students with a form for note-taking while reading dense portions of text, thus providing scaffolded support. These are especially helpful if major concepts, such as the Roman numeral level of the outline, are already filled in. The students can then add other information to the outline as they read. For some students, an outline that is entirely completed may be helpful to use as a guide to reading and understanding the text. Figure 2.5 shows an example of a scaffolded outline for a reading on the circulatory system.

- **Audio Supported Text.** Technology tools have the promise of making teaching more meaningful and rewarding. Through audio supports, teachers can help convey new information to students, scaffolding their understanding of the main concepts. Translation and interpretation tools have improved considerably in the past decade. Teachers can now type a sentence or paragraph about a concept to be studied into a Web site that provides translation services and have the concept rewritten in a student's native language.

FIGURE 2.5 Scaffolded Outline

The Circulatory System

I. Major Organs

   A. Heart
      1. Pumps blood throughout the body
      2. _____
   B. _____
      1. _____
      2. _____

II. Major Vessels

   A. Artery
      1. Takes blood away from heart
      2. _____
   B. Vein
      1. _____
      2. _____
   C. _____
      1. Connects arteries and veins
      2. _____

III. Types of Blood Cells

   A. Red blood cells
      1. _____
   B. _____
      1. Fights disease
   C. Platelets
      1. _____

Many sites offer an audio version students can listen to. Several textbook publishers are providing the text on CD or Web site, too, and some have audio options in English or Spanish. Students are encouraged to listen to the audio text while they follow along in the book. For some students, multiple exposures to the audio version of the text may result in a more thorough understanding. Ideally, audio support should be available for both home and school learning center use.

We want to make sure that we are clear, however, that the native language audio supports are just that: supports. Our goal is to help students understand text and information presented orally in English, and our job is to teach the vocabulary, sentence structure, connections between sentences and paragraphs, and other necessary information to the students so they can increase their independence. But if we can give them the gist of what they will be learning in English beforehand through their native language, we can then build on that (new) prior knowledge, and, with careful lesson planning, advance their language skills and strengthen that content knowledge.

Differentiating Ideas for Multi-level Classes

The Lesson Preparation component offers teachers multiple opportunities to meet the needs of students with different abilities or language proficiency levels in their classrooms. Although it takes time to prepare a lesson for different groups of students, the investment pays off when all your students learn the material and you do not have to reteach.

- The first step is knowing your students: their literacy skills both in English and in their native language, their schooling backgrounds (including the number of full years they have had in school), their learning styles, and multiple intelligences. With this knowledge you can have realistic expectations about what they can accomplish and plan activities accordingly.
- The second step is to consider where in your lesson students will need some differentiated instruction.
  - Is it when you introduce new content? If so, should you use different materials or a different presentation style? Should you modulate your speech? Preteach vocabulary?
  - Is it when the children must perform a task to practice or apply the new information or language goal? If so, you may have to consider how you will group the students. Or you may assign different tasks to different groups (based on language proficiency or learning style, for example). Or you may prepare different handouts.
  - Is it when you are checking for comprehension? Then you might plan leveled questions so you can address children in ways that they will be able to comprehend the question and have a chance to respond. Or you may prorate the assignment students complete (e.g., a one-page report versus a three-page report).

A few specific examples of differentiated activities follow.

- **Differentiated Sentence Starters** (Short, Vogt, & Echevarría, 2011a, pp. 30–31). This technique converts the practice of using teacher-developed leveled questions into sentence starters that the students might use orally or in writing.

    1. Begin with the essential question of a lesson.

        For example: How do animals change as they grow?

    2. Write questions at a variety of levels of difficulty.

        For example: (a) How does a caterpillar change as it grows up? (b) Do all animals look different when they grow up? Explain. (c) Why do animals change as they grow?

    3. Convert the questions into sentence starters.

        For example: (a) When a caterpillar grows up, it . . . . (b) Yes, all animals look different because. . . . [or] No, not all animals look different. For example, ... (c) Animals change as they grow for several reasons. For one, ...

    4. Post the questions and have the students respond, either by self-selecting a sentence starter or being assigned one.

- **Leveled Study Guides.** You can write study guides to accompany assigned text or a unit's topics specifically for diverse students' needs and their stages of language and literacy development. All students are expected to master the key concepts in the text or unit; however, some need support for comprehension and some can delve more deeply into the material. For children who can easily read the text material, write a study guide so they can extend and enrich the subject material, and be sure to include challenging questions or tasks. For those who need a little support, write a study guide with definitions and "hints" for unlocking the meaning to lead them through the text. Include fewer challenging questions and tasks. For some English learners and struggling readers, create a study guide with brief summaries of the text or topic along with more manageable questions and tasks. Questions, tasks, and statements on the leveled study guides can be marked with asterisks as follows (from most manageable to most challenging):

    – All students are to respond to these questions/statements/tasks.

    – Group 1 students are required to complete these questions/statements/tasks.

    – Group 2 students are required to complete these questions/statements/tasks.

    Of course, the option to try the more challenging questions or statements should be open to all students.

- **Highlighted Text.** A few literature anthologies or content textbooks may be marked and reserved for students acquiring English and/or for those with delayed literacy development. Overriding ideas, key concepts, topic sentences, important vocabulary, and summary statements are highlighted (by the teacher or other knowledgeable person, using a highlight pen or highlight tape) prior to the students using the books. Students are encouraged to first read only the highlighted sections. As confidence and reading ability improve, more of the unmarked text is attempted. The purpose of highlighted text is to reduce the reading demands of the text while still maintaining key concepts and information.

Rating Lessons with the SIOP® Protocol

As we mentioned at the start of this chapter, we want to give you the opportunity to learn to use the SIOP protocol, both for your own teaching and for coaching other teachers. So, after we describe each teacher's lesson below, we will ask you to score the SIOP features for this component on a scale of 4–0, with 4 meaning the feature was well implemented and 0 meaning it was not present. You will probably notice that some ratings for the features will seem quite obvious to you (usually those that merit 0, 1, or 4 on the scale), while others will be more challenging.

It is important that you rate each feature as reliably as possible. That is, you need to develop consistency in your rating by having a clear understanding of each feature and how it "looks" during a SIOP lesson. Therefore, it is very important that you discuss with other teachers, coaches, or supervisors how you determined your ratings on the various SIOP features for the lessons depicted in this book. Some teachers work with a partner to establish reliability. A number of schools have SIOP teacher groups that meet to read the scenarios and discuss the ratings. After these groups deepen their understanding of how the features should be implemented, they may watch video clips of teachers delivering instruction and rate those lessons, too. With practice in multiple classes and subject areas and discussion about the ratings you give, you will develop consistency in your ratings. Chapter 11 provides more explanation on scoring and interpreting the SIOP protocol.

Although we organized this book so that you can score the lessons as you read, in real life, you may not want to give scores on each feature, especially as teachers are learning to implement the model. You can record comments and note if a feature is present or absent, and then use the protocol to offer targeted feedback. You will also notice that five of the thirty features have an NA option (see Appendix A). After years of research, we determined that those five (such as Adaptation of Content, in Lesson Preparation) might not be needed in every SIOP lesson. Adaptation of Content, for example, may not be necessary in a class with advanced English learners.

The Lesson

The lesson described below is intended to teach fourth-grade children about the Gold Rush, in particular, about the trails taken by the pioneers to get from the eastern and midwestern parts of the United States to California.

The Gold Rush (Fourth Grade)

The classrooms described in the teaching scenarios in this chapter are in a suburban elementary school with heterogeneously mixed students. English learners represent approximately 30% of the student population, and the children speak a variety of languages. In the fourth-grade classrooms of teachers Ms. Chen, Mrs. Hargroves, and Mr. Hensen, the majority of the English learners are at the intermediate stage of English fluency.

(continued)

> ## The Gold Rush (Fourth Grade) *(continued)*
>
> As part of the state's fourth-grade social studies curriculum, Ms. Chen, Mrs. Hargroves, and Mr. Hensen have planned a unit on the California Gold Rush. The school district requires the use of the adopted social studies series, although teachers are encouraged to supplement the text with primary source materials, literature, illustrations, and realia. The content topics for the Gold Rush unit include westward expansion, routes and trails to the West, the people who sought their fortunes, hardships, settlements, the discovery of gold, the life of miners, methods for extracting gold, and the impact of the Gold Rush.
>
> Each of the teachers has created several lessons for this unit. The first is presented here, a 55–60 minute lesson on routes and trails to the West. Specifically, the content of this lesson covers the Oregon Trail, the Overland Trail, and the route around Cape Horn.

Teaching Scenarios

To demonstrate how Ms. Chen, Mrs. Hargroves, and Mr. Hensen prepared their first lesson on the trails west, we visit them in their fourth-grade classrooms. As you read, consider the SIOP Model features for Lesson Preparation: content objectives, language objectives, appropriate content concepts, supplementary materials, adaptation of content, and meaningful activities.

Ms. Chen

As Ms. Chen began the first day's lesson on the Gold Rush, she referred students to the content objectives written on the board: (1) Find and label the three main routes to the West on a map; (2) Relate one or two facts about each of the three trails based on the text. After reading the content objectives aloud, Ms. Chen then explained the language objectives: (1) Write sentences explaining how the three routes to the West were given their names; (2) Explain how the structure of some words gives clues to their meaning.

Next, Ms. Chen asked the students to brainstorm why people would leave their comfortable homes and travel great distances to seek their fortunes. She listed students' responses on the board and then asked them to categorize the words or phrases, using a List-Group-Label activity. The children determined the following categories: For Adventure, To Get Rich, For a Better Life. Examples of phrases under the first category included *riding in a wagon train, seeing new places, climbing mountains*, and *becoming a gold miner*.

Ms. Chen then assigned her students a quick-write about the Gold Rush. She distributed two or three picture books on the topic for each of the table groups (four or five children per group) and directed students to use their background knowledge, the List-Group-Label categories and phrases, and the books to generate a brief paragraph on the Gold Rush. Students were encouraged to work quietly with a partner, and each pair was expected to have a brief paragraph written for later whole-class discussion.

While the rest of the class were preparing their quick-writes, Ms. Chen asked the six English learners with very limited English proficiency to meet her at the table in the back of the room. For five to seven minutes, she provided the small group of students with a jump-start for the Gold Rush unit they were about to begin. She introduced key vocabulary with illustrations and simple definitions, led the students through a picture walk of two picture books and the textbook chapter, showed the trails on the U.S. map, and talked about where the pioneers began their journey and where they were heading in California. Ms. Chen showed the students some samples of fool's gold (iron pyrite) and asked them how they thought the gold miners were able to get the gold from the earth. After the brief jump-start lesson, Ms. Chen convened the entire class for a brief discussion of the quick-writes and a whole-class introduction to the unit. Several of the groups volunteered to share their quick-writes with the entire class.

Ms. Chen then referred to the key vocabulary she had previously written on the board: Oregon Trail, Overland Trail, Route around Cape Horn. She asked students to think about the names of the trails they were going to be reading about, and she asked, "Why are streets given their names?" She then asked students to call out some of the names of streets on which they lived. They offered First Street, River Avenue, Main Street, and Mill Creek Road, among others. Ms. Chen then suggested that trails, routes, streets, avenues, and highways are frequently named after geographical landmarks. She explained that often we learn about places and surrounding areas by examining their names.

Following a shared reading of the social studies text, Ms. Chen asked the students to examine maps of the United States and the Western Hemisphere on the interactive whiteboard and try to determine why the three main trails to the West had been given their names. The children volunteered appropriate ideas for the first one, the Oregon Trail. Ms. Chen then wrote "Over + land = Overland." One child said, "I get it! They went over the land!" The teacher reinforced this by pointing out the "over the land" route on a map on the whiteboard. She then wrote "Route around Cape Horn" to the side of the Western Hemisphere map and asked students to think about the name's meaning while directing them to look at the map. One child said, "See, the land looks kind of like a horn. And they had to sail around it!" To check understanding, Ms. Chen asked each student to tell a partner in a complete sentence why the three western routes were given their respective names. These reasons were shared with the others in their groups.

Next, Ms. Chen distributed a duplicated map of the Western Hemisphere to each group. She asked three students to come to the wall map and point to the Route around Cape Horn, the Overland Trail, and the Oregon Trail. She then modeled with the interactive whiteboard how to locate and color in the trails, and then directed the students to work together as a team to complete their groups' maps.

In the few remaining minutes, Ms. Chen distributed a skeleton outline of the chapter that students would complete individually the following day. The outline had subheadings labeled for each of the trails: "Location," "Characteristics,"

"Challenges," and "Advantages." She told the groups they would have about 10 minutes to begin working on the outline, using their maps and their text chapter. Ms. Chen wrapped up the lesson by reviewing the content and language objectives and by having several students report a number of facts about each of the trails.

On the SIOP form in Figure 2.6, rate Ms. Chen's lesson on each of the Lesson Preparation features.

FIGURE 2.6 Lesson Preparation Component of the SIOP Model: Ms. Chen's Lesson

4	3	2	1	0
1. **Content objectives** clearly defined, displayed, and reviewed with students		**Content objectives** for students implied		No clearly defined **content objectives** for students

4	3	2	1	0
2. **Language objectives** clearly defined, displayed, and reviewed with students		**Language objectives** for students implied		No clearly defined **language objectives** for students

4	3	2	1	0
3. **Content concepts** appropriate for age and educational background level of students		**Content concepts** somewhat appropriate for age and educational background level of students		**Content concepts** inappropriate for age and educational background level of students

4	3	2	1	0
4. **Supplementary materials** used to a high degree, making the lesson clear and meaningful (e.g., computer programs, graphs, models, visuals)		Some use of **supplementary materials**		No use of **supplementary materials**

4	3	2	1	0	NA
5. **Adaptation of content** (e.g., text, assignment) to all levels of student proficiency		Some **adaptation of content** to all levels of student proficiency		No significant **adaptation of content** to all levels of student proficiency	

4	3	2	1	0
6. **Meaningful activities** that integrate lesson concepts (e.g., interviews, letter writing, simulations, models) with language practice opportunities for reading, writing, listening, and/or speaking		**Meaningful activities** that integrate lesson concepts, but provide few language practice opportunities for reading, writing, listening, and/or speaking		**No meaningful activities** that integrate lesson concepts with language practice

Mrs. Hargroves

Mrs. Hargroves began her lesson on the trails west by stating, "Today you'll learn about the Oregon Trail, the Overland Trail, and the Route around Cape Horn. We'll also be working on maps, and I want you to color the Overland Trail a different color from the color you use for the Cape Horn route. When you learn about the Oregon Trail, you'll complete the map with a third color. By the time you're finished, you should have all three routes drawn on the map using different colors." She held up a completed map for the students to see as an example.

Mrs. Hargroves then presented a brief lecture on the trails west. Using an electronic document reader, she pointed out where the pioneers traveled on the map in the textbook. She referred students to pictures in the book and answered questions. She read the chapter title and the first few paragraphs about the trails west and then assigned the remainder of the chapter as independent reading. She suggested that if students had difficulty with any words, they should hold up their hands and she would circulate to give assistance.

About half the class (mostly the native English speakers) finished reading in 10 to 15 minutes. Some chatted quietly. After about 20 minutes, Mrs. Hargroves asked the class to stop reading. She distributed the U.S. maps and colored pencils and asked the students to work with a partner to complete their maps by locating and coloring in the three trails. When most were finished, Mrs. Hargroves asked three of the students to show and explain their maps to the other students. All maps were then submitted for a grade. At the conclusion of the lesson, students were given the following writing assignment for homework: "If you had been a pioneer, which trail would you have chosen? Why?"

On the SIOP form in Figure 2.7, rate Mrs. Hargroves's lesson on each of the Lesson Preparation features.

Mr. Hensen

Mr. Hensen began his lesson on westward expansion by introducing the topic and asking how many children had been to California. He then asked, "How did you get to California? Did you go by car? By plane? By boat? Or did you go by wagon train? Today you're going to learn how the pioneers made their voyages to California." Mr. Hensen then showed a brief video on the westward expansion. At the end of the video, he introduced the terms Oregon Trail, Overland Trail, and Route around Cape Horn, and then read aloud two paragraphs from the textbook that described the routes. Then he numbered off the students to form six new groups and quickly moved students into the groups. With their team members, students did a Jigsaw activity for the remainder of the chapter, and when they had finished reading, everyone returned to their original home groups to report on what they had read. The English learners with limited English proficiency were partnered with other students during the Jigsaw reading activity.

Mr. Hensen then wrote the names of the three trails on the board, and on his wall map he pointed out where the pioneers had traveled along the three routes. He directed the groups to divide the three trails, with one or two students in each group drawing the Oregon Trail and the other students drawing either the Overland or Cape Horn trails. Their next task was to tell the other students in their group how to

FIGURE 2.7 Lesson Preparation Component of the SIOP Model: Mrs. Hargroves's Lesson

4	3	2	1	0
1. **Content objectives** clearly defined, displayed, and reviewed with students		**Content objectives** for students implied		No clearly defined **content objectives** for students

4	3	2	1	0
2. **Language objectives** clearly defined, displayed, and reviewed with students		**Language objectives** for students implied		No clearly defined **language objectives** for students

4	3	2	1	0
3. **Content concepts** appropriate for age and educational background level of students		**Content concepts** somewhat appropriate for age and educational background level of students		**Content concepts** inappropriate for age and educational background level of students

4	3	2	1	0
4. **Supplementary materials** used to a high degree, making the lesson clear and meaningful (e.g., computer programs, graphs, models, visuals)		Some use of **supplementary materials**		No use of **supplementary materials**

4	3	2	1	0	NA
5. **Adaptation of content** (e.g., text, assignment) to all levels of student proficiency		Some **adaptation of content** to all levels of student proficiency		No significant **adaptation of content** to all levels of student proficiency	

4	3	2	1	0
6. **Meaningful activities** that integrate lesson concepts (e.g., interviews, letter writing, simulations, models) with language practice opportunities for reading, writing, listening, and/or speaking		**Meaningful activities** that integrate lesson concepts, but provide few language practice opportunities for reading, writing, listening, and/or speaking		**No meaningful activities** that integrate lesson concepts with language practice

draw and color their maps, using the map in the text and the language on the board as a guide. Mr. Hensen circulated through the room while the children completed the mapping activity, assisting as necessary. At the lesson's conclusion, students were directed to pass in their maps. Those maps that were not finished were assigned as homework.

On the SIOP form in Figure 2.8, rate Mr. Hensen's lesson on each of the Lesson Preparation features.

| FIGURE 2.8 | Lesson Preparation Component of the SIOP Model: Mr. Hensen's Lesson |

4	3	2	1	0
1. **Content objectives** clearly defined, displayed, and reviewed with students		**Content objectives** for students implied		No clearly defined **content objectives** for students

4	3	2	1	0
2. **Language objectives** clearly defined, displayed, and reviewed with students		**Language objectives** for students implied		No clearly defined **language objectives** for students

4	3	2	1	0
3. **Content concepts** appropriate for age and educational background level of students		**Content concepts** somewhat appropriate for age and educational background level of students		**Content concepts** inappropriate for age and educational background level of students

4	3	2	1	0
4. **Supplementary materials** used to a high degree, making the lesson clear and meaningful (e.g., computer programs, graphs, models, visuals)		Some use of **supplementary materials**		No use of **supplementary materials**

4	3	2	1	0	NA
5. **Adaptation of content** (e.g., text, assignment) to all levels of student proficiency		Some **adaptation of content** to all levels of student proficiency		No significant **adaptation of content** to all levels of student proficiency	

4	3	2	1	0
6. **Meaningful activities** that integrate lesson concepts (e.g., interviews, letter writing, simulations, models) with language practice opportunities for reading, writing, listening, and/or speaking		**Meaningful activities** that integrate lesson concepts, but provide few language practice opportunities for reading, writing, listening, and/or speaking		**No meaningful activities** that integrate lesson concepts with language practice

Discussion of Lessons

1. *Content Objectives Clearly Defined, Displayed, and Reviewed with Students*

Ms. Chen: 4

Mrs. Hargroves: 2

Mr. Hensen: 1

During their planning, Ms. Chen, Mrs. Hargroves, and Mr. Hensen approached the task of writing and delivering content objectives in different ways.

- A review of **Ms. Chen's** lesson plan book indicated the following objectives for her first lessons on the Gold Rush: "Students will be able to (1) identify the three main routes to the West on a map; (2) relate at least one distinct fact about each of the three trails." She wrote the content objectives on the whiteboard and she clearly, explicitly, and simply stated them in a manner that was comprehensible to her students: "Find and label the three main routes to the West on a map; and relate one or two facts about each of the three trails from the text." (See Figure 2.9 for Ms. Chen's lesson plan.) Her lesson received a "4."

- **Mrs. Hargroves** wrote a content objective in her plan book, but not on the board, and she orally stated what she wanted her students to learn and do in simple terms. However, her English learners might have had difficulty understanding the purpose of the activities they were asked to do. Some students may have inferred that the purpose for the lesson was the coloring activity rather than learning where the trails and routes were. Further, the content objectives were not written on the board or overhead for the students to see. Her lesson was rated "2" for this feature.

- A review of **Mr. Hensen's** lesson plan book revealed no content objectives for the Gold Rush lesson on routes and trails. He did not state any content objectives for the students, but just began the lesson with a brief discussion and the video. Some students may have been able to infer the purpose of the map work, but English learners may have been unaware of the purpose of these assignments. His lesson received a "1."

2. *Language Objectives Clearly Defined, Displayed, and Reviewed with Students*

Ms. Chen: 4

Mrs. Hargroves: 0

Mr. Hensen: 2

The three teachers incorporated language objectives into their lesson planning and delivery to varying degrees.

- **Ms. Chen** wrote the following language objectives on the board and read them orally to her students: (1) Write sentences explaining how the three routes to the West were given their names; (2) Explain how the structure of some words gives clues to their meaning. Ms. Chen provided opportunities for students to meet the objectives by encouraging class and small group discussion, assigning sentences about the three trails, and having each student convey important facts related to the lesson. Further, she scaffolded students' understandings of the names of the routes and trails by having them examine the names of familiar street names, and she led them through an analysis of the names of the historical routes, such as "over + land." She pointed out the compound word and supported students' approximations. At the end of the lesson, she orally reviewed the language objectives for the students. Her lesson was rated a "4."

- **Mrs. Hargroves** did not include any language objectives in her lesson plan and she did not suggest any to the students. She did not discuss the meanings of the names or terms used in her demonstration and explanations, nor did

FIGURE 2.9 Ms. Chen's SIOP Lesson Plan

Date: _Feb. 10–11_   Grade/Class/Subject: _4 – Social Studies_

Unit/Theme: _Gold Rush_   Standards: _History—Social Studies 4.3_

Content Objective(s): _Students will find and label 3 routes to West on map;_
SW tell 1–2 facts about each trail

Language Objective(s): _Students will write sentences explaining how 3 routes got_
their names; SW explain how word structure gives clues to meaning

Key Vocabulary	Supplementary Materials
Oregon Trail	Picture books Outlines
Overland Trail	Iron Pyrite
Route around Cape Horn	U.S. map (PowerPoint slide)

SIOP Features

Skel.
Outline
Jumpstart

Preparation
- ✓ Adaptation of Content
- ✓ Links to Background
- ✓ Links to Past Learning
- ✓ Strategies incorporated
  List / Group / Label

Integration of Processes
- ✓ Reading
- ✓ Writing
- ✓ Speaking
- ✓ Listening

Scaffolding
- ✓ Modeling
- ✓ Guided practice
- ___ Independent practice
- ✓ Comprehensible input

Application
- ✓ Hands-on maps
- ✓ Meaningful
- ✓ Linked to objectives
- ✓ Promotes engagement

Grouping Options
- ✓ Whole class
- ✓ Small groups
- ___ Partners
- ✓ Independent

Assessment
- ✓ Individual
- ✓ Group
- ✓ Written
- ___ Oral

Min.	Lesson Sequence
	1. Content/lang. obj.
5	2. Brainstorm — Why would people leave their homes to seek fortunes?
	3. List – Group – Label: Categorize brainstormed words & phrases
10	4. EOs — Quick Write: Gold Rush
	5. ELs — Jumpstart text/ fool's gold/pictures
5	6. Quick Write Share Out
	7. Intro. Vocabulary: Why are streets given their names?
10	8. Shared reading — pp. 124–128
10	9. On map — show trails – How did they get their names?, Discuss compound word structure
	10. Pass out U.S. maps —
	11. Model with interactive whiteboard — Have kids color
5	12. Skeleton Outline — Work in groups – fill in categories –
10	(Start, if time)

Reflections:

It felt a little rushed, but everyone finished the maps. Next time, save Skeleton outlines for 2nd day. Kids loved the fool's gold!

she encourage her students to use the terminology and concepts during discussion. Further, Mrs. Hargroves expected students to read the textbook with very little support. She mostly conveyed information orally, and she expected students to complete the writing assignment as homework with no modeling or assistance. Her lesson received a "0."

- Although **Mr. Hensen** had no stated language objectives, he did write key vocabulary on the board. He scaffolded the mapping activity and the text reading by having the children work in groups and by having each group member explain the map and key words to the others. This activity was appropriate for beginning English learners because they were supported by each other, and their oral explanations were not "public" for the entire class. The lesson would have been more effective had Mr. Hensen explained his language objectives to the children, emphasizing the importance of listening carefully and of giving clear directions. Although one purpose of the lesson was to build listening and speaking skills, the children were not informed of these objectives either orally or in writing. His lesson was rated a "2."

3. *Content Concepts Appropriate for Age and Educational Background Level of Students*

Ms. Chen: 4

Mrs. Hargroves: 4

Mr. Hensen: 4

Each of the teaching scenarios indicates that the three fourth-grade teachers, **Ms. Chen, Mrs. Hargroves,** and **Mr. Hensen,** were teaching a unit on the Gold Rush. The content concepts were appropriate because they are congruent with the fourth-grade state and district standards for the social studies curriculum. Each lesson was rated a "4."

4. *Supplementary Materials Used to a High Degree, Making the Lesson Clear and Meaningful*

Ms. Chen: 4

Mrs. Hargroves: 1

Mr. Hensen: 3

- **Ms. Chen** used a number of supplementary materials to make the content more accessible to the learners: picture books on the Gold Rush, a sample rock of fool's gold, and the maps of the United States and the Western Hemisphere, as well as technology (interactive whiteboard) to model how students might color the trails on their maps. Her lesson received a "4" on this feature.
- **Mrs. Hargroves** used only the electronic document reader and the textbook during her lecture and when the students were coloring their maps. She did not demonstrate, model, or show visuals or other resources to support student learning other than the illustrations in the textbooks. Because Mrs. Hargroves delivered the content orally, some English learners may have had difficulty making connections between the lecture and the text illustrations and maps. Her lesson received a "1."

- **Mr. Hensen's** video enabled his English learners and other students to connect with the pioneers in the Gold Rush, and his use of the wall map enhanced student learning about the location of the three trails. His lesson was rated "3."

5. *Adaptation of Content to All Levels of Student Proficiency*

Ms. Chen: 4

Mrs. Hargroves: 0

Mr. Hensen: 3

- **Ms. Chen** adapted the grade-level content for her English learners and struggling readers in a number of ways. First, she had students brainstorm, categorize, and then quick-write information about the Gold Rush. She then differentiated instruction by providing a "jump-start" for her English learners by preteaching the lesson concepts and key vocabulary. She also had a variety of picture books that were easier to read and more comprehensible than the textbook. In addition, she used a skeleton outline that included key information. The students used this outline to organize their understanding of the content concepts. Her lesson was rated "4."

- **Mrs. Hargroves** did not adapt the content for her English learners, other than by lecturing on the topic. Without any supplementary support except the pictures in the textbook and her oral reading of the first few paragraphs, the English learners may have had difficulty learning key concepts just by listening and reading independently. Further, Mrs. Hargroves did not paraphrase or clarify important points during her lecture, nor did she explain or define key language or vocabulary before or during reading. Her lesson plans made no mention of other ways to adapt the content or text. Her lesson received a "0."

- **Mr. Hensen** provided access to the textbook content through the Jigsaw activity and the video. He grouped the students for their reading so that they read with the support of others and then later conveyed what they had learned to another group of students. However he did not preteach vocabulary they might need to know to fully understand the reading. He also had the students complete their work on the maps in small groups, and he encouraged them to help each other with the assignment. His lesson was rated "3."

6. *Meaningful Activities That Integrate Lesson Concepts with Language Practice Opportunities for Reading, Writing, Listening, and/or Speaking*

Ms. Chen: 4

Mrs. Hargroves: 2

Mr. Hensen: 4

- Recall that **Ms. Chen** asked students to brainstorm what they knew about the Gold Rush in order to activate and build background. She later asked them to name the streets they lived on. Her purpose was to make the names of geographic locations meaningful, connecting to familiar street names and then to routes to California. Her jump-start activity for the English learners included picture walks and discussion of key vocabulary, and the students were able to see and hold iron pyrite, which simulated the feel and look of gold. The picture books supported their learning, and the skeleton outline provided a meaningful way to summarize the key concepts. Students located and colored in the trails on the U.S. maps after Ms. Chen's modeling. Her lesson received a "4."

- **Mrs. Hargroves's** lesson plan included her lecture, the mapping activity, and the independent reading. Locating the trails by coloring the map was meaningful for students if they understood what they were doing; however, if they were unable to access the text or the lecture, the mapping activity may have been irrelevant. Mrs. Hargroves's lesson received a "2." It was teacher centered, with lecture and independent seatwork as the predominant activities. She expected students to complete the homework assignment based only on the information they could gather from the lecture and text. If students did not understand the lecture or comprehend the chapter, it is unlikely that they would be able to write a meaningful essay on what they learned.

- **Mr. Hensen** activated prior knowledge and background when he asked which students had traveled to California. He also showed the video on the westward expansion, incorporated a Jigsaw reading activity, and had the students complete and explain their maps in triads. All of these activities helped make the content concepts more comprehensible for his English learners, and were considered to be meaningful and appropriate. His lesson was rated a "4."

(For more examples of lesson and unit plans in social studies and history for grades K–12, see Short, Vogt, and Echevarría, 2011a.)

Summary

As you reflect on this chapter and the benefits of lesson planning with clear content and language objectives in mind, consider the following main points:

- Lesson Preparation is a critical foundation for delivering a high-quality SIOP lesson. Thoughtful planning leads to effective teaching—but a great plan does not always guarantee a great lesson for English learners. They require sensitive teachers who realize that curriculum must be grade-level appropriate, based on content standards and learning outcomes.

- All SIOP lessons need attention to language with at least one objective devoted to furthering the English learners' academic English development. This should be a learning objective—an achievement target, not an activity—and teachers must teach to the objective during the lesson.

- If children lack background knowledge and experience with content concepts, effective sheltered teachers provide it through explicit instruction, and they enhance student learning with appropriate supplementary materials. They provide scaffolded support by adapting dense and difficult text.

- SIOP teachers situate lessons in meaningful, real-life activities and experiences that involve children in reading, writing, and discussion of important concepts and ideas.

● The principles of effective sheltered instruction and content-based ESL instruction should be reflected in teachers' lesson plans. As we explore the other features of the SIOP Model and see how teachers apply many other important principles in their classrooms, remember that the first step in the instructional process is comprehensive and thoughtful lesson design.

Discussion Questions

1. In reflecting on the content and language objectives at the beginning of the chapter, are you able to:
   a. Identify content objectives for English learners that are aligned to state, local, or national standards?
   b. Incorporate supplementary materials suitable for English learners in a lesson plan?
   c. Select from a variety of techniques for adapting content to the students' proficiency and cognitive levels?
   d. Write language and content objectives?
   e. Discuss advantages for writing both language and content objectives for a lesson and sharing the objectives with students?
   f. Explain the importance of meaningful academic activities for English learners?

2. What are some advantages to writing both content objectives and language objectives for students to hear and see? How might written objectives affect teacher and student performance in the classroom?

3. Think of a lesson you have recently taught or one you might teach. What would be an appropriate content objective and language objective for that lesson?

4. In many elementary schools, one ESL teacher supports English learners from several classrooms, sometimes across different grade levels. How can the ESL and grade-level classroom teachers collaborate to share the responsibility for teaching both language and content objectives to these students? Co-plan a mini-unit in which some lessons will be taught by the ESL teacher and others by the grade-level classroom teacher.

5. Many teachers in sheltered settings rely on paper-and-pencil tasks or lectures for teaching concepts. Think of a curricular area (e.g., science, language arts, math, social studies) and discuss some meaningful activities that could be used to teach a concept in that area. What makes each of these activities "meaningful," and how would they provide language practice?

6. Begin writing a SIOP lesson. Identify the topic and your content and language objectives. Find or create supplementary materials and adapt content as needed. Determine at least one meaningful activity the children can engage in during the lesson. Decide how many class periods will be needed to complete the lesson. When you finish, share your initial lesson plan with a colleague and garner feedback. Revise your lesson.

CHAPTER 3

Building Background

After reading, discussing, and engaging in activities related to this chapter, you will be able to meet the following content and language objectives.

Content Objectives

Identify techniques for connecting students' personal experiences and past learning to lesson concepts.

List elements of academic language and describe its importance for English learners.

Language Objectives

Select academic vocabulary for a SIOP lesson using words from these three groups: content vocabulary, general academic vocabulary, and word parts—roots and affixes.

Write a lesson plan incorporating activities that build background and provide explicit links to students' backgrounds, experiences, and past learning.

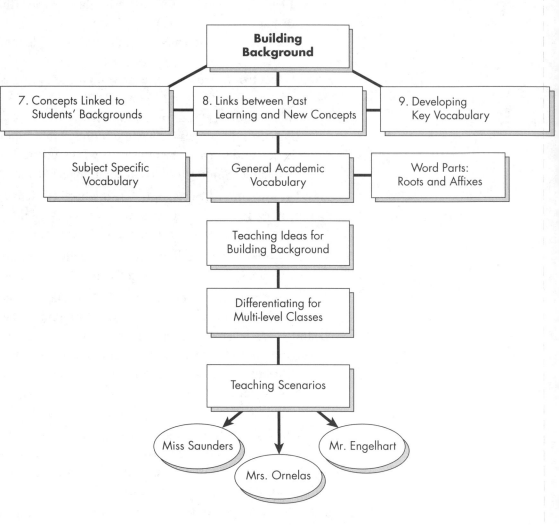

Reflect on two instances when you attended workshops for professional development. During one workshop, you were highly engaged, and you came away from the training renewed and eager to try a new idea or activity. What aspects of this particular workshop clicked for you? Now, recall a workshop during which you were disengaged, bored, and basically unconnected to what the facilitator was talking about. Why was this particular workshop such a unsatisfying experience?

There might be several reasons why there were such differences in your reactions, including the effectiveness of the trainer, the time of day, your physical comfort, and so forth. But consider this other possibility: There was a mismatch between what you know and have experienced with your own students and the concepts and information that were being presented. Your background knowledge and personal experiences differed from the training to the extent that (1) you didn't understand what was being presented; (2) you didn't care about what was being presented because of the mismatch; and/or (3) you couldn't connect with what was being taught, so you turned off and became disengaged. Now ponder what these two workshops would be like if the facilitator were speaking in a language that you do not understand. •

Background

English learners, particularly recent immigrants, are frequently disadvantaged because their schooling experiences (whether they have had little schooling or excellent schooling) may be considerably different from U.S. educational contexts. For example, the K–6 curriculum is quite different from country to country, and depending on circumstances, some students may have experienced interrupted schooling, especially if they have been refugees or lived in remote areas. Further, English learners, including both immigrants and students born in the United States, may lack the academic language and key vocabulary necessary for understanding content information (August & Shanahan, 2010; Donnelly & Roe, 2010). However, do not assume that all English learners lack background experiences and academic language; some students may have rich experiential backgrounds and sufficient academic language in their native language, but they do not know the equivalent English terms and thus are unable to connect with the concepts being taught.

Effective teaching takes students from where they are and leads them to a higher level of understanding (Krashen, 1985; Vygotsky, 1978). Effective SIOP teachers present information in a way that students can understand, bearing in mind their language development needs and any gaps in their educational experiences. In SIOP lessons, new information is explicitly linked to students' backgrounds and experiences, and instructional scaffolding provides students with access to grade-level content concepts. Therefore, this chapter focuses on Building Background, which is closely tied to Lesson Preparation and the teacher's assessment of the students' knowledge of and experience with the topic at hand.

SIOP® FEATURE 7:

Concepts Explicitly Linked to Students' Background Experiences

During the past four decades, researchers have investigated how highly proficient readers and writers process new information (Baumann, 2005; Carrell, 1987; Dole, Duffy, Roehler, & Pearson, 1991). It is a widely accepted notion among experts that a learner's "schemata"—knowledge of the world—provides a basis for understanding, learning, and remembering facts and ideas found in texts. Individuals with knowledge of a topic have better recall and are better able to elaborate on aspects of the topic than those who have limited knowledge of it (Chiesi, Spilich, & Voss, 1979; Vogt, 2005).

Connecting children's experiences to a text, developing background knowledge, and teaching key vocabulary are all effective ways to increase comprehension and achievement (Biemiller, 2005; Echevarría, Short, & Powers, 2006; Stahl & Nagy, 2006). Teachers can assist children in developing background knowledge by:

- Including techniques in lessons such as chapter previews or anticipation guides. As students begin to develop a conceptual framework for their own learning and understanding, they build a repertoire of background experiences from which to draw.

- Recognizing that children from culturally diverse backgrounds may struggle with comprehending a text or concept presented in class because their schemata do not match those of the culture for which the text was written (Anderson, 1984; Jiménez, Garcia, & Pearson, 1996). In the United States, most school reading materials, such as content area texts, rely on assumptions about students' prior knowledge, especially related to curriculum. When introducing a new concept, SIOP teachers often use visuals (pictures, photos, and so forth) to provide context and a reference point for English learners. It's interesting to have students occasionally share in their home languages the name for what the picture represents. Then, the English word can be introduced and explained.

- Acknowledging that many English learners emigrate from other countries and bring an array of experiences that are quite different from those of the majority culture in the United States. Even for those students born in the United States,

FIGURE 3.1 An Example of a Mismatched Schema

A second-grade teacher in a large urban district began teaching map skills, a state history–social studies standard for second grade, by having students identify on a grid some familiar locations and features of their school. The next step of the teacher's lesson plan was to focus on the children's local community and the location and features of the police and fire departments, city hall, post office, community hospital, and so forth. Finally, she planned to work on another social studies standard by talking with the children about those individuals in the community who "make a difference." She intended to connect their contributions with those of some of the historical figures students had learned about previously.

The teacher thought that focusing on the features and locations of the local community would be a relatively simple task for her students. She soon realized, however, that the task was quite difficult for many children, especially her immigrant English learners and others who had scarcely ventured from their own city blocks during their lifetimes. Although the ocean was just a few blocks away, the teacher discovered that some of her young students had never seen it. Also, while many children heard and saw ambulances and fire trucks race frequently by their apartment buildings, they had not seen a fire department or a hospital. These children were unable to engage in a class discussion of the community beyond the school, and they lacked the knowledge and experience needed to sketch a map of it or describe some of the people who worked within their community, except for the small market that was down the street from the school.

This teacher quickly realized that she needed to rethink her lesson plans for this unit, begin again, and determine what her students knew about the concept of "community," including the one in which they lived. Not surprisingly, her students' backgrounds and experiences varied widely. For some who had a large extended family, this defined their "community." For others, they described their community as their home, church, and school. For still others, who had attended the ballet and theater, who regularly shopped with their family at large local malls, and who had siblings who participated in Scouts or Camp Fire, their understanding of "community" was quite different.

culture may have an impact on reading comprehension. Therefore, teaching from a culturally responsive perspective is especially important. Consider this example: As a teacher reads, "The barking dog ran toward the boy on the bike," do all children get a sense of fear or danger? Anderson (1994) questions whether we can assume that "when reading the same story, children from every subculture will have the same experience with the setting, ascribe the same goals and motives to characters, imagine the same sequence of actions, make predictions with the same emotional reactions, or expect the same outcomes" (pp. 480–481). For an actual example of cultural mismatch of schemata that occurred in a second grade classroom, see Figure 3.1.

Teachers of English learners need to be aware that what may appear to be poor comprehension and memory skills may in fact be students' lack of experience or background knowledge associated with or assumed by a message or a text (Bransford, 1994). Further, what might look like a lack of prior knowledge actually may be a lack of accessibility in prior lessons that were taught. Background material may have been "covered," but it was not learned meaningfully. Through the SIOP Model, we urge teachers to activate students' background knowledge explicitly and provide linkages from their experiences to the key concepts. The interactive emphasis of the SIOP Model (see Chapter 6 for specific features) enables teachers to elicit students' prior knowledge and discuss ideas, issues, concepts, or vocabulary that are unfamiliar to them, in order to develop necessary background information.

PD **d** TOOLKIT™ **for SIOP®**

Click on Videos, then search for "Background Experiences and Knowledge" to see Dr. Jana Echevarría give an example of the importance of building background.

Something to Think About

As you begin to write SIOP lessons with techniques to develop students' background knowledge, reflect on the following questions:

- What is meant by activating prior knowledge?
- What is meant by building background?
- How do they differ instructionally?

PD TOOLKIT™ **for SIOP®**

Click on Videos, then search for "Fishing Lesson: Building Background" to hear Dr. MaryEllen Vogt discuss the importance of building background for English learners, and to see two SIOP teachers' plans for developing their students' backgrounds and vocabulary during a lesson.

In the past, we have used the terms "activating prior knowledge" and "building background" somewhat synonymously. However, we now know there are some instructional differences that need to be considered when teaching English learners. All students have prior knowledge gained from schooling and life experiences, and teachers can informally assess what students know and can do, as well as determine any mismatches in schemata through brainstorming, structured discussion, quick-writes, and techniques such as the familiar KWL (Ogle, 1986).

However, if some English learners have little or no prior knowledge about a content topic (e.g., "our community"), brainstorming about it may not be helpful because the brainstormed terms, names, and places may be unfamiliar to some children. Therefore, it is of critical importance that teachers build background using techniques that fill in the gaps, and help students connect what they do know with what is being taught. And when teachers' explanations are made more concrete with supplementary materials (e.g., photos, models, illustrations, etc.), children are more likely to make the appropriate connections.

SIOP — SHELTERED INSTRUCTION OBSERVATION PROTOCOL

SIOP® FEATURE 8:

Links Explicitly Made between Past Learning and New Concepts

PD TOOLKIT™ **for SIOP®**

Click on Videos, then search for "Pitch Lesson" to see how Kendra Moreno helps her students make multiple connections to concepts they have previously studied and what they are learning in today's lesson.

In addition to building background for students, it is also important for teachers to make explicit connections between new learning and the material, vocabulary, and concepts previously covered in class. Research clearly emphasizes that in order for learning to occur, new information must be integrated with what students have previously learned (Rumelhart, 1980). The teacher must build a bridge between previous lessons and concepts and the material in the current lesson. Many students do not automatically make such connections, and they benefit from having the teacher explicitly point out how past learning is related to the information at hand.

Explicit links between past learning and new learning can be made through a discussion—such as, "Who remembers what we learned about? How does that relate to our chapter?"—or by reviewing graphic organizers, previously used class notes, transparencies, or PowerPoint slides related to the topic. By preserving and referring to photos, word banks, illustrations, charts, maps, and graphic organizers, teachers have tools for helping students make critical connections. This is particularly important for English learners who receive so much input through the new language. An explicit, if brief, review of prior lessons focuses on the key information they should remember.

SIOP® FEATURE 9:

Key Vocabulary Emphasized (e.g., introduced, written, repeated, and highlighted for students to see)

Vocabulary development, critical for English learners, is strongly related to academic achievement (August & Shanahan, 2008; Biemiller, 2005; Hart & Risley, 2003; Lesaux, Kieffer, Faller, & Kelley, 2010; Manzo, Manzo, & Thomas, 2005; Zwiers, 2008). In addition, for over 80 years, we have known of the powerful relationship between vocabulary knowledge and comprehension (Baumann, 2005; Stahl & Nagy, 2006). According to Graves and Fitzgerald (2006, p. 122), systematic and comprehensive vocabulary instruction is necessary for English learners because:

- Content area texts that students must read include very sophisticated vocabulary.

- Reading performance tests given to English learners rely on wide-ranging vocabulary knowledge.

- English learners' vocabulary instruction must be accelerated because English learners are learning English later than their native-speaking peers.

- English learners' acquisition of deep understanding of word meanings is very challenging.

According to vocabulary expert Michael Graves (2011, p. 541), "A combination of rich and varied language experiences, . . . teaching individual words, teaching word-learning strategies . . . , and fostering word consciousness . . . are needed in a comprehensive vocabulary program. With tens of thousands of words to learn (something like 40,000 by the time they complete eighth grade), children need many opportunities, many approaches, and lots of motivation and encouragement to build strong vocabularies."

Some studies suggest that a limited number of words should be taught per lesson or per week, and those words should be key words in the text (Beck, Perfetti, & McKeown, 1982). Others recommend teaching English learners the meanings of basic words, such as those that native English speakers know already (Diamond & Gutlohn, 2006; Stahl & Nagy, 2006). In SIOP lessons, teachers select words that are critical for understanding the text or material and provide a variety of ways for students to learn, remember, and use those words. In that way, students develop a core vocabulary over time (Blachowicz & Fisher, 2000; Graves & Fitzgerald, 2006).

Academic Vocabulary

Academic vocabulary is just one aspect of the spectrum of academic language, which includes the language for reading and writing, English grammar, prosody (such as intonation, inflection, and fluency), oral academic discourse, English syntax, and self-talk that promotes thinking and knowing. The terms *academic language* or *academic English* are being widely used to describe vocabulary and language use in U.S. classrooms. Zwiers (2008, p. 20) defines academic language as "the set of words, grammar, and organizational strategies used to describe complex ideas, higher-order thinking processes, and abstract concepts."

Many English learners who have been educated in their native countries come to school in the United States with well-developed vocabularies and an understanding of the academic language of various disciplines. It is important to help these students make connections between what they know about the structure of their home language and what they are learning about English. For example, when appropriate, and depending on your background knowledge about English usage and structure, you can have informal conversations with students about syntax (the word order or the grammatical arrangement of words in a sentence) and pragmatics (how we use language in social, academic, and formal contexts). For beginning English learners, the instruction in English and academic language must be much more explicit and comprehensive. Usually this is provided by the ESL teacher, and it is supported by the elementary or secondary classroom teacher through SIOP lessons.

Academic vocabulary is one important facet of academic language, and it is of critical importance in content classrooms. Most likely, one of the first things you learned when you were preparing to become a teacher was that you needed to teach students key vocabulary words for your lesson topics. While these are certainly important words for English learners to know, there are additional words that they must master in order to succeed academically. The Common Core State Standards for vocabulary development suggest that students must develop proficiency with subject specific as well as other types of academic vocabulary:

> Grades K–5: Acquire and use accurately grade-appropriate general academic and domain-specific words and phrases, including those that signal contrast, addition, and other logical relationships (e.g., *however, although, nevertheless, similarly, moreover, in addition*).
>
> (© Copyright 2010. National Governors Association Center for Best Practices and Council of Chief State School Officers. All rights reserved.)

For better understanding of the varied types of academic vocabulary that teachers need to focus on, especially for English learners, we have classified them into three groups. You probably recognize these three groups because they were introduced in Chapter 1 in the discussion of different types of language objectives. Each should be considered when planning SIOP lessons, when deciding on key vocabulary to teach, and when writing the accompanying language objectives.

1. **Content Vocabulary—Subject Specific and Technical Terms:** These are the key words and terms associated with a particular topic being taught (e.g., for a lesson on the American Revolutionary War: *Redcoats, democracy, Patriots, freedom of religion, Shot Heard 'Round the World, Paul Revere*; for a language arts lesson on parts of speech: *nouns, verbs, adjectives, adverbs*). These words are found primarily in the informational and expository texts that students read, and frequently they are highlighted or in bold in the students' textbooks. In English language arts, they may be terms like *characterization, setting*, and *metaphor*; and while they are not in the fiction passages themselves, they are used to talk about the passages, author's craft, and so on. More important than listing words for students to learn is conveying the importance of knowing particular

words in order to understand a given topic and determining whether a certain word represents a key concept that is being taught (Graves, 2011).

2. **General Academic Vocabulary—Cross-Curricular Terms/Process & Function:** These are academic words students must learn because they are used in all academic disciplines. Often, these words are not explicitly taught; yet, they are the ones that frequently trip up English learners and struggling readers. This category also includes words with multiple meanings. These words may have both a social language and an academic language use, such as *table* and *chair* versus *data table*. Or the word's meanings may differ according to academic subject, such as the distinction among legislative *power*, electrical *power*, and logarithmic *power*.

   a. Cross-curricular terms: Most of the general academic vocabulary terms can be used across the curriculum. They describe relationships (*friendship, conflict, encounter*) and actions (*describe, argue, measure*). They help illustrate information (*chart, model, structure, symbol*) and are used to speculate (*predict, infer*) and conclude (*effect, result, conclusion, drawback*). They are expressions we usually only see in academic text (*In addition to . . . , Moreover . . . , Subsequently . . .*) and terms we might use in casual conversation as well as academic discussions (*situation, circumstances, source, evidence, modify*).

   b. Language processes and functions: A subset of the general academic terms indicates what we want to do with language—the kind of information we convey or receive and the tasks we engage in that require language to accomplish. Some English learners may know the terms in their home languages, but they may not know the English equivalents. Examples of some of these language process and function words that are common in classroom discourse are *discuss, skim, scan, question, argue, describe, compare, explain, list, debate, classify, support your answer, provide examples, summarize, outline, give an opinion*, and so forth. Additional examples are words that indicate transitions and connections between thoughts, such as *therefore, in conclusion, whereas, moreover*, and *furthermore*, and words that indicate sequence such as *first, then, next, finally*, and *at last*. This category also includes the verbs that students encounter in state tests and during other assessments such as *determine, identify, find*, and *contrast*.

3. **Word Parts: Roots and Affixes:** These include word parts that enable students to learn new vocabulary, primarily based upon English morphology. By grade 6, each year students have acquired approximately 800–1,200 words that include roots and affixes. These estimates are based upon *The Living Word Vocabulary* by Dale and O'Rourke (1981). There is no way that English learners can realistically learn all the words they need to know through instruction and memorization. Therefore, all teachers must help students learn that many English words are formed with roots to which are attached prefixes and suffixes (affixes). For example, if a science teacher is teaching photosynthesis, he can help students learn the meaning of *photosynthesis* by introducing the meaning of the root, *photo-* (light). By comparing the words *photosynthesis, photocopy, photograph, photography, photoelectron, photo-finish*, and *photogenic*, students can see how these English words are related by both structure (prefix + root + suffix), and meaning. The root *photo* means "light," thus providing a clue to a word's meaning if it has this root. In fact, in

English, words that are related by structure are usually also related by meaning (Bear, Invernizzi, Templeton, & Johnston, 2011; Helman, Bear, Templeton, & Invernizzi, 2011).

To assist with teaching English word structure, we include in Figure 3.2 some of the most common Latin roots that are found in thousands of English words. The 14 roots with asterisks provide the meaning of over 100,000 words! By adding prefixes and suffixes to many of the words that are included with each root (e.g., *disrespect*ful, *extrac*tion, *inform*ed), you can increase further the number of words on this list.

We urge caution about sharing this list, or others like it, with students. It is not included here as a list for students to memorize the roots, words, and their meanings. Instead, use what students already know about words: If they know how the words *import, export, portable, transport*, and *porter* are all related (they all have to do with carrying something), they can transfer that knowledge to learning the meanings of *important* (carrying value) and *unimportant* (not carrying value). These roots and words should be used for your reference and for helping students understand how roots and affixes work in the English language. (For more information about word parts—morphemes—and English structure, see Bear, Helman, Invernizzi, Templeton, and Johnston, 2011; Bear, Invernizzi, Templeton, and Johnson, 2011; Helman et al., 2011).

One, Two, and Three Tier Words

Another source of words for teaching vocabulary is found in a scheme designed by Beck, McKeown, and Kucan (2002). This scheme is followed in many schools and it includes three tiers of words as described below:

1. Tier One words are common words, such as simple nouns, verbs, high-frequency words, and sight words. Most students know these words conversationally, and usually, it isn't necessary to focus on them instructionally, except for young children who are learning to read. While Beck, McKeown, and Kucan (2002) recommend teachers focus primarily on Tier Two words in their vocabulary lessons, we add a caveat. Teachers of English learners need to be careful about assuming that these students know the Tier One words. Newcomers and emergent speakers, especially, may need explicit instruction and practice with Tier One words. Depending on their ages, they may know the words in their native language, but not their English counterparts.

2. Tier Two words are similar to many of the words in the General Academic Vocabulary—Cross-Curricular Terms/Process & Function category described on p. 71. They are commonly found in school texts but not in general conversation. Stahl and Nagy (2006) refer to them as "Goldilocks words—words that are not too difficult, not too easy, but just right" (p. 133). These are also considered to be the words students need to know for comprehending school texts and achieving academically, and they should be taught explicitly to English learners and to most native-English speaking students.

3. Tier Three words are typically uncommon, found rarely in school texts except in particular contexts, such as a discussion of a specific content-related topic.

FIGURE 3.2 Common Word Roots (Henry, 1990)

There are hundreds of Latin word roots that are used frequently with prefixes and suffixes. This is only a partial list of the most frequently used roots. The roots with asterisks (*) are the 14 roots that provide clues to the meaning of over 100,000 words.

Aud: to hear
Auditory, audible, auditorium, aural, audio

Capit or capt: head, chief, leader
Capital, decapitate, capitol, capitalize, captain, caption, recapitulate

*Cept, cap, ciev, or ceit: to take, to seize, to receive
Capable, capsule, captive, captor, capture, accept, deception, exception, intercept, conception, receptacle, susceptible, perceptive, precept, receive, receipt, deceive, deceit

Cred: to believe
Credit, credential, credible, incredible, creditable, accredit, credence, incredulity

Dic or dict: to say, tell
Dictate, dictator, predict, diction, dictation, contradict, contradictory, edict, indicate, indict, indictment

*Duc, duce, or duct: to lead
Conduct, deduct, educate, induce, introduction, produce, reduce, reduction, reducible, production

*Fac, fact, fic, or fect: to make
Fact, manufacture, faculty, facility, facile, facilitate, satisfaction, factor, beneficiary, amplification, certificate, confection, affect, defective, disinfect, efficacy, magnificent, personification, proficient, sufficient

*Fer: to bring, bear, yield
Refer, reference, confer, conference, inference, suffer, transfer, defer, differ, difference, fertile, fertilize, fertilization, circumference, odoriferous

Flect or flex: to bend
Flex, flexible, flexibility, deflect, inflection, reflect, reflexive, reflective, reflector, circumflexion

Form: to shape
Reform, deform, inform, information, transform, conform, formula, formal, informal, formality, informative

Jac or jec or ject: to throw, lie
Dejected, rejection, adjective, conjecture, eject, injection, interjection, object, objective, project, rejection, adjacent

*Mit or miss: to send
Mission, missile, missive, admit, admission, commit, dismissed, emissary, intermission, intermittent, remiss, remit, remittance, submit, submission, transmit, transmission, emit, permit, permission, permissive

Ped or pod: foot (ped is Latin; pod is Greek)
Pedestrian, pedestal, podium, pedometer, centipede, pedal, expedition, impede, podiatry, podiatrist

Pel or puls: to drive, push, throw
Impulse, compel, compulsion, expel, propel, dispel, impulsive, pulsate, compulsive, repel, repellent

Pend or pens: to hang
Pendant, suspend, suspense, pendulum, pending, dependent, perpendicular, appendix

*Plic or ply: to fold
Implicit, implicitness, explicit, explicate, implication, replicate, complicated, application, ply, apply, imply, reply

Port: to carry
Import, export, portable, transport, porter, deport, report, support, portal, important, importantly, unimportant

*Pos, pon, or pose: to put, place, set
Compose, composite, dispose, disposable, oppose, component, postpone, proponent, deposit, compound, depose, proposal, preposition, disposal, exposition, exponent, expose, impose, suppose, opponent, proposition, position

Rupt: to break
Rupture, disrupt, disruptive, disruption, abruptly, bankrupt, corruption, erupted, eruption, interrupt

*Scrib or script: to write
Scribble, ascribe, describe, description, conscript, inscribe, inscription, superscription, prescribe, prescriptive, script, scripture, transcribe, transcript, transcription

*Spec or spect: to see, watch, observe
Spectator, spectacular, spectacle, respect, spectrum, specter, disrespect, inspect, inspector, retrospective, species, special, specimen

*Sist, sta, or stat: to stand, endure
Persist, consistent, consist, desist, assist, resist, assistant, insist, stamina, constant, circumstance, distant, obstacle, standard, substance

Stru or struct: to build
Structure, structural, construct, construction, destructive, reconstruct, instruct, instructor, obstruct, instrument, construe

*Ten, tent, or tain: to have, hold
Tenant, tenable, tenacity, tenacious, contents, contended, discontented, contentment, intent, maintain, retain, retentive

(continued)

FIGURE 3.2 Common Word Roots (Henry, 1990) *(continued)*

*Tend or tens or tent: to stretch, strain
Intend, intention, intently, extended, tense, intense, pretense, tension, intensity, attention, inattention, unintentionally, distend, detention, détente
Tract: to draw or pull
Tractor, attract, abstract, contract, retract, contractual, detract, distract, extract, subtract, tractable, intractable, traction, protract, protractor
Vert or vers: to turn
Convert, convertible, revert, reversible, extrovert, introvert, divert, avert, aversion, aversive, vertigo
Vis: to see
Visual, visa, visor, vision, visible, visitor, visitation, visualize, invisible, evident, provide, providence

Greek Combining Forms
Beginning: *auto, phono, photo, biblio, hydro, hyper, hypo, tele, chrom, arch, phys, psych, micro, peri, bi, semi, hemi, mono, metro, demo*
Ending: **graph, gram, meter, *ology, sphere, scope, crat, cracy, polis*
Examples: *photograph, microscope, hemisphere, telegram, chronometer, physiology, metropolis, perimeter, archeology, bibliography, democracy, autocrat*

While these words may be interesting, fun to know, and unique to a particular topic, it is recommended that teachers not spend a great deal of time on them. When a Tier Three word is included only once or twice in a story, for example, it's fine to mention the word in its particular context, but then move on.

For more information about Tier One, Tier Two, and Tier Three words, see the book by Beck, McKeown, and Kucan (2002) that includes word lists and a complete discussion of each of the tiers.

Word Consciousness

"The classrooms of teachers who support the vocabulary development of their students are *energized verbal environments*—environments in which words are not only noticed and appreciated, but also savored and celebrated" (Kucan, 2012, p. 361). Stahl and Nagy (2006) suggest the importance of developing students' *word consciousness*, which "is a phrase used to refer to the interest in and awareness of words that should be part of vocabulary instruction. In other words, motivation plays an important role in vocabulary learning, as it does in any other kind of learning" (p. 137).

Activities in which students manipulate words, sort words, laugh and giggle about funny words, and choose words they want to know about are as important for vocabulary growth as the more scholarly aspects of vocabulary teaching and word learning. For example, see if you don't chuckle or eye-roll with the following (Stahl & Nagy, 2006, pp. 147–148):

- A bicycle can't stand alone because it is two-tired.
- Time flies like an arrow. Fruit flies like a banana.

- A chicken crossing the road is poultry in motion.
- Those who get too big for their britches will be exposed in the end.

And how about some of these homographs?

- We polish the Polish furniture.
- He could lead if he would get the lead out.
- The present is a good time to present the present.
- I did not object to the object.

Teaching Academic Vocabulary

In a synthesis of 20 years of research on vocabulary instruction, Blachowicz and Fisher (2000) determined four main principles that should guide instruction.

1. *Children should be active in developing their understanding of words and ways to learn them.* Such ways include use of semantic mapping, word sorts (see Figures 3.3 and 3.4), Four Corners Vocabulary Charts (see Figure 3.5), Concept Definition Maps (see Figure 3.6), and developing strategies for independent word learning.

2. *Children should personalize word learning* through such practices as Vocabulary Self-Collection Strategy (VSS) (Ruddell, 2007) (see Teaching Ideas section, p. 80), mnemonic strategies, and personal dictionaries.

3. *Children should be immersed in words in rich language environments that focus on words and draw students' attention to the learning of words.* Word walls and comparing/contrasting words with the same morphemic element (e.g., (*import, export, portable, transport*) aid students in recognizing and using the words around them.

4. *Children should build on multiple sources of information to learn words through repeated exposures.* Letting students see and hear new words more than once and drawing on multiple sources of meaning are important for vocabulary development. Students should also use the words in speech and writing.

Following a three-year research study, Manyak (2010, pp. 143, 144) developed a framework of vocabulary instruction for English learners and native English speakers in high-poverty schools. The framework includes four components: (1) providing rich and varied language experiences; (2) teaching individual words; (3) teaching word-learning strategies; and (4) developing students' word consciousness. The fast-paced, weekly instructional plan includes:

1. Providing child-friendly definitions (e.g., "*Indifferent* means not caring or not being interested in something.")

2. Providing examples of use (e.g., "Juan was *indifferent* about going with his friends to the movie because it didn't sound interesting to him.")

3. Prompting children to create examples using the word (e.g., "What is something about which you feel *indifferent*?")

Clearly, there is little benefit to selecting 25 to 30 isolated vocabulary terms and asking English learners (and other students) to copy them from the board and look up their definitions in the dictionary (Allen, 2007; Fisher & Frey, 2008b). Many of the words in the definitions are also unfamiliar to these students, rendering the activity meaningless. Although using the dictionary is an important school skill to learn, the task must fit the students' learning and language needs. The number of terms should be tailored to the students' English and literacy levels, and they should be presented in context, not in isolation. Picture dictionaries (definitions are enhanced with pictorial representations) are excellent resources for contextualizing terms. For students with minimal literacy skills, using the dictionary to find words can serve to reinforce the concept of alphabetizing, and it familiarizes them with the parts of a dictionary; however, defining words should not be the only activity used. Effective SIOP teachers support the understanding of dictionary definitions so that the task is meaningful for students. In fact, many effective teachers introduce dictionary skills to students by using words that are already familiar to them.

Teaching Ideas for Building Background

PD **TOOLKIT™ for SIOP®**

Click on Videos, then search for "Activating Prior Knowledge in Kindergarten Math" to see an example of the teacher helping students connect what they've learned previously to the day's lesson.

Additional activities that activate prior knowledge, build students' background knowledge, and develop academic vocabulary include the following:

- **Read aloud** a Big Book, story, article, play, or picture book about the topic to build students' background knowledge, or view a DVD or Internet video on the topic.

- **Digital Jump-starts (DJs)** (Rance-Roney, 2010). Elsewhere in this book (see Chapter 2, Lesson Preparation), we have referred to the powerful effect of jump-starting (also referred to as "front-loading"), where teachers pre-teach a small group of students the concepts, vocabulary, and processes prior to beginning a lesson for the whole class. The purpose is to build background and vocabulary knowledge for students who need extra time and support. Rance-Roney (2010) points out that as effective as jump-starting is, it can cause some management issues for those students who are not working with the teacher in the jump-start group. Therefore, she created "digital jump-starts" that allow students who need the extra time and support to work on a computer to play and replay a reading preview, practice new vocabulary words, and so forth. The DJs can be put on DVDs for home viewing or they can be uploaded to free-access Web sites, such as YouTube. "The unique aspect that sets DJs apart from other reading scaffolds is that with DJs, all of the learning components needed to scaffold reading (i.e., vocabulary, cultural sounds and images, the voice of the teacher (pronunciation and prosody), background information, and schema) are integrated in one product" (Rance-Roney, 2010, p. 388). In the article, you will find several examples of DJs created by teachers of English learners.

- **Plot Chart** (Vogt & Echevarria, 2008). Many (if not most) young English learners are unfamiliar with the fairy tales that are referred to and practiced (for reading fluency and comprehension) in U.S. schools. For children in pre-K to third grade, the Plot Chart provides an opportunity for English learners to learn common fairy tales, and to learn about the elements of short stories, such as character and plot development. For pre-K–2, use four simple boxes on a graphic organizer with the headings *Somebody, Wanted, But, So*. For older children, use a more complex graphic organizer with five boxes: *Somebody, Wanted, So, But, So, In the end*. The Plot Chart is also great for children who may have learned a similar fairy tale in their home language but don't know the English version. Older students who are literate in their first language can write and compare both versions on two Plot Charts. (Did you know that the Cinderella story is found in many versions and languages throughout the world, and was shared with children long before Walt Disney's version—in fact, for hundreds of years?)

Example:

Somebody:	*Goldilocks*
Wanted:	*Some food and a place to rest.*
So:	*She stopped at the bears' house.*
But:	*The bears were not home.*
So:	*Goldilocks found some food that was too hot or too cold, and beds that were too hard or too soft.*
In the end:	*Goldilocks found porridge (or food) and a bed that was just right! Then the bears came home and found her.*

- **Pretest with a Partner**. This activity is helpful for students in grades 2–6 and is appropriate for any subject area. The purpose of Pretest with a Partner is to allow English learners the opportunity at the beginning of a lesson or unit to preview the concepts and vocabulary that will be assessed at the conclusion of the lesson or unit. Distribute one pretest and pencil to each pair of students. The pretest should be similar or identical to the posttest that will be administered later. The partners pass the pretest and pencil back and forth to one another. They read a question aloud, discuss possible answers, come to consensus, and write an answer on the pretest. This activity provides an opportunity for students to activate prior knowledge and share background information, while the teacher circulates to assess what students know, recording gaps and misinformation.

- **Word Clouds** (Dalton & Grisham, 2011, p. 308). To create a word cloud based on the frequency of words in a text, create a template on Wordle (© Jonathan Feinburg; www.wordle.net). Select some interesting text that your students have read, and copy and paste it into the text box on the Web site. You can manipulate the display by selecting a background color, layout, and font. Word clouds enable students to see key words, create headings, and provide prompts for discussion. When students create their own designs, they integrate visual and verbal information, while practicing important digital skills. Like a similar free Web site where students can develop word clouds (www.wordsift.com), Wordle provides support in several different languages, which can be especially helpful for English learners. For an example of a word cloud created on Wordle, see Mrs. Ornelas's lesson in this chapter (Figure 3.8). Note that in the word cloud, the larger the word, the more frequently it has appeared in the text selected for the cloud.

- **Word Sorts** (Bear et. al, 2011; Helman et. al, 2011). During a Word Sort, students categorize previously introduced words or phrases into groups predetermined by the teacher. Words or phrases can be typed on a sheet of paper (46-point type on the computer works well), or they can be duplicated from masters in the book by Bear et al. (2011) or Helman et al. (2011). The teacher or students cut the paper into word strips and then sort the words according to meaning or similarities in structure.

For example, a variety of words in the past tense are listed in mixed order on a sheet of paper (see Figure 3.3). After you orally read and then have children chorally read the words, ask them to cut out each of the words and sort them according to spelling pattern and ending sound. You might wish to differentiate here by having your fluent speakers and capable readers determine for them-

FIGURE 3.3 Word Sorts: Past Tense

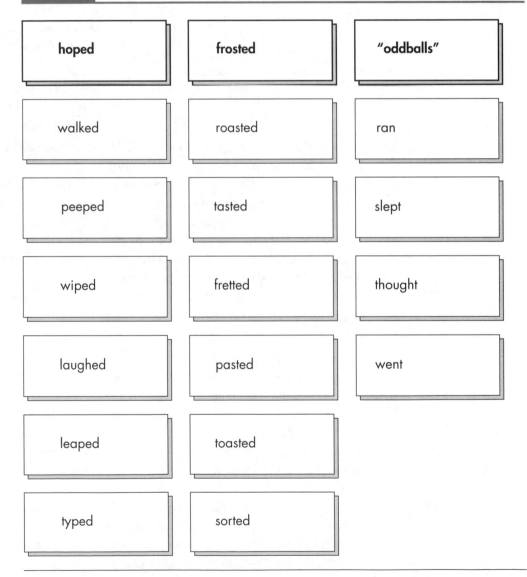

hoped	frosted	"oddballs"
walked	roasted	ran
peeped	tasted	slept
wiped	fretted	thought
laughed	pasted	went
leaped	toasted	
typed	sorted	

selves several possibilities for sorting, such as by ending sound, by words that end in "e" before the "ed" ending is added, and so forth. These children then could do a "word hunt" (Bear et al., 2007; Bear, Helman, Invernizzi, Templeton, & Johnston, 2011) to search for additional words that fit the varied patterns they have identified.

For your English learners and struggling readers, you may wish to engage in a small-group lesson with the sorts to teach and reinforce how the past tense is formed in English words. Contextualize the sorts by providing sentences in which the words are used. For very young students, teachers provide the word cards to eliminate the inordinate amount of time required for children to cut the words themselves.

Other examples of Word Sorts involve words and phrases related to the content concepts being taught, and sounds (such as open/long and closed/short sounds). After students cut apart the words and phrases, have them sort them into groups and identify an appropriate label for each, if they are able to do so (see Figure 3.4). Consider the ways you could differentiate this activity: (1) provide

FIGURE 3.4 Word Sorts: Content Vocabulary

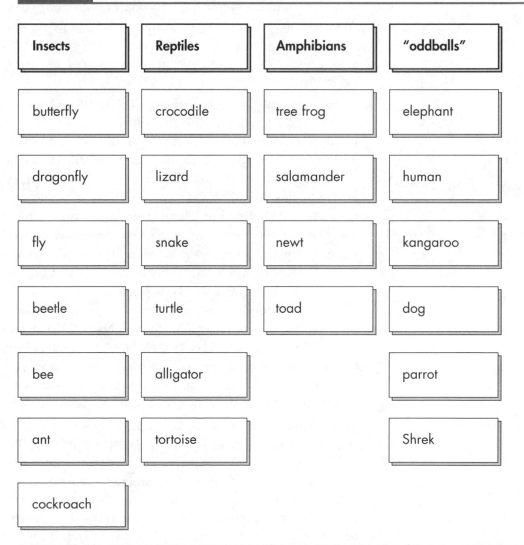

Insects	Reptiles	Amphibians	"oddballs"
butterfly	crocodile	tree frog	elephant
dragonfly	lizard	salamander	human
fly	snake	newt	kangaroo
beetle	turtle	toad	dog
bee	alligator		parrot
ant	tortoise		Shrek
cockroach			

labels for students who may be unfamiliar or shaky with English words for concepts being reviewed; (2) direct students for whom this content sort is quick and easy to www.Wikipedia.org (the free online encyclopedia) and ask them to investigate further what distinguishes insects, reptiles, and amphibians; (3) have students add more columns to the sort (such as mammals and birds) and fill in the columns with appropriate information, using books, Wikipedia, or other resources. Adding the "oddball" column in sorts encourages children to think about both examples and non-examples during the classification activity.

- **Contextualizing Key Vocabulary**. SIOP teachers peruse the material to be learned and select several key terms that are critical to understanding the lesson's most important concepts. The teacher introduces the terms at the outset of the lesson, systematically defining or demonstrating each and showing how that term is used within the context of the lesson. Experienced SIOP teachers know that having students understand completely the meaning of several key terms is more effective than having a cursory understanding of a dozen terms. One way of contextualizing words is to read with students in small groups and, as they come across a term they do not understand, pause and explain it to them, using as many examples, synonyms, or cognates as necessary to convey the meaning. Another way is to embed a definition within a sentence when introducing and reviewing a new word or concept, e.g., *The migratory birds, those that flew in a group from one place to another in autumn, stayed near our lake for several days before flying on.*

- **Vocabulary Self-Collection Strategy (VSS)** (Ruddell, 2007). Following the reading of a content text, students self-select several words that are essential to understanding content concepts. Words may be selected by individuals, partners, or small groups, and they are eventually shared and discussed by the entire class. The teacher and students mutually agree on a class list of vocabulary self-collection words for a particular lesson or unit, and these words are reviewed and studied throughout. They also may be entered into a word study notebook, and students may be asked to demonstrate their knowledge of these words through written or oral activities. Ruddell (2007) has found that when students are shown how to identify key content vocabulary, they become adept at selecting and learning words they need to know, and, given opportunities to practice VSS, comprehension of the text improves (Ruddell & Shearer, 2002; Shearer, Ruddell, & Vogt, 2001; Stahl & Nagy, 2006). The VSS is an effective method for teaching and reviewing content vocabulary because students learn to trust their own judgments about which content words are the most important to learn. This approach is most appropriate for students with high-intermediate and advanced English proficiency and for those in the upper elementary grades.

- **Word Wall**. During a lesson, key vocabulary is reviewed with a word wall where relevant content vocabulary words are listed alphabetically, usually on a large poster, sheet of butcher paper, or pocket chart (Cunningham, 2004). Originally designed as a method for teaching and reinforcing sight words for emergent readers, word walls are also effective for displaying content words related to a particular unit or theme. The words are revisited frequently throughout the lesson or unit, and students are encouraged to use them in their writing and discussions. Cunningham (2004) recommends that teachers judiciously select words for a word wall and that the number be limited to those of greatest importance. We would add that teachers should resist the temptation to have multiple word walls in one classroom because the walls quickly become cluttered with words that are difficult to sort through, especially for English learners. One word wall, carefully maintained and changed as needed, is what we recommend.

- **Personal Dictionaries**. Similar to VSS, personal dictionaries are created as an individual vocabulary and spelling resource for children at all levels of English proficiency, and are generally used with students who have intermediate and advanced English proficiency. English learners read together in pairs or small groups and write unknown words they encounter in their personal dictionaries. The teacher works with each group and discusses the words students have written in their dictionaries, providing correction or clarity as needed. Have young children (K–2) draw a picture to help them remember key words.

- **Four Corners Vocabulary Charts** (Vogt & Echevarria, 2008). These charts provide more context and "clues" than typical word walls, because they include an illustration, definition, and sentence for each vocabulary word (see Figure 3.5). For academic words that are challenging or impossible to illustrate (e.g., *discuss* or *summarize*), simply take a photo of your students during a discussion or when summarizing, and insert the photo as a reminder in the illustration.

- **Concept Definition Map**. The Concept Definition Map is a great way to learn and remember content vocabulary and concepts (Buehl, 2009). For example, in one classroom, the first-grade children were learning about families as their teacher read aloud and discussed several picture books about different kinds of families, including *My Family* by Debbie Bailey and Susan Huszar (1998,

FIGURE 3.5 Four Corners Vocabulary Chart

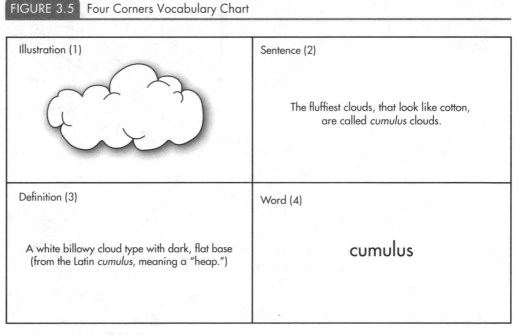

Illustration (1)	Sentence (2)
	The fluffiest clouds, that look like cotton, are called *cumulus* clouds.
Definition (3)	Word (4)
A white billowy cloud type with dark, flat base (from the Latin *cumulus*, meaning a "heap.")	**cumulus**

Vogt & Echevarría, 2008, pp. 40–41

Annick Press); *The Family Book* by Todd Parr (2003, Little, Brown Books for Young Readers); and *Five Little Monkeys Jumping on the Bed* by Eileen Christelow (1989, Clarion). At the beginning of the day's lesson, the teacher introduced a partially completed Concept Definition Map (see Figure 3.6), with the word *Family* in the center box. As the children discussed the different kinds of families they read about, the teacher began filling in some of the boxes in a large Concept Definition Map on chart paper. The next day, after one more story, the children completed their own maps, and used them to write sentences about their own and other families. The teacher honored the fact that English learners, including those who were recent immigrants, knew about families and could contribute what they knew during the class discussions, even if they didn't know some of the English words for the familiar concepts. For upper-grade teachers, even though the Concept Definition Map is a simple graphic organizer, it can be used to discuss complex concepts such as *freedom, democracy, revolution*, or *evolution*, and literary terminology (such as *symbolism* or *irony*). The Concept Definition Map is also an excellent prewriting activity for teaching summarizing. Children begin the summarizing process by organizing content concepts in the graphic organizer. Then sentences can be created from the information in the Concept Definition Map and subsequently written into paragraph form.

FIGURE 3.6 Concept Definition Map

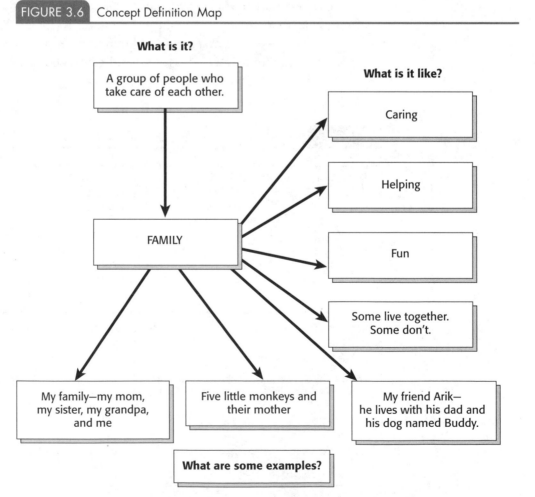

What is it?

A group of people who take care of each other.

What is it like?

Caring

Helping

Fun

Some live together. Some don't.

FAMILY

My family—my mom, my sister, my grandpa, and me

Five little monkeys and their mother

My friend Arik— he lives with his dad and his dog named Buddy.

What are some examples?

- **Cloze Sentences**. Cloze sentences can be used to teach and review content vocabulary. Students read a sentence that has strong contextual support for the vocabulary word that has been omitted from the sentence. Once the meaning of the word is determined and possible replacement words are brainstormed, the teacher (or a student) provides the correct word.

- **Word Generation**. This activity helps English learners and others learn and/or review new content vocabulary through analogy. For example, write *-port* on the board. Invite students to brainstorm all the words they can think of that contain *port*. Examples might include *report, import, export, important, portfolio, Port-a-Potty, Portland, deport, transport, transportation, support, airport*, and so on. Analyze the meaning of each brainstormed word and ask students what they think the root *port* means ("to carry"). Then go back and revisit each word to see if the definition "to carry" has something to do with the word's meaning. Note that we did not define *port* first; rather, we recommend that students generalize meanings of content words from words that they already know that contain the same syllable or word part. Many of the roots found in Figure 3.2 can be used for Word Generation.

- **Word Study Books**. A Word Study Book is a student-made personal notebook containing frequently used words and concepts. Bear et al. (2011) recommend that the Word Study Book be organized by English language structure, such as listing together all the words studied so far that end in *-tion, -sion,* and *-tation.* We support this notion and believe that Word Study Books can also be used for content study where words are grouped by meaning.

- **Vocabulary Games**. Playing games like *Pictionary* and *Scrabble* can help students recall vocabulary terms. Word searches for beginning students and crossword puzzles for more proficient students are additional vocabulary development tools. Software programs are available for teachers or students to create crossword puzzles.

- **Self-Assessment of Levels of Word Knowledge** (Diamond & Gutlohn, 2006, p. 5). As English learners are acquiring vocabulary, it may be helpful for them to self-assess their knowledge of new words. Dale (1965) designated four levels of word knowledge that can be used to describe the extent of a person's understanding of words:

  1. I've never heard or seen the word before.

  2. I've seen or heard the word before, but I don't know what it means.

  3. I vaguely know the meaning of the word, and I can associate it with a concept or context.

  4. I know the word well.

  With effective vocabulary instruction and repeated exposures to unfamiliar vocabulary, students' knowledge of the words increases and they move up the levels from 1 to 4. When teachers introduce the four Levels of Word Knowledge to older students, they can self-assess their knowledge as words are introduced and studied.

Differentiating Ideas for Multi-level Classes

Nearly all of the teaching ideas in the previous section provide ways to differentiate instruction while developing students' background and vocabulary knowledge. The following idea is geared specifically to differentiating according to English learners' levels of English proficiency. (If you need to refresh your memory of these stages, please see the Glossary, p. 309, where they are described.)

- **Differentiated Signal Words**. Signal Words (see Vogt and Echevarría, 2008, p. 36) are an effective way to provide English learners (and other students) with words related to particular language functions, such as comparing/contrasting, determining cause/effect, sequencing events, summarizing, drawing conclusions, making generalizations, etc. Rothenberg and Fisher (2007, pp. 153–154) suggest that signal words can be differentiated for varied levels of language proficiency. For example, for sequencing events, beginning speakers are encouraged to use in their writing and speaking: *first, second, next, later, then.* In addition to these signal words, intermediate speakers are encouraged to use: *while, before, now, after, finally, in the past. . . .* Advanced speakers and older elementary students add the following to their repertoire while writing and speaking about sequential events: *prior to, previously, since, eventually, subsequently.* See Rothenberg and Fisher (2007) for additional examples.

The Lesson

Short Story: *Two Were Left* by Hugh B. Cave (Sixth Grade)

Three teachers in an urban middle school with a large population of English learners are teaching a well-known and suspenseful short story by the author Hugh B. Cave. Although it was written in 1942, it remains an exciting, suspenseful, and intriguing story for upper elementary students. Each of the teachers' self-contained classes in literature includes English learners with a variety of levels of English proficiency. The classes are heterogeneously mixed with native English speakers and English learners, and all students are reading at a variety of reading levels. This story is part of a larger literature unit focusing on stories and poetry, with the theme of "Decisions and Their Consequences."

The short story, *Two Were Left*, begins with a description of a boy named Noni and his devoted husky, Nimuk, stranded on a floating ice island in the sea. It is not evident from the text exactly how they got there, but it is implied that the boy and dog had been with village hunters, and the ice they were on had broken away from the others. Noni and Nimuk had been there for an undetermined time, and both were exhausted, hungry, and increasingly wary of each other. Noni's leg had been

(continued)

Short Story: *Two Were Left* by Hugh B. Cave (Sixth Grade) *(continued)*

hurt at a previous time and he was wearing a simple brace made of a harness and iron strips. The boy decided to make a weapon in case the starving Nimuk decided to attack him. In Noni's village, it was not uncommon to use dogs for food in times of hunger. The story continues as Noni works on making a knife, and boy and dog become increasingly weak. The suspense builds as Noni considers the consequences of attacking his dog. Eventually, he decides he can't possibly kill his beloved dog, and he flings the crude knife away from both of them. It lands point first in the ice some distance away. Nimuk growls in a frightening way, but eventually licks Noni's face and falls, exhausted, by his owner. Sadly, boy and dog cuddle together, unable to save themselves any longer. Not much later, an airplane pilot sees two figures on the ice island and swoops in for a closer look. He settles his plane on the ice and saves an unconscious Noni and his dog, Nimuk. What had caught the pilot's attention was the reflection of a quivering knife stuck in the ice.

In their state, the language arts teachers in grade 6 are expected to address the Common Core State Standards (CCSS, 2010). The following relate to this lesson.

Key Ideas and Details

1. Read closely to determine what the text says explicitly and to make logical inferences from it; cite specific textual evidence when writing or speaking to support conclusions drawn from the text.

2. Determine central ideas or themes of a text and analyze their development; summarize the key supporting details and ideas.

3. Analyze how and why individuals, events, and ideas develop and interact over the course of a text.

Teaching Scenarios

The teachers have prepared their own lesson plans for teaching the short story, *Two Were Left* by Hugh B. Cave. Their individual instructional approaches and SIOP ratings follow.

Miss Saunders

Miss Saunders began her lesson by reviewing with her students the lesson's content objectives (connecting the day's story to the theme of "Decisions and Consequences") and language objectives (reading a story; locating and defining vocabulary words) that were written on chart paper. Next, she asked the table groups to turn over the four photos that were face down on their tables. Each was a photo of Alaska: One was of a glacier, another was of the tundra, the third was of the sea with large, broken pieces of ice floating in it, and the fourth was of an Inuit village. Miss Saunders asked her students to do a Think-Pair-Share and consider what they observed in the photos, what they had questions about, and what they thought life must be like for the people living in the village. She then described her experiences on a vacation to Alaska and showed some of her photos.

Miss Saunders next introduced several vocabulary words that were taken from the story. She mentioned that understanding these words would help students better understand the story. She wrote the following on the board: *Noni, Nimuk, ice island, momentarily, intentions, suspiciously, unconscious.* She explained the first two words were the characters' names in the story. Miss Saunders then distributed copies of the two-page story and asked students to find the remaining vocabulary words in the story. Once they found the words, students were asked to highlight them, and, with a partner, try to define the words using contextual clues. Then, the students, in pairs, were expected to match their informal definitions with those found in the dictionary and make corrections, as needed.

When everyone was finished with the vocabulary assignment, Miss Saunders and the class went over the vocabulary words' definitions. She then asked the students to read the story silently. The evening's homework assignment was to create a "storyboard" of *Two Were Left.* Miss Saunders reminded the class of what the word *sequence* means and that events in a story generally follow in particular order or sequence. She said, "You remember when we talked about this, right?" Her students nodded affirmatively. She then asked the students what the first event was in *Two Were Left.* A student responded that Noni and Nimuk were on a piece of ice that broke off from a larger piece. "That's right, Louis!" She then distributed a large piece of white construction paper to each student with the instructions to fold it into eighths, and draw the first event in the first box in the upper left hand corner. After a few moments, Miss Saunders asked the class to take the construction paper home and to continue making the storyboard sequence by drawing pictures that depicted seven other important events in the story. She quickly went over the day's objectives, with mixed feelings about her students' progress toward meeting them, and the bell rang shortly thereafter.

On the SIOP form in Figure 3.7, rate Miss Saunders's lesson for each of the Building Background features.

Mrs. Ornelas

Mrs. Ornelas began the story, *Two Were Left,* by asking her students to close their eyes for a moment and put their heads down on their desks. She then turned down the lights and turned on a recording of heavy winds blowing. Then, she said in a slow and careful cadence: "Imagine for a moment . . . you are in the Arctic, farther north than Alaska, where the winds blow almost continuously. You live here with your family in a small village. During the winter, it snows every day until there are so many feet of snow piled high that all walking paths are solid ice. The only time there is any natural light is around lunch time and it's only a glimmer; then it becomes black as night once again. In the summer, the sun never sets so you have to put heavy cloth or tarps on window openings so you can sleep. This is your home,

FIGURE 3.7 Building Background Component of the SIOP Model: Miss Saunders's Lesson

4	3	2	1	0	NA
7. **Content explicitly linked** to students' background experiences		**Concepts loosely linked** to students' background experiences		**Concepts not explicitly linked** to students' background experiences	

4	3	2	1	0
8. **Links explicitly made** between past learning and new concepts		**Few links made** between past learning and new concepts		**No links made** between past learning and new concepts

4	3	2	1	0
9. **Key vocabulary** emphasized (e.g., introduced, written, repeated, and highlighted for students to see)		**Key vocabulary** introduced, but not emphasized		**Key vocabulary** not introduced or emphasized

and you share it with your parents and best friend, your dog. You are happy that you have family, good friends, and enough food. However, one day, everything changes. You and your dog become separated from the other hunters in your village and you end up alone on a chunk of ice, floating with only your dog. Think about what you might do in this situation to save yourself."

Mrs. Ornelas then turned off the recording and raised the lights. She turned on the document reader so the students could see the brief paragraph that she had just read to them. She read aloud the directions that followed the paragraph: "With your group members, jot down the ways that your lives are different from this boy's life. Think of as many different things as you can. Now, how are your lives like this boy's life?" Mrs. Ornelas asked each student to draw a Venn diagram graphic organizer (this was familiar to them) on a piece of paper, and as they talked among themselves, they filled out the organizer. The class then briefly reported out what they had discussed.

Mrs. Ornelas then explained the lesson's content objectives (comparing and contrasting their lives with the main character's life; predicting story events in the story) and language objectives (finding examples of foreshadowing in the story; reading the story while confirming or disconfirming predictions). Next, she displayed on the interactive white board a map of the Arctic area, so all students had an idea of the setting for the story they were going to read. Mrs. Ornelas pointed to Alaska and northern Canada, and asked students if they had ever read, seen, or heard anything (other than what she had just read) about this part of the world. One girl said, "I remember when we were studying climate change in Science and we looked at photos of melting glaciers. That's what I thought of when you started telling us your story." Mrs. Ornelas displayed on the white board several large photos of glaciers and said, "You mean these pictures, Esmeralda? You're right. The setting for today's story is very much like what we talked about in science, so think about these photos as you begin reading about the setting in today's story."

Mrs. Ornelas next displayed on the white board the following academic vocabulary words: *predicting* and *foreshadowing*, because these words are critical to understanding the story deeply. She reviewed the meaning of *predicting* because this was a familiar process while reading stories. She then introduced *foreshadowing* by pointing to the word on the board and asking what *fore* made them think of. Someone said "Before?" Another said, "Doesn't it have something to do with golf?" She wrote on the board *foreground* and *forethought*, and asked students to try to figure out the words' meanings, with *fore* meaning "before or in front of"; then she asked them to have a partner conversation about whether the three words might be related because of the prefix *fore*. Mrs. Ornelas walked around the room listening while her students grappled with their task. She then asked the students to share with their partner what *shadowing* might mean. Nearly everyone knew what a shadow was, but they were struggling with the term *foreshadowing*. Mrs. Ornelas asked the students if, when she was reading the brief vignette at the beginning of class, they had formed any ideas of what today's story might be about. Many students' hands flew into the air. After taking a few responses, Mrs. Ornelas told the class, "I used foreshadowing to help you think about the story we're going to read before we actually read it. You're now already making some predictions based upon the hints I provided, right? What are they?"

After taking some responses, Mrs. Ornelas told the students that in the story, *Two Were Left*, the author would also give some hints about what was going to happen later in the story. She said, "These hints are called *foreshadowing*. Throughout our reading, we will make predictions and as we continue, we will either confirm or disconfirm our predictions, sometimes based on the foreshadowing the author provides." Mrs. Ornelas reminded students that they had worked with confirming and disconfirming predictions before in other stories, and she reminded them about how to use the strategy. She also told them that the author's use of foreshadowing would help them predict what would happen in the story. She encouraged them to see if they could find examples of *foreshadowing* and to underline them while they read the story together. Mrs. Ornelas then distributed copies of *Two Were Left* and the class engaged in a familiar group reading activity called the Directed Reading-Thinking Activity (DR-TA) (see Chapter 5, p. 126 for more details).

Mrs. Ornelas began by asking the students to cover with another piece of paper everything but the title, *Two Were Left*. She then asked, "With a title like *Two Were Left*, what do you think this story is going to be about?" The students laughed and said, "About a boy and a dog!" Mrs. Ornelas directed the students to uncover and read the next brief paragraph that provided more information, She then said, "Okay . . . now you have new information. What do you think is going to happen next? Why do you think so?" And off they went, uncovering more and more of the story while reading, predicting, discussing, confirming, and disconfirming their ideas, until Noni and Nimuk were finally rescued. Most students could find some foreshadowing, starting with the title, and some even identified the quivering knife that eventually signaled the pilot. The story concluded with a brief discussion of the unit's theme (Decisions and Consequences) and Noni's decision to throw away the knife. After reviewing their objectives, students and teacher alike agreed that their content and language objectives had been met.

FIGURE 3.8 Wordle Example from *Two Were Left*

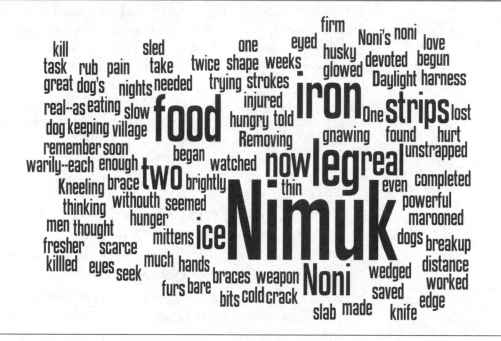

The next day, for a follow-up vocabulary activity, the students in pairs or triads selected their favorite part of *Two Were Left*, and typed it into a word cloud box on the classroom computers. The most frequent words from the story were emphasized on the word clouds. Later, the students discussed how important these words were to the story (see Figure 3.8).

On the SIOP form in Figure 3.9, rate Mrs. Ornelas's lesson for each of the Building Background features.

FIGURE 3.9 Building Background Component of the SIOP Model: Mrs. Ornelas's Lesson

4	3	2	1	0	NA
7. **Content explicitly linked** to students' background experiences		**Concepts loosely linked** to students' background experiences		**Concepts not explicitly linked** to students' background experiences	

4	3	2	1	0
8. **Links explicitly made** between past learning and new concepts		**Few links made** between past learning and new concepts		**No links made** between past learning and new concepts

4	3	2	1	0
9. **Key vocabulary** emphasized (e.g., introduced, written, repeated, and highlighted for students to see)		**Key vocabulary** introduced, but not emphasized		**Key vocabulary** not introduced or emphasized

Mr. Engelhart

Mr. Engelhart began his lesson by telling his students the objectives: *You will learn some new words from the story we are going to read and complete a story plot graphic organizer.* He then distributed a worksheet that had vocabulary word definitions and sentences from the day's story, *Two Were Left.* He gave each student eight index cards so that they could copy the information from the worksheet, one vocabulary word per card so that students would have eight flash cards for practice. The words on the worksheet included the following: *marooned, warily, labored, inventions, thrust, aroused, feebly, quivering.*

The following are examples of four of the vocabulary words, definitions, and sentences that the students copied onto their index cards from the words on the worksheet.

Marooned: to place or leave alone without hope of escape; "And, now, the two, completely alone, *marooned* on the ice, eyed each other warily."

Warily: careful and watchful for danger; "And, now, the two, completely alone, marooned on the ice, eyed each other *warily.*"

Labored: to move with great effort; "He could see hunger and suffering in the dog's *labored* breathing and awkward movements."

Intentions: a planned way of acting; "Closer Nimuk came, aware of Noni's *intentions.*"

After the students had copied the words, definitions, and sentences onto their eight vocabulary cards, Mr. Engelhart distributed copies of the *Two Were Left* story. He then asked for volunteers to take turns reading the story aloud. He directed students to underline the sentences where the eight vocabulary words were found. When the story was completed, Mr. Engelhart asked students how they liked the story, and all said it was good. A discussion followed on what the students liked about the story, and why. A graphic organizer for the story's plot was assigned as homework. He collected the vocabulary cards for checking and concluded the lesson, satisfied that his goals had been met.

On the SIOP form in Figure 3.10, rate Mr. Engelhart's lesson for each of the Building Background features.

Discussion of Lessons

7. *Concepts Explicitly Linked to Students' Background Experiences*

Miss Saunders: 3

Mrs. Ornelas: 4

Mr. Engelhart: 0

- **Miss Saunders's** lesson received a "3" for this feature. She chose to develop students' background knowledge for the story, *Two Were Left,* by showing them photographs of Alaska, similar to the setting of the story. The Think-Pair-Share activity was a good one to choose so that students could share their impressions of the photos with each other and the class. While Miss

FIGURE 3.10 Building Background Component of the SIOP Model: Mr. Engelhart's Lesson

4	3	2	1	0	NA
7. **Content explicitly linked** to students' background experiences		**Concepts loosely linked** to students' background experiences		**Concepts not explicitly linked** to students' background experiences	

4	3	2	1	0
8. **Links explicitly made** between past learning and new concepts		**Few links made** between past learning and new concepts		**No links made** between past learning and new concepts

4	3	2	1	0
9. **Key vocabulary** emphasized (e.g., introduced, written, repeated, and highlighted for students to see)		**Key vocabulary** introduced, but not emphasized		**Key vocabulary** not introduced or emphasized

Saunders's vacation photos and stories were interesting, they didn't directly relate to the setting of the story the students were going to read. Perhaps a video clip from the Internet could have been shown, and, depending on the location of Miss Saunders's school, having the students contrast their living conditions (such as southern California or Florida) to the story's setting would have been meaningful. Also, since the main characters are a boy and a dog, bringing students' feelings about their pets (or others' pets they know) could have prepared them for the emotional aspect of this story.

- **Mrs. Ornelas's** lesson received a "4" for this feature. She spent about 15 minutes activating her students' prior knowledge and building their background about the setting of the story, *Two Were Left*. Because the setting and the situation were so very different from the students' experiences, the time was well spent. It's not just the actual setting that is so different (the Arctic area), but it's also the culture of the people in the story, where dogs aren't pets, but rather commodities that can mean the difference between life and death. (For this story, it might be interesting to mention to students that keeping dogs as pets might also be a cultural difference for other people, including some Asian cultures where dogs are food, and in some Arabic cultures, where neither dogs nor cats are pets.) In the lesson, the students' predictions and ability to grapple with a challenging literary device like foreshadowing were enhanced by the visualization exercise (with students' eyes closed and the wind blowing) and the comparison/contrast of their lives to Noni's via the Venn diagram. Also, the DR-TA is a powerful activity that enables teachers to really understand where students' predictions and ideas are coming from while they're reading. Students use their background experiences and knowledge throughout a DR-TA to make and then confirm/disconfirm their predictions while developing comprehension of the story. (Note that confirming predictions requires citing text evidence, which is a Common Core State Standard.)

- **Mr. Engelhart's** lesson received a "0" for this lesson. He didn't attempt to activate students' background knowledge or build background information related to the story's content concepts or vocabulary. He did state his goals, but these were not written as content and language objectives because the verb *learn* isn't measurable or observable, and "completing a graphic organizer" doesn't indicate the cognitive work the students will be engaged in. When objectives are well written, they provide information that begins to activate prior knowledge and build background knowledge.

8. *Links Explicitly Made between Past Learning and New Concepts*

   Miss Saunders: 1

   Mrs. Ornelas: 3

   Mr. Engelhart: 0

   - **Miss Saunders's** lesson received a "1" for this feature. She made only one reference to the students' past learning and it was nearly at the end of the lesson. When she asked her students if they recalled when they talked about story sequence, the students gamely replied with a unison nod. Because understanding story sequence was critically important for the homework assignment, explicitly reviewing (and if necessary, re-teaching) the steps taught previously (e.g., introduction, rising action, falling action, climax, conclusion; or beginning, event 1, event 2, . . . conclusion) was very important. English learners would have benefitted from working together with the teacher and/or small group to identify the story sequence prior to creating the storyboard. There will also most likely be confusion when doing the homework if the number of boxes (8) doesn't match the number of story events they identify at home.

   - **Mrs. Ornelas's** lesson received a "3" for this feature. She was prepared to make an explicit link between the students' previous learning about the Arctic area and the story they were going to read in this lesson. She had the photos from the Science lesson ready to display on the interactive white board so students could make the connections. It would have been a good idea to be more explicit in reminding students of how readers make predictions, and more importantly, how they could confirm and disconfirm predictions while reading. This was especially important because Mrs. Ornelas was connecting predicting to the author's use of foreshadowing in the story. This might have been confusing to some English learners and struggling readers who still needed more practice in understanding prediction as a metacognitive strategy (see Chapter 5 for more information).

   - **Mr. Engelhart's** lesson received a "0" for this feature because it included nothing to connect past learning to today's lesson in terms of content concepts, vocabulary, or language. Although students may have completed vocabulary cards previously, there was no attempt to connect former vocabulary to today's new words.

9. *Key Vocabulary Emphasized*

   Miss Saunders: 2

   Mrs. Ornelas: 4

   Mr. Engelhart: 1

- **Miss Saunders's** lesson received a "2" for this feature. She selected some interesting and perhaps tricky words from the story for her students to work with. However, the time that was spent on finding informal and formal definitions of these words was not necessarily going to enable the English learners (and other students) to better understand this story. That is, they were not critical to the story's outcome, especially character names, which are easily learned. It would have been more relevant to this particular story and the objectives (sequencing the events in the story) had she spent the time reviewing the academic vocabulary related to sequencing, perhaps with signal words the students could have used on their storyboards (*first, next, then, finally, in the end*, and so forth). She then could have identified and talked about some of the more interesting and challenging words in the story, working with the students to use the context clues for the informal definitions.

- **Mrs. Ornelas's** lesson received a "4" for this feature. She chose to teach explicitly two academic vocabulary words that she felt were essential to fully comprehending the story. One is an important literary term related to author's craft (*foreshadowing*), and the other is a critical strategy for reading (*predicting*). Notice how she introduced these concepts with the visualizing activity. She then divided the word *foreshadowing* into two parts (*fore* + *shadowing*), before writing *foreground* and *forethought* on the board, leading students to generalize the meanings of the three words. There are many other very interesting words in this story, and on the following day, the students worked with them when creating their Wordle designs. Because the Wordle designs emphasized the most frequent words in the passages the students chose, they could readily compare them with the interesting, but less frequently used words.

- **Mr. Engelhart's** lesson received a "1" for this feature. He provided his students with a list of vocabulary words, definitions, and sentences from the story they read, but the students' assignment to copy them onto the flash cards didn't have a clear purpose, and it's unlikely the words carried much meaning for them. Making a connection for the students would have been difficult to do since the words on the worksheet were mostly Tier Three words, somewhat unique for grade 6 students. One exposure to these words would not ensure retention of either the words or their meanings. Mr. Engelhart's students may have enjoyed listening to and reading the story, but his lesson missed many opportunities to develop his students' content and language knowledge.

(For more ideas of lessons and units in English-language arts in grades K–6, please see Vogt, M.E., Echevarría, J., and Short, D. (2010). *The SIOP® Model for Teaching English-Language Arts to English Learners*. Boston: Allyn & Bacon.)

Summary

As you reflect on this chapter and the impact of connecting students' background knowledge and learning experiences to the content being taught, and the importance of explicitly teaching academic vocabulary, consider the following main points:

PD **d** TOOLKIT™ **for SIOP**®

Click on Videos, then search for "Building Background Elementary Lesson" to hear Dr. Jana Echevarría discuss the Building Background Component. You will also see a grade 3 teacher introduce a new short story to her students.

- Explicitly linking a lesson's key content and language concepts to students' background knowledge and experiences enables them to forge connections between what they know and what they are learning.

- In addition, explicitly connecting past content and language learning to a new lesson's content and language concepts assists students in understanding that previous learning connects to today's lesson.

- English learners may have a difficult time with the academic vocabulary of various disciplines. Three types of academic vocabulary discussed in this chapter are: (1) subject-specific and technical vocabulary; (2) general academic: cross-curricular/process/function vocabulary; and (3) word parts: roots and affixes.

- Teaching ideas, such as using visuals to provide concrete meanings, Four Corners Vocabulary charts, differentiated signal words, and Wordle, engage students in interactive practice with words that promotes academic vocabulary development for English learners.

Discussion Questions

1. In reflecting on the content and language objectives at the beginning of the chapter, are you able to:
   a. Identify techniques for connecting students' personal experiences and past learning to lesson concepts?
   b. List elements of academic language and describe its importance for English learners?
   c. Select academic vocabulary for a SIOP lesson using words from these three groups: content vocabulary, general academic vocabulary, word parts: roots and affixes?
   d. Write a lesson plan incorporating attention to building background, links to students' past learning, and key academic vocabulary?

2. Some educators argue the importance of connecting new information to English language learners' own cultural backgrounds in order to make content concepts meaningful. Others disagree, stating that students relate more to popular American influences than they do to their parents' traditional cultural practices. What are some merits and problems with both positions? What about English learners born in the United States who have never lived in their native cultural setting?

3. Think about a joke or cartoon that you didn't understand, such as from a late-show monologue or a political cartoon. Why was it confusing or not amusing? What information would you have needed for it to make sense? What are the implications for teaching content to all students, including English learners?

4. Add to the SIOP lesson you have started. Think about how you will activate students' prior knowledge and build background. What explicit connections to past learning can you make? What are your key academic vocabulary words, and how will you teach them? Choose some techniques or activities for the lesson.

CHAPTER 4

Comprehensible Input

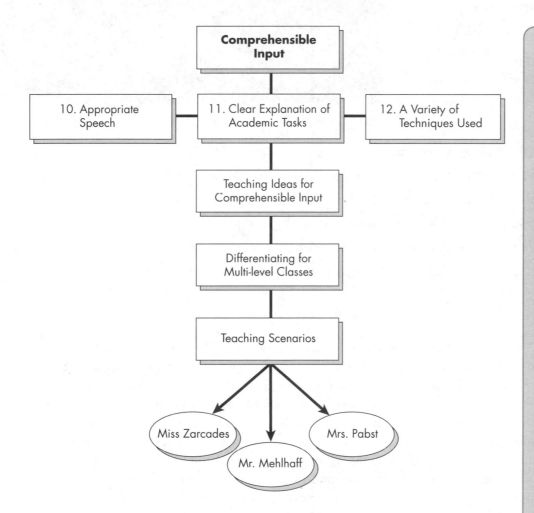

After reading, discussing, and engaging in activities related to this chapter, you will be able to meet the following content and language objectives.

Content Objectives

Identify techniques for presenting content information in ways that children comprehend.

Review various ways to provide directions for completing academic tasks.

Language Objectives

Discuss modifications to teacher speech that can increase student comprehension.

Write the steps needed for students to perform an academic task and have a partner perform each step.

As you look through the features of the SIOP protocol, you will see that they reflect what we know about effective instruction for all students—English speakers and English learners alike. However, implementation of some features is critical for making content understandable for English learners. The features of the Comprehensible Input component make SIOP instruction different from "just good instruction." While English learners benefit from many of the teaching practices that are effective for all students, these children also require modifications to make instruction meaningful (August & Shanahan, 2006, 2010). Making a message understandable for students is referred to as *comprehensible input* (Krashen, 1985). A culturally responsive SIOP teacher takes into account the unique linguistic needs of English learners and modifies teaching accordingly. Whether instruction is for a direct English language development lesson or for a content area lesson that makes subject matter accessible while also developing English language proficiency, comprehensible input techniques are essential. •

Have you ever tried to water ski without a boat? Impossible, right? No matter how badly you want to ski, it can't happen without a boat. A teacher using the features of Comprehensible Input functions as the boat because English learners, no matter how motivated, can't be successful academically if they don't understand what the teacher is saying, what they are expected to do, or how to accomplish a task. Humans don't "pick up" language solely from exposure. For example, many of us have been around speakers of Spanish, Vietnamese, or Farsi, but can't understand anything that is being said. Comprehensible input techniques are necessary to understand the essence of what is being said or presented. A SIOP teacher makes verbal communication more understandable by consciously making modifications based on students' levels of English proficiency.

Background

PD TOOLKIT™ **for SIOP®**

Click on Videos, then search for "Comprehensible Input for English Learners" to see teachers illustrate in their classrooms what comprehensible input is all about as Dr. MaryEllen Vogt describes its tenets.

Children who are expected to learn rigorous content material to meet high academic standards in a language they do not speak or comprehend completely require specialized teaching techniques to make the message understandable. Acquiring a new language takes time and is facilitated by many "clues"—by speech that is geared to individual proficiency levels and by techniques that are used consistently in daily teaching routines.

Comprehensible input is much more than simply showing pictures as visual clues during a lesson. It involves a conscious effort to make the lesson understandable through a variety of means. Communication is made more understandable through speech that is appropriate to students' proficiency levels. The teacher enunciates and speaks more slowly, but in a natural way, for children who are beginning English speakers. More repetition may be needed for beginners and, as students gain more proficiency in English, the teacher adjusts her speech to the students' levels. Teachers will increase students' understanding by using appropriate speech coupled with a variety of techniques that will make the content clear.

These techniques are particularly important as students aim to meet the Common Core State Standards (CCSS) for listening and speaking in each grade level. Across grade levels, the CCSS ask students to comprehend information presented orally and to express their understanding in a variety of ways, such as recounting key ideas and dctails, and paraphrasing or summarizing the information presented. The way information is presented orally will have a significant impact on the degree to which English learners will be able to achieve these standards.

We will discuss a number of ways to make teacher talk comprehensible to students in the next sections. In the scenarios that follow later in the chapter, you will see examples of teachers who use comprehensible input techniques to varying degrees of effectiveness.

SIOP® FEATURE 10:

Speech Appropriate for Students' Proficiency Levels

For this feature, speech refers to (1) rate and enunciation and (2) complexity of speech. The first aspect addresses *how* the teacher speaks and the second aspect refers to *what* is said, such as level of vocabulary used, complexity of sentence structure, and use of idioms.

Children who are at the beginning levels of English proficiency benefit from teachers who slow down their rate of speech, use pauses, and enunciate clearly while speaking. As students become more comfortable with the language and acquire higher levels of proficiency, a slower rate isn't as necessary. In fact, for advanced and transitional students, teachers should use a rate of speech that is normal for a regular classroom. Effective SIOP teachers adjust their rate of speech and enunciation to their students' levels of English proficiency.

Likewise, young learners will respond according to their proficiency level. The following example illustrates the variation in responses that may be expected when

PD TOOLKIT™ **for SIOP®**

Click on Videos, then Search "Communication about 'Island'" for an example of speech that is appropriate for the students' proficiency levels.

students at six different levels of English proficiency are asked to describe the setting in a story. The levels reflect the WIDA performance definitions (http://www.wida.us/standards/elp.aspx).

- Entering: "Cold day."
- Beginning: "Day is cold and there snow."
- Developing: "The day is cold and there is snow."
- Expanding: "The day is very cold and heavy snow is falling."
- Bridging: "It is a cold, winter day and it is snowing more heavily than usual."
- Reaching: "The unusually heavy snow on the day the story takes place causes a number of problems for the characters."

SIOP teachers carefully monitor the vocabulary and sentence structure they use with English learners in order to match the students' proficiency levels, especially with students at beginning levels of English proficiency. The following are ways to monitor classroom speech:

- Ask children for elaboration. Especially with students at intermediate and advanced levels, teachers should frequently ask students to: explain their answers; say it another way; ask why, how, or what if; and show me where that is in the text. They should also require students to connect words, phrases, and short sentences into compound sentences that represent their ideas and thoughts. In this way, students not only use the language but think about how to use it as well.

- Model what you want students to say before having them produce language. For example, in science the teacher might say, "We've been studying that there are many changes that occur in the earth's crust. Some come quickly and others take millions of years. Ask your partner, 'What is one change that comes quickly?'" In this way, students know what to say when they turn to their partners because they have heard correct sentence formation. Providing children with a model of what to say increases the likelihood that on-point discussion will occur.

- Avoid idioms, particularly with beginners. These common sayings that do not have exact translations create difficulty for students who are trying to make sense of a new language. Some common idioms include "below the belt" for unfair; "put one's foot down" meaning to be firm; "see eye to eye" for being in agreement; "get the hang of" meaning to become familiar with; and "get a person's back up" indicating to make someone annoyed. English learners are better served when teachers use language that is straightforward, clear, and accompanied by a visual representation.

- Employ paraphrasing and repetition to enhance understanding. English learners may require repeated exposures to a word in order to hear it accurately since they often lack the auditory acuity to decipher sounds of English words. Then they need to see and hear the words used repeatedly, preferably in a variety of ways. Brain research tells us that repetition strengthens connections in the brain (Jensen, 2005).

- Point out cognates to promote comprehension for children whose native language has a Latin base. For example, using "calculate the mass/volume ratio" (*calcular* in Spanish) may be easier for some students to understand than "figure out the mass/volume ratio." (See Vogt and Echevarría, 2008, for more examples of cognates.)

- Simplify sentence structures to reduce the complexity that some English learners find confusing. Use subject–verb–object with beginning students and reduce or eliminate embedded clauses. For example, in a history lesson, the teacher may use the following complex sentence structure that is difficult to understand: "English colonists brought free enterprise, the idea of owning and controlling their own businesses, from England but because England's leaders wanted the colonies' financial support, laws were passed to limit the free enterprise system in the colonies." It might be better stated as, "English colonists brought the idea of owning and controlling their own businesses from England. This idea is called free enterprise. England's leaders wanted the colonies' financial support, so the laws were passed to limit the free enterprise system in the colonies." Reducing the complexity of language is effective for beginners but should be used judiciously. Oversimplification of spoken or written language eliminates exposure to a variety of sentence constructions and language forms (Crossley et al., 2007), especially complex text called for in the Common Core State Standards.

Using appropriate speech patterns and terms that are easier for English learners to understand contributes to comprehensible input and provides a basis for students to be successful. It is difficult for students to learn if a teacher's way of delivering information is too fast, complex, or inarticulate.

SHELTERED INSTRUCTION
SIOP®
OBSERVATION PROTOCOL

SIOP® FEATURE 11:

Clear Explanation of Academic Tasks

PD **IC** TOOLKIT™ **for SIOP®**

Click on Videos, then search for "Clear Directions for Determining Fact or Opinion" to see an example of clear explanations of academic tasks.

English learners at all levels (and native English speakers) perform better in academic situations when the teacher gives clear instructions for assignments and activities. The more practice students have with the types of tasks found in content classes, the better they will perform in class and the better prepared they will be when they exit the language support program. It is critical for English learners to have instructions presented in a step-by-step manner, preferably modeled or demonstrated for them. Ideally, a finished product such as a business letter, a research report, or a graphic organizer is shown to students so that they know what the task entails. Oral directions should always be accompanied by written ones so English learners can refer back to them at a later point in time as they complete the assignment or task. Children with auditory processing difficulties also require clear, straightforward instructions written for them to see.

According to case study data collected from English learners in sheltered classes (Echevarría, 1998), middle school students were asked what their teachers do that makes learning easier or more difficult. The following are some student comments:

- "She doesn't explain it too good. I don't understand the words she's saying because I don't even know what they mean."

- "She talks too fast. I don't understand the directions."
- "He talks too fast. Not patient."
- "It helps when he comes close to my desk and explains stuff in the order that I have to do it."

It is reasonable to assume that elementary age students would express much the same sentiment if they were able to articulate it in the same way. These students' comments illustrate the importance of providing a clear explanation of teachers' expectations for lessons, including delineating the steps of academic tasks. This point cannot be overstated. In our observations of classes, many "behavior problems" are often the result of students not being sure about what they are supposed to do. A cursory oral explanation of an assignment can leave many children without a clue as to how to get started. The teacher, frustrated with all the chatter, scolds students, exhorting them to get to work. However, students do not know *how* to get to work and oftentimes do not know how to articulate that fact to the teacher. Bottom line: Making expectations clear to students contributes to an effective and efficient classroom (Gibson & Hasbrouck, 2008).

SIOP teachers go over every aspect of the lesson, showing visuals with each step, if needed. For example, in a reading class, the teacher wants students to complete a graphic organizer with information about the characters, setting, problem, resolution of the problem, and theme of a piece of literature the class has been reading. Using this information children will write a summary. Figure 4.1 contrasts clear directions and step-by-step instruction with unclear directions and unguided instruction. Think about the way you present directions to your students.

In the left column, the teacher uses a written agenda so that if students don't understand, weren't paying attention, or simply forgot, they have the written steps to guide them and keep them on task. Depending on the age and proficiency levels of the group, the teacher may need to model one or more of the steps. By the time students complete the graphic organizer, they have received feedback on the accuracy of the information they will use and have seen a model of a partially completed graphic organizer. Likewise, using information in the graphic organizer to write a summary is modeled for them. This type of clear teaching facilitates writing of an accurate, complete summary. In the right column, the teacher gives information and instructions orally, and only a handful of students participate in the discussion. When it is time to complete the graphic organizer, most likely many students are unsure about where to begin or what information is pertinent. Undoubtedly few children will be able to complete the homework assignment.

As a check of how clear your task explanations are, you might write out the directions you would give your students for completing an academic task and ask a colleague to follow them. It can be eye opening!

In the area of writing, children need to be shown very specifically—and have opportunities to practice what has been clearly explained—the essential elements of good writing. Showing students what constitutes good writing, explaining it clearly, and providing opportunities to practice will result in improved writing (Echevarría & Vogt, 2011; Graham & Perin, 2007; Schmoker, 2001). For intermediate and

FIGURE 4.1   Clear Explanation Contrasted with Unclear Explanation

Clear Explanation	Unclear Explanation
The teacher writes on the board: 1. Review your notes from yesterday. 2. Use your notes to answer the five questions on the board. 3. Write your answers on your white board. 4. Complete the graphic organizer. 5. Write a summary of the information contained in the graphic organizer. After giving children a few minutes to review their notes with a partner (more fluent speaker paired with less-proficient; additional information is added as needed), the teacher gives them a set amount of time to answer the first of five questions. She gives them a 30-second signal and then asks the class to "show me" their white boards on which they have written their answers. She can see from a glance at their boards who got it right and who needs assistance or clarification. This process continues until all five questions are answered. The teacher shows a copy of the graphic organizer on the document reader and completes the first part with the class. Then children take the information from the five questions and use it to complete the graphic organizer. Students are allowed to work with a partner on completing the graphic organizer, but the teacher circulates and observes to makes sure that both partners have mastered the content. She asks questions and prompts to ensure understanding. Finally, the teacher models using information in the graphic organizer to write a brief summary and then has students write a summary using their information.	The teacher gives an oral review of what was discussed in the story the previous day. Then she asks a series of questions about the characters, the story's problem, and how the problem in the story was resolved. Several children raised their hands to answer the questions. The teacher talks about the theme and the importance of recognizing a story's theme. Then the teacher hands out a graphic organizer and tells the children that they have 20 minutes to complete it using the story and the information they have talked about. For homework, students are to write a brief summary of the story based on the information.

PD TOOLKIT™ **for SIOP®**

Click on Videos, then search for "Introduction to Comprehensible Input" to hear Dr. MaryEllen Vogt explain how a variety of techniques are used to make the lesson comprehensible.

advanced speakers, focused lessons on "voice" or "word choice" may be appropriate, while beginning speakers benefit from models of complete sentences using adjectives or forming a question.

SIOP® FEATURE 12:

A Variety of Techniques Used to Make Content Concepts Clear

Effective SIOP teachers make content concepts clear and understandable for English learners through the use of a variety of techniques. We have observed some teachers who teach the same way for English learners as they do for native English speakers,

PD TOOLKIT™ **for SIOP®**

Click on Videos, then search for "Comprehensible Input: Lesson in Mandarin" to see Dr. Jana Echevarría present a lesson in Mandarin. What specifically does she do to make her teaching comprehensible?

except that they use pictures for English learners. We believe that the actual teaching techniques a teacher uses have a greater impact on student achievement than do pictures simply illustrating content concepts, without other supports. High-quality SIOP lessons offer students a variety of ways for making the content accessible to them. Some techniques include:

- Use gestures, body language, pictures, and objects to accompany speech. For example, when saying, "We're going to learn about the three forms of water," the teacher holds up three fingers. Showing one finger, she says, "One form is liquid," and shows a glass of water. Holding up two fingers, she says, "the second form is ice," and shows an ice cube. Holding up three fingers, she says, "and the third form is steam," and shows a picture of a steaming cup of coffee. These simple gestures and visual aids assist students in organizing and making sense of information that is presented verbally.

- Provide a model of a process, task, or assignment. For example, as the teacher discusses the process of water taking on the form of ice, she shows or draws a model of the process as it is being described. When students are later instructed to record conditions under which the change in ice from a solid to a liquid is accelerated or slowed, the teacher shows an observation sheet that is divided into three columns on the overhead projector (or document reader or interactive white board). The teacher has a number of pictures (e.g., lamp, sun, and refrigerator) that depict various conditions such as heat and cold. She demonstrates the first condition, heat, with a picture of the sun. She models how students will describe the condition in the first column (e.g., heats). Then she asks students what effect the sun, or heat, has on ice. They answer and in the second column she records how the ice changed (e.g., melted), and in the third column she indicates if the process was accelerated or slowed by the condition (e.g., accelerated). Providing a model as the students are taken through the task verbally eliminates ambiguity and gives the message in more than one way. Students are then able to complete the rest of the worksheet.

- Preview material for optimal learning. When children's attention is focused on the specific material they will be responsible for learning in the lesson, they are able to prepare themselves for the information that is coming, making it more comprehensible for them. Further, they have an opportunity to access prior knowledge and make the connections that they will need to understand the lesson.

- Allow students alternative forms for expressing their understanding of information and concepts. Often English learners have learned the lesson's information but have difficulty expressing their understanding in English, either orally or in writing. Hands-on activities can be used to reinforce the concepts and information presented, with a reduced linguistic demand on these students.

- Use multimedia and other technologies in lessons. Teachers may use transparencies, PowerPoint slides, interactive white boards, a document projector, or relevant Web sites as supplements to a presentation. In so doing, they not only provide more visual support but also model the use of the technology.

- Provide repeated exposures to words, concepts, and skills. English learners are learning through a new language, and in order for the input to be comprehensible, they need repetition. However, excessive practice of a single word or skill can become monotonous and defeat the purpose. Jensen (2005) discusses a process for introducing material repeatedly in a variety of ways. He suggests introducing terms and skills well in advance of learning the material (pre-exposure); explicitly previewing the topic at the start of the lesson; exposing students to the target information (priming); reviewing the material minutes after students have learned it; and allowing students to revise or reconstruct information hours, days, or weeks after the lesson to revisit the learning. Research indicates that teachers ought to provide students with the specifics of what they need to learn—the key details of the unit—and then find ways to expose students to the details multiple times (Marzano, Pickering, & Pollock, 2001).

- Use graphic organizers effectively. New ideas and concepts presented in a new language can be overwhelming for English learners. Graphic organizers take the information, vocabulary, or concept and make it more understandable by showing the key points graphically. To paraphrase the saying "a picture is worth a thousand words," a graphic organizer can capture and simplify a teacher's many potentially confusing words. While graphic organizers are used commonly in school, they are most effective when they match the task and lead to attaining the lesson's objectives. So if the task is learning definitions, then the graphic organizer would be:

	is a		that	

Some graphic organizers may be simple, such as a problem/solution chart or a web with vocabulary definitions. For older children, especially those with learning challenges, some more elaborate graphic organizers such as a Course-Planning Organizer or a Concept Diagram have improved student performance (Deshler & Schumaker, 2006). See Vogt and Echevarría (2008) for many SIOP-appropriate graphic organizers.

- Audiotape texts for greater comprehension. There are a variety of commercially available resources that provide an audio version of a story or book. Publishers often include CDs or Web links to audio versions of text. Also, software exists to create MP3 files by scanning text and reading it aloud. Students can listen to the file on an iPod. An audio version of the text not only allows for multiple opportunities to hear the text, but also it can be adjusted to different proficiency levels. When the teacher (or someone else) records the text him- or herself, the same passage may be read more slowly with clear enunciation for beginning speakers, or synonyms may be substituted for difficult words.

The Comprehensible Input techniques we present in this chapter assist English learners in understanding the lesson's information, especially when it is presented orally. Whether the teacher is giving directions, conveying content information, or teaching a skill or concept—any time a message is delivered verbally—it must be made understandable for all students. Many English learners adapt to the classroom environment by pretending they understand, when, in fact, they may not. SIOP teachers use frequent checks for understanding to gauge how well students comprehend and how speech may need to be differentiated based on proficiency.

Teaching Ideas for Comprehensible Input

In the section that follows, you will find some teaching ideas to help you with preparing SIOP lessons.

- Record step-by-step instructions for completing a task or project, using an electronic tablet application. English learners, individually or in pairs, listen to the instructions as many times as needed, using the speech speed feature to slow the output to their level of understanding. You may also generate questions for partners to ask each other, such as "Which pages do we read before completing the graphic organizer?" or "Are the words we use in the graphic organizer in the reading passage or somewhere else?" In this way, students listen to the instructions again with a focus on specific questions whose answers will help them complete the task. English learners may be unaware that the headings or bolded words in a text are those used to complete a graphic organizer.

- Use sentence strips. This common technique can be used in a variety of ways at all grade levels. In reading/language arts, students can review events in a story by writing each event on a sentence strip, then sequencing the strips to retell the story. This technique can be applied in science to sequence steps in an experiment. For optimal engagement, students in math might work in groups to sequence the steps for problem solving. After the group has put the strips in the correct order, each student takes a strip and lines it up in the order of how the math problem is solved. Other groups provide feedback as to whether the order is correct.

- Show a brief (2–4 minutes) video clip that reinforces the content objective and complements the reading assignment prior to reading a passage of informational text. Have children work in pairs to discuss specific questions about the video clip so that they have a grasp of the big ideas before participating in reading (Reutebuch, 2010).

- Spell difficult words or math formulas to the tune of B-I-N-G-O or another song while clapping out each letter, number, or symbol.

- Make lectures or presentations more compelling to the brain by using objects, photographs, slides, graphs, bulletin board displays, and color. Visuals are important for remembering information. Change things up: Use vivid posters, drawings, videos, and other ways to grab attention (Jensen, 2008).

Differentiating Ideas for Multi-level Classes

We know that most classes with English learners have students with multiple proficiency levels. Even those designated ESL 2, for example, may have some children who have stronger listening skills than writing skills or stronger reading skills than speaking ones. Teachers have at their disposal a variety of ways to differentiate spoken English to make it comprehensible for our diverse English learners. Almost every utterance can be modified in some way to address the variety of proficiency levels of students in your classrooms. Several considerations include the following.

- Use a slower rate, clear enunciation, and simple sentence structure for beginning speakers; use a more native-like rate and sentence complexity for intermediate and advanced speakers of English.

- Remember that you make a huge contribution to your students' attitude toward school. Particularly in the early grades, children's experiences form their impressions about school and learning. Learners in a positive environment are more likely to experience enhanced learning, memory, and self-esteem (Jensen, 2008). Differentiating how information is delivered so that it is comprehensible helps students with lower levels of proficiency feel accepted, understood, and as much a part of the class as native speakers of English.

- Allow students to provide differentiated responses to questions and assignments. For oral responses, provide sentence frames for those children who need them. With written assignments, beginning speakers may require partially completed information (e.g., Cloze procedure),, while advanced speakers may only need a word bank, or other support, to complete the assignment. Level of support should be differentiated so that students at each level of proficiency are able to understand expectations and be successful in lessons.

The Lesson

Economics: Natural Resources and Products (Third Grade)

The following lessons take place in an urban elementary school where English learners make up approximately 30% of the school population. In the classrooms described, there is a mix of language proficiency levels represented, ranging from beginning speakers to advanced English speakers. Students have varying levels of literacy in their native languages.

Teachers in this school have weekly planning time when they co-plan lessons by grade levels. During this time, teachers develop content and language objectives and share ideas for the week's lessons, thus ensuring that they follow similar pacing as they address Common Core State Standards. As you will see, although the objectives are the same, the teachers have their own ways of teaching the lessons.

Third-grade teachers Miss Zarcades, Mr. Mehlhaff, and Mrs. Pabst are all teaching a unit on Economics. The lessons described focus on distinguishing the difference between a natural resource and a product, and address Common Core State

(continued)

Economics: Natural Resources and Products (Third Grade) *(continued)*

Standard, RI.3.4: *Determine the meaning of general academic and domain-specific words and phrases in a text relevant to a grade 3 topic or subject area.* The classes have been studying natural resources, learning about which ones are renewable and non-renewable, and examining the problems associated with scarce resources.

The current lesson takes place over two days. On the first day, the three teachers introduced the lesson by pointing out that we use products every day and that most come from natural resources. They used the example of paper (product) being made from trees (natural resource) and the classes read text about the production of paper. Then the class was told that they would select a product they wanted to research. The vignettes that follow describe Day 2 of the lesson.

The lesson's objectives are:

Content Objective (CO): Students will

- investigate how a product is made and the natural resources used to produce it.
- distinguish between a finished product and a natural resource.

Language Objective (LO): Students will

- write a summary of the production process.
- orally present their research findings.

Teaching Scenarios

To demonstrate how Miss Zarcades, Mr. Mehlhaff, and Mrs. Pabst planned lessons, we look at how each lesson on natural resources and products unfolded in the classroom. As you can see in the lesson descriptions, the teachers varied in the level of support they offered to address the unique language needs of the English learners in their classes.

Miss Zarcades

As was her practice, Miss Zarcades reviewed the content and language objectives she had posted for students. She asked students to read along with her, pointing to each word as she read so that all students, including English learners, could follow along. She began this second day of the lesson by asking each group to quickly say what product they had researched the previous day from texts and Internet sources. Since she had distributed a worksheet to guide—or scaffold—their information gathering, she reviewed on the document reader a sample completed worksheet (production of a pencil). She went through each section, being careful to enunciate clearly and repeat the specific academic vocabulary words that were key terms in the lesson, e.g., renewable resource, product, and production. She paused periodically to make sure that all group members were following along on their own worksheets and checking that they had filled in the section correctly. She told the groups that they had

10 minutes to review their worksheets and add any additional information. She wrote the time the task ended on the white board (e.g., 1:10). During this time, Miss Zarcades circulated around the classroom assisting groups or individuals who needed support.

Next, she distributed poster board and pointed to the samples on the wall that were posted. She instructed groups to draw a similar poster to reflect the production process outlined on their worksheet. Each member of the group was assigned one section of the worksheet to illustrate, e.g., the product, natural resource used in the product, where the natural resource comes from, and if it is a renewable or nonrenewable resource. The groups were given 15 minutes to complete a simple illustration of the process as a visual to accompany their oral presentations. Again, Miss Zarcades wrote the time the task ended on the board (e.g., 1:30). After the posters were completed, the groups gave oral presentations of their projects. Each member of the group told about his or her part of the poster using complete sentences and academic terms. Miss Zarcades had sentence frames written on the white board for those students who needed language support, e.g., "The product we researched was _____." and, "Production of _____ uses _____ resources" (renewable or nonrenewable). After the oral presentations were made, Miss Zarcades played a quick game of naming things and asking students randomly if each were a finished product or a natural resource. Throughout the lesson, Miss Zarcades used language structures and vocabulary that she believed the students could understand at their level of proficiency. For beginning English speakers, she spoke slowly, often contextualizing vocabulary words, and enunciated clearly. Also, she avoided the use of idioms, and when she sensed that students did not understand, she paraphrased to convey the meaning more clearly. At the conclusion of the lesson she reviewed the content and language objectives with her students.

On the SIOP form in Figure 4.2, rate Miss Zarcades' lesson on each of the Comprehensible Input features.

FIGURE 4.2 Comprehensible Input Component of the SIOP Model: Miss Zarcades' Lesson

4	3	2	1	0
10. **Speech appropriate** for students' proficiency levels (e.g., slower rate, enunciation, and simple sentence structure for beginners)		**Speech** sometimes inappropriate for students' proficiency levels		**Speech inappropriate** for students' proficiency levels

4	3	2	1	0
11. **Clear explanation** of academic tasks		**Unclear explanation** of academic tasks		**No explanation** of academic tasks

4	3	2	1	0
12. **A variety of techniques** used to make content concepts clear (e.g., modeling, visuals, hands-on activities, demonstrations, gestures, body language)		Some techniques used to make content concepts clear		**No techniques** used to make content concepts clear

Mr. Mehlhaff

Mr. Mehlhaff began the lesson by reading the content and language objectives. Then he told students to continue researching the products they had started investigating the day before. He had each student select his or her own product and work individually on gathering information. Some of the students seemed lost about how to take text and Internet sources and extract pertinent information. Quite a few sat quietly while others began talking among themselves. Mr. Mehlhaff sensed that children were off task so he stood and gave the directions orally again, speaking rather quickly and curtly. He wrote on the board: *Product, Natural Resources Used*, to help guide students in completing the task. He pointed to the words and repeated that they were supposed to be looking for information about their product (pointed to word) and writing down which natural resources (pointed to word) were used. He gave students more time to "get to work." After a while, he assigned partners and told the class that the partners were going to share information about their products with one another. He reminded them that they needed to use academic language including the specific terms that had been the focus of the lesson. He referred them back to the language objective and read it to them, stressing that he wanted to hear students using key academic terms and phrases. He called on two of the top students in class and asked them to come up and demonstrate what partners were going to do. The students faced each other and Mr. Mehlhaff told one, "Ask him the name of his product" and the student asked his partner who then answered. Next Mr. Mehlhaff prompted, "Now, what about natural resources?" and the student asked his partner which natural resources were used to make the product. After this demonstration, Mr. Mehlhaff told the class that partners were going to follow the same questioning format, asking one another about their products. Students began talking with their partners, asking and answering questions with varying levels of success.

On the SIOP form in Figure 4.3, rate Mr. Mehlhaffs lesson on each of the Comprehensible Input features.

FIGURE 4.3 Comprehensible Input Component of the SIOP Model: Mr. Mehlhaff's Lesson

4	3	2	1	0
10. **Speech appropriate** for students' proficiency levels (e.g., slower rate, enunciation, and simple sentence structure for beginners)		**Speech** sometimes inappropriate for students' proficiency levels		**Speech inappropriate** for students' proficiency levels

4	3	2	1	0
11. **Clear explanation** of academic tasks		**Unclear explanation** of academic tasks		**No explanation** of academic tasks

4	3	2	1	0
12. **A variety of techniques** used to make content concepts clear (e.g., modeling, visuals, hands-on activities, demonstrations, gestures, body language)		Some techniques used to make content concepts clear		**No techniques** used to make content concepts clear

Mrs. Pabst

Mrs. Pabst asked the class to chorally read the lesson's content and language objectives, which were written on the board. She was sure to read slowly so that all students, including English learners, were able to follow along. She asked if there were any questions from the previous day's assignment and requested a show of hands of children who knew what their product was. All children raised hands. The previous day Mrs. Pabst had let students pick a partner and then work in pairs to select a product and gather information about its associated natural resources. Mrs. Pabst told the students that today they would identify where the natural resources came from that were used to make the products. She pointed to the large map on the wall. Children were told that they would create a symbol that represents each resource used in their product. As Mrs. Pabst explained this process, she used her normal, somewhat rapid manner, the same speaking style she used with English-speaking students. Then she passed out paper for making two copies of each symbol—one to put on the large world map and the other for the map key, or legend. She pointed out that a *map legend* is a key to the symbols used on a map. It is like a dictionary so you can understand the meaning of what the map represents. She modeled what the children would complete by showing a symbol for trees (paper products) and placed one on the map where logging takes place and another on the map legend with, "trees for paper production" next to the symbol. Mrs. Pabst then told students to get started working with their partners to create a symbol. After all students had completed this task, Mrs. Pabst had each pair come to the map and tell the name of the product, the natural resource used, and where the natural resource came from. They then put one symbol on the map and the other on the map key. When all students had completed their oral report, Mrs. Pabst reviewed the content and language objectives and asked if they were met.

On the SIOP form in Figure 4.4, rate Mrs. Pabst's lesson on each of the Comprehensible Input features.

FIGURE 4.4 Comprehensible Input Component of the SIOP Model: Mrs. Pabst's Lesson

4	3	2	1	0
10. **Speech appropriate** for students' proficiency levels (e.g., slower rate, enunciation, and simple sentence structure for beginners)		**Speech** sometimes inappropriate for students' proficiency levels		**Speech inappropriate** for students' proficiency levels

4	3	2	1	0
11. **Clear explanation** of academic tasks		**Unclear explanation** of academic tasks		**No explanation** of academic tasks

4	3	2	1	0
12. **A variety of techniques** used to make content concepts clear (e.g., modeling, visuals, hands-on activities, demonstrations, gestures, body language)		Some techniques used to make content concepts clear		**No techniques** used to make content concepts clear

Discussion of Lessons

10. *Speech Appropriate for Students' Proficiency Level (Rate and Complexity)*

Miss Zarcades: 4

Mr. Mehlhaff: 0

Mrs. Pabst: 1

- **Miss Zarcades** was attuned to the benefit of modulating her speech to make herself understood by the children. She slowed her rate of speech and enunciated clearly to accommodate beginning speakers, and she adjusted her speech for the other, more proficient speakers of English. She used a natural speaking voice, but paid attention to her rate of speech and enunciation. Further, Miss Zarcades repeated key academic vocabulary terms, which helps all students, but especially English learners. Finally, she adjusted the level of vocabulary and complexity of the sentences when speaking and also by using sentence frames so that all students could participate at their level of proficiency. For this reason, Miss Zarcades lesson received a "4" for this feature.

- **Mr. Mehlhaff** seemed unaware that his students would understand more if he adjusted his oral presentation to accommodate the proficiency levels of English learners in his class. He gave few instructions to assist students in completing the task, and those instructions he gave did not take into consideration his rate of speech or complexity of speech, variables that impact English learners' ability to comprehend information in class. Also, making sense of written information independently and creating original sentences are inordinately difficult tasks for English learners. Unwittingly, Mr. Mehlhaff set the students up for failure, and then he was frustrated when they were off task. He spoke quickly and curtly, which did not enhance comprehension. Mr. Mehlhaff's lesson was given a "0" for this feature.

- Generally, **Mrs. Pabst's** rate of speech and enunciation was similar to that used with native English speakers. She didn't consciously adjust her speech (rate or complexity) to the variety of proficiency levels in the class, although she did have students chorally read the objectives slowly so all could follow along. Mrs. Pabst could have paraphrased some of her instructions and questions, using simpler sentence structure, when some children struggled to understand. Because Mrs. Pabst made minimal adjustments while speaking to English learners, her lesson received a "1" for this feature.

11. *Clear Explanation of Academic Tasks*

Miss Zarcades: 4

Mr. Mehlhaff: 2

Mrs. Pabst: 3

Making your expectations crystal clear to students is one of the most important aspects of teaching, and when working with English learners, explicit, step-by-step directions can be critical to a lesson's success. It is difficult for almost any student to remember directions given only orally, and oral directions may be incomprehensible to many English learners. A lesson is sure to get off to a rocky start if students don't understand what they are expected to do. Written procedures provide students with a guide.

- **Miss Zarcades'** lesson received a "4" for this feature because she used a teaching style that supported student success by making her expectations for completing academic tasks clear and understandable. She modeled almost every task students were expected to complete. During the lesson she first checked for understanding by using a "popcorn" approach, quickly asking each group the name of their product. Then she modeled for the class a completed worksheet and gave each student a chance to check his or her own work from the previous day. If an individual student or group was confused or had done the worksheet incorrectly, it was important for Miss Zarcades to make sure they all understood what to do and were doing it correctly before the children spent more time on the task. She then provided time to make additions or corrections, and was careful to oversee their work. Throughout the lesson, tasks were modeled so that students at all levels of English proficiency knew the expectations and, with the scaffolding she offered, were more likely to be successful in completing the work. She took into account the linguistic differences in her class and differentiated accordingly. The sentence frames let the students know exactly the kinds of complete sentences that were expected during their oral presentations.

  Using a time management technique, Miss Zarcades wrote the ending time on the board for various tasks. This technique provided students with time boundaries for the tasks—letting them know how much time she expected them to spend—and helped them learn to manage their time. Overall, she understood the value of being explicit in what she wanted the students to do and walked them through each step of the lesson.

- Although **Mr. Mehlhaff** was a veteran teacher, he did not provide the kind of guidance that all students benefit from and that is critical for English learners. He expected young children to work independently, gathering information from text and Internet sources. Exposing students at all levels of English proficiency to complex text is important, but scaffolding is essential to help students access the information. Many students, and especially English learners, were unsure of the expectations or process for completing the assignment. Mr. Mehlhaff attempted to explain further when students were off task by rereading the objectives, but that probably did little to make the task clearer. He did assist students by having two children model how to work in pairs asking questions about the assignment. This gave students an idea about how to conduct their pair work. Thus, Mr. Mehlhaff's lesson was given a "2" for this feature.

- **Mrs. Pabst** first got students focused on the task by reading the objectives and asking them to remember the product they had chosen the previous day. She told them explicitly what they were going to do first: Identify where the natural resources came from that were used to make the products. This kind of clarity helps English learners to know precisely what is expected. In addition, she modeled the task that children were to work on. She showed the symbol she had created to represent paper products and put it on the map, just as they would do when they finished. Even without words, the students, including English learners, could see what the process was: Find out where your natural resource comes from, draw a symbol, and prepare to place it on the map and legend with a brief explanation. The lesson would have received a higher rating had Mrs. Pabst actually modeled or explained how students were to extract information about where the natural resources come from. She said that they would create a symbol to represent it, but didn't sufficiently explain how children would go about finding the information that their symbol would represent. A worksheet to guide them, as Miss Zarcades provided, would have scaffolded the task for students. Mrs. Pabst's lesson received a "3" for this feature.

12. *A Variety of Techniques Used*

Miss Zarcades: 4

Mr. Mehlhaff: 1

Mrs. Pabst: 2

Concepts become understandable when teachers use a variety of techniques, including modeling, demonstrations, visuals, and body language.

- Throughout the lesson, **Miss Zarcades** used a number of techniques that supported students' learning and helped them be successful in completing the assignment. She provided a worksheet to scaffold children's organization of information and she showed the sample completed worksheet, carefully going through each section. All of the visuals she showed and pointed to increased students' comprehension. By giving students a worksheet and poster board for their illustrations, she made the lesson more hands-on and provided more than one way to express the information they had gathered. One can imagine that the atmosphere in Miss Zarcades' class is positive, encouraging, and non threatening for English learners. This kind of environment instills confidence in children about their ability to learn and be successful in school. Because of the variety of effective techniques used, Miss Zarcades' lesson received a "4" for this feature.

- **Mr. Mehlhaff** is a kind and friendly teacher, but he did not use many teaching techniques that increased children's comprehension of the lesson. His teaching style was one of teacher lecture and student performance without scaffolding. He expected young learners to work independently, which is difficult for all children, especially English learners who may not even understand the words in the text. Thus, completing a summary of the natural resources used to produce a product was a nearly impossible task. He modeled how to discuss the information in pairs, but one might expect that few English learners had actually independently gathered sufficient information for the oral exchange. Think about the difference between Miss Zarcades' scaffolded lesson and Mr. Mehlhaff's reliance on independent work. This lesson received a "1" for use of comprehensible input techniques.

- **Mrs. Pabst** used teaching techniques in the lesson, but some of the ones she used were not useful, especially for English learners. First, she asked if there were any questions. Few English learners typically ask for clarification or assistance in front of the class. Then she provided them with the hands-on activity of creating a symbol to place on the map. However, there was no technique used to check for understanding as to whether the children investigated how a product was made and learned about the natural resources used to produce it (the objective). Although she modeled how to create a symbol and place it on the map, she depended on the map symbol activity to guide students' understanding of the content. Instead, she might have used a technique for checking understanding of the production process, or provided an outline or graphic organizer for students to make sense of the information they were expected to gather. Gestures, modeling, hands-on activities, and the like are important for increasing English learners' understanding of the lesson, but these techniques must lead to meeting the lesson's objectives. For these reasons, Mrs. Pabst's lesson received a "2" for this feature.

(For more examples of lesson and unit plans in history/social studies for grades K–6, see Short, Vogt, and Echevarría, 2010.)

Summary

PD **TOOLKIT**™ **for SIOP**®

Click on Videos, then search for "Comprehensible Input" to hear Dr. Deborah Short describe the features of CI and to see a science lesson using comprehensible input techniques.

As you reflect on this chapter and the impact of comprehensible input on learning, consider the following main points:

- Although English learners learn in many of the same ways as fluent English-speaking students, they do require special supports, or accommodations to make instruction understandable (August & Shanahan, 2006; Goldenberg, 2008).
- Effective SIOP teachers constantly modulate and adjust their speech to ensure that the content is comprehensible.
- Concepts are taught using a variety of techniques, including modeling, gestures, hands-on activities, and demonstrations, so that students understand and learn the content material.
- Effective SIOP teachers provide explanations of academic tasks in ways that make clear what students are expected to accomplish and that promote student success.

Discussion Questions

1. In reflecting on the content and language objectives at the beginning of the chapter are you able to:
   a. Identify techniques for presenting content information in ways that students comprehend?
   b. Review various ways to provide directions for completing academic tasks?
   c. Discuss modifications to teacher speech that can increase student comprehension?
   d. Write the steps needed for students to perform an academic task and have a partner perform each step?

2. Have you recently been in a situation where you were not an "insider," and therefore you didn't understand what was being talked about? Compare that situation and your feelings about it to the way language is used in classrooms where there are English learners. What can you do to be a more culturally responsive teacher, making sure all students are able to follow a lecture or discussion?

3. Many times in classrooms, discipline problems can be attributed to students not knowing what they're supposed to be doing. If students don't know what to do, they find something else to do. What are some ways that you can avoid having students become confused about accomplishing academic tasks?

4. If you have traveled in another country, or if you are an English learner, reflect on difficulties you had in understanding others. What are some techniques people used to try to communicate with you? What are some techniques you can use in the classroom?

5. Using the SIOP lesson you have been developing, add to it so that the Comprehensible Input features in the lesson are enhanced.

6. For the economics lesson (natural resources), what are some comprehension checks that are quick, non threatening, and effective for determining if a student is ready to move on?

CHAPTER 5

Strategies

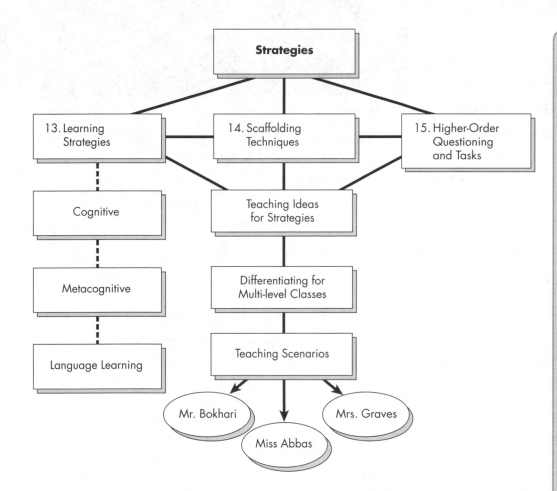

After reading, discussing, and engaging in activities related to this chapter, you will be able to meet the following content and language objectives.

Content Objectives

Select student learning strategies appropriate to a lesson's objectives.

Incorporate explicit instruction and student practice with learning strategies when planning lessons.

Identify techniques for verbal, procedural, and instructional scaffolding.

Language Objectives

Identify language learning strategies to include in lessons.

Write lesson plans that include varied techniques for scaffolding student understandings.

Write a set of questions or tasks on a chosen topic with increasing levels of cognition.

Think about a time when you had to read a challenging text, such as a graduate-level chapter or a computer manual. Because this was required reading, you probably set yourself up for success by sitting in a good chair with proper lighting, with a highlighter, pen or pencil, and sticky notes, or with an e-reader, you activated note-taking so you're all ready to read. As you read, you took notes, highlighted important information, and tagged material that you wanted to find quickly at a later time. If you came across something you didn't understand, you tried a number of different things, such as rereading, checking

the text's glossary, trying to summarize previously read material, generating some questions, using text structures, and/or checking class notes or another source for clarification (McLaughlin, 2010). Why did you employ these learning strategies while reading? Were they taught to you, or did you develop them naturally because you are an avid reader? What other strategies do you employ to help you read and learn more effectively? ●

Background

As introduced in Chapter 3, researchers have found that information is retained and connected in the brain through "mental pathways" that are linked to an individual's existing schemata (Anderson, 1984; Barnhardt, 1997). If schemata for a particular topic are well developed and personally meaningful, new information is easier to retain and recall, and proficient learners initiate and activate their associations between the new and old learning. In cognitive theory, initiation and activation are described as the mental processes that enhance comprehension, learning, and retention of information. Teachers of English learners sometimes have difficulty determining their children's proficiency with learning strategies, especially in the beginning stages of their acquisition of English. Teachers may observe English learners' lower *English* proficiency and misdiagnose it as symptoms of poor or underdeveloped *learning* skills. In this chapter, we discuss the importance of teaching and providing practice with a variety of learning strategies that facilitate the learning process. We also suggest that all children, including English learners, benefit from questions and tasks that involve higher levels of thinking. In order to accomplish these goals, teachers must carefully scaffold instruction for those who need additional support.

SIOP® FEATURE 13:

Ample Opportunities Provided for Students to Use Learning Strategies

There is considerable evidence from research over the past four decades supporting the assertion that explicitly teaching a variety of self-regulating strategies improves student learning and reading (August & Shanahan, 2010; Dole, Duffy, Roehler, & Pearson, 1991; Pressley, 2000, 2002; Snow, Griffin, & Burns, 2005; Vogt & Nagano, 2003). Many of these research studies focused on highly effective readers and learners who use a variety of strategies in an interactive and recursive manner. Paris (2001, p. 89) suggests that self-regulated learning "emphasizes autonomy and control by the individual who monitors, directs, and regulates actions toward goals of information acquisition, expanding expertise, and self-improvement." Chamot (2009, p. 57) suggests that learning strategies are important because:

- Good language learners use task-appropriate and flexible strategies.
- Students who are mentally active and strategic are better learners.
- Learning strategies are particularly effective with academic tasks.
- Learning strategies can be taught and learned.
- Learning strategies can transfer to new tasks.

As English learners develop English proficiency, it is important that their language, literacy, and content instruction include a focus on learning and practicing a variety of learning strategies (Chamot, 2009; Dymock & Nicholson, 2010; National Institute of Child Health and Human Development, 2000; Vogt, Echevarría, & Short, 2010). These strategies can be classified as follows:

1. **Cognitive Learning Strategies.** These strategies help students organize the information they are expected to learn through the process of self-regulated learning (Paris, 2001). Cognitive strategies are directly related to individual learning tasks and are used by students when they mentally and/or physically manipulate material, or when they apply a specific technique to a learning task (Slater & Horstman, 2002). Examples of cognitive strategies include the following (McLaughlin, 2010; Vogt & Shearer, 2011):

   - Previewing a story or chapter before reading
   - Establishing a purpose for reading and/or learning
   - Consciously making connections between personal experiences, beliefs, and feelings and what is learned while reading
   - Using mnemonics
   - Highlighting, underlining, or using sticky notes to identify important information
   - Taking notes or outlining
   - Reading aloud for clarification

- Rereading to aid comprehension
- Mapping information or using a graphic organizer
- Identifying key vocabulary
- Identifying, analyzing, and using varied text structures

2. **Metacognitive Learning Strategies.** The process of purposefully monitoring our thinking is referred to as *metacognition* (Baker & Brown, 1984). The use of metacognitive strategies implies awareness, reflection, and interaction; and strategies are used in an integrated, interrelated, and recursive manner (Dole, Duffy, Roehler, & Pearson, 1991). Studies have found that when metacognitive strategies are taught explicitly, reading comprehension is improved (Duffy, 2002; Snow, Griffin, & Burns, 2005; Vogt & Nagano, 2003). Examples of metacognitive learning strategies include:

- Predicting and inferring
- Generating questions and using the questions to guide comprehension
- Monitoring and clarifying ("Am I understanding? If not, what can I do to help myself?")
- Evaluating and determining importance
- Summarizing and synthesizing
- Making mental images (visualizing)

3. **Language Learning Strategies.** As with other aspects of learning, effective language learners consciously use a variety of strategies to increase their progress in speaking and comprehending the new language (Cohen & Macaro, 2008). Examples of language learning strategies include:

- Applying basic reading skills, such as previewing, skimming, scanning, and reviewing
- Analyzing and using forms and patterns in English, such as the *prefix + root + suffix* pattern
- Making logical guesses based on contextual and syntactic information
- Breaking words into component parts
- Purposefully grouping and labeling words
- Drawing pictures and/or using gestures to communicate when words do not come to mind
- Substituting a known word when unable to pronounce an unfamiliar word
- Self-monitoring and self-correcting while speaking English
- Paraphrasing
- Guessing and deducing
- Imitating behaviors of native English-speaking peers to successfully complete tasks
- Using verbal and nonverbal cues to know when to pay attention

Other language learning strategies include those described as social-affective, such as seeking out conversation partners, taking risks with the new language, practicing English when alone, and combatting inhibition about using English by having a positive attitude. Another important social-affective strategy is asking for clarification, something that is often difficult for English learners.

Whichever sets of strategies are emphasized, learned, and used, it is generally agreed that they can be taught through explicit instruction, careful modeling, and scaffolding (Duffy, 2002). Additionally, Lipson and Wixson (2012) suggest that just teaching a variety of strategies is not enough. Rather, learners need not only *declarative* knowledge (What is the strategy?) but also *procedural* knowledge (How do I use it?) and *conditional* knowledge (When and why do I use it?). Also, it is important that students practice and apply strategies with different tasks and genres.

When teachers model strategy use (such as through think-alouds) and then provide appropriate scaffolding during practice sessions, students are more likely to become effective strategy users (Fisher, Frey, & Williams, 2002; Pressley & Woloshyn, 1995).

Things to Remember about Teaching Learning Strategies

- Many English learners who have been well schooled in their home language probably have developed a variety of learning strategies that they can talk about once they learn the English terms for them. Therefore, it's important to know your students' educational backgrounds and their native language literacy proficiency so you can be aware of what they already know and can do regarding strategy use in their home language.

- Many strategies transfer to learning in the new language. For example, once you know how to find a main idea in a text written in your home language (L1), you can do it with a text in your target language (L2). Likewise, if you know how to make predictions in your L1, you can engage in making predictions in your L2.

- The Common Core State Standards require that students "adapt their communication in relation to audience, task, purpose, and discipline. They set and adjust purposes for reading, writing, speaking, listening, and language uses as warranted by the tasks." (© Copyright 2010. National Governors Association Center for Best Practices and Council of Chief State School Officers. All rights reserved.) This is precisely what it means to be an effective user of reading and language strategies.

- Remember that having students identify and label strategies is not the end goal (Baker, 2008). Instead, the desired outcome is for students to engage in a variety of learning strategies while they're reading, listening, writing, speaking, and working with other students.

- McKeown, Beck, and Blake (2009) found that some students spend so much time focusing on strategic actions that they seem less likely to connect key ideas in the text. "Focusing on strategies during reading may leave students less aware of the overall process of interacting with text, especially in terms of the need to connect ideas they encounter and integrate those ideas into a coherent whole" (p. 246). This can happen when teachers mistakenly focus too much attention on the identification of separate learning strategies, such as, "Today, our goal is to make predictions. Tomorrow, we'll work on making connections." Effective learners use sets of strategies, coordinate them, and shift when appropriate. If one thing doesn't work, good strategy users try something else. What's important is having an overall idea of what it means to be strategic; that is, how to adapt and combine individual strategies within a plan.

- The ultimate goal is for children to develop independence in self-monitoring and self-regulation through practice with peer-assisted and student-centered strategies. Many English learners, however, have difficulty initiating an active role in using these strategies because they are focusing mental energy on their developing language skills. Therefore, effective SIOP teachers scaffold English learners by providing many opportunities for them to use a variety of learning strategies that have been found to be especially effective.

- "[T]he bottom line is that we want our students to do more than recite a list of strategies; we want them to actually *use* the strategies, unprompted—and to do so without having to record the event on a sticky note" (Marcell, DeCleene, & Juettner, 2010, p. 687). So give them time to get good at strategy use. They do not have to learn a new strategy each day. One per week or two is better, especially if they can try to apply the strategies with different texts and genres.

- To assist children in becoming effective strategy users, see the section, Teaching Ideas for Strategies, later in this chapter. In particular, note the following instructional activities: Directed Reading-Thinking Activity (DR-TA), SQP2RS (Squeepers), Question-Answer Relationships (QAR), and Questioning the Author (QtA). Also, see Miss Abbas's lesson on Saving Our Planet in this chapter, and determine which cognitive, metacognitive, and language learning strategies her lesson incorporates.

SIOP® FEATURE 14:

Scaffolding Techniques Consistently Used, Assisting and Supporting Student Understanding

Scaffolding is a term coined by Jerome Bruner (1983) that is associated with Vygotsky's (1978) theory of the Zone of Proximal Development (ZPD). In essence, the ZPD is the difference between what a child can accomplish alone and what he or she can accomplish with the assistance of a more experienced individual. The assistance that is provided by a teacher is called *scaffolding*.

Pearson and Gallagher (1983) described ZPD and scaffolding as the "gradual release of responsibility" (GRR) as it relates to classroom practices. Madeline Hunter (1982) used somewhat different terms to describe the gradual release of responsibility, but her instructional cycle was similar: Input (focused teaching), Demonstration (similar to modeling), Guided Practice, and Independent Practice. Teachers scaffold instruction when they provide substantial amounts of support and assistance in the earliest stages of teaching a new concept or strategy, and then gradually decrease the amount of support as learners acquire experience through multiple practice opportunities with peers. One of the goals of the Common Core State Standards is that students will be able to comprehend independently complex texts across a variety of disciplines.

Therefore, it is essential for all students, including English learners, to have appropriate scaffolded instruction (as needed) that leads to eventual independence.

During a lesson, the gradual release of responsibility is manifested when teachers consciously include the following practices (adapted from Brown, 2008, p. 541):

- Emphasize the role of personal choice, effort, and persistence in enacting learning strategies;
- Motivate students' strategy use by showing how applying strategies improves comprehension and learning;
- Highlight the vital role of prior knowledge activation and connection in learning;
- Explain the benefits of strategy use in general and the value of using specific strategies;
- Mentally model (e.g., think-aloud) to make thinking transparent to students;
- Provide guided and independent practice so that students learn to use strategies when cued by a diverse array of goals, needs, task demands, and texts;
- Promote independent strategy use by gradually shifting responsibility for strategy application to students.

There have been a number of graphics created to represent the gradual release of responsibility (GRR) model as initially conceptualized by Pearson and Gallagher (1983). Do a Web search for "gradual release of responsibility" and you will find several interesting variations. What has been mostly consistent among these variations is that a lesson has "phases" that move from one to another. What has been consistently absent from these charts is teaching that is recursive. The intent of the GRR model is to move from reliance on the teacher to student independence in applying key content concepts and vocabulary, but as we all know, a lesson may not move smoothly from one phase to the next.

Here, we offer a different way of looking at GRR that has at its center recursive teaching that is essential for English learners and struggling students (see Figure 5.1). After explicitly teaching a concept (*I do. You watch and respond.*), students practice what has been taught with assistance from the teacher (*We do together. I help and respond.*). Students who are successful can then practice with other students, with minimal supervision (*You do together. I watch and respond.*). For some students it may be necessary to take a step back and reteach and model before moving again to supported practice. Of course, the goal for all students is independent application of key concepts and vocabulary (*You do independently. I watch and respond.*). However, the process is not linear and it requires differentiated teaching, enabling those who can move forward to do so. But for those who need additional modeling and support, opportunities are provided.

Three Types of Scaffolding

Three types of scaffolding can be used effectively with English learners: Verbal, Procedural, and Instructional.

1. **Verbal Scaffolding.** Teachers who are aware of English learners' existing levels of language development use prompting, questioning, and elaboration to facilitate

FIGURE 5.1 Scaffolding: Gradual Increase of Student Independence

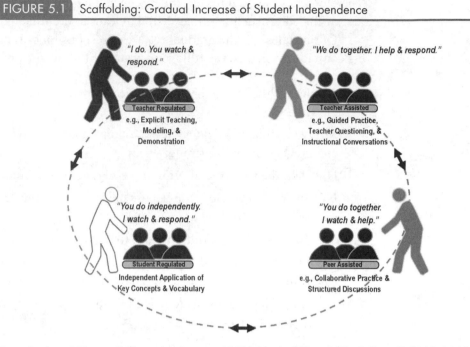

Reproduction of this material is restricted to use with Echevarría, J, Vogt, M.E., & Short, D (2013). Making content comprehensible for English learners. The SIOP Model (4th Ed.) Boston: Pearson/Allyn & Bacon.

students' movement to higher levels of language proficiency, comprehension, and thinking. Effective teacher–student interaction promotes confidence when it is geared to a student's language competence. The following are examples of verbal scaffolding:

- **Paraphrasing.** This is restating a student's response in another form or in other words to clarify and model correct English usage.

- **Using "think-alouds."** These are carefully structured models of how effective strategy users think and monitor their understandings (Baumann, Jones, & Seifert-Kessell, 1993). For example, when teaching students how to preview a story or chapter, the teacher might think aloud as follows: "I like to think about a story or chapter before I read it. I look at the pictures and ask myself what will this be about? What will happen? If I look at the big bold heading at the top of the page, I'll get an idea. The title or heading might be black, or it could be another color. I see here that it's _____.' Now I need to look at other headings on the pages to see if they will help me determine what is important. Usually I think about what I already know about the topic. If I know something about it, it helps me understand better."

- **Reinforcing contextual definitions.** An example is "Aborigines, the people native to Australia, were being forced from their homes." The phrase "the people native to Australia" provides a partial definition of the word "Aborigines" within the context of the sentence.

- **Providing correct pronunciation by repeating students' responses.** When teachers repeat English learners' correct responses, enunciating carefully and naturally, children have an additional opportunity to hear the content information, pronunciation, and inflection. However, in order for children to internalize the gentle corrections, research has shown that the focus should be on form. Saunders and Goldenberg (2010) suggest that dedicating time to work on pronunciation may be beneficial.

- **Slowing speech, increasing pauses, and speaking in phrases.** Teachers provide scaffolding for English learners' language acquisition when they slow down the rate of speech, pause between phrases, and allow children the wait time they may need to process information in English (see Chapter 4 for more information about Comprehensible Input).

- **Eliciting more language and information from the students.** Children often provide one- or two-word responses to teacher questions. Teachers then elaborate. Instead, teachers can ask children to add on, tell more, or explain their ideas more fully, giving them the chance to advance their language skills.

2. **Procedural Scaffolding.** Effective teachers also incorporate instructional approaches that provide *procedural scaffolding*. These approaches include, but are not limited to, the following:

- Using an instructional framework that includes explicit teaching, modeling, and guided and independent practice opportunities with peers, and an expectation for independent application;

- One-on-one teaching, coaching, and modeling;

- Small-group instruction with children practicing a newly learned strategy with another more experienced student;

- Partnering or grouping children for reading and content activities, with more experienced readers assisting those with less experience.

3. **Instructional Scaffolding.** Teachers use *instructional scaffolding* to provide English learners with access to content and language concepts. Examples include:

- Graphic organizers that are used as a prereading tool to prepare children for the content of a textbook chapter. The organizer can also be used to illustrate a chapter's text structure, such as comparative or chronological order (Vogt & Echevarría, 2008).

- Models of completed assignments are instructional scaffolds, too. Teachers can show children sample products, such as posters, booklets, podcasts, and the like, to give them a clear picture of their goal.

As you begin to write SIOP lesson plans, keep this in mind: "A scaffold is a temporary structure that is constructed to help someone complete a task that would otherwise be too difficult to do alone. We use scaffolds frequently in real life. We see scaffolds that are assembled to facilitate erecting or repairing a building; we see scaffolds used by painters to reach areas inaccessible without them; we see scaffolds dangling from high-rise offices that allow window washers to undertake a task unimaginable without such a device. But when the job is completed, scaffolds are dismantled" because they are temporary (Buehl, 2006, p. 1). Most important is that scaffolds in the classroom are used to provide access to grade-level texts and complex concepts. The release of verbal, procedural, and instructional scaffolds is gradual until student independence has been achieved.

SIOP® FEATURE 15:

A Variety of Questions or Tasks That Promote Higher-Order Thinking Skills

Another way that effective SIOP teachers can promote strategy use is by asking questions and providing tasks that promote critical thinking (Fordham, 2006). Nearly 60 years ago, Benjamin Bloom and colleagues (1956) introduced a taxonomy of educational objectives that includes six levels: Knowledge, Comprehension, Application, Analysis, Synthesis, and Evaluation. This taxonomy was formulated on the principle that learning proceeds from concrete knowledge to abstract values or from the denotative to the connotative. For decades, educators have adopted this taxonomy as a hierarchy of questioning that, when used effectively in the classroom, elicits varied levels of student thinking.

In 2001, D. R. Krathwohl (who originally worked with Bloom) and colleagues published a revised taxonomy: *Taxonomy for Learning, Teaching, and Assessing: A Revision of Bloom's Taxonomy of Educational Objectives* (see Anderson & Krathwohl, 2001). In the revised taxonomy, the six levels include (simplified here):

1. Remember
   a. Recognizing
   b. Recalling

2. Understand
   a. Interpreting
   b. Exemplifying
   c. Classifying
   d. Summarizing
   e. Inferring
   f. Comparing
   g. Explaining

3. Apply
   a. Executing
   b. Implementing

4. Analyze
   a. Differentiating
   b. Organizing
   c. Attributing

5. Evaluate
   a. Checking
   b. Critiquing

6. Create
   a. Generating
   b. Planning
   c. Producing

Webb (1997) developed a similar, but more complex system and criteria for aligning standards, teaching, and assessment. The Depth of Knowledge (DOK) model analyzes the cognitive expectations of standards, academic tasks, and assessments. Each DOK level reflects increasingly sophisticated cognitive processes. What distinguishes DOK from Bloom's Taxonomy (and other similar taxonomies) is that DOK relates knowledge levels to curricular activities and assessment in particular content areas (language arts, science, and mathematics). The term *knowledge* broadly encompasses procedural knowledge, declarative knowledge, and conditional knowledge.

Following are the four levels of the Depth of Knowledge Model, along with brief descriptions of each level. (For more information, see www.wcer.wisc.edu/ WAT/index.aspx.)

- **Level 1: Recall.** Requires recall of a fact, information, or procedure (such as identify, list, label, illustrate, measure, report, define, draw, calculate, arrange, match, use, state, repeat, tell, recite)

- **Level 2: Skill/Concept.** Requires both comprehension and subsequent processing of text (such as infer, categorize, collect and display, organize, construct, modify, predict, interpret, distinguish, compare, relate)

- **Level 3: Strategic Thinking.** Requires reasoning, developing a plan or a sequence of steps, some complexity, and more than one possible answer (such as revise, develop a logical argument, assess, apprise, use concepts to solve non-routine problems, compare, critique, formulate, investigate, hypothesize, differentiate, cite evidence)

- **Level 4: Extended Thinking.** Requires thinking and processing multiple conditions of the problem (such as design, connect, synthesize, apply concepts, critique, analyze, create, prove)

Whichever taxonomy, such as Bloom's or Anderson and Krathwohl's, or descriptive framework, such as Webb's DOK, teachers choose to use when designing lessons, it is important to carefully plan higher-order questions and tasks prior to lesson delivery. It is just too difficult to think of them on the spot when you're teaching. Researchers have found that of the approximately 80,000 questions the average teacher asks annually, 80% of them are at the literal level (Gall, 1984; Watson & Young, 1986). This is especially problematic with English learners. As children are acquiring proficiency in English, it is tempting to rely on simple questions that result in yes/no or other one-word responses. It is possible, however, to reduce the linguistic demands of responses while still promoting higher levels of thinking. For example, in a study of plant reproduction, the following question requires little thought: "Are seeds sometimes carried by the wind?" A nod or one-word response is almost automatic if the question is understood. However, a higher-level question such as the following requires analysis, though not a significant language demand: "Which of these seeds would be more likely to be carried by the wind: the round one or smooth one? Or this one that has fuzzy hairs? Why do you think so?" Encouraging children to respond with higher levels of thinking requires teachers to consciously plan and incorporate questions and tasks at a variety of levels.

Teaching Ideas for Strategies

In the section that follows, you will find some teaching ideas to help you with preparing SIOP lessons.

- **Digital Storytelling** (Sylvester & Greenidge, 2009). A digital story combines old and new literacies as children speak, write, and create a multimedia text consisting of still images and a narrated soundtrack. Especially appealing to children who struggle with writing, including some English learners, digital stories provide an exciting, hands-on, and innovative way to create stories. Sylvester and Greenidge (2009) suggest that effective digital stories combine seven elements: point of view, a dramatic question, emotional content, economy (economizing language), pacing (rhythm to hold interest), the gift of voice, and soundtrack (music). Note that these require students to engage with cognitive, metacognitive, and language learning strategies. The authors also include in their article a wide variety of Web sites for creating digital stories, including the Center for Digital Storytelling at www.storycenter.org. There are great examples, articles, and resources on this Web site.

- **Directed Reading-Thinking Activity (DR-TA)** (Ruddell, 2007; Stauffer, 1969; Vogt & Echevarría, 2008). DR-TA is a very effective activity for encouraging strategic thinking while children are reading or listening to narrative (fiction) text. It's especially effective in grades K–8 with the steps given below; only the difficulty level of the text changes. Reading materials (including Big Books for young children) should be rich, interesting, and, if possible, cliff-hanging stories in which there is some question as to how the story may end. Throughout the reading of a story or book, the teacher and students stop periodically and contemplate predictions about what might follow logically in the next section of the text. Begin the lesson with a question about what the class members think the story or book will be about, based on the title. As children respond, include a variety of probes, such as:
  - "With a title like . . . , what do you think this story will be about?"
  - "Let's read to find out."
  - "Did . . . happen? If not, why not?" (revisit predictions)
  - "What do you think is going to happen next? What makes you think so?"
  - "Where did you get that idea?"
  - "What made you think that?"
  - "Tell me more about that . . ."

It is important that you revisit previously made predictions after chunks of text are read so that children come to understand how predictions (and their confirmation or disconfirmation) impact their comprehension. Students can "vote" on which predictions are most likely as they focus their thinking on character (and author) motivations, problems characters face, reasons for characters' behaviors, and how the plot unfolds. Note that DR-TA is also effective in the upper grades for longer novels, with chapter-to-chapter discussions focusing on what children think will happen, what really happened, and why. (See Chapter 3 for a lesson vignette that includes DR-TA for a short story.)

- **SQP2RS ("Squeepers").** This instructional framework for teaching content with expository texts includes the following steps (Vogt, 2000, 2002; Vogt & Echevarría, 2008):

  1. *S*urvey: Students preview and scan the text to be read for about one minute to determine key concepts that will be learned. For children in pre-K–2, preview an informational Big Book with your students.

  2. *Q*uestion: In groups, children generate questions likely to be answered by reading the text; post student questions on chart paper and mark with multiple asterisks those that are frequently suggested by the groups. This is a great opportunity to model for beginning English speakers how questions are formed in English.

  3. *P*redict: As a whole class, children come up with three or four key concepts they think they will learn while reading; the predictions are based on the previously generated questions, especially those marked with asterisks. Model this step with younger children.

  4. *R*ead: While reading (with partners or small groups, or with you in a small group), students search for answers to their generated questions and confirm or disconfirm their predictions; use sticky notes or sticky strips to mark answers to questions and indicate spots where predictions have been confirmed.

  5. *R*espond: Students answer questions (not necessarily in writing) with partners or group members and formulate new ones for the next section of text to be read (if the text is lengthy); then, lead a discussion of key concepts, clarifying any misunderstandings.

  6. *S*ummarize: Orally or in writing, alone or with a partner or group, students summarize the text's key concepts, using key vocabulary where appropriate.

  Read Miss Abbas's lesson later in this chapter to see Squeepers in action. For math, see the adaptation of the Squeepers process in Figure 5.2. For more information on Squeepers, see Vogt and Echevarría (2008).

- **GIST (Generating Interactions between Schemata and Texts).** This summarization procedure assists students in "getting the gist" from extended text (Cunningham, 1982; as cited in Muth & Alvermann, 1999). Together with children, read a section of text (150 to 300 words) displayed on a white board, in a PowerPoint presentation, or in a handout. After reading, assist students in underlining 10 or more words or concepts that are deemed "most important" to understanding the text. List these words or phrases on the board. Without the text, together write a summary sentence or two using as many of the listed words as possible. Repeat the process through subsequent sections of the text. When finished, write a topic sentence to precede the summary sentences; the end result can be edited into a summary paragraph. This technique is also useful

---

FIGURE 5.2 SQP2RS ("Squeepers") for Math

Note that this Squeepers adaptation works well for math lessons. The steps are the same, but how they work in the lesson is slightly different.

SURVEY Before you read, ask yourself: What will this lesson be about? Look at the types of problems you will solve.

QUESTION After your text survey, write 1–3 problems you may be able to solve by the end of this lesson.

PREDICT Predict 1–3 math skills you might need to use to solve the problems in this lesson. What prior knowledge or new knowledge is necessary?

READ Read the lesson.

RESPOND After you read, try to answer the sample questions and confirm your predictions about the necessary math skills.

SUMMARIZE After you read, write a 4-sentence summary:
Sentence 1: The big idea of the lesson.
Sentences 2–4: How would you explain how to solve the problems in this lesson to a classmate who was absent?

(SQP2RS math adaptation created by Karlin LaPorta and Melissa Canham, Downey Unified School District. Used with permission.)

---

when viewing video clips. Students watch, record 10 key words or phrases, and then create summary sentences.

- **Graphic organizers.** A "common strategy to increase the chances that students who are unfamiliar with English will understand lessons sufficiently is to provide scaffolding in the form of visual representations of language . . ." (August & Shanahan, 2010, p. 225). Graphic organizers are schematic diagrams of key concepts and other information, and children use them to organize the information they are learning. Examples include Venn diagrams, timelines, flow charts, semantic maps, and so forth. See Buehl (2009) and Vogt and Echevarría (2008) for more examples.

- **Reciprocal Teaching** (Oczkus, 2010; Palinscar & Brown, 1984). Reciprocal Teaching incorporates four metacognitive strategies that teachers and students practice to improve comprehension of text:
  - Predicting
  - Questioning
  - Clarifying
  - Summarizing

  After students have learned each of the strategies, they work together as a whole class or small group while pausing and identifying each of the strategies as they read together. We have learned through teaching both techniques that when students learn to use the SQP2RS (Squeepers) steps first, they more readily engage in Reciprocal Teaching in small groups. For detailed lesson plans, task cards, and other RT resources, see Oczkus, 2010.

- **Question-Answer Relationships** (Raphael, 1984; Raphael, Highfield, & Au, 2006). Students can become more strategic readers when they learn how to determine the levels of questions they are asked. Some questions can be answered by looking right "In the Book" (*Right There* or *Think and Search*). Other questions need to be answered with prior knowledge and experience, and they'll be found "In My Head" (*Author and Me* or *On My Own*). See a more detailed explanation in Vogt and Echevarría, 2008.

- **Pre-Questioning.** Burke (2002) explains the importance of older elementary students writing their own research questions *before* they use the Internet to find information so that they "steer" rather than "surf" for answers. In science, students could also use the technique prior to making a hypothesis.

- **Questioning the Author (QtA)** (Beck & McKeown, 2008). Successful learners know how to use question-asking to help them construct meaning while they read (Taboada & Guthrie, 2006). They ask questions and challenge what the author says if something does not make sense to them. Beck and McKeown (2002, 2006, 2010) recommend using the instructional approach, Questioning the Author (QtA), to develop children's comprehension of textbook material, which sometimes can be disjointed and lacking in connections between ideas and key concepts. QtA values the depth and quality of students' interactions with texts, and their responses to authors' intended meanings. It assists children in developing the ability to read text closely, as if the author were there to be questioned and challenged.

Differentiating Ideas for Multi-level Classes

Within this component, scaffolding is a focus, and by definition, scaffolding leads to differentiated instruction. One way to scaffold for English learners' varied language development needs while teaching learning strategies is through Strategic Sentence Starters (Olson, Land, Anselmi, & AuBuchon, 2011, p. 251). Giving children sentence starters or frames provides the support many need to be able to participate in literature and content area discussions. The following examples could be printed on small "cue cards" that students select and use as needed.

- *Planning and goal setting*
  - My purpose is . . .
  - My top priority (or most important job) is . . .
  - I will accomplish my goal by . . .
- *Tapping prior knowledge*
  - I already know . . .
  - This reminds me of . . .
  - This relates to . . .
- *Asking questions*
  - I wonder why . . .
  - What if . . . ?
  - How come . . . ?

- *Making predictions*
  - ◆ I'll bet that . . .
  - ◆ I think . . .
  - ◆ If _____, then . . .
- *Visualizing*
  - ◆ I can picture . . .
  - ◆ In my mind, I see . . .
  - ◆ If this were a movie, . . .
- *Making connections*
  - ◆ This reminds me of . . .
  - ◆ I experienced this once when . . .
  - ◆ I can relate to this because once . . .
- *Summarizing*
  - ◆ The basic gist is . . .
  - ◆ The key information is . . .
  - ◆ In a nutshell, this says that . . .
- *Monitoring*
  - ◆ I got lost here because . . .
  - ◆ I need to reread the part where . . .
  - ◆ I know I'm on the right track because . . .
- *Clarifying*
  - ◆ To understand better, I need to know about . . .
  - ◆ Something that is still not clear is . . .
  - ◆ I'm guessing that this means _____, but I need to know . . .
- *Reflecting and relating*
  - ◆ So, the big idea is . . .
  - ◆ A conclusion I'm drawing is . . .
  - ◆ This is relevant to my life because . . .
- *Evaluating*
  - ◆ I like/don't like _____ because . . .
  - ◆ My opinion is _____ because . . .
  - ◆ The most important message is _____ because . . .

The Lesson

The lesson described in this chapter is taken from a fifth-grade reading/language arts theme titled Saving Our Planet.

Unit: Saving Our Planet (Fifth Grade)

The three classrooms described in the teaching scenarios in this chapter are heterogeneously mixed with native English speakers and English learners with varied levels of fluency. The elementary school is in a suburban community with Hispanic English learners constituting approximately 55% of the student population. There are also small numbers of English learners representing other language groups.

Mr. Bokhari, Miss Abbas, and Mrs. Graves are each teaching a reading/language arts unit on Saving Our Planet. The district-adopted reading series is used for most of the instruction for this unit, but teachers are encouraged to supplement the series with relevant trade books when appropriate. For the following two-period lesson, the fifth-grade teachers chose a beautiful informational trade book available in multiple copies from the school library. The book titled *Earth from Above for Young Readers* by Yann Arthus-Bertrand and Robert Burleigh (Harry N. Abrams, Inc., Publishers, 2001), includes stunning photographs taken from the air of interesting and beautiful countries around the world, some of which are in ecological danger. A brief and informative description accompanies each photograph.

The teachers' lessons are designed to address the following state standards for reading comprehension (grade 5):

- Understand how text features (e.g., format, graphics, sequence, diagrams, illustrations, charts, maps) make information accessible and usable.

- Discern main ideas and concepts presented in texts, identifying and assessing evidence that supports those ideas.

- Draw inferences, conclusions, or generalizations about text and support them with textual evidence and prior knowledge.

- Distinguish facts, supported inferences, and opinions in text.

Teaching Scenarios

To demonstrate how fifth-grade teachers Mr. Bokhari, Miss Abbas, and Mrs. Graves designed instruction for their students, including English learners, we look at how each prepared a two-day lesson using the trade book *Earth from Above for Young Readers*.

Mr. Bokhari

Mr. Bokhari began his lesson by distributing two copies of the trade book to the six table groups, which included either four or five students in each group. His 17 English learners were mixed heterogeneously in the class of 33 students. He asked the students, in pairs or triads, to thumb through the book and to use the photos and other textual features (e.g., titles, maps, and illustrations) to predict what they had

FIGURE 5.3 Strategies Component of the SIOP Model: Mr. Bokhari's Lesson

4	3	2	1	0
13. Ample opportunities provided for students to use **learning strategies**		Inadequate opportunities provided for students to use **learning strategies**		No opportunity provided for students to use **learning strategies**

4	3	2	1	0
14. **Scaffolding techniques** consistently used, assisting and supporting student understanding (e.g., think-alouds)		**Scaffolding techniques** occasionally used		**Scaffolding techniques** not used

4	3	2	1	0
15. A variety of **questions or tasks that promote higher-order thinking skills** (e.g., literal, analytical, and interpretive questions)		Infrequent **questions or tasks that promote higher-order thinking skills**		No **questions or tasks that promote higher-order thinking skills**

to do with the unit theme, Saving Our Planet. One student in each group was to be the recorder who would jot down the group's thoughts, and the other group members were to be ready to explain orally how they came up with their predictions. Mr. Bokhari then asked the students to orally report their findings as he wrote them on the white board. Next, he asked the table groups to determine which photographs of six countries depicted in the book they would like to read about—three countries for each pair or triad. Once the children made their selections, they orally read the descriptions of their three countries by taking turns. Students were then directed to find the most important information in each of the three descriptions and write a three-sentence summary. Mr. Bokhari encouraged the students to make connections between what they had been learning about the planet earth and what they were going to read in the book. Next, the partners and triads read their sentences to each other when their group members had completed the summaries. During the second day of the lesson, Mr. Bokhari reviewed each group's summaries and then asked the groups to describe their chosen photographs by orally reading their summaries to the other class members. Each group then voted on their favorite photograph in the book, and a spokesperson gave an oral rationale for the group's choice.

On the SIOP form in Figure 5.3, rate Mr. Bokhari's lesson on each of the Strategies features.

Miss Abbas

Miss Abbas began the lesson by introducing to her 31 students (of whom 22 were English learners at varied levels of English proficiency) the content and language objectives that she had written on sentence strips and placed in a pocket chart (see the following lesson plan—Figure 5.4—for the objectives). She distributed two copies of the book *Earth from Above for Young Readers* to each table group, and reviewed previously taught academic language (*environment, prediction, summarize*). She then reviewed the steps to SQP2RS ("Squeepers"), a process designed to engage students in critical and strategic thinking while reading challenging informational and expository texts (see p. 127). Previously, Miss Abbas had taught, modeled, and provided practice with each of the six sequential steps in Squeepers, so students were able to begin the process with a quick review. Also in an earlier lesson in the reading series, the children had placed sticky notes on a world map designating places on earth where there are current and potential environmental problems. Miss Abbas referred to this map on the wall as she introduced the book that she had distributed, and reminded students of environmental issues they had previously discussed. She then directed students to remember them as they began to **S**urvey this new book to determine what they thought they would learn by reading it and by examining carefully the large photographs and other illustrations. The survey continued for about two to three minutes.

Miss Abbas stopped the surveying, and then directed her students to work with a partner to write two or three **Q**uestions they thought they might find answers to by reading some of the descriptions in the book that accompanied the photographs. Miss Abbas jotted these questions on chart paper, noting with asterisks which questions were asked by more than one group of students. From the questions, the class next predicted five important concepts or ideas they thought they would learn from this book (**P**redict).

Because this book is an informational text that can be challenging for some students, including English learners, Miss Abbas read aloud the first two brief descriptions about New Caledonia and Botswana. She modeled how to review the class list of posted questions to see if any had been answered at this point. When students read a sentence about how hunters pose dangers for elephants in Botswana, several students immediately remarked that this was similar to what they had read earlier in the week when they learned about other endangered species. All partner/triad groups noted this sentence with a sticky note. Miss Abbas then directed the pairs and triads to **R**ead quietly together the descriptions of Mali, Indonesia, Argentina, Côte d'Ivoire, and Brazil. She selected these particular photographs and descriptions because each includes mention of an environmental problem. As students read together, they noted with their sticky notes those sentences that answered their posted questions, as well as some that described an environmental concern. If students finished the reading task, they were encouraged to continue looking through the book, reading about places of interest.

When everyone was finished, Miss Abbas asked each set of partners or triads to return to the country descriptions, as well as the introductory descriptions that she had read aloud, and find important words related to their unit on Saving Our Planet (VSS: Vocabulary Self-Collection Strategy, p. 80). These VSS words were shared with other table members and ultimately with the class, and as Miss Abbas and the students discussed the meanings, the words were posted on chart paper for future reference.

Miss Abbas then directed students back to the questions they had earlier generated to see which had been answered and which remained unanswered. Also, during this **R**esponse time, the children reported what they had discovered while reading and showed in their books where they had marked important information with the sticky notes. They checked their predictions to see if they had been confirmed, and discussed why some were not, such as the author didn't include certain information in the descriptions.

Next, each set of pairs or triads was asked to Summarize in writing (the length depending on levels of English proficiency) the key concepts that had been discussed and learned. Students were encouraged to use in their summaries the chart papers with the questions, predictions, and pages that had been noted with sticky notes, along with the key vocabulary that had been selected during VSS. Miss Abbas spot-checked throughout this final step in SQP2RS to make sure each individual was contributing to the group summary.

To prepare the students for the next day's activity, Miss Abbas taught the meaning of the word *persuade* by providing examples of how someone was trying to persuade another (e.g., persuading someone to buy a particular product, to go on a diet, or to vote for a candidate for office). Finally, Miss Abbas assigned the following questions for students to take home and discuss with their parents or caregivers during the evening. She indicated that the next day's discussion during their reading/language arts block would focus on the responses to the questions. Each group would pool their responses and argue for the environmental issue they thought was most important.

Of the environmental problems described in the book we read today, which do you think are the most important for Saving Our Planet? Why do you think so?

a. Vegetation unable to grow in salt water (New Caledonia).

b. Animals like elephants becoming endangered by humans (Botswana).

c. Agricultural land being used poorly and unwisely (Indonesia).

d. Whales killed for the oil in their bodies (Argentina).

e. Hydroelectric dams flooding needed agricultural land (Côte d'Ivoire).

f. Climate changes resulting because of logging in the Amazon forests (Brazil).

On the SIOP form in Figure 5.5, rate Miss Abbas's lesson on each of the Strategies features.

Mrs. Graves

Mrs. Graves began her lesson by distributing the two trade books to each table group (28 students; 16 of whom were English learners at varied levels of proficiency). She asked each student to complete a quick-write based on the cover photo of the book and the following prompts: Where do you think this photograph was taken? Where do you think the people on the walkway are going? (Note: The colorful photograph, taken from high in the sky, is of Yellowstone Park's hot springs with tourists walking by on a wooden walkway.) After students completed the quick-write, Mrs. Graves asked each child to read his or her writing to the others at their tables. Some students wrote paragraphs, while others wrote only a few words. A few students wrote nothing.

Next, Mrs. Graves directed students to look through the book with other students in their group, find their favorite photographs, and try to figure out what the photos were all about. Because many of the students had reading problems and/or were limited English speakers, Mrs. Graves had students identify the page numbers of their favorite photos, and then she read aloud the descriptions for their favorites. This activity took the entire period on the first day, and most students enjoyed looking at the pictures.

FIGURE 5.4 | SIOP Lesson: Miss Abbas's Lesson Plan

Key: SW = Students will; TW = Teacher will; HOTS = higher-order thinking skills (questions and tasks)

Unit: Saving Our Planet	**Grade: 5**	**Teacher:** Miss Abbas

SIOP® Lesson: Comparing environmental issues in seven countries outside the United States

Reading/Language Arts Content Standards (Comprehension):

2.1 Understand how text features (e.g., format, graphics, sequence, diagrams, illustrations, charts, maps) make information accessible and usable.

2.3 Discern main ideas and concepts presented in texts, identifying and assessing evidence that supports those ideas.

2.7 Draw inferences, conclusions, or generalizations about text and support them with textual evidence and prior knowledge.

2.8 Distinguish facts, supported inferences, and opinions in text.

Key Vocabulary: TW review *environment, prediction, summarize*. Teach meaning of *persuade;* In VSS, SW find key words and phrases in the descriptions.

HOTS:

Of the environmental problems described in the book we read today, which do you think are the most important for Saving our Planet? Why do you think so?

a. Vegetation unable to grow in salt water because of human-made floods (New Calcedonia).

b. Animals like elephants becoming endangered by humans (Botswana).

c. Agricultural land being used poorly and unwisely (Indonesia).

d. Whales killed for the oil in their bodies (Argentina).

e. Hydroelectric dams flooding needed agricultural land (Côte d'Ivoire).

f. Climate changes resulting from logging in the Amazon forests (Brazil).

Visuals/Resources: Yann, Arthus-Bertrand & Burleigh Robert. (2001). *Earth From Above For Young Readers.* New York: Harry N. Abrams, Inc., Publishers.

World map, sticky notes, chart paper, markers, binder paper, copies of questions for homework.

Connections to Prior Knowledge and Past Learning; Building Background:

- Review steps to SQP2RS (Squeepers): Who remembers the steps?
- Review unit theme by referring to world map and sticky notes placed there last week indicating places where serious environmental problems are currently occurring, including the United States.
- Complete the Survey, Question, Predict steps of SQP2RS to narrow focus and build background.
- Introduce book and share introductory information about the photographer, Yann Arthus-Bertrand.
- Review the differences between a *fact* and an *opinion*.

Content Objectives:	Meaningful Activities: Lesson Sequence	Review and Assessment:
1. You will use photographs, maps, and illustrations to predict important information about environmental concerns in several different countries.	• TW post and orally explain content and language objectives.	
2. You will identify key information in written descriptions of five environmental problems.	• TW briefly review meanings of words previously taught: *environment, prediction, summarize*.	
3. You will select what you think is the most important environmental issue facing us today.	• TW review steps of SQP2RS	Add 1-2 minutes to Survey if questions are lacking in substance. Review how to ask appropriate questions based on the text information (Practice and Application).
	• TW distribute copies of books, two/table group.	
	• Introduce the photographer and author: Introduction (pp. 6–9).	
	• TW review how to do a quick survey of informational text (2–3 min).	
	• In partners or triads, SW write 2–3 questions generated from the survey. TW post questions on	

During the second day of the lesson, students were directed to complete independently a Venn Diagram, comparing and contrasting any two photos and countries described in *Earth from Above*. Students had completed Venn Diagrams frequently, so they began working when the graphic organizers were distributed. Mrs. Graves

FIGURE 5.4 SIOP Lesson: Miss Abbas's Lesson Plan (*continued*)

Language Objectives:

1. You will listen to two and will read five descriptions of environmental problems in the world.

2. You will write a brief summary about the environmental issues you read about.

3. You will try to *persuade* others about the environmental issue you think is most important by saying:

"I am going to *persuade* you that the environmental issue that is most important for saving our planet is: _____ because _____.

My reason is a (*fact*) or (*opinion*).

---

chart paper; mark with asterisks the questions generated by more than one group (i.e., 4 asterisks for a question asked by four groups).

- SW predict 3–4 most important concepts we will discuss and learn. TW post on chart paper.
- TW read first two descriptions of New Calcedonia (pp. 10–11) and Botswana (pp. 12–13).
- SW read about Mali (pp. 16–17), Indonesia (pp. 28–29), Argentina (pp. 38–39), Côte d'Ivoire (pp. 44–45), Brazil (pp. 62–63), using sticky notes for noting key ("most important") information.
- VSS: SW find 2–3 vocabulary words or phrases in the seven descriptions that are related to Saving Our Planet Examples: p. 45: *"The vegetation was submerged."* What happened to the plants when the dam was built? Or p. 62: "Here, *as elsewhere, people must weigh the good results against the bad."* What is the meaning of *weigh* in this sentence? (Practice and Application)
- TW will list words/phrases on white board. Explain/discuss as necessary.
- TW lead discussion on posted questions and spots in text with sticky notes. Check back on earlier predictions to see if they were confirmed or disconfirmed (Practice and Application).
- TW review how to use the key information from charts, maps, photographs; VSS words and phrases; and descriptions marked with sticky notes to write brief summaries (suggest at each table which partners or triads need to write paragraphs, which need to write good sentences).
- TW reminds students to take summaries home along with homework questions.
- TW distribute and read aloud questions for homework discussion at home and in class tomorrow. Review the meanings of *fact, opinion.* Teach the meaning of *persuade.* Review sentence stem in language objectives. Chorally read the sentence starter several times for practice. Each student's job tomorrow is to try to *persuade* the others in his or her table group which is the most important environmental issue affecting the countries we read about. You can include your parents' or caregivers' opinions, too. Remember the differences between *facts* and *opinions* when you're trying to *persuade* others.

Check to see if predictions include most important information; if not, add another 1-min. survey.

Spot-check while students are quietly reading to each other to see what they're marking with sticky notes.

Spot-check to make sure all partners or triads are finding key vocabulary and/or phrases. Help with pronunciation and meanings, if necessary.

Are students able to answer their own questions? If not, why not?

Model with think-aloud how to take information from charts, map, and create 2–3 summary statements together with class. Circulate and spot-check while students are writing summaries paragraphs or sentences.

Check understanding of questions, and vocabulary *fact, opinion, persuade.*

Model pronunciation of sentence starter; listen during choral reading.

Ask for student examples of *facts* and *opinions* as review.

Wrap-up:

- Review the three key concepts about the environmental issues identified in the book descriptions: (1) humans flooding agricultural land, (2) animals being endangered by humans, (3) world climate changes because of humans.
- Review key vocabulary on VSS poster; review the meaning of *persuade.*
- Review content and language objectives by showing fingers: 1 = I met this objective, 2 = I'm getting close to meeting the objective, but need more practice; (3) I'm still confused and need some more help.

Lesson plan format created by Melissa Castillo & Nicole Teyechea. Used with permission.

FIGURE 5.5 Strategies Component of the SIOP Model: Miss Abbas's Lesson

4	3	2	1	0
13. Ample opportunities provided for students to use **learning strategies**		Inadequate opportunities provided for students to use **learning strategies**		No opportunity provided for students to use **learning strategies**

4	3	2	1	0
14. **Scaffolding techniques** consistently used, assisting and supporting student understanding (e.g., think-alouds)		**Scaffolding techniques** occasionally used		**Scaffolding techniques** not used

4	3	2	1	0
15. A variety of **questions or tasks that promote higher-order thinking skills** (e.g., literal, analytical, and interpretive questions)		Infrequent **questions or tasks that promote higher-order thinking skills**		No **questions or tasks that promote higher-order thinking skills**

said that the students could talk to each other quietly, but they were to work independently. She collected the graphic organizers at the end of the period so that she could generate a grade for the two-day lesson.

On the SIOP form in Figure 5.6, rate Mrs. Graves's lesson on each of the Strategies features.

FIGURE 5.6 Strategies Component of the SIOP Model: Mrs. Graves's Lesson

4	3	2	1	0
13. Ample opportunities provided for students to use **learning strategies**		Inadequate opportunities provided for students to use **learning strategies**		No opportunity provided for students to use **learning strategies**

4	3	2	1	0
14. **Scaffolding techniques** consistently used, assisting and supporting student understanding (e.g., think-alouds)		**Scaffolding techniques** occasionally used		**Scaffolding techniques** not used

4	3	2	1	0
15. A variety of **questions or tasks that promote higher-order thinking skills** (e.g., literal, analytical, and interpretive questions)		Infrequent **questions or tasks that promote higher-order thinking skills**		No **questions or tasks that promote higher-order thinking skills**

Discussion of Lessons

13. *Ample Opportunities Provided for Students to Use Learning Strategies*

Mr. Bokhari: 3

Miss Abbas: 4

Mrs. Graves: 1

Mr. Bokhari's lesson received a "3" for the learning strategies feature. His students were required to make predictions about the content of the book they were going to read. After reading, the children evaluated the importance of the factual information in the descriptions of the three countries they had selected. While Mr. Bokhari asked the students to "make connections" to earlier learning, he did not provide an example of what he meant, so some English learners (and other students) had difficulty doing this task. Finally, students were asked to summarize the information they had read and orally share it with their table group and ultimately the entire class. Mr. Bokhari's lesson would have been stronger had he asked the students to return to their earlier predictions and confirm or disconfirm them after they had read the text selections.

Miss Abbas's lesson received a "4" for the learning strategies feature because students engaged in using cognitive, metacognitve, and affective strategies throughout. During SQP2RS (Squeepers), students predicted, reexamined their predictions later in the lesson, generated questions about the reading materials, identified important information with sticky notes, read together and noted key points, selected key vocabulary, and wrote a partner or triad summary. Finally, everyone was asked to evaluate the relative importance of six environmental issues found throughout the world. Miss Abbas also encouraged her students to make connections with past learning.

Mrs. Graves's lesson received a "1" for the learning strategies feature. While she attempted to engage the students in making predictions from the cover of the book, many of the English learners (and other students as well) knew little of Yellowstone Park's hot springs, and therefore they were disengaged because they had no idea what the photograph was. Mrs. Graves also asked the students to evaluate their favorite photo of the 34, but because the students weren't expected to read or really learn much of anything from the accompanying descriptions for the photos, the task was more about looking at interesting pictures than engaging in strategic thinking.

14. *Scaffolding Techniques Consistently Used, Assisting and Supporting Students*

Mr. Bokhari: 2

Miss Abbas: 4

Mrs. Graves: 1

Mr. Bokhari missed several opportunities to provide scaffolding for his English learners and struggling readers, and therefore his lesson received a "2" for the scaffolding feature. While he did have the students work in heterogeneous groups, which allowed them to work together and help each other, he did not remind the children how to use the textual features in the book to guide their predictions about the course content. He also could have scaffolded the group's selections of their countries by limiting the number so the task was more manageable, especially because some of the descriptions and photos aren't directly related to the unit theme. Instructional time was not used well by some groups because there were 34 descriptions with appealing photographs in the book, and several groups had a difficult time making their selections. The entire lesson would have been more effective if Mr. Bokhari had modeled exactly what the students were to do, including how to make their selections, how to forge connections with prior learning, and how to use their notes to create their oral summaries. These directions, as well as criteria for selecting the most important information in the descriptions, should have been written and posted for the students' use. This type of scaffolding is critical for English learners and other children who struggle, but it is also helpful for all students.

Miss Abbas's lesson received a "4" for the scaffolding feature. Throughout her lesson, she provided the following scaffolds: (1) posting and orally explaining the lesson's content and language objectives; (2) reviewing essential academic language (prediction, summarize, environment), and teaching what could be new academic language to English learners (persuade); (3) reviewing the steps to SQP2RS (Squeepers); (4) grouping students heterogeneously in pairs or triads; (5) reviewing an earlier lesson by referring back to the world map; (6) introducing the photographer and author information from the book's introduction; (7) encouraging students to survey the text prior to reading; (8) listing the student-generated questions on chart paper and indicating with asterisks which questions had been asked by multiple groups, thereby narrowing the focus of the topic to important information; (9) limiting to five the number of descriptions that groups would read; (10) modeling by reading aloud the first two descriptions before the students read the others; (11) allowing students to find their VSS words, a process Miss Abbas frequently included in lessons after she initially taught the children how to find important words; (12) reviewing and discussing the questions the students had generated earlier; (13) adjusting the final written summary assignment according to the English learners' proficiency levels; (14) allowing all students to use their notes, charts, map, and Squeepers questions and predictions during the group summary writing; and (15) previewing the key question for the following day and allowing students to discuss this with family members at home. Because of the extensive scaffolding throughout the lesson, the children were able to complete the assigned tasks.

Mrs. Graves's lesson received a "1" for the scaffolding feature because her attempts to assist the students actually may have hindered their learning. For example, she assigned a quick-write for everyone. While this activity is generally considered an effective way to activate students' prior knowledge about a topic, it was inappropriate for the selected book because the cover photo was taken from the air and is somewhat difficult to figure out even for those familiar with Yellowstone Park. The quick-write proved especially difficult for the English learners, not only because of their levels of English proficiency, but also because of their lack of prior knowledge about what they were viewing. A more effective activity would have been to allow the students to talk together about the cover photo and pool their ideas and predictions. In addition, many English learners have a very challenging time listening for an entire period while the teacher reads content material aloud. While Mrs. Graves believed she was supporting her English learners by reading the descriptions, in reality, the children were unable to follow what she was saying, even when they had the text in front of them. Remember that there were only two books for each table group, so many students had nothing to look at during the teacher's read-aloud. Finally, even though the students had prior practice with the Venn Diagram graphic organizer, expecting them to complete one based on the photos and the teacher's oral reading of the descriptions was unreasonable, especially when the students could not work together. It appears that the grade, not student mastery of clearly stated objectives, was Mrs. Graves's goal for the lesson.

15. *A Variety of Questions and Tasks That Promote Higher-Order Thinking Skills*

Mr. Bokhari: 2

Miss Abbas: 4

Mrs. Graves: 1

Mr. Bokhari's lesson received a "2" for the tasks that required the students to engage in higher-order thinking. Remember, as you plan lessons according to the SIOP protocol, that even when teachers include higher-order questions and tasks, if an adequate amount of scaffolding isn't included in the lesson, some students will not be engaged in critical thinking. Even the best lesson plan that promotes higher-order thinking will be ineffective in execution if students are unable to complete the tasks that are assigned. This is precisely why the scaffolding feature is included in the Strategies component. See Chapter 8 for a complete discussion of this and other issues during lesson delivery.

Miss Abbas's lesson received a "4" for the higher-order thinking questions and tasks she planned. The steps of SQP2RS (Squeepers) promote critical thinking when students are engaged in predicting, questioning, monitoring their comprehension (when they are searching for answers to their questions and confirming/disconfirming predictions), determining what's really important, and summarizing. Keep in mind that the Squeepers technique can be used with students of all ages, including pre-K and K. The steps remain the same; the text is what changes according to age, English proficiency, and reading level. Also note that the final question of Miss Abbas's lesson that was to be discussed at home and the following day is written at the highest level of Bloom's Taxonomy (Evaluation).

Mrs. Graves's lesson received a "1" for the final feature in the Strategies component. The initial questions in the lesson (Where do you think this photograph was taken? Where do you think the people on the walkway are going?) are thought provoking, but the manner in which they were asked (the quick-write) was inappropriate given the students' varied English proficiency levels. Having the students orally read their quick-writes in front of all classmates is also an ineffective (and frankly deleterious) practice, especially when children are acquiring a new language and/or are having difficulty with reading. Sharing a quick-write with a partner or triad is very different from reading in front of an "audience" of peers. Finally, while Venn Diagrams are intended to promote critical thinking (comparing and contrasting), when assigned as Mrs. Graves did without interaction and as a silent independent task, the graphic organizer became just another classroom worksheet.

(For more examples of SIOP lesson and unit plans in language arts, see Vogt, Echevarria, & Short, 2010.)

Summary

As you reflect on this chapter and the impact of learning strategies, scaffolding, and higher-order thinking questions and tasks, consider the following main points:

- In this chapter, we have described how to promote critical and strategic thinking for all students, but most especially for English learners. Learning is made more effective when teachers actively assist students in developing a variety of learning strategies, including those that are cognitive, metacognitive, and language based. Learning strategies promote self-monitoring, self-regulation, and problem solving.

- Students with developing English proficiency should be provided with effective, creative, and generative teaching while they are learning the language. Therefore, it is imperative that all teachers provide them with sufficient scaffolding, including verbal supports such as paraphrasing and frequent repetition; procedural supports, such as teacher modeling with think-alouds, one-on-one teaching, and opportunities to work with more experienced individuals in flexible groups; and instructional supports such as the appropriate use of graphic organizers and content and text adaptations. Through appropriate and effective scaffolding, English learners can participate in lessons that involve strategic and critical thinking.

- We frequently remind teachers, "Just because the students don't read well doesn't mean they can't think!" A similar adage to this might be said of English learners: "Just because they don't speak English proficiently doesn't mean they can't think!" Therefore, SIOP teachers include in their lesson plans higher-order thinking questions and tasks.

Discussion Questions

1. In reflecting on the content and language objectives at the beginning of the chapter, are you able to:
   a. Select student learning strategies that are appropriate to a lesson's objectives?
   b. Incorporate explicit instruction and student practice with learning strategies when planning lessons?
   c. Identify techniques for verbal, procedural, and instructional scaffolding?
   d. Identify language learning strategies to include in lessons?

e. Write lesson plans that include varied techniques for scaffolding student understandings?

f. Write a set of questions or tasks on a chosen topic with increasing levels of cognition?

2. Describe a learning situation you participated in or observed in which the teacher modeled how to do something. Describe a recent lesson in which you modeled a process, directions students were to follow, or steps for an experiment. What did you have to do to ensure that students could follow your instruction? What worked and what didn't? How could you have made things more clear?

3. If the concept of scaffolding is somewhat new for you, the definition in the glossary may be helpful, as may be the following construction analogy. Picture a high-rise building as it is under construction. As new floors are added, scaffolding is built along the outside of the previously constructed floor (or level). This scaffolding allows access for the construction workers—they need to be able to get into the upper stories in order to continue the building process.

Think of a content topic that you must teach that is challenging to students acquiring English as a second (or multiple) language. What types of scaffolds must you put in place for your students to successfully access your content and language objectives?

4. Here's a factual question a teacher might ask based on a social studies text: "Who was the first president of the United States?" Given the topic of the presidency, what are several additional questions you could ask that promote higher-order thinking? Why is it important to use a variety of questioning strategies with English learners? Use one of the taxonomies (Bloom's [1956] or Anderson & Krathwohl, 2001), or the Depth of Knowledge levels (Webb, 1997) to guide you.

5. The answers to higher-order thinking questions may involve language that is beyond a student's current level of English proficiency. Discuss the advantages and/or disadvantages of allowing English learners to use their native language for part of the lesson, if doing so enables them to participate at a higher cognitive level.

6. Using the SIOP lesson you have been developing, add meaningful activities that augment learning strategies. Determine how to scaffold English learners' access to your objectives. Write several higher-order thinking questions or tasks for your lesson.

CHAPTER 6

Interaction

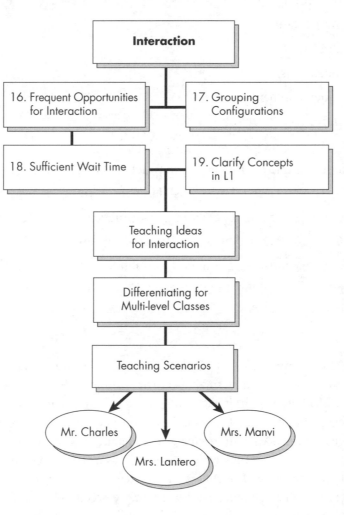

After reading, discussing, and engaging in activities related to this chapter, you will be able to meet the following content and language objectives.

Content Objectives

Select a variety of activities that promote interaction and incorporate them into lesson plans.

Design grouping structures that support lesson content and language objectives.

Identify techniques to increase wait time.

List ways that CCSS collaborative discussions are aligned with the Interaction component.

Identify resources to support student clarification in the native language.

Language Objectives

Explain in writing the purpose of student–student interaction for language development.

Describe techniques to reduce the amount of teacher talk in a lesson.

Practice asking questions that promote student elaboration of responses.

Having opportunities to talk about concepts, ideas, and information, especially when using academic terms, is beneficial for all children. However, for English learners to become fluent in academic English, they need to be provided with structured opportunities in all subject areas to practice using the language. Because of the large number of English learners in schools today, *all* teachers are teachers of English language development, even if students also have access to excellent ESL specialists. The integration of language development across the curriculum is vital. For children learning in and through a new language—

English—teachers must create ample opportunities to practice using *academic* language, not just social English. It is recommended that English learners as young as kindergarten spend about 90 minutes per week working together in pairs, practicing and extending material already taught (Gersten, Baker, Shanahan, Linan-Thompson, Collins, & Scarcella, 2007). And the language must be meaningful to children; it is not just the quantity of exposures to English that affects learning, but the quality as well (Wong-Fillmore & Valadez, 1986). ●

For many teachers it may be challenging to move from presenting whole-class instruction to providing small-group opportunities. Sharing responsibility for learning with children working in small groups or with partners is an adjustment for many teachers, but it can make a significant impact on learning. Researchers have found that English learners were more engaged academically when working in small groups or with partners than they were in whole-class instruction or individual work (Brooks & Thurston, 2010). For students to connect with school and engage in learning at a level that will result in high achievement, we need to provide them with opportunities to interact with one another, to discuss and "puzzle over" genuine problems (Wiggins & McTighe, 2008). In this chapter, we present ways that teachers can use interaction to launch students to higher levels of English proficiency, improve academic outcomes, and meet standards including the Common Core State Standards.

Background

"Use it or lose it" is a saying that conveys what we know from our own experience in learning a second language. If one doesn't practice using the language, it is difficult to maintain it. But what about learning a language in the first place—does speaking it help to develop the language? The answer is a resounding "Yes!" The role that conversation plays in the process of second language teaching and learning is clear. But discussion also offers important benefits for learning in general. As Gerald Graff puts it, "Talk—about books and subjects—is as important educationally as are the books and subjects themselves" (2003, p. 9).

The issue is, why are there so few opportunities for students to interact in typical classrooms? Studies indicate that in most classrooms, teachers dominate the linguistic aspect of the lesson, leaving students severely limited in terms of opportunities to use language in a variety of ways (Goodlad, 1984; Marshall, 2000). In a study of programs for English learners (Ramirez, Yuen, Ramey, & Pasta, 1991), it was found that the classes were characterized by excessive teacher talk. When students were given the chance to respond, it usually involved only simple information-recall statements, restricting students' opportunity to produce language and develop complex language and thinking skills. In our own work, we observe teachers doing a significant amount of talking at children rather than providing the impetus for a discussion or sharing and then allowing the children to talk to one another.

There are many benefits to having students actively engaged in interaction around subject matter. Some include:

- **Deeper understanding of text.** When teachers use thoughtful questioning to promote discussion, it encourages students to discuss what the passage is about and to think about the text at deeper levels (Echevarría, 1995b; Saunders & Goldenberg, 1999). Also, new understandings are constructed through interactions (McIntyre et al., 2010).

- **Oral language development.** Being exposed to and interacting with language that is just beyond their independent speaking levels move students to higher levels of language proficiency. However, these interactions must be carefully planned and carried out to yield gains in oral language (Saunders & Goldenberg, 2010).

- **Brain stimulation.** Interesting, engaging activities, including discussions, play an important role in learning. When students are engaged and their brains are activated, more of the pleasure structures in the brain fire than when students are simply asked to memorize information (Jensen, 2008; Poldrack, Clark, Pare-Blagoev, Shohamy, Creso Moyano, Myers, & Gluck, 2001).

- **Increased motivation.** Interaction with others is an important component of reading instruction that increases motivation and comprehension (Guthrie & Ozgungor, 2002).

- **Reduced risk.** The typical question-answer sessions in which teachers call on students may be threatening to children, particularly those unprepared to respond. Some students cannot focus on the content in this setting because it triggers the brain's "threat response" (Jensen, 2005, 2008). Having young students talk in pairs or in small groups minimizes the risk and allows ideas to flow more easily.

- **More processing time.** Children need time to process after learning. Direct instruction should be limited to short increments followed by time for discussion.
- **Increased attention.** Use of pairs or teams can heighten attention levels. Students may be asked to work together to compare/contrast material learned, group and regroup the material, resequence it, or retell it from another point of view (Marzano, Pickering, & Pollock, 2001).

Unfortunately, these practices tend not to be prevalent in classrooms with English learners.

We find that it is both interesting and helpful to analyze actual transcripts from lessons to demonstrate the kind of teacher dominance that is so common in classrooms. The following transcripts are from a pilot SIOP study (Echevarría, Greene, & Goldenberg, 1996) in sixth-grade social studies classes. The teachers were videotaped teaching the same content about consumerism to English learners, with the first using a typical approach found in mainstream classes and the other using the SIOP Model approach. Both classes had approximately 25 students, and in this lesson students were learning how to read labels on clothing and on a bottle of antiseptic.

Mainstream Lesson

TEACHER: Look at the piece of clothing at the bottom. It says *(he reads)*, "This shirt is flame-resistant," which means what?

STUDENT: Could not burn.

STUDENT: Won't catch fire.

TEACHER: It will not burn, won't catch fire. Right *(continues reading)*. "To retain the flame-resistant properties"—what does "to retain" mean?

STUDENT: *(unintelligible)*

TEACHER: To keep it. All right. *(He reads)* "In order to keep this shirt flame-resistant wash with detergent only." All right *(he reads)*. "Do not use soap or bleach. Tumble dry. One hundred percent polyester." Now, why does it say, "Do not use soap or bleach"?

STUDENT: 'Cause it'll take off the . . .

TEACHER: It'll take off the what?

STUDENTS: *(fragmented responses)*

TEACHER: It'll take off the flame-resistant quality. If you wash it with soap or bleach, then the shirt's just gonna be like any old shirt, any regular shirt, so when you put a match to it, will it catch fire?

STUDENT: No.

TEACHER: Yes. 'Cause you've ruined it then. It's no longer flame-resistant. So the government says you gotta tell the consumer what kind of shirt it is, and how to take care of it. If you look at any piece of clothing: shirt, pants, your shirts, um, your skirts, anything. There's always going to be a tag on these that says what it is made of and how you're going to take care of it. Okay. And that's for your protection so that you won't buy something and then treat it wrong. So labeling is important. All right. Let's review. I'll go back to the antiseptic. What did we say indications meant? Indications? Raise your hands, raise your hands. Robert?

STUDENT: What's it for.

TEACHER: What is it for, when do you use this? Okay. What do directions, what is that for, Victor?

STUDENT: How to use . . .

TEACHER: How to use. Okay, so indications is when you use it *(holds one finger up)*, directions is how you use it *(holds another finger up)*, and warnings is what?

STUDENTS: *(various mumbled responses)*

TEACHER: How you don't use it. This is what you don't do.

The teacher in this case tended to finish sentences for the students and accept any form of student comment without encouraging elaborated responses. In examining the exchanges, what did the teacher do when students gave partial or incorrect answers? He answered the question himself. Students learn that they can disengage because the teacher will continue with the "discussion."

SIOP® Model Lesson

TEACHER: Most clothing must have labels that tell what kind of cloth was used in it right? Look at the material in the picture down there *(points to picture in text)*.[1] What does it say, the tag right there?

STUDENT: The, the, the . . .

TEACHER: The tag right there.

STUDENT: *(Reading)* "Flame-resis . . ."

TEACHER: Resistant.

STUDENT: "Flame-resistant. To retain the flame-resistant properties, wash with detergent only. Do not use soap or bleach. Use warm water. Tumble dry."

TEACHER: "One hundred percent . . ."

STUDENT: "Polyester."

TEACHER: Now, most clothes carry labels, right? *(pointing to the neck of her sweater)*. They explain how to take care of it, like dry clean, machine wash, right? It tells you how to clean it. Why does this product have to be washed with a detergent and no soap or bleach?

---

[1]The teacher explained then that they would be doing an activity in which they would read labels for information.

STUDENT: Because clothes . . .

TEACHER: Why can't you use something else?

STUDENTS: *(several students mumble answers)*

STUDENT: *(says in Spanish)* Because it will make it small.

TEACHER: It may shrink, or *(gestures to a student)* it may not be . . . what does it say?

STUDENT: It's not going to be able to be resistant to fire.

TEACHER: Exactly. It's flame-resistant, right? So, if you use something else, it won't be flame-resistant anymore. How about the, uh, look at the *antiseptic (holds hands up to form a container)*—the picture above the shirt, the antiseptic?

STUDENT: Read it?

TEACHER: Antiseptic *(Teacher reads)* and other health products you buy without a prescription often have usage and warning labels. So what can you learn from this label? Read this label quietly please, and tell me what you can learn from the label. Read the label on that antiseptic. *(Students read silently.)*

TEACHER: What can you learn from this label?

STUDENT: It kills, oh I know.

TEACHER: Steve?

STUDENT: It kills germs.

STUDENT: Yeah, it kills germs.

TEACHER: It kills germs. You use it for wounds, right? What else?

STUDENTS: *(various enthusiastic responses)*

TEACHER: One person at a time. Okay, hold on. Veronica was saying something.

STUDENT: It tells you in the directions that, you could use it, that like that, 'cause if you use it in another thing, it could hurt you.

TEACHER: It could hurt you. Okay, what else? Ricardo?

STUDENT: If you put it in your mouth, don't put it in your mouth or your ears or your eyes.

TEACHER: Very good. Don't put it in your mouth, ears, and eyes. Okay, for how many days should you use it? No more than what?

STUDENT: No more than 10 days.

STUDENT: Ten days.

TEACHER: So don't use it—you have to follow what it says so don't use it more than 10 days. Now, the next activity you're going to do . . .

The SIOP teacher allowed for a balance of teacher-to-student talk and encouraged student participation. She asked questions, waited for students' responses, and restated or elaborated on the responses. In this case, what did the teacher do to elicit answers to the question? She scaffolded the answer by encouraging the students to think about it, prompting them to give their responses.

The features of the SIOP Model within the Interaction component are designed to provide teachers with concrete ways of increasing student participation and developing English language proficiency. When implemented consistently, these practices will facilitate students' ability to meet the Common Core State Standards, especially in the areas of listening and speaking.

SIOP® FEATURE 16:

Frequent Opportunities for Interaction and Discussion Between Teacher/Student and Among Students, Which Encourage Elaborated Responses About Lesson Concepts

Oral Language Development

This SIOP feature emphasizes the importance of balancing linguistic turn taking between the teacher and students, and among students. It also highlights the practice of encouraging children to elaborate their responses rather than accepting yes/no and one-word answers, even from the youngest learners. As noted in the CCSS, "students must have ample opportunities to take part in a variety of rich, structured conversations" ().

The findings of the National Literacy Panel on Language Minority Children and Youth () revealed the important relationship between oral proficiency in English and reading and writing proficiency. Specifically, reading comprehension skills and writing skills are positively correlated with oral language proficiency in English (Geva, 2006), two areas that are particularly challenging for English learners and are reflected in the Common Core State Standards. Solid reading comprehension is the foundation for achievement in nearly every subject area in school, and writing proficiency in English is an essential skill as well. Some other important findings include:

1. There has long been recognition that language, cognition, and reading are intimately related (Tharp & Gallimore, 1988). As one acquires new language, new concepts are developed. Think about your own language learning with respect to understanding computer functions. Each new vocabulary word and term you learn and understand (e.g., *hard drive, thumb drive, memory*, and *terabyte*) is attached to a concept that in turn expands your ability to think about how a computer works. As your own system of word-meaning grows in complexity, you are more capable of using the self-directed speech of verbal thinking ("Don't forget to save it on the thumb drive to take to work."). Without an understanding of the words and the concepts they represent, you would not be capable of thinking about (self-directed speech) or discussing (talking with another) computer functions.

2. Language proficiency is a precursor for effective reading comprehension. Because an understanding of language makes acquiring knowledge possible, deriving meaning from texts in English will be extremely challenging for English

PD TOOLKIT™ for SIOP®

Click on Videos, then search for "Strategies to Develop Academic Language" to hear two teachers discuss the importance of opportunities for discussion and interaction.

PD TOOLKIT™ for SIOP®

Click on Videos, then search for "Eliciting Interaction" to see an example of student-to-student interaction.

learners who may have difficulty reading unfamiliar words or comprehending their meaning.

3. Researchers who have investigated the relationship between language and learning suggest that interactive approaches—where there is more balance in student talk and teacher talk—are effective in promoting meaningful language learning opportunities for English learners (Cazden, 2001; Echevarría, 1995b; Echevarría & Short, 2010; McIntyre, Kyle, & Moore, 2010; Saunders & Goldenberg, 2007, 2010; Tharp & Gallimore, 1988; Walqui, 2006). Called *collaborative conversations* (grades K–2) or *collaborative discussions* (grades 3–6) in the Common Core State Standards, teaching approaches that emphasize oral language development and promote meaningful discussions around academic topics and texts have also been called *instructional conversations* (ICs) (Goldenberg, 1992–93) and *academic conversations* (Zwiers & Crawford, 2009). This mode of instruction has some of the following characteristics:

- Emphasizes active student involvement and meaningful language-based teaching. Instructional conversations have been defined as having a number of elements that are consistent with other discussion-based methods (Goldenberg, 1992–93). Essentially it is talking about text, which provides opportunities for using language to learn language and concepts.

- Differs from typical teaching because most instructional patterns in classrooms involve the teacher asking a question, the student responding, and the teacher evaluating the response and asking another question (Cazden, 2001). In contrast, in the typical format of an IC:

  a. The teacher begins by introducing the group to a theme or idea related to the text, then relating the theme to students' background experiences.

  b. Next, the teacher shows the text to be read and asks prediction questions.

  c. As the text is read, the teacher "chunks" the text into sections to provide maximum opportunity for discussion, constantly relating the theme and background experiences to a text-based discussion.

  d. Students are asked to support their comments with evidence from the text. Figure 6.1 illustrates the contrast in approaches.

FIGURE 6.1   Contrast Typical Instructions with IC

Typical Instruction	*Instructional Conversation*
Teacher-centered	Teacher facilitates
Exact, specific answers evaluated by the teacher	Many different ideas encouraged
No extensive discussion	Oral language practice opportunities using natural language
Skill-directed	Extensive discussion and student involvement
Easier to evaluate	Draw from prior background knowledge
Check for understanding	Student level of understanding transparent
Mostly literal level thinking and language use	Fewer black and white responses
	Mostly higher level thinking and language use

A conversational approach is particularly well suited to English learners who frequently find themselves significantly behind their peers in most academic areas, usually due to low reading levels and underdeveloped language skills. ICs provide a context for learning in which language is expressed naturally through meaningful discussion. Further, the skills developed through ICs meet the Common Core State Standards in the area of *Comprehension and Collaboration* in English Language Arts, *Speaking and Listening*. The following examples are taken from fourth grade, but are similar across all elementary grade levels.

SL.4.1. Engage effectively in a range of collaborative discussions (one-on-one, in groups, and teacher-led) with diverse partners on *grade 4 topics and texts,* building on others' ideas and expressing their own clearly.

SL.4.2. Paraphrase portions of a text read aloud or information presented in diverse media and formats, including visually, quantitatively, and orally.

SL.4.3. Identify the reasons and evidence a speaker provides to support particular points.

A rich discussion, or conversational approach, has advantages for teachers as well and contributes to a culturally responsive classroom. Through discussion teachers can more naturally activate the class's background knowledge as they encourage students to share their knowledge of the world and about how language works. When teachers and young students interact together, it fosters a supportive environment and builds teacher–student rapport. Also, when working in small groups with each child participating in the discussion, teachers are better able to determine individual levels of understanding; weak areas are made transparent.

As mentioned previously, however, teachers typically do most of the talking in class. Of course, teachers have knowledge to share and discuss with children, but consistent teacher dominance reduces the opportunities children have to participate fully in lessons by discussing ideas and information, and practicing English as they express their ideas, opinions, and answers.

Effective SIOP teachers:

- Structure their lessons in ways that promote student discussion, and they strive to provide a more balanced linguistic exchange between themselves and their students. It can be particularly tempting for teachers to do most of the talking when students are not completely proficient in their use of English, but these students are precisely the ones who need opportunities to practice using English the most.

- Encourage elaborated responses from students when discussing the lesson's concepts. The teacher elicits more extended student contributions by using a variety of techniques that will take students beyond simple yes or no answers and short phrases (Echevarría, 1995b; Goldenberg, 1992–93). Some of these techniques include asking students to expand on their answers by saying, "Tell me more about that"; and by asking direct questions to prompt more language use such as, "What do you mean by . . . ?" or "What else . . . ?" Another technique is to provide further information through questions such as "How do you know?" "Why is that important?" "What does that remind you of?"

- Use techniques such as offering restatements to scaffold replies: "In other words . . . is that accurate?" and frequently pausing to let students process the language and formulate their responses. If an English learner is obviously unsure about what to say, teachers call on other students to extend the response: "Vesna said . . . can you add to that?"

It takes time and practice for these techniques to become a natural part of a teacher's repertoire. The teachers with whom we've worked report that they had to consciously practice overcoming the temptation to speak for students or to complete a child's short phrase. The preceding transcript shows how the first teacher spoke for students instead of encouraging students to complete their thoughts. The following segment from the transcript provides another example.

TEACHER: What do "directions" . . . what is that for, Victor?

STUDENT: How to use . . .

TEACHER: How to use. Okay, so "indications" is when you use it, "directions" is how you use it, and "warnings" is what?

STUDENTS: *(various mumbled responses)*

TEACHER: How you don't use it. This is what you don't do.

In this segment, the mainstream teacher could have encouraged a more balanced exchange between himself and the students. First, he did not encourage students to completely express their thoughts; he accepted partial and mumbled answers. Second, he answered for the students, dominating the discussion. It is easy to imagine how children could become uninterested, passive learners in a class in which the teacher accepts minimal participation and does the majority of the talking.

The SIOP teacher approached students–teacher interaction differently:

TEACHER: What can you learn from this label?

STUDENT: It kills, oh I know.

TEACHER: Steve?

STUDENT: It kills germs.

STUDENT: Yeah, it kills germs.

TEACHER: It kills germs. You use it for wounds, right? What else?

STUDENTS: *(various enthusiastic responses)*

TEACHER: One person at a time. Okay, hold on. Veronica was saying something.

STUDENT: It tells you in the directions that, you could use it, that like that, 'cause if you use it in another thing, it could hurt you.

TEACHER: It could hurt you. Okay, what else? Ricardo?

STUDENT: If you put it in your mouth, don't put it in your mouth or your ears or your eyes.

TEACHER: Very good. Don't put it in your mouth, ears, and eyes. Okay, for how many days should you use it? No more than what?

STUDENT: No more than 10 days.

STUDENT: Ten days.

TEACHER: So don't use it—you have to follow what it says, so don't use it more than 10 days. Now, the next activity you're going to do . . .

The SIOP teacher let the students have time to express their thoughts (e.g., student says, "It kills . . . It kills germs."). The teacher could have completed the sentence for the student, but she waited for him to finish his thought. Also, the SIOP teacher encouraged and challenged the students more than the mainstream teacher did by asking twice, "What else?" Finally, the teacher nominated students who volunteered to talk and repeated what they said so that the class could hear a full response (e.g., Veronica).

Culturally responsive SIOP teachers plan instruction so that students have opportunities to work with one another on academic tasks, using English to communicate. Through meaningful interaction, students can practice speaking and making themselves understood. That implies asking and answering questions, negotiating meaning, clarifying ideas, giving and justifying opinions, and more. Students may interact in pairs, triads, and small groups. Literature circles, think-pair-share, Jigsaw readings, debates, and science experiments are only a sample of the types of activities teachers can include in lessons to foster student–student interaction. An interactive approach has been shown to improve the achievement of young English learners with learning disabilities (Echevarría, 1995b) as well as typically developing English learners (Dockrell, Stewart, & King, 2010; Saunders & Goldenberg, 2007; Van de Pol, Volman, & Beishuizen, 2010).

SIOP® FEATURE 17:

Grouping Configurations Support Language and Content Objectives of the Lesson

PD TOOLKIT™ **for SIOP®**

Click on Videos, then search for "Interaction and Cooperative Learning" to see Dr. MaryEllen Vogt explain the importance of opportunities for students to interact with each other during a lesson. Classroom examples are included.

In order to meet Common Core state Standards, especially for Speaking and Listening, teachers provide a variety of grouping configurations including whole class, partners, and small group. The intent of CCSS is to engage students more directly in learning by having a balance of teacher presentation and productive group work by students. The benefits of a balanced approach include the following:

- Varying grouping configurations—by moving from whole class to small group, whole class to partners, and small group to individual assignments—provides students with opportunities to learn new information, discuss it, and process it. Organizing children into smaller groups for instructional purposes provides a context that whole-class, teacher-dominated instruction doesn't offer.

- Allowing students to work together to critique or analyze material, create graphic representations of vocabulary terms or concepts, or summarize material makes information more meaningful and increases learning.

- Pacing delivery of instruction appropriately increases retention. According to brain-based learning expert Eric Jensen, "Given what the research shows, it should be apparent that presenting more content per minute or moving from one piece of learning to the next too rapidly, virtually guarantees that little will be learned or retained" (2005, p. 43).

- Changing grouping structures and activities enhances learning. It is recommended that when working with young learners, content, lectures, and cognitive activities should be limited to 5–10-minute periods each. These focused learning periods should be followed by interactive activities such as pair-shares or model building (Jensen, 2008).

In Chapter 5 of this book we present a process for teaching that slowly and purposefully shifts the workload from teacher to students and requires a variety of grouping configurations. As seen in Figure 5.1, "Scaffolding: Gradual Increase of Student Independence," the teacher uses a variety of groupings such as presenting information to the whole class and explicitly teaching part of the lesson, followed by a different grouping configuration in which students are given an opportunity to collaborate (students discuss ideas and information they learned during explicit teaching and guided instruction—not new information—and practice using academic English). Then, when students have acquired sufficient background knowledge and language, they apply the information individually. Varying grouping structures provides more interaction, and students have more opportunities to participate actively in the lesson. In contrast, when students aren't learning, it is often because there has not been the critical scaffolding that Figure 5.1 represents. That is, teachers go directly from "I do it . . . you watch" to "You do it alone . . . I watch."

In small guided instruction groups, the teacher naturally differentiates instruction as she works on focused skill instruction, language development, and/or assessment of student progress. Small-group instruction provides more opportunity to discuss text (Saunders & Goldenberg, 2007, 2010) and increases reading achievement (Vaughn, Linan-Thompson, Kouzekanani, Bryan, Dickson, & Blozis, 2003). While the teacher is working with one group, the other students can work on familiar material in small groups, with a partner, or individually either at their desks or at work stations. Activities may include listening to recorded stories (at listening centers, on computers, or via electronic notebooks), reinforcing skills with computer games, creating graphic representations of vocabulary terms or concepts, summarizing material, practicing word sorts, or reading self-selected leveled readers. These activities are purposeful and meaningful, and they lead to increased learning. In our work, we have seen this type of grouping work successfully with all elementary school grades. In their book, Gibson and Hasbrouck (2008) provide a wealth of ideas for grouping effectively, including how to organize the classroom and schedule and how to use a rotation chart for flexible grouping.

But not just any kind of grouping works well. It is important to acknowledge the following information about grouping and think about it as you work with instructional groups.

- Grouping by ability, which divides children for instruction based on their perceived capabilities for learning (low group, average group, high group) has serious academic and social effects for students who are not in the top group, (Callahan, 2005; Hiebert, 1983; Lucas, 1999). Futrell and Gomez (2008) make this point: "We cannot ignore the fact that for more than five decades, ability grouping has resulted in separation of students by race, ethnicity, and socioeconomic status. Many studies have confirmed that minority and low-income students of all ability levels are overrepresented in the lower tracks and underrepresented in the higher tracks" (p. 76).

- English learners, who learn from exposure to good language models, are often shut out of the groups with rich academic learning opportunities. In fact, in some schools, it has become common practice to group English learners with low-achieving students regardless of their academic ability and performance. This practice deprives English learners of the opportunity to learn grade-level academic skills and language.

- When working with low-achieving groups, teachers have been found to talk more, use more structure, ask lower-level questions, cover less material, spend more time on skills and drills, provide fewer opportunities for leadership and independent research, encourage more oral than silent reading, teach less vocabulary, and allow less wait time during questioning. In addition, they spent twice as much time on behavior and management issues (Oakes, 1985; Vogt, 1989).

- All children, including English learners, benefit from instruction that frequently includes a variety of grouping configurations. Whole-class groups are beneficial for introducing new information and concepts, modeling processes, and review. Flexible small groups promote the development of multiple perspectives and encourage collaboration. Partnering encourages success because it provides practice opportunities, scaffolding, and assistance for classmates (Flood, Lapp, Flood, & Nagel, 1992; Nagel, 2001; Tompkins, 2006).

Effective SIOP classes are characterized by a variety of grouping structures, including individual work, partners, triads, small groups of four or five, cooperative learning groups, and whole class. Groups also vary because they may be homogeneous or heterogeneous by gender, language proficiency, language background, and/or ability. The decisions teachers make about how to group students should be purposeful, not arbitrary.

A case can be made for grouping children by how well they speak English during literacy instruction (Uribe & Nathenson-Mejía, 2008), but the teacher needs to be aware of each student's individual skill profile. For example, when working on fluency, English learners with strong decoding skills would not read the same text as an English learner who is still working on mastering phonics. Advantages of grouping English learners together are that teachers can target specific language instruction and students are more apt to take risks in their second language. However, grouping students from very different grade levels (i.e., second through fifth grade) together based on language proficiency should be discouraged because these learners have very different social and academic needs (Uribe & Nathenson-Mejía, 2008).

There are other times that grouping by language proficiency level is useful. For example, if a teacher's goal is for students at beginning levels of English proficiency to practice using a particular language structure such as the present progressive (-*ing*) form within the context of a social studies lesson, then those students may be grouped together for that lesson. Likewise, when developing the skills of students with low levels of literacy, it makes sense to have those with similar ability grouped together for a particular lesson. Assigning all English learners to the same group regularly is *not* good practice, especially when total responsibility for teaching is turned over to a paraprofessional. In SIOP classes, English learners are given the same access to the curriculum and the teacher's expertise as native English-speaking students.

Using a variety of grouping configurations facilitates learning in a number of ways.

- It helps to maintain student interest because it is difficult for some students to stay focused when the teacher relies almost exclusively on whole-class instruction or having children work individually.

- Moving from whole class to small groups or partners adds variety to the learning situation and increases student involvement in the learning process.

- It provides much-needed movement for learners. When children are active, their brains are provided with the oxygen-rich blood needed for highest performance. Movement may be especially important for learners with special needs (Jensen, 2005).

It is recommended that at least two different grouping structures be used during a lesson, depending on the activity and objectives of the lesson.

SIOP® FEATURE 18:

Sufficient Wait Time for Student Responses Consistently Provided

Wait time is the length of time between utterances during an interaction. In classroom settings, it refers to the length of time a teacher pauses between asking a question and soliciting a response. In a review of studies on wait time, it was revealed that after a teacher asks a question, students must begin a response within an average time of one second. If they do not, the teacher repeats, rephrases, asks a different question, or calls on another student. Further, when a student makes a response, the teacher normally reacts or asks another question within an average time of 0.9 seconds (Rowe, 2003).

Wait time varies by culture; it is appropriate in some cultures to let seconds, even minutes, lag between utterances, while in other cultures utterances can even overlap one another. In U.S. classrooms, the average length of wait time is clearly *not* sufficient. Imagine the impact of wait time on English learners who are processing ideas in a new language and need additional time to formulate the phrasings of their thoughts. Research supports the idea of wait time and has found it to increase student discourse and more student-to-student interaction (Honea, 1982; Rowe, 2003; Swift & Gooding, 1983; Tobin, 1987).

Effective SIOP teachers are culturally responsive and consciously allow children to express their thoughts fully, without interruption. Many teachers in U.S. schools are uncomfortable with the silence that follows their questions or comments, and they immediately fill the void by talking themselves. This situation may be especially pertinent in SIOP classes where English learners need extra time to process questions in English, think of an answer in their second language, and then formulate their responses in English. Although teachers may be tempted to fill the silence, English learners benefit from a patient approach to classroom participation, in which teachers wait for students to complete their verbal contributions.

While effective SIOP teachers provide sufficient wait time for English learners, they also work to find a balance between wait time and moving a lesson along. Some youngsters may become impatient if the pace of the class lags. One strategy for accommodating impatient students is to have them write down their responses while waiting, and then they can check their answers against the final answer.

SIOP® FEATURE 19:

Ample Opportunity for Students to Clarify Key Concepts in L1 as Needed with Aide, Peer, or L1 Text

Best practice indicates that English learners benefit from opportunities to clarify concepts in their first language (L1). In fact, the National Literacy Panel on Language Minority Children and Youth found that academic skills such as reading taught in the first language transfer to the second language (August & Shanahan, 2006). Although SIOP instruction involves teaching subject-matter material in English, children are given the opportunity to have a concept or assignment explained in their L1 as needed. Significant controversy surrounds the use of L1 for instructional purposes, but we believe that clarification of key concepts in students' L1 by a bilingual instructional aide, peer, or through the use of materials written in the students' L1 provides an important support for the academic learning of those students who are not yet fully proficient in English.

This feature on the SIOP may have "N/A" circled as a score because not all SIOP classes need to use students' L1 to clarify concepts for them (especially for advanced English learners).

However, with Web sites offering word translation capabilities and bilingual dictionaries available in book and computer program formats, all SIOP classrooms have access to resources in most of the students' native languages.

Teaching Ideas for Interaction

In the section that follows, you will find some teaching ideas to help you with preparing SIOP lessons.

- With appropriate supervision, children can interact with each other through a class electronic list, shared research files on a school network, or a planned pen pal e-mail or video camera exchange on the computer with another class elsewhere in the world.

- In a discussion of the importance of movement for learning at all ages, Jensen (2005) suggests a number of games such as rewriting lyrics to familiar songs in pairs or teams as a content review, then performing the song; playing Simon Says using content such as "Point to Rome. Point to the first country the Romans conquered," etc.; or role-plays, charades, or pantomime to review main ideas or key points.

- Children may interact by sharing their expertise. In an Expert Stay & Stray activity, students work in small groups on an assignment, such as completing a chart summarizing the steps to solving math problems or key points from a unit of study. Students in the group number off. The teacher calls a number, e.g., #4, and student #4 takes his or her group's chart and goes to another table and shares the information with the new group. Then the student remains with the new group as the teacher calls another number, e.g., #1. Student #1 takes the chart of the student who shared (#4)—which encourages students to listen carefully—and goes to a new group and shares the information from the chart. This activity provides students with an opportunity to discuss the information while completing the chart, then to share the information orally while others listen attentively, and to paraphrase someone else's explanation of the chart. It can be adapted to any content area or elementary grade level.

- Start the class each day with children in pairs and have them tell each other the day's content objective in a Partner Share. Then they move to find another partner and tell them the language objective.

- An activity appropriate for all levels and most content areas is called Dinner Party (or Birthday Party for K–2). For instance, during reading instruction, students would respond to the prompt: "Suppose you could have a dinner party for authors or poets that we have studied. Whom would you invite? Why would you select them? What would be the seating order of the guests at your table, and why would you place them in that order? What do you think the guests would talk about during dinner? Include specific references to the authors' lives and works in your response." The purpose is for students to act out the questions by assuming personas, such as characters in novels, scientists, historical figures, or artists. During each Dinner Party, specific content from texts must be included and the characters must respond to each other as realistically and accurately as possible (Vogt & Echevarría, 2008).

- The time-tested activity of using Dialogue Journals provides students with an opportunity to interact through writing about topics of interest or those related to lessons. Journaling is typically between teacher and child as they share ideas. Students learn from teachers as they model appropriate written text, and teachers learn about their students' ideas and ways of expressing themselves.

- To support English learners, allow the techniques made popular by a television show: "50-50" and "phone a friend." Children who are unsure of an answer or unable to articulate it well might ask to choose between two possible responses provided by the teacher (50-50) or ask a classmate for help (phone a friend). However, to ensure practice with the language, the original child must give "the final answer" to the teacher.

Differentiating Ideas for Multi-level Classes

We know that most classes with English learners are made up of children with multiple proficiency levels. Even those designated ESL 2, for example, may have some children who have stronger listening skills than writing skills or stronger reading skills than speaking ones. Teachers have at their disposal a variety of ways to differentiate spoken English to make it comprehensible for our diverse English learners. The Interaction component lends itself well to meeting the variety of instructional needs and proficiency levels of students in your classrooms. Several considerations include the following.

- Use sentence frames for both oral and written answers. "It has often been said that teachers, rather than students, use academic language in the classroom. However, our students won't learn academic vocabulary solely by listening to us; they need to practice using it themselves" (Donnelly & Roe, 2010, p. 135). Sentence frames have been mentioned several times in this book as effective ways to scaffold English learners while they are acquiring their new language. Donnelly and Roe (2010, p. 132) suggest that teachers write sentence frames according to their students' English proficiency by:

  1. Writing sentences that express a language function (e.g., compare/contrast), and replacing target language with blanks.
  2. Replacing target words with blanks.
  3. Creating a word bank or a list of words that were eliminated from the original sentences.

What is left are sentence frames with fill-in spaces that are differentiated for different language levels. Lower level frames are not as complex as those for more English-proficient students. For example: The expected outcome for students at levels 2, 3, and 4 working with comparison/contrast might be:

Level 2. Sentence frame with vocabulary underlined: *Carrots are <u>orange</u>. Peas are <u>green</u>.* (simple sentence)

Sentence frame with vocabulary removed: _____ are _____.

Level 3. Sentence frame with vocabulary underlined: *<u>Carrots</u> and <u>peas</u> are both <u>vegetables</u>, but <u>carrots</u> are <u>root vegetables</u> and <u>peas grow on vines</u>.* (comparative sentence)

Sentence frame with vocabulary removed: _____ and _____ are both _____, but _____ are _____ and _____.

Level 4. Sentence frame with vocabulary underlined: *The main difference between <u>carrots</u> and <u>peas</u> is that <u>carrots</u> are <u>root vegetables</u> while <u>peas grow on vines</u>.* (complex comparative sentence)

Sentence frame with vocabulary removed: The main difference between _____ and _____, is that _____ are _____, while _____.

Sentence frames can use familiar content such as illustrated above, or they can use specific topics that are being studied. Other language functions, such as cause/effect, problem/solution, and so forth can serve as the basis of the differentiated sentence frames.

As you can see, less proficient children use sentence frames to participate in discussions, Dialogue Journals, and written work. More proficient speakers have a model of correct syntax to assist their contributions.

- Allow older students to choose between two or more assignments to complete. When students have options, they are more engaged, feel more confident, and perform better (Sparks, 2010). Some children may opt for an oral presentation to demonstrate their knowledge rather than a written assignment. Lower proficiency students may be more comfortable with a different mode of assignment than more proficient students, and having some control over their learning may increase their achievement.

- Pair students with more proficient speakers to scaffold their participation. More proficient speakers have an opportunity to practice using academic English and negotiating meaning with peers while less proficient students have the support needed to complete academic tasks.

- Differentiate wait time by becoming accustomed to allowing more wait time for beginning English speakers and those students who require more time for processing information. More advanced speakers will require less wait time.

- Partner students together who speak the same primary language for native language support as needed.

The Lesson

Unit: Addition and Subtraction (First Grade)

The first-grade teachers in this chapter, Mr. Charles, Mrs. Lantero, and Mrs. Manvi, work in a suburban school that has a 24% EL population. Their classes have an even distribution of English learners, each with approximately 10% ELs. Most of these students are at the intermediate to advanced-intermediate levels of English proficiency and still benefit from having teachers use SIOP techniques to increase their understanding of lessons.

The teachers in this school plan math units around the district's content standards. The lessons described in the scenarios that follow are part of a unit on addition and subtraction sums to 12. The standards in this lesson are related to number sense and mathematical reasoning. Students are to learn the addition facts (sums to 20) and the corresponding subtraction facts and commit them to memory. The teachers each have their own methods for teaching addition, as seen in the lessons that follow.

Teaching Scenarios

Mr. Charles

Mr. Charles began the lesson by explaining to the first-grade children that they were going to learn about different ways to do addition. He reviewed vocabulary that had been taught previously, such as *addends* and *sums*. He then engaged the children in a discussion about what information they knew about addition that had been learned previously, and he provided an adequate amount of time for the children to respond. He then asked the children when they would use addition in their everyday lives. Some of the children volunteered information about going to the grocery store or the bank and how they might have to use addition to solve problems. Mr. Charles then showed the children an addition problem on the overhead and asked them to work with a partner to figure out how they might solve the problem. He picked a student to come up to the overhead to solve one of the problems. (He chose the student by picking a name that had been written on a tongue depressor to ensure that he would call on a variety of children—not just the ones who raised their hands.) He also asked the student to underline the addends and circle the sums in the problem. To engage the whole class, Mr. Charles asked the children to raise their hands if they thought the student had the correct answer.

Mr. Charles continued the lesson by asking a volunteer to give a number from one to eight. He then had the children write the number on their paper, then draw the same number of shapes as the number they had written, using the color blue. Mr. Charles checked to make sure the children understood the directions, and he stopped at each child's desk to see how he or she was doing. He then asked the children to draw two more shapes, using the color yellow. He checked all students' work by circulating around the room. He asked the children to count all the blue and yellow shapes and to write an addition problem to illustrate what they had done. Mr. Charles asked the children to check with a partner to see if their problem was done correctly. He then engaged the children in a discussion of how pictures can help you find the answer to "how many in all." The discussion was balanced between the teacher and the students, and Mr. Charles asked for some examples of the kinds of pictures that they might draw to help them solve addition problems. He reminded the children to check for the addends and the sums in their problems.

Mr. Charles then had the children work in pairs. He distributed a paper plate and clothespins to each pair of students. He told the children to clip four clothespins on the top edge of a paper plate and three on the bottom. He then instructed the students to write an addition sentence for the clothespins and solve it ($4 + 3 = 7$). Mr. Charles called on children to explain how they found the answer. He asked a child who understood the concept to model putting clothespins on the plate and writing a corresponding addition sentence. He then asked another child to answer the addition problem provided by the previous child.

Next, Mr. Charles told the children that they would be taking the clothespins off their plates and making up a new problem using a different number of clothespins. He explained that he would like one partner in the group to tell the other partner how many clothespins to place on the top and how many to place on the bottom,

FIGURE 6.2 Interaction Component of the SIOP Model: Mr. Charles's Lesson

4	3	2	1	0
16. Frequent opportunities for **interaction** and discussion between teacher/student and among students, which encourage elaborated responses about lesson concepts		**Interaction** mostly teacher-dominated with some opportunities for students to talk about or question lesson concepts		**Interaction** teacher-dominated with no opportunities for students to discuss lesson concepts

4	3	2	1	0
17. **Grouping configurations** support language and content objectives of the lesson		**Grouping configurations** unevenly support the language and content objectives		**Grouping configurations** do not support the language and content objectives

4	3	2	1	0
18. Sufficient **wait time for student responses** consistently provided		Sufficient **wait time for student responses** occasionally provided		Sufficient **wait time for student responses** not provided

4	3	2	1	0	NA
19. Ample opportunities for students to **clarify key concepts in L1** as needed with aide, peer, or L1 text		Some opportunities for students to **clarify key concepts in L1**		No opportunities for students to **clarify key concepts in L1**	

thus giving the children an opportunity to practice their English with each other. The children exchanged paper plates, and one partner was responsible for writing the addition problem.

Mr. Charles finished the lesson with a review of what the students had learned about addition and asked for volunteers from the class to give some examples of addends and sums.

On the SIOP form in Figure 6.2, rate Mr. Charles's lesson on each of the Interaction features.

Mrs. Lantero

Mrs. Lantero introduced the lesson on addition by giving an example of how she used addition to count and add the playground equipment that they had in their classroom. On an overhead projector transparency, she drew a picture of five balls, three jump ropes, and three hula hoops. She called on students to come up to the overhead to solve the problem and demonstrate how they counted all the objects that she drew. She made an effort to call on a wide variety of students to respond and explain their answers. She asked students to explain how they answered the question "How many in all?" Several students raised their hands to volunteer. She then asked the students to give some examples of how they use addition in their everyday lives. She instructed individual students to come up to the overhead to write an addition problem using pictures to represent the numbers (e.g., four flowers + two trees). Mrs. Lantero then told the students that they were going to practice using addition to solve problems. She wrote an addition problem on the overhead (3 + 4 = 7). She asked the class if they could solve the problem and explain their work, then called on a volunteer to do so.

Mrs. Lantero gave a description of "counting on," a strategy that teaches what the next number is regardless of where the child starts counting. The children had previously learned this strategy. She asked the children, "How do you count on in the addition problem (9 + 1 =)?" She instructed the children to talk to the person next to them and gave adequate time for the discussion. Mrs. Lantero wrote some additional problems on the overhead and showed the students how to solve the various problems. Mrs. Lantero then gave the class a brief review of some of the strategies that they had used previously to solve addition problems, such as counting on and using doubles. Mrs. Lantero spent the next five minutes solving various addition problems on the overhead and calling on individual students who raised their hands to give the answer. At times she encouraged the students to elaborate on their responses and to explain how they solved the problem. After Mrs. Lantero was sure that the students had a clear understanding of addition, she had the children get into groups of three to complete the workpage from their textbook, helping one another as needed. At the end of the lesson the teacher reviewed the concepts of addends and sums and asked students to explain their answers.

On the SIOP form in Figure 6.3, rate Mrs. Lantero's lesson on each of the Interaction features.

Mrs. Manvi

Mrs. Manvi introduced the lesson on addition by having the students open their math book to a specific page on addition. She reviewed with the class what they had learned in the previous day's lesson and picked a student in the class to tell what they had learned. She asked the students if they had any questions, and when none of the children raised their hands, she continued her lesson. Mrs. Manvi had the children count in unison from one to thirty. Then she asked the students to come up with some examples using addition facts to add numbers and she called on two volunteers to provide examples. Next, Mrs. Manvi demonstrated some addition problems on the overhead. To engage the students in prior learning, she asked the students to provide descriptions of the word "addition." She reviewed the strategies of counting on and drawing pictures to help determine the correct answers to the problems. Mrs. Manvi tried to encourage the children to raise their hands if they did not understand how to do the addition problems. She continued the lesson, providing many examples to the children.

Mrs. Manvi had the students take out their workbooks and told them to do two pages of addition. She walked around the room to make sure that the students were on task and to see if anyone needed extra support. Mrs. Manvi realized that the students were having difficulty, so she drew some examples on the board using pictures and asked the children if they had any questions. She again encouraged the children

FIGURE 6.3 Interaction Component of the SIOP Model: Mrs. Lantero's Lesson

4	3	2	1	0
16. Frequent opportunities for **interaction** and discussion between teacher/student and among students, which encourage elaborated responses about lesson concepts		**Interaction** mostly teacher-dominated with some opportunities for students to talk about or question lesson concepts		**Interaction** teacher-dominated with no opportunities for students to discuss lesson concepts

4	3	2	1	0
17. **Grouping configurations** support language and content objectives of the lesson		**Grouping configurations** unevenly support the language and content objectives		**Grouping configurations** do not support the language and content objectives

4	3	2	1	0
18. Sufficient **wait time for student responses** consistently provided		Sufficient **wait time for student responses** occasionally provided		Sufficient **wait time for student responses** not provided

4	3	2	1	0	NA
19. Ample opportunities for students to **clarify key concepts in L1** as needed with aide, peer, or L1 text		Some opportunities for students to **clarify key concepts in L1**		No opportunities for students to **clarify key concepts in L1**	

to raise their hands if they were having problems. Mrs. Manvi then worked through the problems one at a time on the overhead and had the children check their work. She noticed that one student in particular was coming up with incorrect responses, so she focused her attention on that child and tried to help the child solve the problem correctly.

When she was confident that the students understood addition, Mrs. Manvi assigned homework that night so they could practice some more addition problems.

On the SIOP form in Figure 6.4, rate Mrs. Manvi's lesson on each of the Interaction features.

Discussion of Lessons

16. *Frequent Opportunities for Interaction and Discussion Between Teacher/Student and Among Students*

Mr. Charles: 4

Mrs. Lantero: 2

Mrs. Manvi: 0

FIGURE 6.4 Interaction Component of the SIOP Model: Mrs. Manvi's Lesson

4	3	2	1	0
16. Frequent opportunities for **interaction** and discussion between teacher/student and among students, which encourage elaborated responses about lesson concepts		**Interaction** mostly teacher-dominated with some opportunities for students to talk about or question lesson concepts		**Interaction** teacher-dominated with no opportunities for students to discuss lesson concepts

4	3	2	1	0
17. **Grouping configurations** support language and content objectives of the lesson		**Grouping configurations** unevenly support the language and content objectives		**Grouping configurations** do not support the language and content objectives

4	3	2	1	0
18. Sufficient **wait time for student responses** consistently provided		Sufficient **wait time for student responses** occasionally provided		Sufficient **wait time for student responses** not provided

4	3	2	1	0	NA
19. Ample opportunities for students to **clarify key concepts in L1** as needed with aide, peer, or L1 text		Some opportunities for students to **clarify key concepts in L1**		No opportunities for students to **clarify key concepts in L1**	

Although interaction among students is important for learning new concepts and practicing English, the teachers varied in the opportunities they provided to their students.

- **Mr. Charles** planned a lesson that had frequent opportunities for interaction, so his lesson received a "4" on the SIOP protocol for this feature. He used a variety of techniques that ensured participation from the whole class, such as calling on children by selecting sticks (tongue depressors) with their names written on them; asking students to work with partners to solve problems; involving students in a discussion; and having students work in pairs for practice with addition sentences represented by clothespins, writing the sentence, and coming up with the sum.

- **Mrs. Lantero's** lesson was heavily teacher controlled, although she did attempt to involve the children in discussion and did call on volunteers to come to the overhead. (Often it is the students who least need the practice using English that are called upon to participate in the lesson.) She also had students work in groups of three, although completing a workpage from the textbook isn't an optimal activity for interaction because it is basically an individual paper-and-pencil activity. Since Mrs. Lantero made an attempt to provide interaction, her lesson received a "2" for this feature.

- **Mrs. Manvi's** lesson received a "0" for this feature because she used a traditional whole-group format for teaching her first graders. This format severely restricted opportunities for students to discuss the concepts and ask for clarification as needed. It is very difficult to determine the needs of students and gauge their understanding when teaching the way Mrs. Manvi did.

17. *Grouping Configurations Support Language and Content Objectives of the Lesson*
Mr. Charles: 4
Mrs. Lantero: 2
Mrs. Manvi: 0

- Rather than having students in structured groups interact to solve problems, **Mrs. Lantero** and **Mrs. Manvi** solved problems on the overhead in front of the whole class. Whole-group instruction has a role to play, but it should not be used extensively because it limits opportunities for students to ask questions, discuss ideas, and clarify information. English learners and students who struggle academically may find whole-group instruction intimidating, as undoubtedly was the case with Mrs. Manvi's lesson. Although she asked several times if students had questions, nobody was willing to speak up in the whole-group setting. So, Mrs. Manvi's lesson received a "0" for this feature. Because Mrs. Lantero used both whole-group and partner work, her lesson received a "2" for grouping.

- **Mr. Charles's** lesson, on the other hand, received a "4" for this feature because he was aware of the importance of having students interact with the material (creating problems and solving them) and one another (practicing English). He had students work in pairs and small groups throughout the lesson, which provided optimal opportunity for interaction.

18. *Sufficient Wait Time for Student Responses Consistently Provided*
Mr. Charles: 4
Mrs. Lantero: 4
Mrs. Manvi: 0

- Both **Mr. Charles** and **Mrs. Lantero** interacted with students in a way that gave them time to formulate their thoughts and express them in English. These teachers recognized English learners' need to have a little extra time when participating in class, so they both received a "4" on the SIOP for Wait Time. **Mrs. Manvi**, on the other hand, had students count in unison, so the pace was set by the more proficient speakers, leaving the others with no time to think about the next number. Also, when she did call on students, she was looking for specific answers to be given quickly to the whole class. Therefore, she received a "0" on the SIOP for Wait Time.

19. *Ample Opportunities for Students to Clarify Key Concepts in L1*
Mr. Charles: NA
Mrs. Lantero: 3
Mrs. Manvi: 0

- The students in **Mr. Charles's** class had enough contextual clues throughout the lesson—coupled with intermediate English proficiency—that they did not need to use their primary language (L1). Therefore, Mr. Charles received an "NA" on the SIOP.

- **Mrs. Lantero** permitted the students to complete the worksheet together, which provided the opportunity for discussing and clarifying concepts in the students' native language if necessary. However, because opportunities for interaction were limited, there may have been a need for students to use L1 more extensively, which is why Mrs. Lantero received a "3" on the SIOP.

- **Mrs. Manvi** did not provide opportunities for students to interact with one another, so their L1 could not be used even if it would have helped scaffold their understanding.

(For more examples of lesson and unit plans in mathematics, see Echevarría, Vogt, and Short, 2010c.)

Summary

PD **TOOLKIT™ for SIOP®**

Click on Videos, then search for "Overview of the Interaction Component" to hear an overview and to see a math classroom where students are interacting.

As you reflect on this chapter and the benefits of interaction for English learners, consider the following main points:

- You should create ample opportunities for English learners to practice using academic English among themselves and with you, the teacher. Children should elaborate their comments and responses, not provide one- or two-word answers.

- The Common Core State Standards require that students must have ample opportunities to take part in a variety of rich, structured discussions—as part of a whole class, in small groups, and with a partner.

- Incorporating a number of grouping configurations into lessons facilitates using English in ways that support the lessons' objectives and develop children's English proficiency.

- Using a Gradual Increase of Student Responsibility approach ensures that a variety of groups are used in a lesson.

- For most teachers, it is challenging to balance the amount of teacher talk and student participation. Effective SIOP teachers plan for and incorporate structured opportunities for children to use English in a variety of ways.

- It may be beneficial for children to use their native language to clarify directions and express their ideas. However, the teacher may need to help them articulate their ideas in English, particularly as they advance in their proficiency levels.

Discussion Questions

1. In reflecting on the content and language objectives at the beginning of the chapter, are you able to:
   a. Select a variety of activities that promote interaction and incorporate them into lesson plans?

b. Design grouping structures that support a lesson's content and language objectives?

c. Identify techniques to increase wait time?

d. Identify resources to support student clarification in the native language?

e. Explain in writing the purpose of student–student interaction for language development?

f. Describe techniques to reduce the amount of teacher talk in a lesson?

g. Practice asking questions that promote student elaboration of responses?

2. Think of a content concept that you might be teaching. Describe three different grouping configurations that could be used for teaching and learning this concept. How would you organize the children in each group? How would you monitor student learning? What would you want students to do while working in their groups? How would the grouping configurations facilitate learning for English learners?

3. Either film your own classroom while you're teaching a lesson or observe another teacher's classroom for a 15-minute segment. Estimate the proportion of teacher talk and student talk. Given the ratio of teacher–student talk, what are some possible ramifications for English learners in the class?

4. What are some ways that CCSS collaborative discussions are aligned with the Interaction component?

5. Young English learners are often reticent to contribute to class discussions. An important role for a SIOP teacher is to encourage English learners to participate in nonthreatening ways. What are some specific techniques you can use to encourage children to elaborate on their responses and express their thoughts fully? What can you do to ensure sufficient wait time for children to formulate and express their thoughts?

6. Using the SIOP lesson you have been developing, add activities and grouping configurations to enhance interaction.

CHAPTER 7

Practice & Application

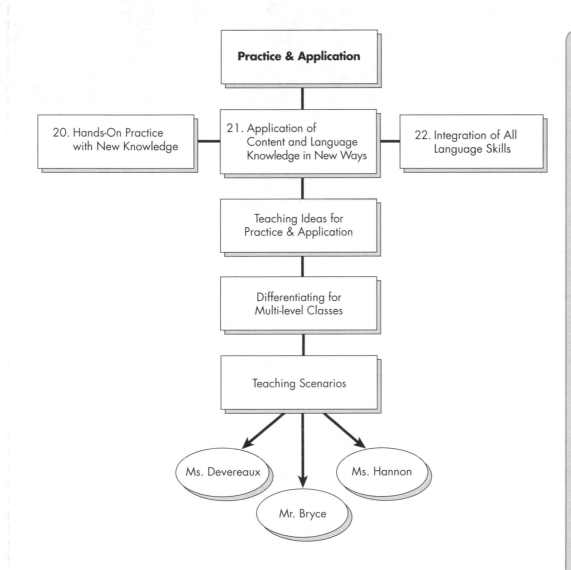

Practice & Application

20. Hands-On Practice with New Knowledge

21. Application of Content and Language Knowledge in New Ways

22. Integration of All Language Skills

Teaching Ideas for Practice & Application

Differentiating for Multi-level Classes

Teaching Scenarios

Ms. Devereaux

Mr. Bryce

Ms. Hannon

After reading, discussing, and engaging in activities related to this chapter, you will be able to meet the following content and language objectives.

Content Objectives

Identify a variety of ways for students to enhance their learning through hands-on practice.

Create application activities that extend the learning in new ways and relate to language or content objectives.

Language Objectives

Design activities that integrate different language skills as students practice new content knowledge.

Discuss the importance of linking practice and application activities to specific lesson objectives.

One common memory that most adults share is of learning to ride a full-sized bike. Even after riding smaller bicycles with training wheels, most of us were unprepared for the balancing act required for us not to fall down when riding a regular bike. If you had a parent or older brother or sister who talked you through the process, showed you how to balance, and perhaps even held on to the bike while you were steadying yourself, your independent practice time with the big bike was probably enhanced. Talking about the experience, listening to someone else describe it, observing other riders, and then

practicing for yourself all worked together to turn you into a bicycle rider. That feeling of accomplishment, of mastering something new through practice and applying it to a bigger bike, or perhaps a motorcycle in later years, is a special feeling that most of us have experienced as learners.

Background

Up to this point in a SIOP lesson, a teacher has introduced content and language objectives, built background or activated prior knowledge, introduced key vocabulary, selected a learning strategy and higher-order questions for students to focus on, developed a scaffolding approach for teaching the new information, and planned for student interaction. In the Practice & Application component, the teacher gives the students a chance to practice with the new material, and, with careful teacher oversight, demonstrate how well they are learning it. In the same lesson or a subsequent one, the teacher plans a task so students can apply this new knowledge in new ways. It is well established that practice and application help one master a skill (Fisher & Frey, 2008a; Jensen, 2005; Marzano, Pickering, & Pollock, 2001). For SIOP instruction, however, both the practice and application tasks should also aim for practice of all four language skills: reading, writing, listening, and speaking.

For English learners, this stage of a SIOP lesson is very important, especially for academic language development. As Saville-Troike (1984) pointed out, both language and academic learning occur through language use in the classroom. Second language acquisition research has shown repeatedly that for an individual to develop a high level of proficiency in a new language, he or she must have opportunities not only for comprehensible input (Krashen, 1985) but also targeted output (Swain, 1985), namely oral and written practice. In a synthesis of 20 years of research on oral language development, Saunders and O'Brien (2006) conclude that English learners "are most likely to use the language used to deliver instruction in their interactions with peers and teachers" (p. 41). They further explain:

> [W]hile use and exposure are necessary conditions, they may not be sufficient conditions, especially when it comes to achieving higher levels of proficiency involving more academic uses of language. The content and quality of L2 exposure and use are probably of equal, if not greater, importance than L2 exposure and use per se (p. 41).

For SIOP teachers, this means that we need to carefully choose the activities we include in our lessons.

- Some activities may build foundational language knowledge, especially for young learners who enter school with few pre-academic experiences or newcomers to the United States who have had significant interruptions in their educational backgrounds.

- Some activities must strengthen the students' progress in meeting or mastering the content and language objectives. If a language objective calls for third-grade students to argue a point of view, for example, then an activity might have the children write a letter to the editor of a school or local newspaper on the content topic of the lesson (or a related one for application), such as the nutritional value of school lunches for a health unit.

- Some activities must advance student proficiency in using English. Zwiers and Crawford (2009) and Seidlitz (2008) recommend teaching sentence stems and language frames to help students articulate their thoughts and ideas. These frames link to language functions, and activities can be created to encourage more sophisticated use of these frames over time. For example, students may progress from expressing an opinion as "I believe that_____" to "In my opinion, _____ is right/wrong because _____" and finally to "My prediction for the main character was _____ but in the next chapter I read that _____."

If the class includes students with multiple language proficiency levels, the Practice & Application component of the SIOP Model is the ideal place to differentiate instruction. In the lesson on school lunches mentioned above, the teacher might facilitate a whole-class brainstorming of an argument to make (e.g., occasional sweets, more vegetarian options). Students share ideas, including information about their meals at home, and the teacher generates a list. Next, the class selects one idea as a model and discusses pros and cons for the argument. The teacher might review language frames and key words to use in the argument and in the conclusion. Then, some advanced-level students might write individual letters, intermediate-level students might write with one partner or two, and beginners might work with the teacher to prepare a group letter.

Indeed, it is within this component that teachers can incorporate activities that explore project-based learning, different learning styles, and cultural perspectives (Nieto & Bode, 2008), multiple intelligences (Gardner, 1993), or other methods for meeting the different language needs of students (Echevarría, Short, & Vogt, 2008; Tomlinson, 2005; Vogt & Echevarría, 2008). As teachers plan these practice and application activities, they should consider the structure of the task and degree of difficulty for the resulting product, the grouping configurations, the type of feedback that will be provided so it is geared to proficiency level, and the expectations for student achievement (Vogt, 2012).

In this chapter, we discuss how sheltered language and content teachers provide English learners with the types of hands-on experiences, guidance, and practice that can lead to mastery of content knowledge and higher levels of language proficiency. The teaching vignettes demonstrate how three second-grade classroom teachers, all of whom have large numbers of English learners in their classes plus a few newcomers, designed science lessons on weather precipitation.

SIOP — SHELTERED INSTRUCTION OBSERVATION PROTOCOL

SIOP® FEATURE 20:

Hands-On Materials and/or Manipulatives Provided for Students to Practice Using New Content Knowledge in the Classroom

As previously mentioned, riding a bike is usually preceded by practicing with training wheels and working with a more experienced bike rider. Obviously, the more practice one has on the bike, the more likely one is to become a good bike rider. Now think about learning to play a musical instrument.

Some years ago, an entrepreneur decided to market a piano-teaching course that included a cardboard sheet printed with piano keys. Students were supposed to practice the piano on the paper keyboard by following the directions printed in the course manual. The black-and-white keys on the keyboard were printed, and dotted lines represented where students were supposed to place their fingers during practice sessions. It was little surprise that the paper keyboards didn't catch on even though the course manual clearly described in incremental steps how to play the piano, because even with hours of practice on the paper keyboard, students were still unable to play the piano well. In this case, it wasn't just the *practice* that was important. Without hearing the sounds during practice, learning to play the piano was an artificial and nearly impossible task.

When learning to ride a bicycle, play the piano, or explain the difference between a concave and convex lens, students have a greater chance of mastering content concepts and skills when they are given multiple opportunities to practice in relevant, meaningful ways. When this practice incorporates "hands-on" experiences including manipulatives, practice sessions are enhanced. Madeline Hunter (1982), a renowned expert in teaching methods, coined the term *guided practice* to describe the process of the teacher leading the student through practice sessions prior to independent application. She suggested that we keep the following four questions (and their answers) in mind as we plan lessons involving hands-on practice for students (pp. 65–68):

PD **Id** TOOLKIT™ **for SIOP®**

Click on Videos, then search for "Kindergarten Comparing Objects" to see students using manipulatives to practice new knowledge.

1. How much material should be practiced at one time? *Answer:* A short meaningful amount. Always use meaning to divide your content into parts.

2. How long in time should a practice period be? *Answer:* A short time so the student exerts intense effort and has intent to learn.

3. How often should students practice? *Answer:* New learning, massed practice. Older learning, distributed practice. [Hunter explains that massed practice means several practice periods scheduled close together. Distributed practice means spacing practice periods farther and farther apart, such as when we review previously learned material.]

4. How will students know how well they have done? *Answer:* Give specific knowledge of results (i.e., specific feedback).

Although all students benefit from guided practice as they move to independent work, English learners make more rapid progress in mastering content objectives when they are provided with multiple opportunities to practice with hands-on materials and/or manipulatives. These may be organized, created, counted, classified, stacked, experimented with, observed, rearranged, dismantled, and so forth. We would also include kinesthetic activities in a broad definition of this feature. Manipulating learning materials is important for English learners because it helps them connect abstract concepts with concrete experiences. Furthermore, manipulatives and other hands-on materials reduce the language load for students. Children with beginning proficiency in English, for instance, can still participate and demonstrate what they are learning.

Obviously, the type of manipulative employed for practice depends on the subject being taught. For example, in a math class in which children are learning to draw geometric shapes, content objectives might justify paper-and-pencil practice. However, if it is possible to incorporate hands-on practice with manipulatives (e.g., tangrams in this example), students' learning will probably be enhanced.

Being told how to ride a bike or play the piano, reading about how to do so, or watching a video of someone else engaged in bike riding or piano playing is much different from riding down the sidewalk or listening to musical sounds you have produced yourself. Whenever possible and appropriate, use hands-on materials for practice.

SIOP® FEATURE 21:

Activities Provided for Students to Apply Content and Language Knowledge

We all can recall our own learning experiences in elementary, middle, and high school, and the university. For many of us, the classes and courses we remember best are the ones in which we applied our new knowledge in meaningful ways. These may have included activities such as writing a diary entry from the perspective of a character in a novel, creating a semantic map illustrating the relationships among complex concepts, or completing comprehensive case studies on children we assessed and taught. These concrete experiences forced us to relate new information and concepts in a personally relevant way. We remember the times when we "got it," and we remember the times when we gave it our all but somehow still missed the target.

PD TOOLKIT™ for SIOP®

Click on Videos, then search for "Applying Concepts: First Grade" to see a class applying their new content and language knowledge.

Hunter (1982) recognized this: "The difference between knowing how something should be done and being able to do it is the quantum leap in learning . . ." (p. 71).

For students acquiring a new language, the need to apply new information is critically important because discussing and "doing" make the abstract concepts more concrete. We must remember that we learn best by involving ourselves in relevant, meaningful application of what we are learning. Application can occur in a number of ways:

- Students can organize new information on a graphic organizer and then use that for review.

- Students can be asked to generate solutions to real-life problems. These solutions may represent multicultural viewpoints.

- Students can plan for and hold a debate on a current event.

- Students may discuss a scientific theory in class (e.g., Life existed on Mars in the past) and then write their opinion on the topic in a journal.

For English learners, application must also include opportunities for them to practice language knowledge in the classroom. For example, it is appropriate, depending on students' language proficiency, to ask them to explain a process to a peer using a newly learned sentence structure or explain the steps in their solution to a math word problem using key terms. Activities such as describing the results of an experiment in writing, retelling a story but with a different ending, acting out an historical event, or creating a video "selling" a learning strategy all help English learners produce and practice new language and vocabulary, as long as they are in a supportive environment. These activities are also appropriate for struggling learners and other children.

In Chapter 5 we presented a model for scaffolding that shows how a teacher can gradually increase the students' responsibility for learning and doing, and we argued that collaborative practice and structured conversations along with recursive teaching are important bridging steps between guided practice and independent work. Through collaborative learning, students support one another in practicing or applying information while the teacher assists as needed. Some children may be able to move on to independent work, but others may need some targeted reteaching by the teacher.

SIOP® FEATURE 22:

Activities Integrate All Language Skills

Reading, writing, listening, and speaking are complex cognitive language processes that are interrelated and integrated. As we go about our daily lives, we move through the processes in a natural way, reading what we write, talking about what we've read, and listening to others talk about what they've read, written, and seen. Most young children become grammatically competent in their home language by age five, and their continuing language development relates primarily to vocabulary, more sophisticated grammar usage (e.g., embedding subordinate clauses), and functional as well as sociocultural applications of language (e.g., adjusting one's language to a particular audience, developing rhetorical styles) (Peregoy & Boyle, 2005). Proficiency in reading and writing is achieved much later, and differences exist among individuals in levels of competence. Students especially need to learn academic language for use in school settings (see Chapter 1 for a detailed discussion).

Some English learners may achieve competence in written language earlier than oral language; others may become proficient speakers before they read and write well (August & Shanahan, 2006). But it is important to realize that the language processes—reading, writing, listening, and speaking—are mutually supportive. Although the relationships among the processes are complex, practice in any one promotes development in the others (Hinkel, 2006).

Effective SIOP teachers understand the need to create many opportunities for English learners to practice and use all four language processes in an integrated manner. Throughout the day, these teachers offer their children varied experiences such as:

- Linking oral discussions of essential questions to reading selections;
- Structuring interaction with peers;
- Guiding students to use sentence starters and signal words;
- Providing children with the chance to listen and react to peers' ideas;
- Asking students to write about what is being learned.

We do want to clarify two things about language development as part of the Practice & Application component:

1. Although all identified language objectives in a lesson need to be practiced and applied as the lesson advances, not all language skills that are practiced need to be tied to an objective. In other words, a language objective represents a key skill, language structure, or strategy the teacher plans to teach and intends for students to learn. In a SIOP lesson, the teacher teaches to this objective and assesses, formally or informally, how well students are meeting it. The objective may focus on one language domain, such as writing, but in the course of the lesson, students may have additional opportunities to read, speak, and listen. These should be carefully planned, but need not be assessed in the same way an objective would be.

2. Teachers are sometimes unsure about whether to correct English learners' language errors during practice time (Peregoy & Boyle, 2005). In general, consider children's stages of English language development when deciding whether to correct them. For beginning English speakers, errors may be developmental and reflect children's native language use (e.g., not remembering to add past tense inflected endings to English verbs). Other errors may deal with placement of adjectives, sentence structure, plurals, and so forth. Research on error correction indicates that impromptu corrections are less effective than setting aside a portion of a lesson to focus on the grammatical forms or usage issues that arise (Ellis, 2008).

If errors impede oral communication, you can gently correct children by restating the sentence in proper form. Otherwise, leave the errors alone. If errors are in a written product that is to be displayed, you may want to work with the student to edit it. If you notice, however, that many students make the same error and it does not seem to be due to the language acquisition process, it is reasonable to plan a minilesson on the issue for a later class period. What is most important is that you be sensitive to errors that might confuse communication; corrections usually can be modeled in a natural and nonthreatening way.

Teaching Ideas for Practice & Application

In the section that follows, you will find some teaching ideas to help you develop practice and application activities for SIOP lessons:

- **Manipulatives and Movement.** Have children play with and manipulate objects or themselves instead of doing paper-and-pencil tasks for practice. For example, have students form a physical timeline about Ancient China with their bodies rather than complete a timeline worksheet. Some students might have a card displaying a date; others would have one displaying an event. The students would organize themselves, first pairing the dates and events, and then forming the human timeline in the front of the room.

- **Hands-On Games.** Educational, engaging, and fun games provide opportunities to practice or apply new content and language learning. For example, depending on the children's language levels, bingo could be played in the typical manner—the students hear a number or word spoken aloud and mark its written form on the bingo card. Or definitions, synonyms, or antonyms could be read aloud, and students would find the corresponding term. In Piece O' Pizza, individual students or small groups create a pizza slice with information that differs from that of their peers. They put their slices together to address the main points of a key topic. See *99 Ideas and Activities for Teaching English Learners with the SIOP® Model* (Vogt & Echevarría, 2008) for more games.

- **Electronic Games.** Use PowerPoints or Web sites to build electronic game boards for *Jeopardy!* or *Who Wants to Be a Millionaire?* or similar games. These games allow for differentiation as less proficient or less knowledgeable children can choose easier questions in the *Jeopardy* game or choose to "take the money" and stop advancing in the *Millionaire* game.

- **Foldables and Flip Charts.** Foldables and flip charts involve folding and cutting paper and offer a hands-on way for students to organize information. They can be made in various ways. With one type, a sheet of paper is held in a landscape orientation and then folded in half lengthwise (hot dog fold). The front half is then cut into a number of flaps (e.g., 3), with the cut going up to the fold. On the outside front, a key word (e.g., *element, compound, mixture*) may be placed on each flap. When each is lifted, a definition may be written on the top half and a picture may be on the bottom half. (For numerous examples, see Zike, 1994, 2004.)

- **Character Diaries.** Students take the role of a character from a novel, an historical figure, a person in the news, or an object, such as a good moving from manufacture or harvest to market. They create several entries in a diary, writing in the voice of that person/item, and including key events. Teachers may add other requirements to apply specific language objectives such as use of descriptive language, use of past tense or if-then clauses, or use of a key language frame.

- **Reader's Theater and Role-Plays.** Children can build oral fluency, reinforce content knowledge, and practice language structures and academic vocabulary through Reader's Theater (Short, Vogt, & Echevarría, 2011a, pp. 58–60). Teachers create scripts on particular topics to be performed by small groups of students. The teacher may model the script before the students are assigned roles and perform. Role-plays are more informal, with children taking roles and deciding what they want to say while acting out a fictional, historical, or current event.

- **Numbered Heads Together** (Kagan, 1994). Students number off and form equal-size groups. The teacher poses a question and the members in each group work together to determine an answer. Each member should know the answer, but the teacher calls only one number and that individual responds.

Differentiating Ideas for Multi-level Classes

The Practice & Application component offers teachers a relatively easy way to meet the needs of students with different abilities or proficiency levels in their classrooms. Consider the five options below when you want to adjust activities for your multi-level classes (Echevarría, Short, & Vogt, 2008; Tomlinson & Imbeau, 2010; Vogt, 2000).

1. **Group with a purpose.** Arrange students by language proficiency, learning style or multiple intelligences, demonstrated ability, perceived ability, or another reasoned way. Mix groups from time to time. Rotate roles so the more proficient students produce work or perform first and thus act as peer models for others.

2. **Differentiate the tasks.** Give each group a similar, yet specifically designed and equivalent task. Explain each group's assignment clearly, making sure it is as demanding as the others. An "easy" task may be as cognitively demanding to lower proficiency students as a "hard" task is to native English speakers.

3. **Use motivational strategies.** Learn what will motivate your students to perform to their ability. The following may be considered:
   - *Extrinsic:* Actual, physical rewards (stars, points, etc.) for accomplishing a task
   - *Intrinsic:* The mental and emotional "reward" for accomplishing a task
   - *Task engagement:* Positive feeling from being part of something that is stimulating, interesting, and do-able
   - *Cooperative, competitive, individualistic:* The three most common classroom goal structures; each has a role, but cooperative goal structures tend to be the most motivational for students
   - *Ego involvement:* Positive feeling about self when able to complete a task

4. **Use leveled questions to engage all learners.** As mentioned previously in Chapter 5, teachers tend to ask higher-level questions more frequently to high-performing students, and more literal-level questions to low-performing students. Instead, know your children's language levels (beginning, intermediate, etc.). Prepare a hierarchy of questions so that students of all proficiency levels are able to participate—simplify word choice and structure in questions for newcomers and beginners. Allocate turns, monitor turn taking, and make sure you allow enough wait time for less proficient students to respond. Be sure all children are given the chance to be involved.

5. **Select resources for differentiation.** Find leveled readers on the same or related topics. Bookmark Web sites and utilize native language Web sites or translations. Check the readability of texts you ask students to read. Use wordless books or photo journals with newcomers. Design activities at multiple levels of difficulty, such as the scaffolded cloze shown in Figure 7.1, a vocabulary worksheet with a word bank and a companion one without, or a writing assignment with different required lengths or research sources.

A few specific examples of activities follow:

- **Scaffolded Cloze Activities.** Consider a mixed fifth-grade math class with native English speakers and English learners. For a listening cloze dictation, the native English speakers might record what the teacher says as a regular dictation. The English learners might have two different dictation forms with more or fewer words already written down. (See Figure 7.1.) All the students listen to the paragraph the teacher reads on adding fractions, and all participate in the listening task, but the task format is differentiated to the students' English abilities.

FIGURE 7.1 Scaffolded Listening Cloze Dictation Forms

More Proficient Students	*Less Proficient Students*
Fill in the blanks with the missing words while the teacher reads a passage aloud. You will hear the passage twice.	Fill in the blanks with the missing words while the teacher reads a passage aloud. You will hear the passage twice.
In order to _____ two fractions, they must have the same _____. If the _____ are the same, you add the _____ together, but you don't _____ the denominator. For example, $\frac{3}{8}$ + _____ equals _____. Sometimes the answer is not in the simplest ____. In that case, you have to _____ it, or reduce it. You have to find a/an _____ fraction. When we simplify _____, we get ____.	In order to add two fractions, they must have the same _____. If the denominators are the same, you add the _____ together, but you don't change the denominator. For example, $\frac{3}{8}$ + $\frac{3}{8}$ equals _____. Sometimes the answer is not in the simplest form. In that case, you have to _____ it, or reduce it. You have to find an equivalent _____. When we simplify $\frac{6}{8}$, we get _____.

Written cloze activities can be differentiated in a similar way so that some students fill in the blanks with words they generate and others draw from a word bank.

- **Information Gap Activities.** These activities, which include jigsaws, problem solving, and simulations, are set up so each student (generally in a group) has one or two pieces of information needed to get the full picture of a topic or event, or solve a puzzle, but not all the necessary information. Children must work together, sharing information while practicing their language, negotiating, and critical thinking skills. Teachers differentiate by assigning the amount and complexity of the specific pieces of information to students according to their language proficiency, background knowledge, and interests.

The Lesson

Unit: Weather (Second Grade)

The three second-grade classrooms in these teaching vignettes are located in an urban elementary school in the Northeast. Approximately 40% of the 24 students are English learners from multiple-language backgrounds, including Spanish, Cape Verdean, and Haitian Creole. They range in proficiency from beginner to advanced. In each class, one to three students is a recent arrival with limited formal schooling. The other students in the class are native English speakers.

The state does not have standards for science in grade 2 because statewide testing does not begin until grade 3. However, the district has a curriculum framework that the teachers follow. The state does have English language proficiency standards for grades pre-K–12.

The second-grade teachers in these scenarios have been teaching a unit on the weather. They have had two days of instruction prior to the lessons described here. The students have been introduced to types of weather, the seasons, and the concept of temperature.

Teaching Scenarios

Ms. Devereaux

Ms. Devereaux entered class wearing a raincoat holding an open umbrella above her head. "What is the weather outside?" she asked. "Raining," shouted several second graders. She then took a piece of ice out of a container. "What weather does this remind you of?" "Winter" said one student. "Winter is a season," Ms. Devereaux replied. "I want to know the weather. Think about the forms of water we studied yesterday." One young girl said, "Ice." "Yes, it is ice," replied the teacher, "Can you also think of another kind of precipitation?" (She paused for several seconds.) "I'll give you a hint. It rhymes with *tail*." Sensing the students were still unsure, she told them to open their notebooks and find the weather words. One student finally said "hail" and Ms. Devereaux acknowledged he was right.

Ms. Devereaux pointed to the objectives on the board and told the students to copy them while she got supplies ready. The objectives were:

Content objective: We will identify types of weather.

Language objective: We will describe weather using adjectives.

Ms. Devereaux then showed the students the props they would use that day: a microphone, a map of their state, and a pointer. She asked the children to raise their hands if they had ever watched the news on television. Then she asked them to keep their hands up if they watched the weather broadcast. She called on one child with his hand still up to tell about a broadcast he saw. "The lady talked about the clouds and the rain." Ms. Devereaux replied, "Yes, she probably told you the temperature for the day and how cloudy it was and when the rain would come. Also she probably gave a prediction about the amount of rain and whether it would be windy or not. I bet she pointed to the weather map and showed you how a storm was moving across our state. Well, that's what I want you to do today in your groups."

She told them they could work with whomever they wanted in groups of three or four. They should prepare a two-minute broadcast about the weather, and they could decide what type of weather they would report on. She told them that when they performed their broadcast, they could use the props and she would record them with her digital camera.

Ms. Devereaux circulated among the groups and noticed that the English learners were mostly all together in three groups. All three groups planned to do a broadcast about rain. She tried to encourage them to do another form of weather, "What about snow? Or fog?" The students said they didn't know what to say about those. "I not see snow," said a newcomer student from Cape Verde who had only been in the United States for one week.

After 10 minutes of planning, the groups began to present their broadcasts. Ms. Devereaux noticed that the groups with the English learners had very little to say. One young broadcaster's statements were representative of all the English learner groups. "It is raining tomorrow. You get wet. Bring umbrella to school." She was disappointed that they weren't more descriptive about the upcoming weather and didn't seem excited about the activity, even though she was filming them.

On the SIOP form in Figure 7.2, rate Ms. Devereaux's lesson on each of the Practice & Application components.

Mr. Bryce

Mr. Bryce reminded the second graders of the lesson they had started the day before. He showed some pictures of different types of weather and had students try to identify the types of precipitation with a partner. He had previously paired his three newcomers with the most advanced English learners in the class. He continued by reading the objectives aloud from the board:

FIGURE 7.2   Practice & Application Component of the SIOP Model: Ms. Devereaux's Lesson

4	3	2	1	0	NA
20. **Hands-on materials and/or manipulatives** provided for students to practice using new content knowledge		**Few hands-on materials and/ or manipulatives** provided for students to practice using new content knowledge		**No hands-on materials and/or manipulatives** provided for students to practice using new content knowledge	

4	3	2	1	0	NA
21. Activities provided for students to **apply content and language knowledge** in the classroom		Activities provided for students to **apply either content or language knowledge** in the classroom		No activities provided for students to **apply content and language knowledge** in the classroom	

4	3	2	1	0
22. Activities integrate all **language skills** (i.e., reading, writing, listening, and speaking)		Activities integrate some **language skills**		Activities do not integrate **language skills**

Content objective: We will distinguish among different forms of precipitation.

Language objective: We will write opinion sentences about the weather using the word "because."

He said, "Let's think, what do our objectives mean? Who can explain them? Look at the verbs in our objectives. What does *distinguish* mean? Tell a partner." The students spoke softly in pairs and then several raised their hands.

"It means to tell them apart," said one young girl.

"Can anyone add on?" asked Mr. Bryce.

"To tell how rain and snow are different," responded a boy.

"Right" replied Mr. Bryce. "And what does our language objective tell us?"

"We are going to write today," said another boy.

Mr. Bryce extended this, "Yes. We will write sentences with the word *because*. Our sentences will give us more information, more details about our opinions. Who can remind me what an opinion is?"

Mr. Bryce began the first activity. He asked two students—one an English learner, the other a native English speaker—to find the word cards about precipitation on the word wall that they had been studying. The children selected *rain, hail, snow, ice, mist*, and *fog* and brought the cards to him. He posted them across the board and checked that the students remembered the words by having six volunteers come up and quick-draw a picture of the water form next to the word.

Next, he explained the task. The students were to choose one of these words and write a sentence using the word on an index card, which he provided. Using an electronic document reader, he displayed a sentence frame they could

Teaching Scenarios

use: "I like _____ because _____." and reminded the students that they were going to write sentences with details—with more information.

He then revealed the first part of the sentence.

I like wind

He said, "This tells you one thing, but you want to know more. Why do I like wind?" He revealed the next word.

I like wind because _____.

He asked a few volunteers to suggest a reason. He acknowledged their ideas and then revealed the rest of the sentence.

I like wind because the leaves dance.

Mr. Bryce explained that using *because* gives more details. It can tell why something happened or why someone did something. He asked the students to take turns asking their partners if they like wind and telling why or why not. As children conversed, he moved among the three pairs with the newcomer students and checked on their comprehension and ability to formulate the question and response.

Mr. Bryce next gave the students a few minutes to write their own opinion sentences, again helping the newly arrived children. Then, he asked them to stand and form two rows (A and B), facing each other, to perform a Conga Line. At his signal, the students took turns reading their cards to their partner in the opposite row. At the next signal, the students in Row A took one step to their left and faced a new partner in Row B to read with. Mr. Bryce repeated this process two more times and then had the students return to their seats. Because the students were familiar with the activity, the process took only eight minutes. He asked students to share one idea they heard. He also asked if any of the students had changed their sentences after reading it to a partner. Two students explained how they improved their idea based on feedback from a classmate. He gave the class two minutes to edit their sentence if they wanted.

Mr. Bryce introduced the next activity. In heterogeneous groups of four, the children would design a Wacky Weather! poster. They would choose a form of precipitation to depict in a wacky way. Then, they would write a caption for the picture, using a sentence with *because*. He showed a sample poster of people wearing bathing suits and standing in the snow. The caption read: "The people are surprised because it is snowing at the beach." He asked the students to generate some wacky weather ideas related to the six precipitation words that he listed on the board. He then assigned a type of precipitation to each of the six groups, giving the potentially more difficult types (*mist, fog*) to groups with more proficient students. He told them that they could choose one of those ideas or think of a new one in their groups. He informed the materials managers of each group that once they had finished a draft poster on scrap paper, they could come to him for chart paper and markers to create the final poster. He stated that he expected they would complete the posters the next day.

4	3	2	1	0	NA
20. **Hands-on materials and/or manipulatives** provided for students to practice using new content knowledge		**Few hands-on materials and/ or manipulatives** provided for students to practice using new content knowledge		**No hands-on materials and/or manipulatives** provided for students to practice using new content knowledge	

4	3	2	1	0	NA
21. Activities provided for students to **apply content and language knowledge** in the classroom		Activities provided for students to **apply either content or language knowledge** in the classroom		No activities provided for students to **apply content and language knowledge** in the classroom	

4	3	2	1	0
22. Activities integrate all **language skills** (i.e., reading, writing, listening, and speaking)		Activities integrate some **language skills**		Activities do not integrate **language skills**

On the SIOP form in Figure 7.3, rate Mr. Bryce's lesson on each of the Practice & Application components.

Ms. Hannon

Ms. Hannon greeted her second graders when they returned from lunch and reviewed the day's objectives on weather precipitation terms by asking the students questions about types of weather and weather words. The children copied the objectives in their notebooks:

> **Content objective:** We will identify types of precipitation: *rain, hail, snow, ice, mist*, and *fog*.
>
> **Language objective:** We will write words and phrases that describe weather.

Ms. Hannon divided the class into six groups, each with at least one native English speaker and one English learner. She pointed out the six concept maps posted on chart paper around the room and explained the task. Each group would receive a concept map (see Figure 7.4). They would have five minutes to complete it and then they would place their maps back up on the walls. Next, they would move around the room in a Carousel fashion, with each group having two or three minutes at each map to add ideas before moving on to the next map at her signal. "Do you remember how we did the Carousel when we studied animals?" she asked and most of the students responded "Yes."

FIGURE 7.4 Precipitation Concept Map

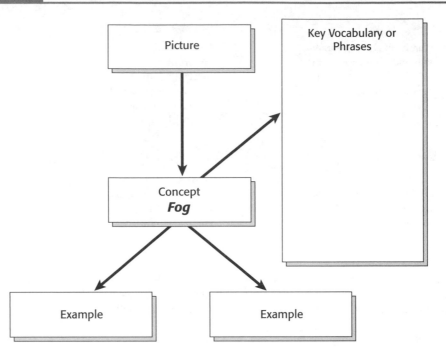

Ms. Hannon distributed the concept maps to the student groups and they began work. As she circulated, she noticed that the children had many things to write down for some maps, like those for snow and rain, but less for others. She hoped that the Carousel activity would generate more ideas. After the allotted time, she had the groups post their maps and begin the Carousel. She reminded them that when a group reached a map, the students were to discuss their ideas, and then the recorder would add to the concept map. She noticed that her two newcomers stood back from their groups, however, not contributing anything.

After about 15 minutes, the groups returned to their original map, and she asked the reporter from each group to read what was written. This process started well, but after the first two maps, the students began to fidget. To maintain order, she ended this reading aloud after the third group finished and had everyone sit down.

She told the students that for the next activity they would write about their favorite type of weather. She told them to think of the six types of precipitation they studied and choose one. In a paragraph they were to write what they liked about that type of weather and why. They could use the words and ideas on the concept maps. The students worked on this task for about 10 minutes, although some of the English learners, including her two new students, struggled to write even one initial sentence. She talked to several of these students individually to get them started. When the time for science ended, she told the class to complete the paragraph for homework.

On the SIOP form in Figure 7.5, rate Ms. Hannon's lesson on each of the Practice & Application components.

4	3	2	1	0	NA
20. **Hands-on materials and/or manipulatives** provided for students to practice using new content knowledge		**Few hands-on materials and/ or manipulatives** provided for students to practice using new content knowledge		**No hands-on materials and/or manipulatives** provided for students to practice using new content knowledge	

4	3	2	1	0	NA
21. Activities provided for students to **apply content and language knowledge** in the classroom		Activities provided for students to **apply either content or language knowledge** in the classroom		No activities provided for students to **apply content and language knowledge** in the classroom	

4	3	2	1	0
22. Activities integrate all **language skills** (i.e., reading, writing, listening, and speaking)		Activities integrate some **language skills**		Activities do not integrate **language skills**

Discussion of Lessons

Ms. Devereaux, Mr. Bryce, and Ms. Hannon taught lessons with similar objectives in their weather unit, but they used different activities and supports with varying results. As you read our ratings, compare them to your own and those of colleagues.

20. *Hands-on Materials and/or Manipulatives Provided for Students to Practice Using New Content Knowledge*

Ms. Devereaux: 0

Mr. Bryce: 4

Ms. Hannon: 3

    Ms. Devereaux's lesson was primarily an application activity, but it was evident by the outcome that her students, in particular the English learners, needed some practice time first. This lesson received a score of "0" for practice using new content knowledge. The class didn't review the weather terms other than *rain* and *hail* with Ms. Devereaux's real objects. The fact that the students didn't recall *hail* without considerable prompting should have indicated to her that they were not ready to jump into a broadcasting activity. Further, there were no occasions for students to practice descriptive words that they might associate with different types of weather and there was no targeted support for her newcomer student.

    Mr. Bryce's lesson received a "4" for hands-on practice with new content knowledge. Knowing that his second graders didn't like to sit at their desks for long periods of time, he used the Conga Line technique. He also carefully paired his newcomers with advanced learners to support their understanding of the weather concepts. First, he had students practice writing sentences using a *because* clause (which had been modeled) and a precipitation term. The students thought of a term they preferred and wrote the sentence independently. Then, they took turns reading their sentences to partners as they moved in the Conga Line.

Ms. Hannon's lesson received a score of "3" for hands-on practice. Her concept map activity offered the students a chance to review and organize information they had about types of precipitation. It was hands-on and kinesthetic, which is beneficial with young children, especially after lunchtime. The students focused on one type initially and then had a chance to review other groups' work and add to their maps. The activity had to be cut short during the reporting stage, however, because the students lost concentration when the activity lasted too long. Also the newly arrived students were not actively engaged.

21. *Activities Provided for Students to Apply Content and Language Knowledge*

Ms. Devereaux: 1

Mr. Bryce: 4

Ms. Hannon: 2

Ms. Devereaux's lesson received a "1" for application of language and content knowledge. Although she had an interesting plan to have the students act as weather broadcasters, she did not prepare them well for the role. She asked a few students to talk about a weather report they'd seen on the television news, but she provided most of the details. Also, she did not make sure all the students were familiar with that type of broadcast. If she had shown a brief video clip, she would have modeled the activity for the students and thus given them a greater chance at being successful. Doing so might have helped her meet the language and content objectives. As it was, no attention was given to the language objective. No practice time was devoted to reviewing adjectives that could be used with weather terms.

Mr. Bryce's lesson received a "4" for this application feature. After the Conga Line practice with the new sentence structure and the precipitation terms, he had students apply their language and content knowledge to a poster. The second graders enjoyed doing something amusing—in this case, designing a Wacky Weather! poster. It gave them a chance to consider characteristics of weather that are unexpected and also prompted them to write another sentence using a *because* clause. This activity used hands-on materials and had students working in small groups so that those with stronger academic language skills could support those with weaker ones. Mr. Bryce also checked in with the newcomer students to help them accomplish the assigned tasks.

Ms. Hannon's lesson received a "2" for activities that apply language and content knowledge. She asked students to write a paragraph about their favorite type of precipitation, which would have been a good application task if it had been executed well. Unfortunately, Ms. Hannon did not scaffold the writing process. She provided no model paragraphs, nor did the students, as a class or in a group, brainstorm ideas or list information that could be included. The newly arrived students would have really benefitted from modeling. Her instructions were delivered only orally and the language objective was implicit, not explicit. The concept maps had information the students could draw from, but because they remained on the walls, the students did not make much use of them. When the English learners were unable to do the task well, she did not reconsider and pull them aside to work in a small writing group with her. This situation was an obvious opportunity for her to differentiate instruction for the English learners. Instead, she talked to them one by one. Finally, she moved the completion of the task to a homework assignment, which was unlikely to yield success for the children learning English as a new language if they were not sure how to complete the task in class.

22. *Activities Integrate All Language Skills*

Ms. Devereaux: 2

Mr. Bryce: 3

Ms. Hannon: 3

Ms. Devereaux's lesson received a "2" for integrating all four language skills. The students focused only on listening and speaking as they prepared and then delivered their weather reports. No reading was required; even if some students wrote a transcript of what they intended to say, it was not part of the instructions to the children.

Mr. Bryce's lesson received a "3" for integrating all four language skills in the lesson. The second graders had multiple opportunities to listen and speak (during the Conga Line, while at work in their groups, when the class was generating ideas for the poster) and to write (the *because* sentence and the poster caption). There was less reading in this particular lesson, although they did read the precipitation word cards, the ideas listed on the board, and their sentences aloud. In the next lesson, they will do a Gallery Walk activity whereby each group posts its poster and the students circulate on their own to view them and read the captions. Students will put a dot sticker on two posters they think are the wackiest.

Ms. Hannon's Concept Map/Carousel activity prompted students to practice all four language skills because they had to discuss ideas for the map and record those ideas, read what others had written on their maps and extend the ideas, and then listen while some students spoke during the reporting phase. The paragraph writing task was also intended to apply writing skills to the science topic. The lesson received a "3" on this feature of the SIOP component, however, because the reporting phase of the Carousel and the paragraph writing were not well accomplished.

(For more examples of lesson and unit plans in science for grades K–12, see Short, Vogt, and Echevarría, 2011b.)

Summary

As you reflect on this chapter and the impact that practice and application has on learning, consider the following main points:

- With any type of new learning, children need practice and application of newly acquired skills to ensure mastery of content concepts.

- You should plan a variety of hands-on activities and materials, including manipulatives, to enable students to forge connections between abstract and concrete concepts in a less language-dependent way.

- When you create application activities to extend learning, be sure to relate the activities to both the content and the language objectives.

- Because children have different preferred learning styles, when teachers use different modalities for instruction and encourage students to practice and apply new knowledge through multiple language processes, they have a better chance of meeting students' needs and furthering both their language and content development.

Discussion Questions

1. In reflecting on the content and language objectives at the beginning of the chapter, are you able to:
   a. Identify a variety of ways for your students to enhance their learning through hands-on practice?
   b. Create application activities that extend the learning in new ways and relate to language or content objectives?
   c. Design activities that integrate different language skills as children practice new content knowledge?
   d. Discuss the importance of linking practice and application activities to specific lesson objectives?

2. Compare and contrast the following two teachers' approaches to teaching a lesson on nutrition.
   a. One teacher's approach involves a lecture, a diagram of the USDA's Food Plate, and a list of appropriate foods for each group. Students are then tested about their knowledge of the percentages of each food type they should eat at a meal.
   b. The other teacher's approach begins with each student maintaining a food diary for a week. Copies of the Food Plate are distributed and explained, and all students must analyze their food consumption according to the national recommendations. With a partner, students must design a nutritionally sound weekly menu for each day of the following week, and they must be prepared to defend their food choices to peer group members.

Which approach to teaching this content concept is most appropriate for English learners? How do you know? Be as specific as you can.

3. One way to ensure practice and application of new knowledge is through project-based learning. Develop a unit project that children in one of your courses can build incrementally as the series of lessons progresses over several days or weeks. Identify the steps to completion that children will accomplish in each lesson of the unit. If you can collaborate with another teacher (i.e., a classroom teacher with an ESL teacher), divvy up tasks to provide targeted support for the English learners. Plan a culminating presentation or performance that will enhance language practice.

4. English learners benefit from the integration of reading, writing, listening, and speaking during a lesson. What adjustments and techniques can a teacher use to provide successful experiences for students with limited English language proficiency while they read, write, listen, and speak about new information they are learning? Include specific activities and examples in your answer.

5. Elementary teachers are responsible for incorporating rigorous state standards, such as the Common Core, for English language arts and mathematics in their instruction. How is it possible to provide direct application and hands-on practice for lessons? What can teachers do to alleviate the conflict between "covering the content" and making it "accessible" for English learners?

6. Using the SIOP lesson you have been developing, write some activities for your students to practice and then apply the key language and content concepts.

CHAPTER 8

Lesson Delivery

After reading, discussing, and engaging in activities related to this chapter, you will be able to meet the following content and language objectives.

Content Objectives

Monitor lessons to determine if the delivery is supporting the objectives.

List strategies for improving student time-on-task throughout a lesson.

Generate activities to keep English learners engaged.

Language Objectives

Discuss characteristics of effective SIOP lesson delivery.

Explain how a focus on a lesson's objectives can aid in pacing.

Evaluate a situation in which a lesson plan is not enacted successfully and explain what might have gone wrong and what could be improved.

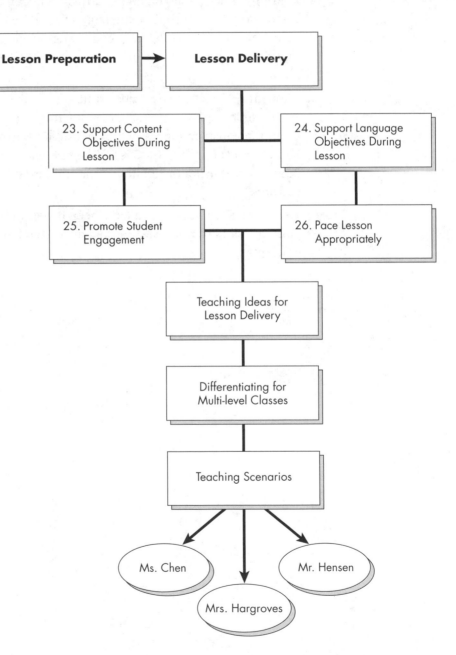

Lesson Preparation → Lesson Delivery

23. Support Content Objectives During Lesson

24. Support Language Objectives During Lesson

25. Promote Student Engagement

26. Pace Lesson Appropriately

Teaching Ideas for Lesson Delivery

Differentiating for Multi-level Classes

Teaching Scenarios

Ms. Chen

Mrs. Hargroves

Mr. Hensen

Background

As we have mentioned, good preparation is the first step in delivering a lesson that leads to student learning. However, a lesson can go awry, even if the plan is well written. Activities might be too easy or too difficult for the students. The lesson might be too long or too short. A child might ask an interesting but tangential question, and the ensuing class discussion consumes 10 unexpected minutes. The Lesson Delivery component of the SIOP Model is included to remind teachers to stay on track, and in this chapter we provide some guidance for doing so.

This chapter addresses the way a lesson is delivered, how well the content and language objectives are supported during the lesson, to what extent students are engaged in the lesson, and how appropriate the pace of the lesson is to students' ability levels. You will see that this chapter parallels Chapter 2, Lesson Preparation, because the two components are closely related. The effectiveness of a lesson's delivery—the level of student participation, how clearly information is communicated, students' level of understanding reflected in the quality of their work—often can be traced back to the preparation that took place before children entered the classroom. We will meet the teachers from Chapter 2 again in the Teaching Scenarios and discuss how their level of preparation was executed in their lesson delivery.

SIOP® SHELTERED INSTRUCTION OBSERVATION PROTOCOL

SIOP® FEATURE 23:

Content Objectives Clearly Supported by Lesson Delivery

As we discussed in Chapter 2, content objectives must be stated orally, and they must be displayed for students and teachers alike to see. From the content perspective, this is no longer an unusual proposition. Since the No Child Left Behind Act has raised the level of school accountability, teachers and principals are more comfortable with posting objectives tied to state standards. Districts in the 46 states that have adopted the Common Core State Standards for language arts and mathematics were already rewriting curriculum at the time this book was being revised and so content objectives for those subjects are likely to be similar across states. We caution against any inclination to list the standard in an abbreviated form, like CC.W.2.2 (for a Grade 2 writing standard), as an objective because it would be meaningless to the children and it is unlikely to be at the level of a lesson goal. For young learners it may appear as gibberish. Rather, written, child-friendly objectives serve to remind us of the focus of the lesson, providing a structure to classroom procedures.

Schmoker (2011) calls for more focus in classroom instruction. He proposes "simplicity, clarity and priority" regarding learning goals. He recommends "whole class lessons focused on a clear learning objective in short instructional 'chunks' or segments, punctuated by multiple cycles of guided practice and formative assessment ('checks for understanding')" (pp. 20–21). We know that written objectives allow students to know the direction of the lesson and help them stay on task. SIOP teachers who attend to their lesson objectives make sure there are times during the lesson when some explicit instruction takes place that targets the objectives and other times when students have the opportunity to practice and make progress toward meeting those objectives. Throughout the lesson and at its conclusion, the teacher and children can evaluate the extent to which the lesson delivery supported the content objectives.

SIOP® FEATURE 24:

Language Objectives Clearly Supported by Lesson Delivery

PD TOOLKIT™ for SIOP®

Click on Videos, then search for "Lesson Delivery to Support Language Objectives" to see how a teacher addresses the language objective explicitly in the lesson.

As you now know, language objectives are an important part of effective SIOP lessons. Teachers and students benefit from having a clear language objective that is written for them to see and that can be reviewed during the lesson. The objective may be related to an English language proficiency standard such as "Students will compare/contrast attributes of three-dimensional shapes from labeled models or charts (e.g., A _____ is like a _____ because _____.)" (WIDA Consortium, 2007, p. 35); or it may be related to teachers' scope and sequence of language skills that their own students need to develop, such as "Students will state an opinion and give reasons to support the opinion." No matter which language objective is written for a lesson, as we stated in Chapter 2, a teacher needs to address it explicitly during instruction. For example, if first graders in a language arts lesson have to "retell a story" as their language objective with *The Hungry Caterpillar* by Eric Carle, then we expect the teacher will spend some time teaching or reviewing *how* to retell with students, perhaps using a different, familiar story, and also reviewing the number words and names of the objects that the caterpillar ate.

Meeting Content and Language Objectives

A SIOP lesson is effective when it meets its objectives. Although we have experienced some teacher reluctance to write both kinds of objectives for each lesson and to post them for the children, our research results give evidence of their value (Short, Fidelman, & Louguit, 2012). When presenting a SIOP lesson, the objectives should be:

- **Observable**—the learning goals are able to be noticed by an observer, in terms of the activities students are asked to accomplish and the questions and comprehension checks the teachers ask.

- **Measurable**—there is a way to assess whether students met the objectives, or made progress toward meeting them.

- **Assessed**—the objectives are reviewed at the end of the lesson and the class determines if they were met.

Some teachers have explained that they don't want to write out and discuss the objectives with the students because they can't write them in a manner that students understand or because they fear not completing the full lesson. Both of those arguments are easily overcome with practice and support. A SIOP coach or a fellow SIOP teacher can give guidance on writing student-friendly objectives. The students themselves will confirm if they understood the objective when it is presented in class. And as a teacher gets to know his or her students, writing for their age and proficiency level becomes easier.

If the problem is that the objectives are not being met by the end of the lesson, then the teacher and students can discuss why as they review them. It may be that the activities took longer than planned or class discussions veered off track, but the presence of objectives can actually impose discipline on the pacing of each lesson. If a teacher consistently does not meet objectives, however, it may also be that too many objectives have been planned for the time frame of the lesson, or that time is lost during activity transitions or at the start or end of the period.

We acknowledge that it takes time to determine good objectives for every lesson, but the investment in writing them and then teaching to them pays off in student achievement.

SIOP® FEATURE 25:

Students Engaged Approximately 90% to 100% of the Period

This feature in the Lesson Delivery component calls on teachers to engage students 90% to 100% of the class period. By this we mean that the students are paying attention and on task. It does not mean they need to be highly active (writing, reading, moving) the entire time, but they are following the lesson, responding to teacher direction, and performing the activities as expected. When students are in groups, all are participating. Lessons where students are engaged less than 50% of the time are unacceptable. This situation tends to occur when teachers have not provided clear explanations of the assignment or have not scaffolded the process well. If students don't know what to do, they will find something else to do, and then misbehavior or inattention ensues.

Engagement, motivation, and cultural responsiveness are important factors in successful lessons—for both native and non-native English-speaking children (Nieto & Bode, 2008; Turner, 2007). When learners are actively engaged, they are involved in tasks that challenge them and allow them to gain confidence. Younger learners prefer tasks with objects they can manipulate or movements they can perform, as well as puzzles and learning games. They will listen to or try to read texts above their level in subject matter that captures their imagination. Offering choices in tasks, texts, or partners, setting up learning centers, and differentiating instruction are key methods for accommodating classrooms with English learners of varying proficiency levels as well as those with both native English speakers and English learners. It is often through such modifications to a curriculum that student engagement can be enhanced (Buck, Carr, & Robertson, 2008; Tomlinson, 2005).

English learners are the students who can least afford to have valuable time squandered through boredom, inattention, socializing, and other off-task behaviors. Time also is wasted when teachers are ill prepared; have poor classroom management skills; spend excessive amounts of time making announcements and passing out and collecting papers; and the like. The most effective teachers minimize these behaviors and maximize time spent actively engaged in instruction. English learners who are working to achieve grade-level competence benefit from efficient use of class time. Further, many of these learners have had uneven schooling experiences, missing time in school due to circumstances beyond their control, and are then further disadvantaged by inefficient use of class time. Investing in a slower pace in the first quarter of the year often pays off later because children then know the task procedures and classroom routines and have better academic language skills.

There are three aspects to student engagement that should be considered during a lesson: (1) allocated time, (2) engaged time, and (3) academic learning time (Berliner, 1984).

1. *Allocated time* reflects the decisions teachers make regarding the amount of time to spend studying a topic (e.g., math versus reading) and a given academic goal (e.g., how much time to spend on reading comprehension versus decoding skills). As we have discussed throughout this book, effective sheltered instruction teachers plan for and deliver lessons that are balanced between teacher presentation of information and opportunities for students to practice and apply the information in meaningful ways.

2. *Engaged time* refers to the time students are actively participating in instruction during the time allocated. The engaged time-on-task research has consistently concluded that the more actively students participate in the instructional process, the more they achieve (Schmoker, 2006). Instruction that is understandable to English learners, that creates opportunities for students to talk about the lesson's concepts, and that provides hands-on activities to reinforce learning captures students' attention and keeps them more actively engaged.

3. *Academic learning time* focuses on students' time-on-task, when the task is related to the content and language objectives they will be tested on. Creative, fun activities are not effective if they are unrelated to the content and language objectives of the lesson. But equally, "skill and drill" exercises on discrete points (e.g., past tense verb endings) and endless multiple-choice practice tests are not engaging, thus reducing academic learning time. SIOP teachers maximize the academic learning time for their students, as shown in Figure 8.1.

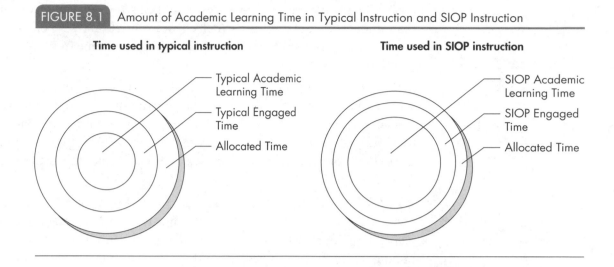

FIGURE 8.1   Amount of Academic Learning Time in Typical Instruction and SIOP Instruction

Time used in typical instruction

- Typical Academic Learning Time
- Typical Engaged Time
- Allocated Time

Time used in SIOP instruction

- SIOP Academic Learning Time
- SIOP Engaged Time
- Allocated Time

Student engagement is also enhanced when students have a focus for their work. According to Leinhardt and colleagues (1982):

> When teachers spend their time and energy teaching students the content the students need to learn, students learn the material. When students spend their time actively engaged in activities that relate strongly to the materials they will be tested on, they learn more of the material (p. 409).

SIOP teachers therefore need to be explicit in their expectations and make certain that their English learners understand which content and language objectives will be the focus of upcoming assessments.

SIOP® FEATURE 26:

Pacing of the Lesson
Appropriate to Students' Ability Levels

Pacing refers to the rate at which information is presented during a lesson. The pace of the lesson depends on the nature of the lesson's content, as well as the level of students' background knowledge. When working with English learners, it can be challenging to find a pace that doesn't present information too quickly yet is brisk enough to maintain students' interest, especially when a variety of English proficiency levels are represented in the same classroom. Finding an appropriate pace requires practice, but becomes easier as teachers develop familiarity with their students' language and academic skills.

- *Elementary teachers* know, for instance, that the attention span of a kindergartener or first grader is much shorter than that of a fifth grader, so they adjust their lessons accordingly. A practice activity may last only five to seven minutes in the primary grades, where in the upper grades it could last 20. They also chunk important information in smaller conceptual units and allot time for processing the material taught in the new language between the chunks. Because many elementary teachers have a less rigid bell schedule than secondary teachers (i.e., students do not typically switch classes at a set time per period), on some days, certain lessons may extend beyond the normal time frame to cover the material.

- *Middle and high school content area teachers* are often constrained by the school's bell schedule and the district's curriculum pacing guide. However, teachers cannot move so quickly through the curriculum that they leave their English learners behind. They may need to carefully select the most important concepts to spend some extra time on and adjust their planning accordingly.

- *ESL teachers* can augment instructional time. When a grade-level or subject area teacher collaborates with the ESL teacher, both language and content instruction benefit. The ESL teacher might introduce key vocabulary and build background on topics before they are covered in the content classroom, or provide additional practice and application activities afterward. This supports the student's content learning. It also supports the acquisition of academic English and motivates English learners because they cover grade-level material in the ESL class and understand more in the content class. (See Lacina, New Levine, and Sowa, 2006 for examples of ESL–elementary classroom teacher partnerships.)

In classes with native English speakers and English learners, it can take some effort and experience to pace the lessons well. Investing in instructional routines and teaching task procedures during the first quarter of the year are two strategies that will reap dividends later. Most learners enjoy working with peers, so collaborative learning projects with tasks geared to proficiency level and interest are beneficial. On occasion, interdisciplinary projects could be planned, such as a project on Volcanoes Around the World that involves science (e.g., the steps in forming a volcano and leading to an eruption), math (calculating temperature of lava and rate of lava flow), geography (e.g., locations of active and dormant volcanoes), and reading (e.g., stories about volcanoes). Such projects not only spiral the content but also introduce and reinforce key language terms, functions, and sentence structures, allowing English learners time over the course of a unit and across several content areas to develop the academic English skills they need for success.

One important fact to remember is this: If a teacher wastes five minutes of a class period daily, perhaps by starting the lesson late or finishing early, over the course of 180 days, 15 hours of instructional time will be lost! Often, simple routines can help the pacing: a basket by the door where students deposit homework when they enter or class work when they leave, a materials manager for each group of desks who distributes books or worksheets to everyone in the group, routinized activities that do not need directions explained each time, and/or a classroom timer set to ring when an activity should end. If you finish a lesson early, don't let students chat or do homework; instead, play a game to review vocabulary or key concepts. We need to maximize the way we use time when we have English learners in the classroom.

The Relationship Between Lesson Preparation and Lesson Delivery

PD **TOOLKIT**™ **for SIOP**®

Click on Videos, then search for "Kindergarten Teacher Reflects on Her Lesson Delivery" to listen to a teacher discuss her planning to meet the Lesson Delivery features.

Now that you have read about the features of this component, you can see that strong, thoughtful lesson preparation is critical to effective lesson delivery. Without the planning necessary to make the content truly comprehensible for the diversity of English learners in your class and without considering which aspects of academic English they need to learn or practice in your given lesson, your lesson may fly over their heads and a day during which they could be learning may be wasted.

Figure 8.2 shows how the features of Lesson Preparation influence the features of Lesson Delivery. The content and language objectives written on a lesson plan need to be presented and practiced in a way to support student learning. Not all students may master the objectives the first day they encounter them, but all students should make progress toward mastery. Just writing a content and a language objective on your lesson plan is not sufficient; you have to "deliver" on those learning goals.

Next, you can see how student engagement depends in large part on what content you teach, how you adapt that content, what supplementary materials you include, and what activities you ask students to perform. English learners are motivated to learn what their English-speaking peers are learning. Sometimes, in order to provide that grade-level content in a comprehensible way, you will have to adapt it. You will decide whether the adaptation is through the texts they are reading (e.g., utilizing a book with a lower reading level) or the tasks they are being asked to do, but if the material is at or a little above their level of understanding, they can be engaged with it. And of course, the planned lesson tasks play a critical role in student engagement. "Skill and drill" exercises turn everyone off—English speakers and English learners alike. Creative activities related to the objectives that include plenty of language practice do not.

Finally, we have to consider how the choices we make when planning a lesson affect the pacing. If students use supplementary materials and the content has been adapted to their levels, they are better able to move through the materials with

FIGURE 8.2 The Relationship Between Lesson Preparation and Lesson Delivery

Lesson Preparation	Lesson Delivery
Plan for content objectives ⟶	Support learning of content objectives
Plan for language objectives ⟶	Support learning of language objectives
Address grade-level content	
Use supplementary materials	Promote student engagement
Use adapted content	Pace the lesson appropriately
Plan meaningful activities with language practice	

occasional support from the teacher. If, however, those materials are above their level, the lesson and class discussions will get bogged down. More time will be spent explaining what something means than applying or extending the information. Likewise, if the activities are not meaningful or clearly explained, students may exhibit off-task behavior or dawdle while trying to complete the assigned work.

Teaching Ideas for Lesson Delivery

The following ideas can help a teacher check on student progress toward meeting objectives and promote student engagement:

- **Think-Pair-Share** (Lyman, 1981). This tried and true technique is an excellent means for teachers to monitor student understanding of the content or language objectives. Instead of asking questions to the whole class and calling on two or three students to respond, the teacher asks everyone to think of an answer or respond to a prompt, and tell it to a partner. Then, the teacher calls on some students to share their responses with the whole class. This relatively simple and quick technique gives *all* of the students a chance to think and speak about the topic, instead of just two or three. A variation called **Think-Pair-Square-Share** asks partners to pair up (square = four students) before the whole-class sharing out.

- **Chunk and Chew** (see Vogt & Echevarría, 2008, p. 164 and Short, Vogt, & Echevarría, 2011a, pp. 66–68). To maintain the goal of chunking new information, this technique encourages teachers to pause after every 10 minutes of input to give students time to talk with a partner or in a small group about what they have just learned. In SIOP lessons, the student talk is carefully structured by the teacher in the lesson plan with specific prompts and/or sentence starters.

- **Roam and Review.** At the end of a lesson, the teacher may pose a reflection question (e.g., "What was the most important thing you learned today?" or "What surprised you in our studies today?") and have students think silently, then stand and roam the classroom, discussing their ideas with classmates. This is unstructured; students can roam and talk to whomever they choose.

- **Podcasts.** Students prepare a two- to three-minute oral summary on a topic they have selected or the teacher has assigned. They rehearse and then record it on a podcast or an audio file for use on the class computer.

- **TV Talk Show.** A wonderful project that addresses content and language objectives (particularly listening and speaking ones) and engages students is the TV talk show (Cloud, Healey, Paul, Short, & Winiarski, 2010; Herrell & Jordan, 2008). Small groups plan a talk show on a topic with multiple parameters that they have studied. One student is the host and interviewer; others are the guests. For example, after studying extreme weather phenomena, one guest might be an expert on hurricanes, another on blizzards, a third on earthquakes, and a fourth on tornadoes. The talk shows could be videotaped for later viewing and analysis by the teacher or the students. The analysis might look at how well the students spoke, used key vocabulary, responded to host questions, and so forth.

- **Writing Headlines.** Students try to capture the essence of a day's lesson, section of a text read, video watched, or information presented orally in a newspaper headline. Teachers can encourage students to use descriptive language and focus on word choice to create compelling headlines.
- **E-Journals and Wiki Entries.** The teacher can have students write in an e-journal daily or once a week to reflect on what they have been learning. At the end of a unit, the teacher might ask students to write an online entry for a class wiki that presents key information on a topic being studied.

Differentiating Ideas for Multi-level Classes

As teachers deliver their lessons, they need to be cognizant of the learning process all of their students experience. The following ideas will help teachers differentiate activities among multi-level students as well as gauge which students are meeting the objectives and which need more assistance.

- **Pro-Rate the Task.** The product of a task need not be exactly the same across students. The more advanced students are in their knowledge or language skills, the more they can be asked to do. In classes with both English learners and English speakers, a teacher might explain to English speakers that even if an assigned task for the English learners seemingly has less required output, it still is as cognitively challenging (or more) as the task for English speakers because the English learners are doing the work in a language they are still mastering.
- **Radio Advice Line.** The teacher can select two or three of the more advanced learners to be the radio show host. Other children can draft questions they have on a topic, perhaps as a review or a way to seek clarification. They "call in" to pose the questions to the radio hosts, who take turns responding. The teacher can monitor what questions are being asked and which students seem to have a good or poor sense of the lesson's objectives.
- **Projects.** One of the best ways for students to work at their own ability level, language level, and interest level is through projects. Projects also offer a meaningful way to determine whether students can apply information they are learning and can tap into their creativity too.
- **Varying Comprehension Checks.** Teachers can modulate the questions they ask of students according to their levels of language proficiency. In addition, when teachers know that some children are having more difficulty than others, they can check in with them more frequently. In Chapter 5, Figure 5.1, we presented a scaffolding graphic that showed the teacher watching and helping as needed while students worked collaboratively or independently. At these points in a lesson, the teacher can offer more assistance to those who are struggling while letting the others continue to work on their own.

- **Scale of Student Mastery.** The teacher can keep track of how students are progressing in mastering the language and content objectives of a unit. At set moments of time (e.g., Day 1, Day 3, Day 7), the teacher records a score for the students' progress. The score might be on a continuum of 1–5, with 5 being mastery, or it might be a symbol like /, √, and +.

The Lesson

Unit: The Gold Rush (Fourth Grade)

The classrooms described in the teaching vignettes in this chapter are all located in a suburban elementary school with heterogeneously mixed students. English learners represent approximately 30% of the student population, and the children speak a variety of languages. In the fourth-grade classrooms of teachers Ms. Chen, Mrs. Hargroves, and Mr. Hensen, the majority of the English learners are at the intermediate stage of English fluency.

As part of the fourth-grade social studies curriculum, Ms. Chen, Mrs. Hargroves, and Mr. Hensen have planned a unit on the California Gold Rush. The school district requires the use of the adopted social studies series, although teachers are encouraged to supplement the text with primary source materials, literature, and realia. The content topics for the Gold Rush unit include westward expansion, routes and trails to the West, the people who sought their fortunes, hardships, settlements, the discovery of gold, the life of miners, methods for extracting gold, the impact of the Gold Rush, as well as other topics.

Each of the teachers has created several lessons for this unit, beginning with a lesson plan (approximately 45 minutes per day) on routes and trails to the West. Specifically, the content of this lesson covers the Oregon Trail, the Overland Trail, and the Route around Cape Horn.

Teaching Scenarios

These scenarios continue the lessons presented in Chapter 2. To refresh your memory about each lesson on westward expansion and the Gold Rush taught by Ms. Chen, Mrs. Hargroves, and Mr. Hensen, we summarize them in the sections that follow. (See Chapter 2, Teaching Scenarios, for a complete description of the three lessons.)

Ms. Chen

Ms. Chen began the lesson on westward expansion by reading aloud the content and language objectives for the day.

Content Objectives

1. Find and label the three main routes to the West on a map.
2. Relate one or two facts about each of the three trails from the text.

Language Objectives

1. Write sentences explaining how the three routes to the West were given their names.
2. Explain how the structure of some words gives clues to their meaning.

After a whole-class brainstorming and List-Group-Label activity about why people leave their homes and move to new locations, Ms. Chen assigned most of the class a quick-write on the Gold Rush. She then provided a "jump-start" for the English learners with very limited proficiency by introducing key vocabulary, passing around iron pyrite ("fool's gold"), looking together at a map of the trails west, and viewing several pictures of pioneers and Gold Rush characters.

Following this, Ms. Chen introduced the key vocabulary to the entire class, and discussed why roads, streets, and trails have particular names. She pointed out the three trails west on interactive whiteboard maps, discussed their names, and explained how the Overland Trail's name was a compound word that gave clues to its meaning (over + land = overland).

Next, Ms. Chen distributed copies of maps and modeled on the interactive whiteboard how to use colored pencils to color in the maps. Students worked together in small groups to complete their maps. Finally, with a few minutes remaining in the period, Ms. Chen distributed a skeleton outline of the chapter that the students had read. The outline's headings (Locations, Characteristics, Challenges, and Advantages) provided an organizer for the information, and in groups, students began working together to fill in the outline. The lesson concluded with a review of the content and language objectives. Then, several students volunteered to report on a number of facts about each of the trails.

On the SIOP form in Figure 8.3, rate Ms. Chen's lesson for each of the features in Lesson Delivery. Be able to defend your ratings and discuss them with others, if possible.

Mrs. Hargroves

Mrs. Hargroves began her lesson on the trails west by stating, "Today you'll learn about the Oregon Trail, the Overland Trail, and the Route around Cape Horn. We'll also be working on maps, and I want you to color the Overland Trail a different color from the color you use for the Cape Horn route. When you learn about the Oregon Trail, you'll complete the map with a third color. By the time you're finished, you should have all three routes drawn on the map using different colors." She held up a completed map for the students to see as an example.

Following a brief lecture on westward expansion, Mrs. Hargroves directed students to the respective chapter in the text and also displayed it using the electronic

FIGURE 8.3 Lesson Delivery Component of the SIOP Model: Ms. Chen's Lesson

4	3	2	1	0
23. **Content objectives** clearly supported by lesson delivery		**Content objectives** somewhat supported by lesson delivery		**Content objectives** not supported by lesson delivery

4	3	2	1	0
24. **Language objectives** clearly supported by lesson delivery		**Language objectives** somewhat supported by lesson delivery		**Language objectives** not supported by lesson delivery

4	3	2	1	0
25. **Students engaged** approximately 90% to 100% of the period		**Students engaged** approximately 70% of the period		**Students engaged** less than 50% of the period

4	3	2	1	0
26. **Pacing** of the lesson appropriate to the students' ability levels		**Pacing** generally appropriate, but at times too fast or too slow		**Pacing** inappropriate to students' ability levels

document reader. Students looked at the illustrations and she responded to questions they had. She began reading the chapter, and after a few minutes, she directed students to complete the reading independently. She circulated through the room, answering questions and helping with difficult words. After 20 minutes, Mrs. Hargroves stopped the reading, distributed colored pencils and maps, and asked students to complete the maps with partners. When the maps were completed, she collected them and assigned a brief essay on the topic "If you had been a pioneer, which trail would you have chosen? Why?"

On the SIOP form in Figure 8.4, rate Mrs. Hargroves's lesson for each of the Lesson Delivery features.

Mr. Hensen

Mr. Hensen began his lesson by asking how many of the students had traveled to California. They discussed the various modes of transportation used by students who had visited the state, and then Mr. Hensen linked their responses to the travel modes of the pioneers. Following a video on the westward expansion, he introduced the key vocabulary for the day's lessons (Oregon Trail, Overland Trail, Route around Cape Horn).

4	3	2	1	0
23. **Content objectives** clearly supported by lesson delivery		**Content objectives** somewhat supported by lesson delivery		**Content objectives** not supported by lesson delivery

4	3	2	1	0
24. **Language objectives** clearly supported by lesson delivery		**Language objectives** somewhat supported by lesson delivery		**Language objectives** not supported by lesson delivery

4	3	2	1	0
25. **Students engaged** approximately 90% to 100% of the period		**Students engaged** approximately 70% of the period		**Students engaged** less than 50% of the period

4	3	2	1	0
26. **Pacing** of the lesson appropriate to the students' ability levels		**Pacing** generally appropriate, but at times too fast or too slow		**Pacing** inappropriate to students' ability levels

Next, Mr. Hensen read aloud two paragraphs from the textbook chapter. He then numbered students off into six groups, assigned different sections of the text to the newly formed groups, and engaged them in a Jigsaw reading activity for the remainder of the chapter. English learners were partnered with more proficient English readers for the Jigsaw activity. After the Jigsaw groups completed their reading, they regrouped to share what they had learned from the assigned text. At least one student from each of the Jigsaw groups was placed in the new home groups so chapter sections were fully covered. Again, English learners had support from students with greater English proficiency.

Mr. Hensen then directed the students in their home groups to divvy up the three trails. Some students were asked to draw the Oregon Trail on a map, and the other students were to draw either the Overland or Cape Horn trails. Their next task was to show the other students in their group how to locate, draw, and color the trails on their maps, using the map in the text and their reading as a guide. Mr. Hensen circulated through the room, assisting as necessary, while the children completed the mapping activity. At the lesson's conclusion, students were directed to pass in their maps. Those maps that were not finished were assigned as homework.

On the SIOP form in Figure 8.5, rate Mr. Hensen's lesson for each of the Lesson Delivery features.

4	3	2	1	0
23. **Content objectives** clearly supported by lesson delivery		**Content objectives** somewhat supported by lesson delivery		**Content objectives** not supported by lesson delivery

4	3	2	1	0
24. **Language objectives** clearly supported by lesson delivery		**Language objectives** somewhat supported by lesson delivery		**Language objectives** not supported by lesson delivery

4	3	2	1	0
25. **Students engaged** approximately 90% to 100% of the period		**Students engaged** approximately 70% of the period		**Students engaged** less than 50% of the period

4	3	2	1	0
26. **Pacing** of the lesson appropriate to the students' ability levels		**Pacing** generally appropriate, but at times too fast or too slow		**Pacing** inappropriate to students' ability levels

Discussion of Lessons

23. *Content Objectives Clearly Supported by Lesson Delivery*

Ms. Chen: 4

Mrs. Hargroves: 1

Mr. Hensen: 3

Clearly, we believe (and our research supports it) that teachers must include content and language objectives in every lesson, not only for planning and teaching, but also for the students, especially English learners. They need to have a clear, explicit understanding of what the expectations are for a lesson. Recall that only Ms. Chen wrote her content and language objectives on the board and read them aloud for her students. While Mrs. Hargroves had a content objective (but no language objective) written in her plan book, she stated her plans for the day orally to her students, without clearly defining their learning objectives. Mr. Hensen had neither content nor language objectives written in his plan book, yet he appeared to have a clear idea of where he was going with his lesson. However, at the outset of the lesson, his plans may not have been clear for some students.

In this component of the SIOP Model (Lesson Delivery), we move beyond having the content and lesson objectives written in plan books and on the board (or chart paper or transparency). Rather, the focus here is on whether the lesson delivery matches the stated (or implied, in Mr. Hensen's case) objectives.

- From the beginning of the lesson, **Ms. Chen** had a clearly defined content objective, and her lesson delivery supported it. Her focus on the three routes to the West was supported by (1) activating students' prior knowledge about why people leave their homes and move to a new location (brainstorming and List-Group-Label); (2) engaging some students in a quick-write about the Gold Rush, so that she could have a few minutes to preteach (jump-start) the English learners a topic about which they probably had little prior knowledge; (3) the shared reading of the textbook chapter; (4) the mapping activity; and (5) the skeleton outline that compared and contrasted the three trails. The lesson was rated a "4" for supporting content objectives.

- In contrast, **Mrs. Hargroves's** lesson received a "1" on this feature. As you may recall, she did not write an objective on the board, and she hurriedly stated what she wanted the students to do for the lesson. What is also problematic about her lesson is that the coloring of the maps seemed to be what was important to her, rather than her confirmation that each student understood the information about the trails west. Students were expected to read the chapter independently, which was most likely impossible for struggling readers and the English learners.

     Further, her lecture may have been difficult for her English learners to follow. The writing assignment, while a worthwhile topic ("If you had been a pioneer, which trail would you have chosen? Why?"), was not scaffolded, so it may or may not have been appropriate for her students, depending on their English proficiency and their ability to access the information in the text. Therefore, her lesson delivery did not support well her intended content objective.

- Although **Mr. Hensen** did not state the objectives, they were implied and supported by his lesson. For example, at the end of the period, he asked several students to report on some differences among the trails; this initial feedback provided information about whether the students had met the day's objective. His constant monitoring and the various grouping activities provided additional information about who was meeting the objective and who was having difficulty. He might have added a quick group-response activity (pencils up/ pencils down) to determine if all students understood the differences among the trails. The skeleton outline to be completed the following day would provide him with definitive information about his students' meeting of the content objectives. Had Mr. Hensen written his objectives on the board and reviewed them with his students, his lesson would have received a "4" for this feature. Because he did not, his lesson received a "3" for supporting content objectives.

24. *Language Objectives Clearly Supported by Lesson Delivery*

   Ms. Chen: 4

   Mrs. Hargroves: 0

   Mr. Hensen: 2

- **Ms. Chen's** lesson was rated "4" on this feature. Language objectives were clearly written and stated, and students had several opportunities to meet them. During the discussion of the street names, students had a chance to talk about why and how streets and routes were named. Additionally, students were asked to use complete sentences.

- **Mrs. Hargroves** did not write or state any language objectives. Although she did assign a reading and writing activity, the text was inaccessible for many of the students, so the writing activity would be difficult, if not impossible, for them to complete. Moreover, as we pointed out in Chapter 2, a language activity is not the same as a language objective. Her lesson received a "0" for supporting language objectives.

- **Mr. Hensen** did not write or state his language objectives, but as with the content objectives, they were implied. He engaged students in a Jigsaw activity for reading the text, and then they returned to their home groups and explained what they had learned from the reading. His lesson received a "2."

25. *Students Engaged Approximately 90% to 100% of the Period*

Ms. Chen: 4

Mrs. Hargroves: 1

Mr. Hensen: 4

- **Ms. Chen** is an enthusiastic teacher who plans lessons that use each minute of class time to its fullest. As illustrated in the lesson, Ms. Chen spent time presenting materials and she allowed students to work together. They eagerly participated in whole-group and small-group discussions, and Ms. Chen made sure they were on task as she walked around the room. In addition, the content of the lesson was directly related to the district's content standards on which the students will be assessed at the end of the unit.

  Her lesson received a "4" for this feature because it met all the criteria for active student engagement: She used the allocated time in an effective way, basing the lesson on the text, teaching outlining and mapping skills, providing opportunities for interaction and application of concepts, and so forth. Students were active and on task throughout, and the material was relevant to the assignment.

- Recall that **Mrs. Hargroves** read part of the text chapter aloud, which cut its substantial length. She then allotted 20 minutes for students to read the remaining portion of the text chapter. Many students completed the reading in about 10 minutes. Some began talking among themselves, while others were trying to finish the reading. Overall, students were engaged less than 50% of the period. During Mrs. Hargroves's lecture on westward expansion, many students were disengaged except when she used the electronic document reader and discussed the illustrations and the trails on the map in the text. This lesson received a "1" for engaging the students.

- **Mr. Hensen's** students were actively engaged throughout the lesson. From the opening question about trips to California through the video and the Jigsaw activity, all students were held accountable for learning the material. During the map activity, students not only located and colored a trail, but were also responsible for assisting each other in finding, drawing, and coloring the additional trails. This lesson was rated a "4" for this feature.

26. *Pacing of Lesson Appropriate to Students' Ability Levels*

Ms. Chen: 4

Mrs. Hargroves: 1

Mr. Hensen: 3

- **Ms. Chen** understood that the English learners in her class may have needed a slower pace than the native English speakers. Therefore, she provided a jump-start minilesson that enabled them to keep up with the whole-class activities. She also moved the pace along by reading aloud and doing a shared reading of the text. In this way, she scaffolded instruction for the English learners, and all students were able to work at roughly the same pace. The groups for the map activity included four to five students with both native English speakers and English learners who assisted one another as needed. Her lesson received a "4" for pacing.

- The pacing of **Mrs. Hargroves's** lesson was slow and monotonous at times, especially when she lectured, yet she covered material too quickly at other times. Many students were off task because of the problematic pace of the lesson. Her lesson received a "1" for pacing because it was inappropriate for the students' ability level—too slow to maintain interest and too quick for English learners to understand the information presented orally.

- **Mr. Hensen** included discussions, videos, a Jigsaw reading activity, group work, and map coloring; some students, especially the English learners, may have felt a bit rushed to accomplish all of these tasks. However, he also provided substantial scaffolding and did allow students to complete their maps at home. The students participated well and understood most concepts. This lesson was rated a "3."

(For more examples of lesson and unit plans in social studies and history for grades K–12, see Short, Vogt, and Echevarría, 2011a.)

Summary

As you reflect on this chapter and the impact of effective lesson delivery, consider the following main points:

- The importance of setting and meeting objectives cannot be overemphasized. Many teachers may feel comfortable having a general objective in mind and moving along with a lesson's flow, but that approach is not helpful for English learners.

- If you plan objectives, you have to teach to them. Delivering a lesson geared to objectives allows the teacher to stay on track, and lets the children know what is important to focus on and remember.

- By incorporating a variety of techniques that engage students throughout the lesson, teachers not only give students opportunities to learn, practice, and apply information and language skills, but also help to ensure the students meet the lesson's objectives.

• An appropriate pace for a lesson is critical for English learners. Information that is presented at a pace suitable for native English speakers may render that information meaningless, especially for beginning English speakers. Finding the right pace for a lesson depends in part on the content of the lesson and students' prior knowledge about the topic. Effective SIOP teachers use instructional time wisely.

Discussion Questions

1. In reflecting on the content and language objectives at the beginning of the chapter, are you able to:
   a. Monitor lessons to determine if the delivery is supporting the objectives?
   b. List strategies for improving student time-on-task throughout a lesson?
   c. Generate activities to keep English learners engaged?
   d. Discuss characteristics of effective SIOP lesson delivery?
   e. Explain how a focus on a lesson's objectives can aid in pacing?
   f. Evaluate a situation where a lesson plan has not been enacted successfully and explain what might have gone wrong and what could be improved?

2. Reflect on a lesson that you taught or observed that did not go well. What happened? When did it go awry? Can you identify a feature in Lesson Delivery that might have caused the lesson to be less successful? Or a feature from another SIOP component? In retrospect, how might your delivery of the lesson have been improved?

3. Suppose three new students, all with limited English proficiency, joined a fifth-grade class midyear. The other students in the class include a few former English learners and native English speakers. What are some language objectives the teacher could write for each of the following content concepts?
   a. Trade routes across the Sahara
   b. Expansion of the Roman Empire

   How might the teacher pro–rate the tasks associated with the language objectives to meet the different academic development needs of the students?

4. How does an elementary teacher or supervisor determine whether a majority of students, including English learners, are engaged during a lesson? What techniques could be used to sustain engagement throughout the period? What should the teacher do if he or she senses that students are off task? Why is sustained engagement so critical to English learners' academic progress?

5. Look over a SIOP lesson you have been working on. Write down the amount of time you expect each section (or activity) of the lesson to take. Teach the lesson and compare your expectations with reality. Do you have a good handle on pacing? If not, review your lesson for tightening or extending. What can you add or take away? List some routines you could implement in your classroom so you do less talking, or less distributing and collecting. Share with a colleague your ideas for maximizing time-on-task and student engagement.

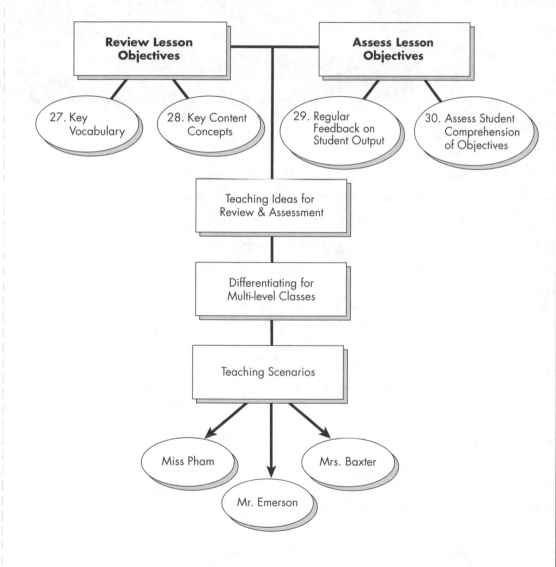

CHAPTER 9

Review & Assessment

After reading, discussing, and engaging in activities related to this chapter, you will be able to meet the following content and language objectives.

Content Objectives

Analyze the context of your classroom to provide more appropriate instruction for your English learners and other students.

Identify the challenges in assessing content and language learning of students with limited English proficiency.

Determine opportunities for reviewing and assessing key vocabulary and key content concepts in your lesson plan.

Language Objectives

Provide effective academic oral and written feedback to English learners during a lesson.

Compare and contrast characteristics of informal and formal assessments.

Explain the meaning of the following assessment terms: *formal assessment, informal assessment, authentic assessment, multidimensional, multiple indicators.*

Over the years, teachers have asked us why Review & Assessment is the eighth component in the SIOP Model. Usually the question is preceded by a comment such as, "Shouldn't the assessment of students' strengths and needs come before any instruction?" Our response is always, "Of course!" Clearly, assessment and instruction are inexorably linked (Vogt & Shearer, 2011). Effective SIOP teachers use assessment findings to plan their lessons according to children's needs and strengths, review children's progress toward meeting content and language objectives throughout each lesson, and evaluate how effectively their lessons have  been delivered. In this component we focus on a very important aspect of teaching: being aware of your children's learning by checking for understanding and assessing their comprehension of concepts and language, and adjusting instruction accordingly. In this chapter, we provide a discussion of the features of Review & Assessment, so with the increasing emphasis on assessment in schools today, we begin with a discussion of different types of assessment. ●

Background

Throughout this book, we have discussed many aspects of the classroom context that impact the achievement and language development of English learners. These include:

- lesson-based content and language objectives
- explicit links between a lesson and students' background knowledge
- instructional methods and materials for vocabulary and content concepts
- curriculum modifications and adaptations
- varied grouping structures
- patterns of interaction between the teacher and students and among students
- appropriate pacing and wait time during a lesson
- comprehensibility
- scaffolding techniques
- student engagement

Each of these aspects, along with other factors (e.g., classroom management and room organization), determines the classroom context for English learners and your other students.

Click on Videos, then search for "Assessment and Instruction" to see an example of the relationship between assessment and instruction.

PD **TOOLKIT™ for SIOP®**

Perhaps it is not surprising that effective SIOP teachers consider the context of the classroom when planning opportunities to review and assess student comprehension of a lesson's language and content concepts. These teachers plan so that their students eventually will reach independence in applying language and content concepts (as depicted in Figure 5.1 in Chapter 5). It is likely that some children will need substantial vocabulary and concept review, along with additional practice before they reach the goal of independence. With ongoing assessment throughout a lesson, teachers are able to ascertain who is ready to move on and who needs further reteaching, review, and practice.

Classroom Context and the Review & Assessment Component

When considering classroom context as you plan for review and assessment throughout a lesson, think about each of your students, both those who perform satisfactorily and those who struggle with your lessons. For those who are having little or no difficulty, there probably is a match between the classroom context (such as the aspects listed previously) and your children's needs. However, for those students who struggle, there could be a mismatch between the classroom context and the students' academic and language needs. With data-driven, culturally-responsive instruction, guided by periodic review and assessment, students are more likely to achieve an instructional match in your classroom.

The following questions may help you locate possible areas of match and mismatch. Keep in mind that there may be other areas of instruction that you need to explore (e.g., classroom management and room organization), but these questions can get you started (Echevarría & Vogt, 2011, p. 45; Vogt & Shearer, 2011, p. 94). For those of you who are in schools with Response to Intervention (RTI), the following questions can be part of the progress monitoring process.

1. Is there a match between the student and a classroom context? If so, what needs to be continued? (*Informal measures such as teacher observation and in-class assignments provide information, as well as more formal measures, such as unit exams and standardized test scores.*)

2. Is there a mismatch between the student and the classroom context? (*Again, observations and student work samples are a start; additional information, such as English proficiency level, information about L1 language and literacy acquisition, and the student's educational history may be needed.*)

3. If there is a mismatch, what could create a better match for the student? (*Check the student's L2 reading and math abilities to determine areas of mismatch with instructional materials; determine if the student is understanding task directions; and determine what is preventing success with in-class and out-of-class assignments.*)

4. How can you tell whether the changes you are making are achieving a closer match for the student in question? (*Use formative assessments such as teacher*

observation, in-class and out-of-class assignments; and summative assessments, such as periodic measures of language and literacy proficiency, end-of-chapter or unit tests.)

When review and assessment are linked to instruction that targets a lesson's content and language objectives, you are better able to answer these questions. Just as students need to know what the objectives are for a lesson, they also need to be informed about how they will be assessed on them. Both formative and summative assessment of students' progress provides information about whether it is appropriate to move on or whether it is necessary to reteach and review.

Formative and Summative Assessment

Historically, educators have blurred somewhat the line between assessment and evaluation, generally using the term *evaluation* for both formative and summative judgments. The teacher's role in evaluation was primarily as an "evaluator," one who conveyed a value on the completion of a given task. This value was frequently determined from the results of periodic quizzes, essays, reports, oral or written presentations, or tests that served as the basis for report card grades in elementary and secondary schools.

Today, however, educators distinguish between assessment and evaluation (Lipson & Wixson, 2012; Vogt & Shearer, 2011). *Assessment* is defined as the gathering and synthesizing of information concerning students' learning, while *evaluation* is defined as making judgments about students' learning. The processes of assessment and evaluation can be viewed as progressive: first, assessment; then, evaluation. Formative and summative assessments that are multi-faceted and attentive to the various contexts of a student's life (e.g., home, school, culture, native language, and literacy development in both L1 and L2) provide relevant and practical information to the teacher about how to design appropriate and culturally relevant content and language instruction for linguistically and culturally diverse students.

Informal Assessment

Informal assessment measures are generally used by teachers to gather data about their students' academic and language performance in the classroom. Effective classroom assessment is *informal*, *authentic*, and *multidimensional*, with *multiple indicators* that reflect student learning, achievement, and attitudes (Lenski, Ehlers-Zavala, Daniel, & Sun-Irminger, 2006; McLaughlin, 2010; O'Malley & Pierce, 1996; Vogt & Shearer, 2011). These qualities are described as follows:

PD **TOOLKIT™ for SIOP®**

Click on Videos, then search for "Introduction to Review and Assessment" to see how a teacher includes authentic assessment as she and her students collect evidences for their portfolios.

- **Informal assessment** involves on-the-spot, ongoing opportunities for determining the extent to which students are learning content. These opportunities may include teacher observations, anecdotal reports, teacher-to-student and student-to-student conversations, quick-writes and brainstorming, or any number of tasks that occur within regular instruction and are not intended to be graded or evaluated according to set criteria.

- **Authentic assessment** is characterized by its application to real life, where students are engaged in meaningful tasks that take place in real-life contexts.

- **Multidimensional assessments** are usually part of authentic assessments because teachers use different ways of determining student performance. These may include written pieces, audiotapes, student and parent interviews, videotapes, observations, creative work and art, discussion, performance, oral group responses, and so forth.

- **Multiple indicators** are specific evidences students complete that are related to a lesson's content and language objectives. They provide a teacher with several ways of looking at a student's language proficiency and content knowledge. For example, a student may demonstrate proficiency with a language objective through a piece of writing, active participation in a group activity, or insightful questions asked during discussion. The teacher thus has more than one piece of evidence indicative of progress toward mastery of a particular objective.

This approach to informal assessment is congruent with RTI (progress monitoring), the Common Core State Standards (high academic standards for all students), culturally-responsive teaching, and, of course, the SIOP Model.

Formal Assessment

Formal assessments can be formative (to achieve a baseline or beginning point) or summative (to determine progress over time). One type is standardized and norm-referenced, and it ranks students' scores in comparison to a normed group of students. Another type of standardized measure is criterion referenced. These tests measure students' performance as compared to a set of academic skills or objectives (Rothenberg & Fisher, 2007, p. 79).

Generally, formal assessments are used by schools and districts to look at academic trends over time and to identify subgroups of students who are performing unsatisfactorily. Because these assessments are considered to have "high stakes," there is a great deal of pressure on teachers to have high-performing students. So, what does this have to do with the SIOP Model? English learners are at a particular disadvantage when they are taking a standardized test that presumes the test taker is English proficient. One important thing that you, as a teacher of English learners and struggling students, can do is to explicitly teach, model, and provide practice with the general academic words (cross-curricular/process/function) that are described in Chapter 3 (pp. 72–73). These are frequently the types of words that are used in standardized test questions.

SIOP® FEATURE 27:
Comprehensive Review of Key Vocabulary

During class, English learners receive 20 to 30 minutes or more of input in a new language. Unless the teacher takes the time to highlight and review key information and explicitly indicate what students should learn, English learners and other students may not understand the lesson's focus. Students, especially those at the early stages of English acquisition, devote considerable energy to figuring out at a basic level what the teacher is saying or the text is telling them. These students are much less able to evaluate which pieces of information and which vocabulary terms, among all the input they receive, are important to remember. That is why the teacher must take the time to review key vocabulary and key concepts throughout a lesson and as a wrap-up at the end.

We know that students with robust vocabularies are more successful in school. Therefore, it stands to reason that teachers would want to revisit and review key words each day and make sure students are adding to their vocabulary knowledge. Researchers differ on the number of exposures that students need to internalize words at a deep level, but all agree the number is high, over 40 and up to 160! Repetition isn't simply about having students write words repeatedly. Rather, it is important to use the words in a variety of ways during a lesson, referring to the word on the board, on charts, on word walls, and so forth. Encourage students to use the key words or terms in their discussions and hold them accountable for doing so ("I noticed that in your group all of you used our three key words in your conversation!").

There is a variety of ways to effectively review academic vocabulary with students during a lesson, including the following (see the Teaching Ideas section in this chapter for additional ways to provide vocabulary review):

- Use analogies, the process of relating newly learned words to other words with the same structure or pattern. For example, previously we gave the example of the root *photo* (meaning light) in a lesson on photosynthesis, and suggested referring students to other words with the same word root (e.g., *photography, photocopy*).

- Point out multiple meanings, such as those that have one meaning in conversational English (e.g., "The laundry *product* I'm looking for in the supermarket is one that includes both detergent and bleach"), and another that is discipline-specific (e.g., "The *product* of 25 × 4 is 100").

- Point out synonyms and antonyms for key vocabulary, when possible. Four-corner charts can be helpful for review when they include (1) the vocabulary word, (2) a synonym, (3) an antonym, and (4) "what the word is not." For example: (1) *animal*, (2) *mammal*, (3) *puppet*, (4) *reptile*. A math example is: (1) *fraction*, (2) *portion*, (3) *whole*, (4) *a whole number*.

- Draw students' attention to how words are used in various contexts (pragmatics), because they may differ across cultures and languages. For example, a discussion of human reproduction is appropriate in an upper grade science lesson but may be very inappropriate at a family gathering. As we move throughout our day, whatever the context, we continually adjust our speech, facial expressions, and body language accordingly. It's important to talk to students about how language is used in different contexts and how something that might be appropriate in one context may be inappropriate in another.

- As mentioned previously, repetition of academic words and terms has benefits to students. Provide multiple exposures to new terminology to build familiarity, confidence, and English proficiency. Words and concepts may be reviewed through paraphrasing, such as "Remember to *share your ideas;* that is, if you have something you want to say, tell it to the others in your group." Another example of a paraphrase (and contextualized sentence) is *"The townspeople were welcoming as they invited the visitors to their homes*. They were welcoming as they invited soldiers into their homes." Paraphrasing as review provides an effective scaffold for English learners, especially after words and phrases have been previously defined and discussed in context.

- A final vocabulary review is also necessary at the conclusion of a lesson. Students might share understandings with a partner while you check their explanations; write a quick definition (in student-speak) on individual whiteboards and hold them up to show you; do a quick match of words and definitions on an interactive whiteboard; write 2–3 sentences including the words on tickets-out cards that you collect as they leave the classroom (or before transitioning to a new subject); and so forth. What is important is that you plan for the final review just as you plan for the other activities in your lessons.

Please remember that effective review does not include the "dreaded word list" described in Chapter 3, nor the equally ineffective assignment of having students write vocabulary or spelling words 10 (or more) times each. Research findings are very clear—isolated word lists and dictionary definitions alone do not promote vocabulary and language development. Rather, provide as many exposures as possible to new, important words through meaningful tasks that incorporate multiple modalities (reading, writing, illustrating, acting out, using sentence frames, and so forth).

SIOP® FEATURE 28:

Comprehensive Review of Key Content Concepts

Just as it is important to review key vocabulary periodically throughout a lesson and at its conclusion, it is also essential that English learners have key content concepts reviewed during and at the end of the lesson. Understandings are scaffolded when you stop during a lesson and briefly summarize key content concepts covered to that point. For example, in a lesson on Egyptian mummification, you might say something like the following: "Up to this point, we learned that little was known about Mummy No. 1770 until it was donated to the museum. After the scientists completed the autopsy, in which they took a very close look at the mummy's insides, they discovered three important things. Who remembers what they were?" This type of review is usually informal, but it must be stated carefully so students know exactly what to recollect. Ideally, the review leads into the next section of the text or to a discussion: "Let's read this next section to see what else the scientists learned." Or, if predictions about an upcoming section of a text have been made or hypotheses about an experiment developed, teachers can refer to these afterward and confirm or disconfirm them when the time is right.

One of the great benefits of having posted content and language objectives is that you can, at any time, refer to them during a lesson. We all know how easy it is to "bird-walk," a term coined by Madeline Hunter (1982). An eager student's hand goes up, you call on him or her, and for the next several minutes you hear a story about something that is only marginally (or not at all) related to the topic at hand. Other students chime in with their experiences, and before you know it, the period is ending. By referring, as needed, to your objectives during the lesson, it's much easier to stay on track, and students begin to distinguish between contributions that may or may not be appropriate to the lesson's topic.

One favorite wrap-up technique of SIOP teachers is Outcome Sentences. A teacher can post sentence starters on the white board or chart paper, such as:

I wonder . . .

I discovered . . .

I still want to know . . .

I learned . . .

I still don't understand . . .

I still have a question about . . .

Something I will remember is . . .

PD TOOLKIT™ for SIOP®

Click on Videos, then search for "Assessing Understanding: Phonics" to see an example of assessing students' understanding.

Children take turns selecting and completing an outcome sentence orally or in writing. They can also confer with a partner before responding.

A more structured review might involve students summarizing with partners, writing in a journal, or listing key points on the interactive white board. Toward the end of the lesson, a final review helps English learners assess their own understandings and clarify their misconceptions. Students' responses to a review can guide a teacher's decisions about what to do next, such as administering a summative assessment or, if needed, additional reteaching and assessing.

SIOP® | **SHELTERED INSTRUCTION OBSERVATION PROTOCOL**

SIOP® FEATURE 29:

Regular Feedback Provided to Students on Their Output

Periodic review of language, vocabulary, and content enables teachers to provide specific oral and written academic feedback to students to clarify confusing points and to correct misconceptions and misunderstandings. Effective feedback for English learners:

- **Supports and validates.** In order for English learners to receive teacher feedback, they must be able to provide output. Quiet, shy, and unconfident students can go unnoticed, and sometimes their coping strategies mask weaknesses in language production. Throughout this book we have suggested ways to encourage student interaction and participation. Perhaps the most important way to do so is through being supportive and validating when students do interact, participate, and engage meaningfully.

- **Is specific and academically oriented.** While support and validation are certainly important, how we do both is critical. For some teachers, it's almost a habit to say, "Good job!" or "Nice work!" or "Well done!" While these comments feel good when students hear them, they don't provide much information about what was good about the job or nice about the work. English learners and students who struggle need very specific academic feedback, and for some, it is best if it is given in private. They need to know exactly what they did that's right so they can do it again and/or build upon it. For example, teachers can model correct English usage when restating a child's response: "Yes, Amelia Bedelia really does want to do what's right." Paraphrasing also supports children's understanding and validates answers if we add after the paraphrase, "Is this what you're thinking (or saying)?" If English learners are only able to respond to questions in one or two words, you can validate their answers in complete sentences: "You're right! Amelia *does* get confused, or mixed up sometimes!" Also, consider that some immigrant students, who have gone to school in very different contexts, especially benefit from specific feedback as they are learning to negotiate a new educational environment.

- **Focuses on both content and language.** Many English learners plateau at the intermediate level, in part because they are exited prematurely from ESL programs, but also because when they are exited they don't have teachers who continue to develop language while teaching content. Therefore, try to encourage these students to use increasingly sophisticated words, phrases, and sentence structure by modeling their use in your teaching and during teacher-student conversations. Remember to continue to provide scaffolds as you did when these students had lower levels of English proficiency.

- **Includes modeling.** Teachers can model correct English usage when restating a student's response: "Yes, you're correct that the scientists *were confused* by the skull lying next to the mummy." Overly correcting English learners' grammar and pronunciation tends to shut them down. Therefore, simply restating the sentence with correct form, while validating, provides feedback that is instructive and helpful. However, if you want the students to start using the correct pronunciation or structure, you need to dedicate some time to teaching and practicing them. An explicit focus on form makes more of a difference than a teacher-corrected restatement of a student's response (Saunders & Goldenberg, 2010).

- **Includes paraphrasing.** Paraphrasing also supports students' understandings and validates answers if we add after the paraphrase, "Is this what you're thinking (or saying)?" If you know that some students are only able to respond to questions in one or two words, you can extend their responses in complete sentences: "Yes, *embalming* is the process of preserving bodies." But, always give students a chance to elaborate on their own first, with phrases such as, "Tell me more about that."

- **Includes facial expressions and body language.** A nod, smile of support, pat on the shoulder, or encouraging look can take away fear of speaking aloud, especially for students who are beginning to develop English proficiency. At the same time, a teacher's facial expressions and body language that convey frustration, impatience, or ambivalence speak volumes to a student who is trying to learn challenging content and a new language at the same time.

- **Can be provided by students for each other.** Partners or groups can discuss among themselves, giving feedback on both language production and content understanding to each other, and then report back to the whole class. The teacher can facilitate effective feedback by providing appropriate modeling of how it is done. Sentence frames also assist students in getting started: "What you said was really interesting, because _____"; "One word that you used that helped me understand your point was _____"; "One question I have about what you said is _____."

SIOP® FEATURE 30:

Assessment of Student Comprehension and Learning of All Lesson Objectives throughout the Lesson

The purpose of this section is to offer suggestions for SIOP lessons and recommendations for how to assess the degree to which individual students meet or are making progress toward meeting a lesson's content and language objectives. What is different for most teachers is that we are used to assessing students at the end of a lesson with a culminating (summative) activity in which students apply what they have learned during the lesson (e.g., a pop quiz, writing assignment, worksheet, and/or other activity). However, with the SIOP Model, teachers are encouraged to assess students whenever they have an opportunity, such as in the following:

1. The lesson begins with an activity that activates children's prior knowledge and experience, and provides an opportunity to build background for those who need it. This presents a great opportunity to assess who may lack background information about the topic and/or have difficulty with the content and language concepts in the forthcoming lesson.

2. During the lesson, while students are practicing and applying the lesson's key vocabulary and concepts, there is another opportunity to see who may need more review or reteaching. Informal assessments come into play here, including teacher observation, spot-checking with individuals, using group response techniques (such as thumbs up/down, individual white boards), conversations with students about their progress, and so forth.

3. At the end of the lesson, SIOP teachers assess which students have met the content and language objectives by reviewing them with the class. This final review of all content and language objectives is critically important. It provides you with information to guide the planning of your subsequent SIOP lesson. See suggestions for soliciting student responses to this review in the Teaching Ideas section of this chapter.

Some teachers who are learning to implement the SIOP Model express concern about having varied assessments throughout a lesson, in part because of the perceived amount of work it takes to create them, and also because some believe it is unfair if students are not assessed equally. While acknowledging this, we also believe that for English learners, assessment adaptations must be made if teachers are to ascertain accurately the extent to which lesson objectives and standards are met. Often, English learners do know the information on which they are being assessed, but because of language proficiency issues, including vocabulary, reading, and writing, they are unable to demonstrate their knowledge fully.

Therefore, to the extent possible, children should be assessed on their personal progress to determine if learning has taken place. In sheltered classes in particular, where students may have different levels of language proficiency, the value of this becomes apparent. If teachers gather baseline data on what their students know and can do with the content information before instruction occurs, and then assess what they know and can do during a lesson and after its conclusion, they can identify student growth more accurately.

Teaching Ideas for Review & Assessment

Review and assessment can be accomplished with individual or group activities. Group response techniques quickly inform a teacher about how well each student is progressing, and they are especially sensitive to the needs of English learners.

- **Handheld Devices.** At the time of this writing, there are a number of electronic resources that can be used with informal review and assessment. Handheld devices, such as clickers and classroom performance tools, can be used in many ways, including recording student responses, learning about concepts in measurement, practicing multiplication tables, and taking notes, to name a few. Teachers can use clickers for a group review: students hold their clickers and respond to a prompt with multiple-choice options. The computer records and displays the class results, along with the correct answer. Teachers can pose yes/no, true/false, or multiple-choice questions and students respond anonymously. The data are quickly collated and displayed so the teacher and students can see the number of correct responses and determine how many students might need reteaching. The exciting thing is that by the time this book is published, there will most likely be a whole new range of electronic resources to guide assessment and instruction!

- **Teachability.** Teachability (www.teachability.com) is a free, moderated chat room that focuses on particular topics of interest to teachers. For example, there is (at the time of this writing) a "community" for educators who are involved in the RTI process, including assessment and progress monitoring. There is another community of educators who are interested in learning effective ways to use handheld devices in the classroom. There is also a community to discuss issues related to teaching English learners. Check out Teachability for other chat rooms that may be of interest to you.

- **Word Study Books.** For young children (pre-K–grade 2), Word Study books can include the child's own illustrations as mnemonics (pictures to remember word meanings and usage), and/or rebus pictures for definitions (difficult words are represented by simple drawings, usually provided by the teacher). As children are learning to write, they can use their own Word Study books as references for spellings and meanings of the words to which they have had exposure. Usually, words are organized by the alphabet, but some teachers prefer to have them organized by sounds (such as open/long sounds or closed/short sounds, initial consonants, blends, digraphs, etc.).

- **Vocabulary Journal.** Rothenberg and Fisher (2007, p. 158) suggest a Vocabulary Journal for particular subject areas. One section of the journal might focus on multiple-meaning words. For example, a math journal might have four columns labeled with "Word," "Common Definition," "Math Definition," and "Where I Found It." The student might fill in the columns as follows: Word: *"prime"*; Common Definition: *"The best"*; Math Definition: *"A number that can only be divided by itself and 1"*; Where I Found It: *"In our textbook."* The Word Study Book and the Vocabulary Journal provide students with the opportunity to review words any time they wish.

- **Non-Print Review.** Students should be encouraged to review and practice words and idioms in non-print ways as well. Students may draw a picture to depict a concept or to remember a word. They may demonstrate the meaning through physical gestures or by acting out several words within the context of a role-play. The technique works well with primary grades and can be used for phonemes as well as words.

- **Games.** Playing *Pictionary, Bingo, Jeopardy,* and charade-like games at the end of a lesson can stimulate an engaging review of newly learned vocabulary and key concepts.

- **Rubrics.** Often, rubrics (such as the SIOP protocol) are used to ascertain a developmental level of performance for a particular goal, objective, or standard. For example, on a developmental rubric, student performance may be characterized as "emergent," "beginning," "developing," "competent," or "proficient." Other rubrics may communicate evaluative information, such as "inadequate," "adequate," "thorough," or "exceptional." Whichever rubric is used, the results of assessment and evaluation are often shared with other interested stakeholders, such as parents and administrators, as well as with the students themselves.

- **Thumbs Up/Thumbs Down.** Generally, this is used for questions that elicit "agree/disagree" responses. (If students agree, they raise their thumbs.) It can also be used for yes/no questions or true/false statements. Older students may be more comfortable responding with "pencils up/pencils down" (point of pencil up or down). Students can also indicate "I don't know" by making a fist, holding it in front of the chest, and wiggling it back and forth. The pencil used by older students can also be wiggled horizontally to indicate that the answer is unknown.

- **Number Wheels.** As a low-tech alternative to handheld devices, number wheels are fun to use and provide the teacher with immediate information about students' comprehension of content concepts. A number wheel is made from tag board strips (5″ × 1″) held together on a metal ring fastener. Each strip has a number printed on it, with 0 to 5 or 0 to 10, or a–d, depending on your needs and students' ages. Students use their individual number wheels to indicate their answers to questions or statements that offer multiple-choice responses. Possible answers are displayed on the board, chart paper, or pocket chart, and the teacher asks the questions or gives the statements orally. For example, if you were teaching a lesson on possessives, you could write the following on the board:
  a. boys
  b. boy's
  c. boys'

Each child has a number wheel and you say, "Show me the correct use of the word 'boys' in the following sentences. Remember that you can show me a '0' if you don't know the answer. 'The little boy's dog was hungry and was barking.' Think. Get set. Show me." Children then find the number 2 strip, and holding their number wheels in front of their chests, they display their answers. They repeat the process as you give the next sentence. Be sure to give the cues (Think, Get Set) before giving the direction, "Show me!" You may think that number wheels are only appropriate for younger students, but middle school and high school students enjoy working with them, too, and they provide you with much needed information about students' understandings of language and content concepts.

- **Response Boards.** Dry-erase boards can be used for group responses. Each student has a board and writing instrument. You ask a question and students respond on their boards and then turn them to face you when you say, "Show me!" Older students enjoy working with the dry-erase boards and will willingly use them in a classroom in which approximations are supported and errors are viewed as steps to effective learning. Dry-erase boards (12″ × 12″) can be inexpensively cut from "bathroom tile board," which is available at home and building supply stores; laminated tag board or plastic insert sleeves also can be used in the same way.

- **Numbers 3, 2, 1 for Self-Assessment** (Vogt & Echevarría, 2008). It's one thing for the teacher to assess student progress toward meeting objectives; it's something entirely different for students to assess their own progress and understandings. From our experience teaching students of all ages, when we ask English learners (and native speakers as well) if they have met a particular objective, the usual response is generally a grunt, a nod, or a "Yeah," often in unison. As an alternative, this activity is a quick and easy way to have students self-assess the degree to which they think they have met a lesson's content and language objectives. At the end of the lesson as you review the objectives with the students, ask them to indicate with one, two, or three fingers how well they think they met them:

3 = I fully met (or can do) the objective.

2 = I'm making progress but I need more help (or practice) to meet the objective.

1 = I didn't (or can't) meet (or do) the objective.

Depending on how students indicate their understandings of a lesson's key concepts (the objectives), the teacher can reteach, provide additional modeling, group students for further instruction and practice, and so forth. We have found that self-assessments that are directly related to a lesson's content and language objectives are far more informative than the typical students' "yeah" or "no" or "sorta" comments that arise when teachers ask the class whether the lesson's objectives have been met.

- **On-the-Spot Assessment.** This is another low-tech, but effective, method of gathering on-the-spot information when observing students while they work independently or in groups. Put several pages of sticky address labels (3″ × 5″ or a size of your choice) on a clipboard. As you walk around the room and observe what a particular student is doing, jot brief notes on a sticky note, along with the student's name. At a later time, you can transfer the day's notes to students' assessment files by attaching them to pages used for this purpose. You will end up with a consecutive list of observation notes that can be used for parent, ESL, or IEP conferences, and/or for grading purposes. The great thing about this idea is that you don't have to transfer your notes by writing, or input anything into the computer (unless you want to).

- **Stock Market** (grades 3–6). Stock Market is great for an end-of-unit review prior to an exam because it provides the teacher with information about student misconceptions, factual errors, etc. It's also lots of fun!

  1. Prepare *Monopoly* or other "play" money in denominations of 5, 10, 20, 50, 100.

  2. Generate content questions (some from an actual quiz or test you're going to give) so that you can assess your students' readiness to take the test. Mix challenging and easier questions so that you'll have at least 10–15 to choose from, depending on the grade you teach.

  3. Also write some trivia questions of interest to the grade level of your students (such as the principal's first and last name; the U.S. President's first name, the street name where your school is located, the correct spelling of the school's name, etc.). Students also enjoy questions about popular culture, such as the names of musicians, actors, etc., but take care to ask questions on varied topics so that your immigrant English learners are not disadvantaged because they lack background knowledge about American popular culture.

  4. On Stock Market day, group students heterogeneously (4–5 per group). This is very important so that all groups have a mix of kids, languages, abilities, etc.

  5. Provide each table group with one worksheet with two columns:

     a. for dollar "investments"

     b. for students to write answers to the questions you will be asking

  6. Each group receives $25. A recorder for the group must write an "investment" dollar amount on the Stock Market worksheet prior to the teacher's asking a question. Groups cannot risk more than 50% of what they have in their group's "bank." For example, if they have $120, the most they can invest is $60. You don't want to have any group "go broke" so they can't continue to play.

  7. Ask the question (either content-related or trivia). After students have jotted their group answer on the worksheet, walk around to each group and assess whether the response is correct or incorrect. If a group's answer is correct, the "bank" pays; if not, the "bank" (you, the teacher) takes the investment.

  8. Use both content and trivia questions, and alternate frequently, but don't let students know which type of question will be asked. If students miss

several content questions in a row, you know you'll need to do some reteaching later. To keep everyone in the game, switch to some easier trivia questions that all groups are sure to answer correctly.

9. Reward groups that are behaving well and are cooperating by secretly slipping them some extra play money. It's also fun to give bonuses ($25 or more) to groups for providing the correct spelling of answers to particular questions, either trivia or academic content. You don't need to "fine" groups for misbehavior or spelling; just reward or bonus them when they're on task, working well together, and conscientiously answering the questions.

10. If a group falls perilously behind, slip them some money so they won't go broke. If you do this discreetly, no one notices and the group receiving the bank's assistance won't say a word. For older students, you can call it a "loan," and require payment with interest.

11. Make the final question about content (not trivia) and tell groups they can invest all or some of their earnings—it's their choice. After the question is asked and answered, the group with the most money in the end is declared the winner for that day's Stock Market.

Differentiating Ideas for Multi-level Classes

The Center for Intercultural and Multilingual Advocacy (CIMA) at Kansas State University, based on recommendations made by Deschenes, Ebeling, and Sprague (1994), summarized types of assessment adaptations that permit teachers to more accurately determine students' knowledge and understanding. We have modified them somewhat to enable teachers to more accurately assess and give grades (when necessary) to English learners in a culturally-responsive way.

- **Range.** Adapt the number of items the English learner is expected to complete, such as even or odd numbers only (see Leveled Study Guides in Chapter 2 as another example). Determine percentages of correct responses based on the number of items assessed.

- **Time.** Adapt the amount of time the English learner has for completing a task, such as providing more processing time and/or breaking tasks into manageable chunks. Unless there is a requirement to have a timed test, allowing additional time should not impact a student's score or grade.

- **Level of support.** Adapt the amount of scaffolding provided to an English learner during assessments by asking an aide, peer assistant, or parent volunteer to read and/or explain the task, or even read aloud (and translate, if necessary and possible) the items for the assessment. Remember the difference between assessing an English learner's ability to *read* and follow *written* directions and his or her ability to complete a task or answer questions about a content topic. If you are looking for a student's content knowledge (not his or her ability to read directions), it is fine to have someone else help with reading or clarifying what the expectation for the task is.

- **Difficulty.** Adapt the skill level, type of problem or task, and the process for how an English learner can approach the task, such as allowing a calculator, dictionary, or simplified instructions. Once again, you are not reducing the expectation that the English learner should know the material—you're just making it easier for him or her to demonstrate understandings.

- **Product.** Adapt the type of response the English learner is allowed to provide, such as permitting drawings, a hands-on demonstration, a verbal response, or, if necessary, a translated response. Whereas native speakers may be required to write a paragraph summary or essay, it may be reasonable for an English learner to submit an illustration, poster-board explanation, or other kind of product that doesn't rely so much on sophisticated English usage.

- **Participation.** Adapt the degree of active involvement of students in assessment, such as encouraging individual self-assessment, assistance in creating rubrics, and cooperative group self-assessment. As you have read often in this book, content learning is enhanced for all students, but especially for English learners, through interaction and group work. English learners can certainly be involved in their own assessment progress, particularly in the upper grades.

- **Role.** When students are working in collaborative groups, they often assume roles, such as recorder, time keeper, reader, discussant, and so forth. While it is important for English learners to be able to participate fully, some roles (such as timekeeper) require less language. Of course, when a student gains language proficiency, he or she should be encouraged to take on a role that requires reading and writing.

The Lesson

Measurement and Geometry: Concepts of shorter/taller; lighter/heavier; holds less/holds more (Kindergarten)

The classrooms described in the vignettes in this chapter are in a small rural elementary district in the midwestern United States. Until recently, there were very few children whose home language was not English. However, there has been a substantial increase in the number of children coming to kindergarten with little or no English, and now approximately 30% of the children in the district's four elementary schools speak Spanish as their primary language. Nearly all of these children are native born, and most of their parents are immigrants from Central America and Mexico.

Most of the children do not have any formal preschool experiences, although some attended the day care facility at the recently built meat-packing plant where their parents currently work. In addition to the children who live in town, a large number of children, both English speaking and Spanish speaking, are regularly bused to school from farms and neighboring small towns. The three kindergarten classes depicted here have an average of 25 students.

The three kindergarten teachers, Miss Pham, Mr. Emerson, and Mrs. Baxter, teach mathematics each day after the reading/language arts block. The lessons described in the vignettes were designed to meet the following state Mathematics Content Standards for Kindergarten: Measurement and Geometry.

1.0 Students understand the concept of time and units to measure it; they understand that objects have properties, such as length, weight, and capacity; and that comparisons may be made by referring to those properties.

1.1 Compare the length, weight, and capacity of objects by making direct comparisons with reference objects (e.g., not which object is shorter, longer, taller, lighter, heavier, or holds more).

Teaching Scenarios

The following vignettes illustrate how Miss Pham, Mr. Emerson, and Mrs. Baxter review vocabulary and key concepts, and assess student learning in their kindergarten math lessons. Each of the lessons was planned to last approximately 20 to 30 minutes. The kindergarten classes are full day with substantial Title I funding, so instructional assistants are available, but not on a full-time basis. Because nearly all of the parents are employed, classroom volunteers are available infrequently.

Miss Pham

Miss Pham's lesson began with the children on the rug. She had a portable white board and markers, and she had written the following words on the board: *taller, shorter, lighter, heavier, holds less, holds more*. She had placed several objects on a table near the white board, including one large can of tomato juice, one small can of tomato juice, one large drinking glass, and one small drinking glass. She introduced the words on the board by asking the children if anyone recognized any of them. Several of the English-speaking children raised their hands, and Miss Pham called on them for their responses. The selected children who speak English read some of the words they recognized. Next, Miss Pham read all of the words and asked the children to chorally read them after her. Nearly all the children were able to echo-read each of the words as the teacher pointed to them.

Then, the teacher pointed to the tomato juice cans and asked the class which can was taller and which was shorter. Again, several hands were raised. Miss Pham called on these children, and one by one they came to the table. As before, all of the children who volunteered were native English speakers. The teacher asked, "Which can is taller?" and a student pointed to the large can of tomato juice. She then asked, "Which can is smaller?" and the next child pointed to the small can of tomato juice. Miss Pham smiled and said, "Very good." She then asked for two more volunteers who came to the table, and Miss Pham asked, "Which can is heavier?" and the first child pointed to the large can of tomato juice. The next child pointed to the small can when Miss Pham asked, "Which can is lighter?" The same routine was followed when the teacher asked the children, "Which of these glasses, the taller one or the shorter one, will hold more tomato juice?" Again, two volunteers (both of whom speak English fluently) came forward and each pointed to the respective glass. Miss Pham smiled warmly and said, "Good job, class!"

At this point, the children were directed to return to their desks. Miss Pham distributed a math worksheet with three lines of illustrations that were of familiar objects. The teacher orally presented the following directions while she pointed to the worksheet: "On the first line, cross out the picture of the *taller* item. On the second line, cross out the *heavier* item. On the third line, cross out the item that *holds more*. When you are finished, you may take out your crayons and color the pictures on the worksheet."

The children began working. Some made X's on the correct illustrations, while others looked around and followed the lead of the students who understood what to do. These students marked the same pictures as the other children. When some were finished and began coloring, others observed this and they also began coloring the pictures on their worksheets. When all children appeared to have marked their worksheets and were coloring, Miss Pham called the end of the period and the children turned in their work for the lesson.

One the SIOP form in Figure 9.1, rate Miss Pham's lesson for each of the Reviews & Assessment features.

Mr. Emerson

Mr. Emerson also began his lesson on the rug. Referring to a pocket chart, Mr. Emerson pointed to, orally read, and explained the math lesson's content objective:

- We will *compare* people and objects to see which are *taller* and which are *shorter*.

He then read and explained the language objectives:

- We will learn the difference between the words *taller* and *shorter*.
- We will create a sentence using "_(blank)_ is *taller* than _(blank)_."
- We will write a sentence using "_(blank)_ is *shorter* than _(blank)_."

Mr. Emerson held up pictures of a watermelon and a tennis ball. He reminded the students that in their last math lesson, they had talked about the words *bigger* and *smaller*. He wrote the words on the white board. He then asked each child to think-think-think (they all followed his lead and tapped their index fingers on their temples) and decide which is bigger: a *watermelon* or a *tennis ball*. The unanimous

4	3	2	1	0
27. Comprehensive **review** of key vocabulary		Uneven **review of** key vocabulary		No **review of key vocabulary**

4	3	2	1	0
28. Comprehensive **review** of key content concepts		Uneven **review of** key content concepts		No **review of key content concepts**

4	3	2	1	0
29. Regular **feedback** provided to students on their output (e.g., language, content, work)		Inconsistent **feedback** provided to students on their output		No **feedback** provided to students on their output

4	3	2	1	0
30. **Assessment of student comprehension and learning** of all lesson objectives (e.g., spot checking, group response) throughout the lesson		**Assessment of student comprehension and learning** of some lesson objectives		No **assessment of student comprehension and learning** of lesson objectives

decision was that the watermelon was bigger. He asked the students to think-think-think about which object was smaller; again there was a unanimous vote for the tennis ball. He reviewed with the children the word *compare* that they had used previously; they had just *compared* the watermelon and tennis ball to see which was *bigger* and which was *smaller*. "Today," he said, "we will *compare* people and objects, and use the words *taller* and *shorter*." He pointed once again to the words *taller* and *shorter* in the lesson's objectives.

Next, Mr. Emerson asked two of the boys (one taller than the other) to stand up. He asked the children, in pairs, to think and talk about different ways they could *compare* these two friends. He asked the partners to put their thumbs together (up high so he could see) when they were finished with the task. Mr. Emerson also asked the two boys who were standing to think and talk about the same question.

After about two minutes, Mr. Emerson asked the children what they talked about with their partners. One child said, "They're both boys." "Yes," Mr. Emerson confirmed, "they are both boys." Another student suggested, "They both have brown hair." Again, Mr. Emerson repeated the response, "Yes, they both have brown hair." One of the boys standing in front of the class said, "I'm shorter than Jed is." Mr. Emerson said, "Yes, Julio is shorter than Jed! And Jed is taller than Julio!" The children all giggled.

Mr. Emerson then asked all the children to stand with their partners. On chart paper, he had written the following: "_____ is *taller* than _____." He introduced the sentence stem and said that it could be used to *compare* two people or other objects. Mr. Emerson then asked the students to read (nonreaders could echo-read) the words *is, taller,* and *than* several times. Further, he explained that in English we can talk about a person as being *short* and we also talk about a person as being *tall*. He motioned with his hands what *short* would look like and then he motioned what *tall* would look like. Mr. Emerson explained that when we compare the height of two people, we can use the words *taller* and *shorter* (and he pointed again to the words in the language objectives). He used the words again in the sentence: "Jed is taller than Julio. Julio is shorter than Jed."

Next, Mr. Emerson asked the children to sit back down on the rug. He then asked all the students to stand up if they thought they were *tall*. Several students stood. Mr. Emerson then asked all the "tall children" to sit down except for two, one of whom was considerably taller than the other. He then pointed to the word *taller* as he wrote it on the white board and asked, "Who is *taller*? Raphael or Isabelle?" As he asked the question, Mr. Emerson held his hand over each child, emphasizing the difference in their heights. He asked the children to "vote" on who they thought was *taller*, Raphael or Isabelle. Mr. Emerson then asked the students on the rug to use the sentence starter, as he pointed with a pointing stick to the words on the chart paper, "I think _____ is taller than _____." He also asked Raphael and Isabelle to practice saying the same sentence, using their first names.

The children practiced with their partners saying the sentence starter several times, including Raphael and Isabelle's names. During this time, Mr. Emerson walked the perimeter of the rug and listened carefully to what the students were saying, intervening when necessary. The teacher then asked each set of partners to chorally use the sentence starter, inserting the names of the respective children, until everyone had a chance to practice the sentence in front of the other class members.

Mr. Emerson then asked two other children to stand, one of whom was considerably shorter than the other. He asked the class to talk with their partners and *compare* Graciela and Blaine, to see who was *shorter*. The children chatted and put their thumbs together when they were finished. Mr. Emerson flipped the chart paper and a new sentence starter appeared: "_____ is *shorter* than _____." The children repeated the earlier practice round with Mr. Emerson closely monitoring their responses, which was followed by each partner saying together the sentence with *shorter*.

Next, Mr. Emerson asked the children to return to their table groups. He provided each table group with several small trees and bushes (such as one would find in a crafts store). He asked each table group (three to four children) to sort the trees and bushes from tall to short (notice he was careful not to use *tallest* to *shortest* at this time). Once the children had finished this task, he asked them to again use the sentence starters to *compare* the trees, but this time they were to write the words into the blanks on the sentence starters. He modeled with a tree and a bush and used the sentence starters he had written on sentence strips on chart paper: "This tree is *taller* than this bush. This bush is *shorter* than this tree."

While the children were working, Mr. Emerson walked the room, monitoring and providing feedback, such as, "You two are working so well together. Can you show your sentences to your other table group members?" "Wonderful! I just heard you use the words *taller* and *shorter* correctly. You are doing a great job of *comparing* your tree and bush!" "Oops, let's check your spelling of the word *taller*. Can you find the word on the chart? Show me . . . that's right! Now, do you see what needs fixing? Good, now it's correct!"

FIGURE 9.2 Review & Assessment Component of the SIOP Model: Mr. Emerson's Lesson

4	3	2	1	0
27. Comprehensive **review of key vocabulary**		Uneven **review of key vocabulary**		No **review of key vocabulary**

4	3	2	1	0
28. Comprehensive **review of key content concepts**		Uneven **review of key content concepts**		No **review of key content concepts**

4	3	2	1	0
29. Regular **feedback** provided to students on their output (e.g., language, content, work)		Inconsistent **feedback** provided to students on their output		No **feedback** provided to students on their output

4	3	2	1	0
30. **Assessment of student comprehension and learning** of all lesson objectives (e.g., spot checking, group response) throughout the lesson		**Assessment of student comprehension and learning** of some lesson objectives		No **assessment of student comprehension and learning** of lesson objectives

At the end of the lesson, Mr. Emerson brought the children back to the rug. He reviewed the meanings of the words *compare, taller,* and *shorter* with the class. Finally, he reviewed the lesson's objectives, asking the children to respond with a silent cheer for each objective if they thought they had met it. The classroom resounded with silent, kindergarten cheers. Mr. Baxter concluded the lesson with, "Yes, I agree. You all met the objectives by *comparing* the children and the trees and shrubs, by using our key words *taller* and *shorter* when you were saying the sentences. Later, you used the words in your sentences. You also worked very well with your partners and groups. Nice job, kindergartners!"

On the SIOP form in Figure 9.2, rate Mr. Emerson's lesson for each of the Review & Assessment features.

Mrs. Baxter

Mrs. Baxter decided to teach the math lesson using Cuisenaire Rods to develop the math concept of comparison. First, she brought the children to the rug and explained that they were going to be learning about the words *longer* and *shorter*. She didn't write the words on the board because she believed that doing so would only confuse her kindergartners, especially the English learners; they didn't know how to read English words yet. She began by introducing how Cuisenaire Rods are used, and she held up several of the colorful rods as examples. She told the students, "Some of these rods are long and others are short. Some are fat and others are thin." The children nodded in agreement. "Today we are going to compare the sizes of these rods, using the words *longer* and *shorter*." She then asked the children to return to their desks. She distributed a worksheet with drawings that represented the various sizes of the Cuisenaire Rods:

On each desk was a box with some Cuisenaire Rods, and the children began dumping them out. Mrs. Baxter directed the students to find the sizes of the rods that fit into the diagrams on the worksheet. Most students did this with ease and began playing with the rods, using them to stack and sword fight. The teacher brought the kindergartners back to attention and she asked them to look at their papers with the rods. She then asked which of the rods was the *longer* one and which was the *shorter* one. One of the boys responded by pointing to the longest rod on the paper and saying, "Teacher, this one is *longerest* and this one is *smallerest*." Mrs. Baxter said, "Okay, let's use the words *longer* and *shorter*." She then held up two rods, one considerably longer than the other. She said, "See, this rod is taller so it is *longer* than the *shorter* one." The child persisted, "Yep, that's what I said. It's bigger." At this point, Mrs. Baxter realized the children were confused. "Okay," she said, "let's just use two rods. Pick any two off your paper and put them like this. She held two different-size rods up next to each other. "Which is *longer* and which is *shorter*?" Some of the children placed their rods like this:

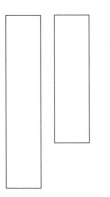

When Mrs. Baxter asked these children to move the second rod down so one looked "taller" than the other, the children became more confused. She decided at that point that kindergartners were not really ready for Cuisenaire Rods *or* superlatives in English, and they all took an early recess.

On the SIOP form in Figure 9.3, rate Mrs. Baxter's lesson for each of the Review & Assessment features.

| FIGURE 9.3 | Review & Assessment Component of the SIOP- Model: Mrs. Baxter's Lesson |

4	3	2	1	0
27. Comprehensive **review of key vocabulary**		Uneven **review of key vocabulary**		No **review of key vocabulary**

4	3	2	1	0
28. Comprehensive **review of key content concepts**		Uneven **review of key content concepts**		No **review of key content concepts**

4	3	2	1	0
29. Regular **feedback** provided to students on their output (e.g., language, content, work)		Inconsistent **feedback** provided to students on their output		No **feedback** provided to students on their output

4	3	2	1	0
30. **Assessment of student comprehension and learning** of all lesson objectives (e.g., spot checking, group response) throughout the lesson		**Assessment of student comprehension and learning** of some lesson objectives		No **assessment of student comprehension and learning** of lesson objectives

Discussion of Lessons

27. *Comprehensive Review of Key Vocabulary*

Miss Pham: 2

Mr. Emerson: 4

Mrs. Baxter: 1

In her lesson, **Miss Pham** introduced the challenging academic vocabulary by having those students who could already read the words do so for the other children. She also pronounced the words, followed by the children's echo-reading of the words. For the children who are native English speakers already familiar with the words and concepts Miss Pham was presenting, this quick review might have been adequate. However, for English learners and other children unfamiliar with English comparatives (e.g., *taller, heavier*), the very brief introduction was inadequate. Miss Pham did provide familiar, concrete examples with the tomato juice cans and drinking glasses to illustrate the challenging academic vocabulary, yet the only children who had an opportunity to demonstrate their understandings were the ones who clearly understood the concepts. By not providing many more opportunities for students to practice with the concrete examples, Miss Pham had little idea of which children comprehended the vocabulary and which did not. Her lesson received a "2" for this feature.

Mr. Emerson's lesson received a "4" for the comprehensive review of vocabulary feature. At the beginning of the lesson, he reviewed the academic vocabulary by going over the language objectives. He reviewed the words *compare, bigger, smaller* from a previous lesson before teaching the new and related words. He provided multiple opportunities for the children to practice using the words, and while they were practicing, he was able to monitor and correct, if needed. Because all students were engaged with every part of the lesson, he had ample opportunities to observe informally which students were having difficulty with pronunciations and usage. Even though many of the kindergartners could not read the words in the objectives and sentence stems, Mr. Emerson provided practice in speech-to-print match, a very important prereading and vocabulary learning skill. At the end of the lesson, Mr. Emerson reviewed once again the academic vocabulary for the day when he reviewed the language objectives.

Mrs. Baxter's lesson received a "1" for this feature. Unfortunately, she did not believe that kindergarten children were ready to begin using print because many were still nonreaders. Therefore, she did not have her objectives, vocabulary words, or directions for the day's activity on the board. She did, however, state the words *longer* and *shorter* for the children. However, the children did not understand why they were "playing" with the Cuisenaire Rods or why it was important to use the words *longer* and *shorter*. Instead of realizing that the children didn't understand what they were supposed to do, stopping, and going back to introduce the lesson objectives and explicitly teach the math lesson's academic language, both the teacher and children eventually gave up.

28. *Comprehensive Review of Key Concepts*

Miss Pham: 2

Mr. Emerson: 4

Mrs. Baxter: 1

Miss Pham's lesson received a "2" for this feature. The worksheet activity, intended for use as an assessment of the children's understandings of the academic language and key concepts of the math lesson, was largely ineffective because, once again, the children who already understood the vocabulary and concepts zipped through it; those who did not understand were able to mimic what the others were doing. In the end, Miss Pham had little idea of whether her English learners and struggling students had made any progress toward mastering the standards that guided her lesson planning. This happens too often when teachers assess responses only from those who volunteer, and when their activities, such as the worksheet, do not really provide assessment information about who understood key concepts and who did not.

Mr. Emerson's lesson received a "4" for this feature. As with vocabulary, Mr. Emerson reviewed the content concepts from the previous lesson before beginning with the new lesson. It was essential that the children understand what it means to *compare* (especially in math), so his examples were concrete and meaningful. Now that they understood the fundamentals (*bigger, smaller, taller, shorter*), they could move to the next steps (*heavier, lighter, holds more, holds less*), all of which involved more comparisons. In his lesson, Mr. Emerson carefully developed each level of learning, and he did so by continuing to review prior to moving to the next step. The practice activities, with the whole class, partners, and small groups enabled the teacher to assess on the spot and provide intervention as necessary. By continuing to develop these measurement and geometry concepts in a purposeful and sequential manner, all of Mr. Emerson's students, including his English learners and struggling learners, had the opportunity for success with the content concepts and with English language development.

Mrs. Baxter's lesson received a "1" for this feature. She made two attempts with the Cuisenaire Rods to have the students place their rods in different positions, but because she did not have clear content objectives for the lessons, the students didn't understand the purpose for what they were doing. The Cuisenaire Rods were also new to the children; they represented a novelty and seemed like blocks to play with rather than learning tools. Mrs. Baxter first could have used the rods on an overhead projector to demonstrate precisely what the children were to do with them. She could have said, "Let's *compare* these rods. Notice how this rod is *longer* than this rod. Notice how this rod is *shorter* than this rod. No matter how I place the rods, this one will always be *longer* than this rod. Watch while I move them. Now, let's *compare* them again." If Mrs. Baxter had provided explicit instruction and modeling, the children would have been able to practice with the rods, and she would have had an opportunity to review and assess their understandings.

29. *Regular Feedback Provided to Students on Their Output*

Miss Pham: 2

Mr. Emerson: 4

Mrs. Baxter: 1

Miss Pham's lesson received a "2" for this feature because she did attempt to provide feedback to those students who volunteered to come to the table and point to the respective objectives. However, "Very good!" and "Good job!" are comments that are ubiquitous in many classrooms, but they provide very little information to English learners about what the children did to deserve the warm smile and congratulations. Miss Pham could have followed the accolades with specific academic feedback such as, "Good job! You listened carefully for the word *taller* and then you compared the two cans. You saw that one can is definitely *taller* than the other." Holding up the two cans of tomato juice so all students could clearly compare them would have provided even more effective and specific feedback.

Mr. Emerson's lesson received a "4" for this feature because all of his feedback to his students was specific and academic. From the beginning of the lesson, he repeated his students' responses, extending each of them. He let his students know exactly what they had done correctly so they could repeat the behavior at another time. At the end of the lesson, after the children's attainment of the objectives, Mr. Emerson paraphrased the objectives one more time, repeating and reviewing the key vocabulary and content concepts that were the goals for the lesson.

Mrs. Baxter's lesson received a "1" for this feature because she provided little academic feedback to her students. She repeated and corrected one child's incorrect English, but because the other students had little opportunity to demonstrate their understandings, other feedback was not provided.

30. *Assessment of Student Comprehension and Learning of All Lesson Objectives*

Miss Pham: 2

Mr. Emerson: 4

Mrs. Baxter: 0

Miss Pham's lesson received a "2" for this feature because her objectives were not made clear to her students, and in reality, Miss Pham may not have been clear about them herself. Had she clearly thought through what her *lesson objectives* were (not just the state standards), she probably would have seen that it was unrealistic to expect her young students, especially the English learners, to be able to master the academic language and key concepts all in one lesson without considerable scaffolding. Each of the vocabulary words and math concepts should have been introduced, practiced, reviewed, and assessed before she moved on to the other vocabulary and concepts. Additionally, while part of this lesson could have been taught effectively with the whole class, many of the students would have benefitted from differentiated, small-group instruction and practice. "Backwards planning" (thinking ahead of time about what students really need to know and be able to do in order to accomplish this day's objectives), and then assessing and reteaching when students are not understanding, are critical elements of effective SIOP lessons.

Mr. Emerson's lesson received a "4" for this feature. Throughout the lesson, Mr. Emerson reviewed the progress his students were making toward meeting the objectives. He modeled what he wanted his students to do, he provided students with the opportunity to model with each other, he had his students work in pairs to practice further, and then he had the students practice their sentences orally with the entire class. Following the oral practice, the students then wrote sentences by using the sentence starter and filling in the appropriate words (*taller, shorter*), which were listed on the board. Note also that even though he was teaching math concepts, all of his students were expected to read, write, listen, and speak during this lesson, thus developing concurrently math content and English language proficiency.

Mrs. Baxter's lesson received a "0" for this feature. Because she did not have explicit content and language objectives, her lesson was poorly designed and executed. She didn't have a clear idea of what she wanted to teach and what her students should learn. Given the short attention spans of kindergartners and the ease with which they can move off task, along with the lack of an understandable purpose for an activity, the children created their own goals. By the end of the lesson, Mrs. Baxter had underestimated both the learning capacity of her children and the potential benefits of manipulatives like Cuisenaire Rods.

(For more examples of lesson and unit plans in math, see Echevarría, Vogt, and Short, 2010c).

Summary

As you reflect on this chapter and the impact and role of review and assessment of vocabulary, and content and language objectives, consider the following points:

- Review and assessment are integrated processes, essential for all students, but they are critical to the success of English learners.
- Informal assessment is attentive to the classroom context, is authentic and multidimensional, and includes multiple indicators of students' performance.
- Effective SIOP teachers carefully plan for review and informal assessment of key vocabulary throughout a lesson and at its conclusion.
- Formal assessments (e.g., standardized tests) require that students understand and apply content knowledge on tests that have high stakes. Therefore, it is important to teach, review, and assess English learners' understandings of the cross-curricular/process/function words and terms that are often found in test questions.
- At the conclusion of a SIOP lesson, teachers assess the degree to which students have met all content and language objectives.
- Most important, review and assessment guide teaching and reteaching, inform decision making, lead to supportive and academic feedback, and provide for fair and comprehensive judgments about student performance.

Discussion Questions

1. In reflecting on the content and language objectives at the beginning of the chapter, are you able to:
   a. Analyze the context of your classroom to provide more appropriate instruction for your English learners and other students?
   b. Identify the challenges in assessing content and language learning of students with limited English proficiency?
   c. Determine opportunities for reviewing and assessing key vocabulary and key content concepts in your lesson plan?
   d. Provide effective academic oral and written feedback to English learners during a lesson?
   e. Compare and contrast characteristics of informal and formal assessments?
   f. Explain the meaning of the following assessment terms: *formal assessment, informal assessment, authentic assessment, multidimensional, multiple indicators*?

2. Many teachers introduce key vocabulary at the beginning of the lesson, but often neglect to revisit the new terms systematically throughout the lesson and review them at its conclusion. How can you ensure that a SIOP lesson's key academic vocabulary is reviewed at the end of each lesson? Describe a variety of ways you would review the terms, as well as the techniques you could put in place to build a vocabulary review into each lesson. Which of the activities introduced in this chapter would you select? Why?

3. Research has shown that gratuitous compliments to students (e.g., "Good job" or "Keep up the good work") do little to motivate them or assist with their learning. Instead, teachers should give regular, substantive feedback to students on their verbal contributions and on their academic work. What are some ways to provide constructive, specific academic feedback to students? Consider class size and English proficiency levels as you answer this question.

4. Reflect on the ideas presented in this chapter, as well as all the other activities you have used to assess student learning of specific lesson objectives. How much time do you think you should allocate for review and assessment during each lesson? What if you discover (as is often the case) that some students are ready to move on, while others need more review and/or reteaching?

5. Using the SIOP lesson you have been creating, provide specific provisions for students at varying levels. Plan multiple indicators throughout the lesson that will enable you to assess on-the-spot progress toward meeting the lesson's content objectives. Then determine what you will do for (1) independent or partner work for students who are ready to move on and (2) a reteaching or review minilesson for those who need additional assistance from you. This is probably the most challenging aspect of providing differentiated instruction, not only for English learners, but for all students. How will you assess who is ready to move on? How will you assess the students in the reteaching/review group to determine if and when they're ready to move on? What will you do if a few students are still struggling? These are the *big* questions to ask (and answer) when planning for a lesson's review and assessment.

CHAPTER 10

Issues of Reading, RTI, and Special Education for English Learners

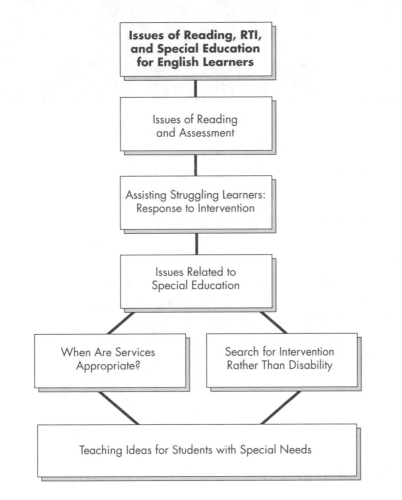

Issues of Reading, RTI, and Special Education for English Learners

Issues of Reading and Assessment

Assisting Struggling Learners: Response to Intervention

Issues Related to Special Education

When Are Services Appropriate?

Search for Intervention Rather Than Disability

Teaching Ideas for Students with Special Needs

After reading, discussing, and engaging in activities related to this chapter, you will be able to meet the following content and language objectives.

Content Objectives

Explain how linguistic differences in home languages and English can affect English learners' reading and writing development.

Describe in-class supports and/or modifications that content teachers can provide to English learners and struggling readers.

Delineate a sequence of steps involved in an effective RTI process to ensure appropriate services for English learners.

Language Objectives

Discuss with a group how to plan appropriate instruction for English learners who may have reading and learning difficulties.

Write a lesson plan that develops vocabulary and reading proficiency for English learners who struggle to read and learn.

In our work with teachers and administrators throughout the United States, a persistent question concerns appropriate instruction for English learners who exhibit difficulties with reading and learning. Teachers often feel ill prepared to provide content instruction for these children because they're not sure whether a student's difficulty is due to a reading problem, a learning disability, lack of schooling, or limited English proficiency. Response to Intervention (RTI) was developed, in part, to more accurately identify learning disabilities. In this chapter we provide a brief overview of RTI and we discuss issues of assessment, identification, and instruction for children who may be experiencing reading and/or learning problems. With more rigorous Common Core State Standards in place, a process for addressing causes and solutions for a child's struggles will be all the more important. ●

Although it is beyond the scope of this book to provide a comprehensive treatment of this topic, we hope this chapter will stimulate your thinking and discussion with colleagues about these issues, especially as they affect English learners. We begin with a discussion of reading development and assessment for English learners, and examine how RTI provides assistance to teachers and learners alike. We then move on to issues related to special education. (For a full discussion of RTI, see *Response to Intervention (RTI) and English Learners: Making It Happen* [Echevarría & Vogt, 2011]. For a discussion of special education and English learners, see Echevarría and Graves, 2010.)

Issues of Reading Development and Assessment

Teachers face many challenges related to the literacy development of English learners. The task of teaching English learners to read is made difficult in part due to the complexity of learning to read and write in a language they do not understand completely. However, it is not always possible for children to learn to read in their primary language at school. Therefore, teachers must find ways to help their students learn to read and write in English at the same time they are learning to speak and understand the language.

Children who are particularly likely to have difficulty with learning to read in the primary grades are those who begin school with less prior knowledge and skill in relevant domains, most notably general verbal abilities, the ability to attend to the sounds of language as distinct from its meaning, familiarity with the basic purposes and mechanisms of reading, and letter knowledge. Children . . . with limited proficiency in English . . . are particularly at risk of arriving at school with weaknesses in these areas and hence of falling behind from the onset (Snow, Burns, & Griffin, 1998, p. 5).

Research suggests that English learners need systematic, high-quality literacy instruction from the start. According to the Report of the National Literacy Panel on Language-Minority Children and Youth (August & Shanahan, 2006),

> Instruction that provides substantial coverage in the key components of reading—identified by the National Reading Panel (NICHD, 2000), such as phonemic awareness, phonics, fluency, vocabulary, and text comprehension—has clear benefits for language-minority students . . . but [these components are] . . . not sufficient—for teaching language-minority students to read and write proficiently in English. Oral proficiency in English is critical as well—but student performance suggests that it is often overlooked in instruction (August & Shanahan, 2006, p. 4).

To improve English learners' oral proficiency, the following suggestions are offered:

- Engage children in "picture walks" where English learners and native speakers take turns describing a book's illustrations, which they use to predict the story's content before reading (Lenters, 2005).
- Provide repeated readings of highly predictable picture or pattern books so that English learners can internalize and then orally produce the patterns, rhyming words, and rhythm.
- Record the reading of stories that can be listened to, then retold by English learners as they refer to pictures they have drawn about the story's content.
- Use the Language Experience Approach (LEA) to record on chart paper English learners' dictated short stories and/or experiences, such as what occurred during a recent field trip or their description of an event at school or home. After the dictation, the text is used for repeated readings, discussion, and instruction. LEA is very effective for developing oral language proficiency, vocabulary, and an understanding of English sentence structure. It is recommended that students have their own copies of the dictated texts so they can underline words they recognize each time they orally and silently reread their stories (Rasinski & Padak, 2004; Stauffer, 1980).

English learners may also need explicit instruction in the aspects of English that differ from their native languages, including the phonology (sounds), morphology (roots and affixes), and syntax of English (sentence structure) (Goldenberg, 2008).

A challenge that is particularly acute when teaching immigrant English learners to read in English is determining their reading proficiency. Children who arrive in the United States with well-developed reading skills in their native language have mastered many of the essentials of reading (Tabors & Snow, 2005), such as:

- They have learned that print carries meaning.
- If their home language is alphabetic, they have learned that phonemes (sounds) are represented by graphemes (letters and letter combinations), and that when put together these graphemes create words and meaning (the alphabetic principle).
- They have also learned the syntax (sentence structure) of their first language, and although they may be challenged by learning English syntax, they can use their knowledge of their first language's structure to make connections with English.
- Also, once students have learned what it means to strategically comprehend text in their native language, they are able to transfer cognitive, metacognitive, and language learning strategies from their home language to English (August, 2006; August & Shanahan, 2006; Genesee, Lindholm-Leary, Saunders, & Christian, 2006; Goldenberg, 2008; Gutiérrez, 2004; McLaughlin, 2012).
- English learners whose first language is non-alphabetic (such as Mandarin) will need to learn an alphabetic sound–symbol system in order to speak, read, and write English, but they will carry over to their new language their understandings of the reading and writing processes.

Therefore, students who read satisfactorily in their primary language do not have to relearn how to read or write. However, they do need to learn English. With comprehensible input and explicit instruction in the structure of English, they have a better chance of transferring their existing reading skills to the reading of English.

For example, for students whose primary language is Spanish, there are many cognates that link English vocabulary and spelling with Spanish (*estudiar* = study; *excepción* = exception). Using dictionaries in Spanish, English, French, and German as resources helps students make these connections as they explore similarities in these languages (Helman, Bear, Templeton, & Invernizzi, 2011).

It is also clear that English learners need to be immersed in print, with many opportunities to read books, stories, and informational texts that are at or a little above their level, ideally in their home language as well as in English (Krashen, 2003). English learners benefit when they learn to read and write in both their native language and in English (August & Shanahan, 2006; Genesee, Lindholm-Leary, Saunders, & Christian, 2006; Goldenberg, 2008; Slavin & Cheung, 2004).

In contrast to those English learners who have well-developed literacy skills in their primary language, other students enter U.S. schools with little or no reading instruction in their primary language, or they find reading and writing very difficult. These students are often referred to special education programs inappropriately, when other interventions may be more appropriate, such as longer exposure to high-quality, scaffolded instruction; more direct, small-group, or individual instruction; or referral to a reading specialist. It is important that teachers know whether their English learners can read in their primary language and that they are able to ascertain whether difficulty in content class work may be the result of a reading problem or a lack of English proficiency. If a particular child speaks a language that differs from other children in the school, it may be necessary for a community member who speaks the language to share reading material in the student's native language so that his or her literacy skills can be assessed.

Estimating Students' Reading Levels

Many teachers, rightly, want to know the "reading level" of their students. This information helps the teacher match texts to students' abilities. For example, if a fifth-grade student is reading at approximately the third-grade reading level, he is likely to have difficulty comprehending his fifth-grade social studies textbook without instructional modifications and scaffolding. Either the too-difficult text will need to be adapted or the student will require considerable assistance in accessing the content information from the text.

It is challenging enough to teach struggling readers who are native English speakers. With English learners, the struggle is compounded. According to Tabors and Snow (2005), "Knowing what a child knows—and in what language—is necessary before any informed placement or program decisions can be made. Often, however, assessment—if it occurs at all—only occurs in English, providing no information about possible early literacy strengths that have been developed in the child's first language" (p. 263).

Classroom teachers and reading specialists use a variety of assessments to determine their students' reading proficiency. However, commonly used assessments that yield a particular reading level (such as fourth grade) may be inappropriate for English learners (Jiménez, 2004; Vogt, 2014). For example, a common diagnostic instrument for assessing students' fluency and comprehension is an informal reading inventory (IRI). During this assessment, a student reads a series of increasingly difficult, leveled passages silently or orally. The teacher or reading specialist marks reading errors, asks comprehension questions, and, based on the student's reading proficiency, determines approximate *independent, instructional*, and *frustration* reading levels.

Think of your own reading.

- If you read for pleasure and enjoy lying in a hammock with a favorite book during the summer, you'll most likely select an *independent*-level text that doesn't require you to look up the meaning of words, take notes, or work very hard while reading. If you're reading at an independent level, you can read 100% of the words in a text without assistance (Treptow, Burns, & McComas, 2007).

- If you're taking a graduate course, your textbook should be at your *instructional* level. You expect to have assistance from your professor, and after a lecture or class discussion on the topic, the text is more accessible for you. If you're reading at the instructional level, you can read, with assistance, 93% to 97% of the words in the text (Treptow et al., 2007).

- You may experience *frustration*-level reading when you read detailed and complex directions that accompany a new electronic gadget, confusing income tax forms, or a text on a subject about which you have very little knowledge or experience. If you understand fewer than 90% of the words in a text, you're experiencing frustration reading and, even with assistance, you'll probably have trouble (McLaughlin, 2012; Treptow et al., 2007).

We know that it is futile to assign any students, native English speakers and English learners alike, text that is written at their frustration level (Snow, Burns, & Griffin, 1998). Instead, we need to select texts that are written at the students' instructional level, if possible, and that account for children's different experiential bases (Goldenberg, 2008), and then provide additional assistance so that the text becomes accessible. If this level and type of text isn't available, then we must adapt the grade-level text through rewriting, providing a detailed study guide, highlighting the key concepts, or providing detailed marginal notes (as discussed in Chapter 2). Without these, the instructional- and frustration-level texts will be largely inaccessible, especially for English learners.

It's important to remember that successful reading of any text is also dependent on a number of other variables, including familiarity with the topic being read, vocabulary knowledge, the flexible use of a variety of reading skills and strategies, motivation, and purpose setting. For students who are reading in their native language, these variables are relatively easy to assess, and the selection of appropriate text materials can be made with a reasonable amount of confidence. However, many of our usual battery of reading assessments may not yield reliable results for English learners, and selection of appropriate texts is considerably more difficult. A child who is assessed at grade level in his native language may be assessed as reading at a considerably lower level in English. Using results from an IRI or a standardized achievement test in English might suggest that the child has a serious reading problem. However, if he doesn't have difficulty reading in his native language, it's unlikely he'll have a serious reading problem in his new language. Likewise, if the child has a reading problem in his first language, he may very well have difficulty reading in English.

So how do we determine whether a student's academic difficulties are due to a reading problem or a lack of English proficiency? First, we need to recognize that the phonology of a student's native language may differ substantially from that of English. Although we may teach phonics explicitly and effectively, some English learners may not hear or be able to reproduce the sounds of English because these sounds do not exist in their primary language. The consonant sounds may be considerably different, the number of vowels may vary, and such things as vowel combinations, commonly found in English (*ea, ie, oa*), may be nonexistent in the students' home languages (such as Spanish).

As an example, consider Figure 10.1 and Figure 10.2 (Au, Garcia, Goldenberg, & Vogt, 2005). These represent just a few of the differences in consonants and vowels in English that may give speakers of other languages difficulty.

It's not just the sound system (the phonemes) that can cause difficulty for English learners. Because of English orthography (the spelling system), some English learners may have difficulty learning to read and write the language. Orthographies of various languages are described in terms of whether they are *transparent*, with highly regular words that are easy to decode (such as Spanish and Italian), or they are *deep* or *opaque*, with correspondences between letters and sounds that are much less direct (such as French and English). A language like German is considered to

FIGURE 10.1 Table of Selected Consonant Sounds

Key:
1 = Often a problem
2 = May be a problem at beginning of words
3 = May be a problem at the end of words

Consonant Sound	Arabic	Chinese	Hmong	Khmer	Russian	Spanish	Vietnamese
/b/		2	1		3	3	3
/ch/							1
/d/		2			3	3	3
/g/	1	2	1	1	3	3	3
/j/			1	1		1	1
/k/					2	2	2
/p/	1				2	2	2
/sh/				1		1	1
/t/					2	2	2
/th/	1			1	1		1
/th/	1	1		1	1	1	1
/v/	1	1				1	3
/z/		1		1		1	1

Adapted from Au, Garcia, Goldenberg, & Vogt, 2005, pp. R5–R6

FIGURE 10.2 Vowel Sounds

Language	Features
Arabic	8 vowels and diphthongs (compared to 20 in English) Possible confusion: Short vowels
Chinese	Fewer vowel sounds in Chinese than English Chinese is a tonal language. Each syllable pronounced with a particular tone that gives it its meaning.
Hmong	6 pure vowels and 7 diphthongs Hmong is a tonal language. Each syllable pronounced with a particular tone that gives it its meaning.
Khmer	16 vowels and 11 diphthongs Possible confusion: Short vowels that don't exist in Khmer (as in *bat, bet, bit*)
Russian	No diphthongs in Russian Possible confusion: Difficulty with /ûr/ after /w/ as in *work, word*; short vowels, such as short ă and ĕ
Spanish	5 pure vowel sounds and 5 diphthongs Possible confusion: Sounds of long ē, long ō (as in *pool*); short *oo* (as in *pull*)
Vietnamese	Complex vowel system with 11 pure vowels and many more diphthongs and triphthongs Possible confusion: May simplify long vowels in English; variations in the length of vowels in English may be confusing because in English they don't carry a difference in meaning

Adapted from Au, Garcia, Goldenberg, & Vogt, 2005, p. R12

be *semitransparent* because its orthography lies somewhere between deep and transparent (Helman et al., 2011). The point is that some students who have a primary language that is transparent (such as Spanish) may have a difficult time learning a language that is deep (such as English). However, in some studies that compare orthographic knowledge, bilingual learners have been found to negotiate satisfactorily between their languages and literacies (Tolchinsky & Teberosky, 1998). Rather than being confused by orthographic differences, these students can apply what they know about the structure of their primary language to the language they are learning.

English Learners and the Common Core State Standards for Reading, Writing, Listening, and Speaking

With the Common Core State Standards now adopted by the majority of states, it is imperative that all students, including English learners and those who are struggling with reading and writing, be provided with appropriate reading instruction that focuses on, among other things, close reading of texts. Following are some ideas for elementary teachers about providing the instruction and opportunities for English learners and other students to meet these challenging literacy standards, especially for informational texts (Buehl, 2009; Calkins, Ehrenworth, & Lehman, 2012; Ruddell, 2007; Vogt & Shearer, 2007, 2011).

1. *Implement the SIOP Model's 30 features to a high degree* and your students will be reading, writing, listening, and speaking throughout the day. As you've read throughout this book, developing English proficiency takes practice, practice, and more practice using the language.

2. *Engage your students in reading more high-quality, high-interest, nonfiction texts.* In many elementary classrooms, the preponderance of text material is narrative fiction. Teachers and children alike love a good story, but with the focus of CCSS on close reading of expository texts, it's important to balance your instruction and children's practice with plenty of interesting and motivating nonfiction texts. It's not enough for students to thumb through a magazine or informational book—instead, it's about the volume of nonfiction texts that students are actually *reading*. This requires having available an ample number of independent or "just-right" books from which students can choose to read. In order to move toward the close reading of complex texts as required by CCSS, students need to practice reading independent level texts and then work up to more challenging texts, without having to complete a worksheet. Rather, engage your students in talking about the text, the big-picture ideas, and the ideas they found compelling. Why was this text so interesting? What did it make you think about? What do you think the author's intention was as he wrote this piece? In part, close readings require students to "read beyond the information on the printed page or screen, and critically analyze the author's message" (McLaughlin, 2012). These kinds of conversations can begin with young children during and after teacher read-alouds of nonfiction texts that are about two grade levels above the students' reading levels. Children can listen to and talk about texts

that are too difficult for them to read independently, and when you engage them in critically thinking about something you've read, you're preparing them to engage in the same kind of thinking when they're able to read more challenging texts. (See Calkins, Ehrenworth, and Lehman, 2012, for specific ideas about how to find appropriately leveled texts and how to "nudge" students toward increasingly challenging reading material that requires close reading and structured discussion.)

3. ***Provide children with explicit and focused strategy comprehension instruction that is embedded in rich content and relevant texts.*** This can occur throughout the day in each subject area when you include primary sources and other interesting texts that provide the opportunity for students to work on the comprehension and learning strategies described in Chapter 5 (Strategies).

4. ***Engage your students in rich collaboration that promotes motivation and self-directed learning.*** Think about the SIOP component of Interaction and the Common Core Standards for listening and speaking. To meet the CCSS standards, students must learn to engage meaningfully with the teacher and with each other. Teach older students how to engage in discussions and instructional conversations about what they read (see Chapter 4), and model skills such as how to articulate positions, defend statements with specific evidence from the text, and analyze the author's perspective. Some students will benefit from relevant sentence frames during this instruction and practice: "From the text, I learned. . . ."; "I think _____ because in the text, I read that _____"; "I don't believe _____, because _____"; "The most important point the author made was _____ because _____"; "In the text I read that _____, but I question that because _____."

So what do we do about those who *are* confused, and despite appropriate instruction in English, reading, and language arts, are not making satisfactory progress? First, as discussed in Chapter 9, it's important to examine the students' present classroom context as it relates to literacy strengths and needs. The following questions might guide this inquiry:

1. What evidence do you have that a particular student is having difficulty with reading?

2. Do you have any evidence that this student has difficulty reading in his or her home language? If not, how might you gather some? If you are not fluent in the student's language, is there another student who is? Is there a community liaison or family member who can provide information about the student's L1 literacy development?

3. If your evidence points to a reading problem, what instructional supports and/or modifications have you and other teachers tried to accommodate the student's needs?
   a. Are the student's teachers adapting content and texts to provide greater accessibility (see Chapter 2)?
   b. Are the teachers using instructional techniques that make the content and expectations understandable for English learners (see Chapter 4)?

c. Are the student's teachers incorporating cognitive, metacognitive, and language learning strategy instruction in the ESL, language arts, and content subjects (see Chapter 5)?

d. Are the student's teachers scaffolding instruction through flexible grouping that promotes interaction between the teacher and students, and among students (see Chapters 5 and 6)?

e. Are the student's teachers providing multiple opportunities for practice and application of key content and language concepts (see Chapter 7)?

f. Are the student's teachers using effective assessment to determine what the student knows and can do related to content and language objectives, and to plan subsequent reteaching lessons (see Chapter 9)?

At this point, we hope you're getting the idea that appropriate instruction for this student involves all of the components of the SIOP Model—those listed above as well as appropriate pacing, meaningful activities, sufficient wait time, and so forth. Certainly, a child with reading problems will benefit from the effective practices advocated in the SIOP Model as he or she receives an appropriate intervention for the reading problems.

Will this type of instruction overcome a serious reading problem? Probably not, although research on effective literacy instruction for young English learners is consistent with the features of the SIOP Model (Graves, Gersten, & Haager, 2004). But here's the key: If you (and your colleagues) have done all you can to provide effective English language development and content instruction using the SIOP Model and a child is still struggling with reading (or math), it may be appropriate and important that the student receive intervention. This might be provided by the teacher in the classroom, a reading specialist, or another service provider. And that brings us to Response to Intervention.

Assisting Struggling Learners: Response to Intervention

Response to Intervention (RTI) is a multi-tiered service delivery model that is used to identify at-risk learners early and to provide effective instruction in general education first (typically called Tier 1), followed by targeted intervention as needed (Tier 2 and/or Tier 3). Generally it consists of skill screening for all students, close monitoring of student progress, and the use of interventions to bolster student achievement. RTI is founded on the principle that *all children can learn* (Echevarría & Hasbrouck, 2009) and is designed to reduce the number of students eligible for and in need of special education services (often Tier 3 or another level of intervention). As you can see in Figure 10.3, all students receive high-quality core instruction in general education, while some receive additional services for as long as there is evidence that they need those services. The focus is on finding ways to change instruction (or student behaviors) so the learner can be successful. RTI involves documenting a change in behavior or performance as a result of intervention and assessments. In the IDEA 2004 reauthorization (Individuals with Disabilities Education Act), RTI was approved as an option for schools to use,

FIGURE 10.3 Response to Intervention: A Recursive Process

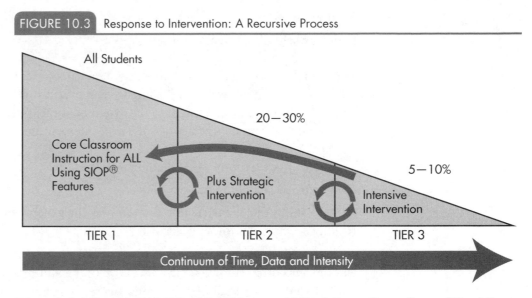

Echevarría, J. & Vogt, M. (2011) *RTI and English Learners: Making It Happen.* Boston: Pearson/Allyn & Bacon

and resources may be allocated from a number of sources such as Title I and special education funds (Tilly, 2006).

Tier 1 represents general education. Beginning in the general education classroom, teachers use evidence-based practices that work for the individual student and monitor each student's progress. Since the SIOP Model has been found to be effective with all learners—and is essential for English learners—its features should be implemented consistently to provide high-quality instruction for all students. The importance of high-quality Tier 1 instruction cannot be overstated:

> Within RTI, the frontline of prevention is Tier 1, or the general education classroom, where every student regardless of ability is to receive *high-quality* instruction. Thus, the preventive possibilities of RTI are only as good as the Tier 1 supports classroom teachers provide students (Brozo, 2010, p. 147).

Children in Tier 1 who are not keeping up may need extra support, such as some of the supplemental supports listed below. For many students, the extra attention will be enough to catch them up.

- specialized materials
- small-group or individualized instruction
- family involvement
- primary language support
- explicit teaching of learning strategies for students who need assistance in "learning how to learn"
- more intensive English language development
- modification of assignments

- counseling services
- Saturday school or after-school sessions

However, a subset of students (approximately 20% to 30%) who have received effective instruction may require more intensive interventions to meet their learning needs (Tier 2). Interventions should, to the extent possible, be scientifically validated through research. Some characteristics of Tier 2 intervention include:

- small-group, classroom-based reading intervention
- homogeneous grouping by area of need
- focused and targeted instruction delivered by the general education teacher, reading specialist, or other specialist
- explicit reading instruction that emphasizes key features important for English learners and other students, including developing and practicing oral language, key vocabulary, interaction, phonemic awareness, phonics, fluency, comprehension strategies, and so forth

The differences between Tier 1 and Tier 2 are the individualized nature of the instruction, the level of intensity of the intervention, and the frequency of assessments. Based on progress monitoring, the RTI team may find some students (approximately 5% to 8%) who have had systematic, effective interventions, yet do not respond (Leafstedt, Richards, & Gerber, 2004; Rinaldi & Samson, 2008). These students are eligible for Tier 3, which may include special education services. Few students would be in this category, and this consideration is based on a student's documented response to general education and Tier 2 interventions, along with the team's informed determination that an additional level of support is needed to increase achievement.

One of the main advantages of an RTI model is its emphasis on ensuring appropriate learning opportunities for all children, beginning in the general education classroom. All children receive instruction in the core curriculum, even those who receive additional services. In other words, Tiers 2 and 3 do not compensate for ineffective Tier 1 instruction. By focusing on interventions rather than learning problems, more students' needs will be met in the least restrictive environment, and decisions about student placement will be based on documented evidence over time.

Issues Related to Special Education

The previous discussion of reading is closely related to any discussion of special education because approximately 80% of referrals to special education are for reading problems. It is critically important that school personnel provide the support and assistance necessary when English learners exhibit learning difficulties, and exhaust every option through an RTI process before considering referral to special education. As mentioned, many reading difficulties can be ameliorated when they are identified early and when appropriate support is provided to the student. However, there are students with disabilities in our schools who have the right to an appropriate individualized education, and so it is equally important to identify those students for services.

In this section we touch on a variety of issues that teachers and administrators should think about when considering special education for English learners. Some issues include:

- **Overrepresentation.** The overrepresentation of culturally and linguistically diverse (CLD) students in high-incidence special education programs (e.g., intellectual disabilities, learning disabilities, and emotional disturbance) has been a serious concern for decades (Artiles, 1998; Dunn, 1968; Vasquez III et al., 2011). One of the issues related to overrepresentation is that "increasing diversity of student population, increasing number of primary languages spoken in many schools, and states raising the bar of the achievement expected of all students has placed additional demands on educators who are ill prepared to teach CLD learners or infuse appropriate practices to meet their needs" (Vasquez III et al., 2011, p. 85). Teachers may believe that special education is the only way to provide extra assistance to underachieving students. Further, teachers may have low expectations for CLD students or may misread their abilities due to their lack of understanding of cultural and linguistic differences.

- **Underrepresentation.** It should be mentioned that English learners are also sometimes underreferred for special education services for some of the following reasons: (1) teachers may delay referral so that children have ample opportunity to learn English, which deprives them of valuable early intervention; (2) low expectations allow English learners to languish without services; or (3) district policies require an arbitrary amount of time (e.g., 12–18 months before starting the identification process) to pass before students can be referred for the services they need (Echevarría, Powers, & Elliott, 2004; Limbos & Geva, 2002). Hispanic students are underrepresented in some regions of the United States (Skiba et al., 2008) and Asian/Pacific Islanders are significantly underrepresented throughout the United States (Cortiella, 2011).

- **Cultural differences.** Another factor may be that the classroom is not culturally responsive, leading to a mismatch between CLD learner characteristics and the materials and teaching methods presented in school, which contributes to underachievement among this group of students (Powers, 2001; Vogt & Shearer, 2011). Much of what students understand and are able to do in school is based on their culture and background, and most academic tasks and curricula reflect middle-class values and experiences (see Chapter 3 for more discussion). Reliance on paper-and-pencil tasks, independent reading of dense text in upper grades, and information presented orally are only some of the types of academic tasks that may create difficulties for English learners. Also, students who are culturally and linguistically diverse may not have the requisite background knowledge and experience to perform well academically, nor do they have behaviors that are consistent with the expectations of school. In general, students achieve better educational outcomes if they have been reared in a culture that has expectations and patterns of behaviors that are consistent with those of their new school (Comer, 1984). If that is not the case, then instruction such as that characterized in the SIOP Model provides the best opportunity for English learners to participate successfully in the academic program of school.

- **Underachievement.** Poor performance that often leads to special education referral and placement may also be explained by factors such as the effects of low teacher expectations (Jensen, 2008), poor study habits and poor time management, cultural differences in students' and teachers' behavioral expectations (Vasquez III et al., 2011), language differences (Cummins, 1984; Echevarría & Graves, 2010), and poverty (Smith, 2009). In fact, twice as many students in low-SES schools are placed in classes for learning disabilities than those from high-SES districts (Lynch, 2000). Obviously, all the complexities of underachievement cannot be ameliorated with good instruction alone; however, quality of instruction is a variable that makes a difference, and it is something that is under the control of school personnel.

- **Increased inclusion.** Teachers may be tempted to refer English learners who struggle academically to special education services, thereby relegating responsibility for meeting these students' needs to special education teachers. They expect these specialists to "fix" the problem. In reality, special education services are part of a comprehensive education plan for students who are eligible for services. Most students with learning disabilities spend the majority of their school day in the general education classroom. In fact, over 60% of students with learning disabilities spend 80% or more of their in-school time in general education classrooms (Cortiella, 2011), so all teachers share responsibility for these students.

- **Better training for school personnel.** Professional preparation programs for all school personnel should address effective instruction for English learners—general education, special education, reading specialists, school psychologists, and administrators. However, there has not been considerable progress in incorporating practices for addressing diverse learners into preservice general education or special education programs. There have been numerous calls for change, but few actual changes (Trent et al., 2008). Preparing general education and special education personnel to work together effectively with English learners begins at the preservice level. Teacher preparation programs (general and special education) that address issues of diversity, social equity, second language acquisition, culturally relevant instruction methods, and empirically supported interventions contribute to a teaching force that implements meaningful and appropriate instruction for students with differing abilities (Echevarría & Graves, 2010). Working effectively with diverse populations should be a priority for teacher preparation programs, especially given demographic trends. Further, RTI is becoming common practice in schools, and when intervention is necessary, it should be provided by a well-trained specialist who has a strong background in literacy and understands the needs of English learners (Vaughn & Ortiz, 2011).

- **Need for improved teaching.** Teachers and administrators in general education often fail to provide effective instruction in reading and math—content areas basic to learning in other areas—and also fail to manage their classrooms effectively (Orfield, Losen, & Edley, 2001). This is more often the case in urban schools where children have the greatest needs. When teachers feel unprepared to work with students who struggle academically or who exhibit inappropriate classroom behaviors, referral to special education is often the first option to which they turn. In many ways, a teacher is the key to a child's success or failure. Students' interactions with their teachers can be either disabling or empowering, and the quality of teacher–student interactions has a significant impact on academic performance and classroom behavior (Kea & Utley, 1998). In a study on teacher–student interaction (Yoon, 2008), it was found that when teachers treat English learners with respect and have positive interactions with them, English-speaking peers follow suit. In addition, English learners participate in class to a greater extent and learning opportunities are enhanced in such settings.

Effective SIOP teachers are culturally responsive; they reflect on their practice and are mindful of the interaction between the learner and the instructional setting, materials, and teaching methods, and they make adjustments as needed to facilitate learning. The importance of context to learning cannot be overstated; characteristics of the classroom and school can increase the risk for academic and behavior problems. Teachers need training in understanding the interaction between learning and context, avoiding the deficit model that views academic and behavior problems as a within-child problem. We have empirical and anecdotal evidence that many academic and behavioral difficulties can be attributed to the impact of the instructional setting (teacher, materials, methods) on the student, rather than some inherent problem of the learner.

PD **TOOLKIT™** **for SIOP®**

Click on Videos, then search for "Special Education: Elementary" to hear a general education teacher and a special education teacher discuss how they meet the needs of special education students in a first grade classroom.

In fact, in our observation of classrooms, it seems that the best option for struggling students may be the type of program offered to our most capable students. In those classes, teachers tend to capitalize on children's strengths; validate cultural and linguistic differences as resources; provide positive behavior supports; allow students time to interact and discuss ideas; and teach in creative, stimulating ways. Too many classes for low-performing students are devoid of an excitement for learning, and teachers often have low expectations for students' potential.

Special Education Services: When Are They Appropriate?

Special education services are designed to provide children who have identified disabilities with the support they need to be successful in school. Of the 5.9 million students with various kinds of disabilities who receive special education services, 42% have learning disabilities (LD). Although learning disabilities are real and last throughout one's life span, it is one of the disability categories in which identification is based on the judgment of school personnel rather than that of a medical professional—and the determination can be subjective. Some other "judgmental" categories include behavior disorders, language impairments, attention deficit hyperactivity disorder, and mild intellectual disability.

Actual learning disabilities are believed to be caused by differences in brain structure and function, and they affect the brain's ability to store, process, or communicate information. They may be passed from one generation of a family to the next, and may also be caused by prenatal and birth problems, childhood experiences of traumatic injuries, severe nutritional deprivation, and exposure to poisons, including lead. However, they are not the result of low intelligence; intellectual disability; emotional disturbance; or cultural, environmental, or economic disadvantages. Some other facts about learning disabilities include the following (Cortiella, 2011):

- Males comprise almost two-thirds of school-age students with LD who receive special education services.

- Conditions such as ADHD, autism, and intellectual disabilities are frequently confused with LD.

- The cost of educating a child with LD is 1.6 times the expenditure for a general education student.

- In 2008, 62% of students with LD spent 80% or more of their in-school time in general education classrooms, double the amount of time spent in 2000. Increasingly, general education teachers are responsible for the progress of all their students, with the support of specialists.

- Students with LD are retained in their grade much more often than those without disabilities. Also, they are involved in school disciplinary actions at a much higher rate than their peers who do not have disabilities.

- Only a small percentage—estimated at between 25% and 35%—of students with LD are being provided with assistive technology to support their instruction and learning.

It is easy to see the complexities involved in providing appropriate services to English learners who may have learning disabilities. Disproportionate representation of minority students in special education is most pronounced among the judgmental disability categories. For example, almost 24% of Hispanic students are labeled as having learning disabilities, although they account for only about 21% of the population, while 52.5% of white students have the LD label, but they make up 56.5% of the population (Cortiella, 2011).

The characteristics of students in mild to moderate disability categories are not as easily identifiable as they are in students with more significant disabilities and therefore require subjective judgment. Research indicates that it is very difficult for school personnel to distinguish between the challenges associated with acquiring a second language and those related to a language-based learning disability (Klinger & Harry, 2006; Lesaux & Geva, 2006; Skiba et al., 2008). The distinctions can be fairly subtle, as you can see in Figure 10.4. The subjectivity of identification is exacerbated because mild to moderate disabilities do not have a clear biological cause, prompting some to argue that the disabilities themselves are socially constructed (Barnes, Mercer, & Shakespeare, 1999). What is considered "normal" is influenced by a number of factors, including culture, age, community practice, point in history, and school expectations. The labels associated with mild disabilities may be assigned

FIGURE 10.4 Causes of Confusion in Assessing Students with Language Differences and/or Language Learning Disabilities

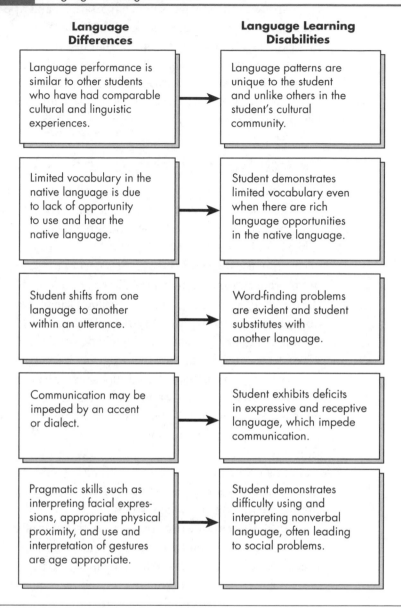

arbitrarily and are subject to extreme variability in identification rates. For example, only 1.8% of Asians and Pacific Islanders are identified as LD, but they comprise 4.7% of the population (Cortiella, 2011).

In determining whether a student qualifies for special education services, we need to ensure that the student has been provided ample opportunity to respond to effective instruction and intervention and that an appropriate process of progress monitoring and intervention has been followed. The reality is that a number of variables affect what happens once a child experiences considerable difficulties in the general education program—academic, behavioral, or both. For English learners, low English language proficiency, gaps in educational experience, and cultural differences influence the referral process. Moreover, teachers have a tremendous impact on who is referred and who is not. Research indicates that two factors influence referral: (1) teacher tolerance and (2) the interaction of perceived student ability or behavior with the teacher's own expectations and approach to instruction and classroom management (Podell & Soodak, 1993). Subjectivity is part of the evaluation process—including whom to test, what test to use, when to use alternative assessments, and how to interpret the results (Losen & Orfield, 2002). So if teachers have an understanding of cultural and linguistic differences and the modifications those differences require, effective instruction and intervention in the general education classroom is more likely.

Search for Intervention Rather Than Disability

When English learners struggle in school, they are referred to a site-based team that considers the reason for the referral and makes recommendations for interventions to be implemented in the general education program (Ortiz, 2002; Rinaldi & Samson, 2008). A site-based team approach offers the best way to address problems the student is experiencing because the team knows the context of the school and has the potential to provide appropriate, effective instructional interventions for English learners, especially when the membership of the team is diverse and includes individuals who are knowledgeable about issues related to diverse learners. Parents should also be included on the team since they offer valuable insight into their child's development and home life (Klinger & Harry, 2006). Rather than regarding the struggling learner as having an inherent problem, the team searches for instructional solutions that will accelerate the student's learning.

Site-based intervention teams have been shown to decrease referral and special education placement (Fuchs, Fuchs, & Bahr, 1990; Ysseldyke & Marston, 1999), and even to reduce disproportionate referrals of minority students to special education (Powers, 2001). Too often, when students struggle, the focus is on naming the student's problem rather than searching for solutions. The first step in considering intervention for struggling students should be to examine the quality of instruction in the general education classroom.

If the student does not make progress after intensive intervention and progress monitoring have been tried and documented, the student would be considered for special education services. All students placed in special education programs have gone through a referral, assessment, and placement process. In those states with an effective RTI process in place, failure to respond to intensive intervention would suffice for qualification. In others, a full battery of assessments is completed to determine eligibility for special education services.

Once it has been determined that a child qualifies for special education services, his or her individualized educational plan (IEP) will include instructional strategies and modifications that are tailored to demonstrated needs, including English language development (Echevarría, Powers, & Elliott, 2004). Further, instruction needs to be evidence based. Kretlow and Blatz (2011) identify the ABC's of evidence-based practice for special education teachers.

- Access evidence-based practice through journals and online resources such as the IRIS Center (http://iris.peabody.vanderbilt.edu/index.html) and Current Practice Alerts Teaching LD (www.teachingld.org/ld_resources/alerts/default.htm).

- **B**e careful with fidelity by implementing the practice in the way it was designed and tested through research. With the SIOP Model, we found that student achievement was directly linked to how well teachers implemented the model with fidelity (Echevarría, Richards-Tutor, Chinn, & Ratleff, 2011).
- Check student progress at regular intervals using progress monitoring and curriculum-based assessment.

Kretlow and Blatz (2011) conclude—and we concur—that "using evidence-based practices with fidelity and ongoing progress monitoring gives students with disabilities the best chance at achieving their goals" (p. 18).

Teaching Ideas for Students with Special Needs

In the section that follows, you will find some teaching ideas to help you prepare lessons that are designed for students who receive special education services.

- **Collaborative Strategic Reading (CSR).** This research-based intervention has been successfully implemented and studied in culturally and linguistically diverse, inclusive classrooms from fourth grade through middle school (Klingner & Vaughn, 1999, 2000; Klingner, Vaughn, Argüelles, Hughes, & Ahwee, 2004; Klingner, Vaughn, & Schumm, 1998). CSR includes strategies for summarizing information, asking and answering questions, monitoring comprehension and taking steps to improve understanding, and peer discussion. The structure of CSR is divided into before, during, and after reading activities.
- **Implement SIOP components.** The SIOP Model is effective for children with learning differences. In studies that included students with learning disabilities, students made significant growth in writing when teachers used the SIOP Model (Echevarría, 1998; Richards & Funk, 2009).
- **Use assistive technology.** Students with severe reading disabilities may benefit from computer programs that can scan words and "read" them aloud via synthesized voices, some of which sound almost human. Also, voice recognition software can help children who have trouble writing their ideas down on paper by pen or typing. It allows them to talk into a microphone and immediately see their words on screen. Some programs use visual prompts and templates to help organize thoughts, improve writing skills, and keep track of tasks. The effectiveness of such programs has yet to be determined for individual students, especially for those who have difficulty with numerous visual cues.
- **Focus students' attention.** Limit the clutter and excessive visual stimuli in the classroom. While we advocate word walls and other visuals to assist students in information recall and vocabulary development, they must be used with discretion. Students with disabilities may have difficulty focusing on important posted information when they are distracted by artwork and projects hanging around the room.
- **Use repetition.** Students will retain more information if it is repeated and reviewed frequently. Poor memory is often a characteristic of children with special needs, especially memory that is associated with symbols (e.g., letters and numbers).

- **Allow extra time for students to process information.** Students with learning differences are often just processing a question by the time the answer is given. Teachers may use strategies such as asking a question, letting the student know he or she will be asked for the answer, and then coming back to the student.

- **Scaffold assessment to measure understanding.** Students' disabilities can interfere with their demonstration of knowledge and understanding. These children may have difficulty with learning vocabulary, expressing their ideas, or using language adequately. Rather than asking a student to write an explanation of a concept, have him list the features of the concept or label a graphic organizer that is provided; ask the child to complete an outline rather than generate a summary or essay; or have the child select examples from a list provided instead of asking him to produce examples.

- **Differentiate the curriculum to students' needs.** Modify the number of items the learner completes; increase the amount of personal assistance; provide different materials to meet a learner's individual needs; or allot a different amount of time for learning, task completion, or testing.

- **Be sensitive to frustration levels.** Children with special needs often have a lower frustration threshold than typical learners, which may result in outbursts or giving up. A structured learning environment, scaffolded instruction, and opportunities to experience success help alleviate frustration.

All of these suggestions for assisting children with learning and behavior problems have commonalities: They must be used consistently; data are used to monitor student learning; student well-being is the focus; and there is a commitment to enhancing learning for all students.

Summary

As you reflect on this chapter and the issues of reading, RTI, and special education for English learners, consider the following points:

- Traditional reading assessments, such as informal reading inventories and phonics tests, may be inappropriate for English learners. Teachers are cautioned to not over-generalize the results of these assessments.

- Linguistic differences between students' home languages and English may cause English learners difficulty with literacy development. When classroom teachers implement the features of the SIOP Model, many children with reading and learning difficulties find success. Very often, students' academic difficulties have more to do with the curriculum, teaching methods, and classroom setting than with any disability the child may have.

- The SIOP Model provides teachers with a guide to lesson planning and delivery that offers an instructional program appropriate for *all* students in their classes: those with limited English proficiency, those who excel academically, those who are performing at grade level, those with low academic levels, those who find reading difficult, those who have experienced persistent failure, those who work hard but continue to struggle academically, and those with problematic behaviors.

- The result of an effective RTI process is that (a) fewer children from diverse backgrounds are inappropriately identified as disabled and (b) those who require special education services will have IEPs that include instructional strategies and modifications tailored to their demonstrated needs (Echevarría, Powers, & Elliott, 2004).

- Effective instruction and intervention offer supports to struggling students. Most importantly, we want to avoid labeling children with reading problems or disabilities and instead provide them with the most appropriate and effective instructional context possible.

Discussion Questions

1. In reflecting on the content and language objectives at the beginning of the chapter, are you able to:
   a. Explain how linguistic differences in home languages and English can affect English learners' reading and writing development?
   b. Describe in-class supports and/or modifications that content teachers can provide to English learners and struggling readers?
   c. Delineate a sequence of steps involved in an effective RTI process to ensure appropriate services for English learners?
   d. Discuss with a group how to plan appropriate instruction for English learners who may have reading and learning difficulties?
   e. Write a lesson plan that develops vocabulary and reading proficiency for English learners who struggle to read and learn?

2. Select an English learner in your class who is having difficulty with reading and/or content learning. Reread the questions in this chapter on pages 245–246. Begin with the first question:
   a. What evidence do you have that a particular student is having difficulty with reading? Try to provide answers to the other questions as they relate to your identified student.
   b. If questions 1a–e are answered negatively, what are the implications for your instruction of this student, and for the other teachers who work with him or her?
   c. Now examine Figure 10.4. From your work with this student, using your best guess as well as any assessment findings you have—including a measure of English language proficiency that you may need to obtain from your school's ESL specialist—see if any of the descriptions of Language Differences and/or Language Learning Disabilities match your student.
   d. If he or she is very young (four to seven), you might want to consider this: Snow, Burns, and Griffin (1998) recommend that very young English learners who haven't learned to read in their native language should learn to speak English first before they are taught to read in English.

    e. For older English learners (grades 4–8), what are some possible next steps for meeting students' language, literacy, and academic needs?

3. In this chapter we have discussed some of the reasons why minority children, including many English learners, are over- and underrepresented in special education. How can RTI help ensure that English learners are receiving an appropriate education and that proper services are offered as needed?

4. How would you respond to a teacher who says, "Well, if I follow the SIOP Model and make sure my English learners are able to access content using these activities, techniques, and approaches, my on-level kids and native English speakers will be bored."

    a. Do you agree with this statement? Why or why not? What research presented in this book supports your position?

    b. How can teachers with only a few English learners in their classrooms organize instruction so that all students' needs are met?

    c. Which, if any, of the activities, methods, or SIOP features in this book are inappropriate for some students, such as accelerated learners?

    d. Recent research has shown that all students benefit from high-quality SIOP Model lessons. But from our experience, some teachers think otherwise. Prepare a response to these teachers' concerns.

CHAPTER 11

Effective Use of the SIOP® Protocol

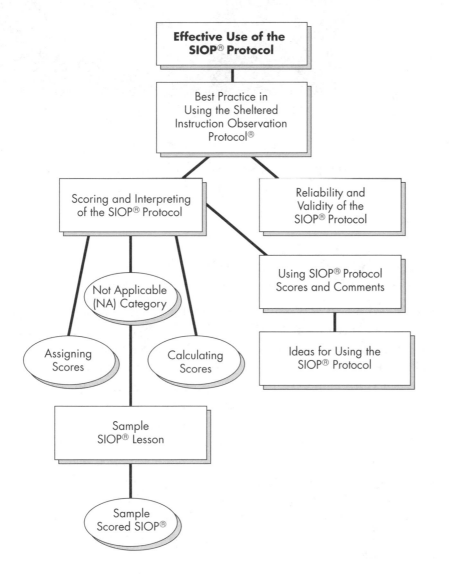

Effective Use of the SIOP® Protocol

Best Practice in Using the Sheltered Instruction Observation Protocol®

Scoring and Interpreting of the SIOP® Protocol

Reliability and Validity of the SIOP® Protocol

Not Applicable (NA) Category

Using SIOP® Protocol Scores and Comments

Assigning Scores

Calculating Scores

Ideas for Using the SIOP® Protocol

Sample SIOP® Lesson

Sample Scored SIOP®

After reading, discussing, and engaging in activities related to this chapter, you will be able to meet the following content and language objectives.

Content Objectives

Examine how all the SIOP features fit into one lesson plan.

Use the Sheltered Instruction Observation Protocol to score and assess a teacher's lesson.

Language Objectives

Discuss SIOP scores at a post-observation conference with the teacher whose lesson was rated.

Explain the value of observing and rating teachers over time on the SIOP.

Since its inception, the SIOP Model has been used as a lesson planning and instructional delivery system for teaching English learners effectively. Sample lesson plan formats can be found in Chapter 2, in Appendix B, and at www.siop.pearson.com.

The SIOP protocol, our observation instrument, has also been useful to educators in a number of ways. The SIOP Model and protocol have been used in school districts and universities around the country since the 1990s with measurable success. We have interviewed many school personnel who have told us their

stories of SIOP implementation (Echevarría, Short, & Vogt, 2008). From their stories and our experience with SIOP professional development, we suggest the following uses of the SIOP protocol. •

Best Practice in Using the SIOP® Protocol

PD **TOOLKIT**™ **for SIOP**®

Click on Videos, then search for "Using the Protocol" to hear a SIOP coach describe how the protocol was used to improve teaching.

Initially we developed the SIOP protocol because we found that school personnel and researchers wanted and needed an objective measure of high-quality sheltered instruction for English learners. Over time, uses of the SIOP protocol have expanded.

The SIOP protocol provides a tool for gauging the quality of teaching. Qualitative and quantitative information written on the protocol documents lesson effectiveness and shows areas that need improvement. This information may be used by teachers, administrators, university faculty, and researchers.

Teachers find the SIOP protocol useful for improving their own practice through self-reflection and/or peer coaching. Some schools reported that their teachers regularly used the protocol to reflect on their lessons, completing the protocol after they taught a specific lesson. More effective is the practice of videotaping lessons and scoring the lessons on their various SIOP features. The objectivity the camera provides is valuable to teachers in recognizing their areas of strength as well as areas that need attention.

Some elementary schools used peer coaches to assist teachers in SIOP implementation. In one school district, a coach modeled a SIOP lesson for a group of three to five peers. Using the SIOP protocol with the rating numbers removed, the group debriefed the lesson and discussed the components of the SIOP. The focus of the debriefing and discussion was around the comments written on the protocol. Participants wrote what they saw the coach do and described it on the protocol under each corresponding feature. At the conclusion of the session, one of the teachers in the group volunteered to model a lesson during the following quarter (two-month period). Because of the nonevaluative nature of the feedback, it wasn't difficult to get teachers to volunteer. The coach assisted the teacher volunteer in planning the lesson that was later modeled for the group. Feedback from the group was always limited to positive comments and a discussion of how the lesson matched SIOP features. After each teacher in the group had a turn at modeling a SIOP lesson for the group, the individuals then became coaches for another small group of teachers. In this way, a large number of teachers learned and practiced using the SIOP Model and had the opportunity to understand the model deeply (Echevarria, Short, & Vogt, 2008).

A number of sources have reported that schoolwide use of the SIOP Model and protocol provides a common language and conceptual framework from which to work and develop a community of practice. School site administrators commented that the features of the SIOP bring together in one place many of the ideas and techniques staff have learned through district professional development efforts. For example, a school staff may have received inservice training in use of technology, Thinking Maps, or differentiated instruction, but teachers may struggle with how to incorporate these varied ideas into their daily teaching practice. The SIOP Model provides a framework for systematically addressing and incorporating a variety of techniques into one's teaching practice.

The SIOP protocol is useful for administrators because it provides them with a way of understanding instruction for English learners. Administrators typically do not have the same opportunity to learn about effective instruction for English learners as do the teachers on their staff (Short, Vogt, & Echevarria, 2008). Yet the administrator is responsible for observing and providing feedback to teaching personnel. The SIOP protocol gives administrators a means for providing clear, concrete feedback to the teachers they observe. The format allows for rating of lessons but, more important, has space for writing comments that will be constructive for improving instruction for English learners.

University faculty have also found the SIOP Model and protocol to be useful in courses that specifically address the needs of English learners. Faculty who supervise field experience find that the SIOP protocol assists in providing concrete examples of techniques necessary for making instruction comprehensible for English learners and developing their English proficiency. Feedback on the rating and comments sections of the instrument assists student teachers in their professional development.

Finally, the SIOP protocol is a tool researchers can use to determine the extent to which SIOP instruction is implemented in a given classroom. It can also be used to measure consistency and fidelity of implementation.

Scoring and Interpreting the SIOP® Protocol

The heading on the first page of the SIOP protocol is fairly self-explanatory (see Figure 11.1). It is intended to provide a context for the lesson being observed. There is space for the observer's name and the date of the observation. Other information,

FIGURE 11.1   SIOP® Heading

The Sheltered Instruction
Observation Protocol (SIOP®)
(Echevarria, Vogt, & Short, 2000; 2004; 2008)

Observer(s): _____   Teacher: _____
Date: _____   School: _____
Grade: _____   Class/Topic: _____
ESL Level: _____   Lesson: Multiday   Single-day
                                                      (circle one)

Total Points Possible: 120 (Subtract 4 points for each NA given) _____
Total Points Earned: _____   Percentage Score: _____

Directions: Circle the number that best reflects what you observe in a sheltered lesson. You may give a score from 0–4 (or NA on selected items). Cite under "Comments" specific examples of the behaviors observed.

such as the teacher's name, school, grade of the class being observed, ESL level of the students, and the academic content area, is also included. We recognize that an observation at one point in time does not always accurately represent the teacher's implementation of SIOP strategies and techniques. Therefore, there is a place for the observer to indicate if the lesson is part of a multiday unit or is a single-day lesson.

In using the SIOP protocol, we have found that it is most useful to videotape a lesson and analyze it later. Teachers, supervisors, and researchers alike have found this to be an effective way of recording and measuring teachers' growth over time. The tape number may be written on the heading to indicate its corresponding lesson.

Finally, there is a box for the total score the teacher received on the SIOP. It is most useful to represent a teacher's score as a percentage because NA (not applicable) affects a total score number (see the next section for an explanation of scoring).

When scoring a lesson is appropriate, an observer may assign scores in a number of ways: (1) during the observation itself, as individual features are recognized; (2) after the observation, as the observer reflects on the entire lesson, referring to observational field notes; or (3) after the observation while watching a videotape of the lesson. The third option is often useful so that the teacher and observer are able to share the same point of reference when discussing the lesson.

It is important to stress that not all features on the SIOP will be present in every lesson. However, some features, such as items under Lesson Preparation, Comprehensible Input, Interaction, and Review/Assessment, are essential for each lesson. Over the course of time (several lessons, a week), all features should be represented in one's teaching.

Assigning Scores

An observer determines the level of SIOP implementation, guided by the scenario descriptions in this book. Each chapter's scenarios were designed to show a clear example for each feature, with scores ranging from 4 to 0. The SIOP protocol provides a five-point scale as well as space for qualitative data. It is recommended that the observer use the "Comments" section to record examples of the presence or absence of each feature. That way, both the observer and the teacher have specific information, besides a score, to use in their post-lesson discussion. More information may be added to the Comments section during the post-lesson review of the

SIOP protocol so that elements of the discussion are recorded for future reference. Also, these comments are useful as subsequent lessons are planned. In any case, sufficient notes with examples of how the feature was addressed should be included to provide concrete feedback with each score.

Naturally, there is an element of subjectivity to interpreting the features and assigning scores. Observers must be consistent in their scoring. For example, one person may think that for Feature #3 (Content concepts appropriate for age and educational background level of students), only grade-level materials are appropriate, while another observer may feel that the same content found in materials for lower grade levels can be used because of the students' low reading levels or because students have interrupted educational backgrounds. In either case, observers must be consistent in their interpretation and scoring across settings.

We suggest that to assist in more accurate scoring, the observer ask the teacher for a copy of the lesson plan in advance of observing the class. Ideally, the teacher and observer would meet for a pre-observation conference to discuss the lesson plan and provide the observer with background about the lesson. In this way, the observer is better able to score the lesson, especially the Preparation section and NA items.

Not Applicable (NA) Category

The Not Applicable (NA) scoring option is important because it distinguishes a feature that is "not applicable" to the observed lesson from a score of "0," which indicates that the feature should have been present but was not. For example, Mr. Leung taught a five-day unit on the solar system. During the first few lessons of the unit, Mr. Leung concentrated on making the rather dense information accessible to his students. He adapted the text to make it understandable for them and provided ample opportunities for students to use strategies. On the final day of the unit, an observer was present. Mr. Leung wrapped up the unit by having the students complete an enjoyable hands-on activity wherein they applied the concepts they had learned. It was obvious that the students had learned the content and were able to use it in the activity. However, because of the nature of that particular lesson, there was no observed adaptation of content (Feature #5). Mr. Leung was not penalized by receiving a score of "0" because the lesson did not lend itself to that item and because Mr. Leung had covered that item on another day. A score of NA would be correct in this case.

In the case of Mrs. Nash, however, it would be appropriate to score this feature as "0." Mrs. Nash also taught a unit on the solar system. On the first day of the unit, she showed a video about the solar system and had a brief oral discussion following the movie. The next day an observer was present as she read from the text and then had students answer chapter questions. There was no evidence that any of the content had been adapted to the variety of student proficiency levels in her class. In fact, many students appeared to be confused as they tried to answer questions based on readings from the grade-level textbook.

The distinction between a "0" and "NA" is an important one because a score of "0" adversely affects the overall score for the lesson, while an "NA" does not because a percentage is to be used.

Calculating Scores

There are 30 features on the SIOP, each with a range of possible scores from 0 to 4, or NA. After scoring each feature, the observer tallies all numeric scores. The score is written over the total possible score, usually 120 (30 features × a score of 4). So an example of a total score would be written 115/120. Because of the NA, adding the individual scores for a grand total is meaningless. It is more informative to know the total score based on the total possible score.

Let's take a step-by-step look at how a lesson's total score is calculated.

Mr. Leung's lesson received a score of 4 on 20 features, a score of 3 on 5 features, a score of 2 on 4 features, and 1 NA. The sum of those scores is 103.

$$20 \times 4 = 80$$
$$5 \times 3 = 15$$
$$4 \times 2 = 8$$
$$\textbf{Total score} = \overline{\textbf{103}}\textbf{/116}$$

The score of 116 was derived in this way: If the lesson had received a 4 on each feature of the SIOP (a perfect score), it would have had a total score of 116.

$$29 \times 4 = 116$$

The number of features is 29 instead of 30 because one feature was not applicable (NA); the lesson was rated on only 29 features.

Mr. Leung's lesson received a total score of 103/116. The total score can be converted to a percentage, if that form is more useful. Simply divide the numerator by the denominator: $103 \div 116$. In this case, the SIOP was implemented at a level of 88%. You can see the importance of distinguishing between a score of 0 and NA. For Mr. Leung's lesson, a 0 score would have changed the total score from 88% to 85%. Let's see how.

$$20 \times 4 = 80$$
$$5 \times 3 = 15$$
$$4 \times 2 = 8$$
$$1 \times 0 = 0$$
$$\textbf{Total score} = \overline{\textbf{103}}\textbf{/120}$$

The highest possible score on the SIOP for all 30 features is 120 (30 items × a score of 4). If Mr. Leung's lesson were rated on all 30 features, the total score would be 103/120, or 85%.

The step-by-step process for tallying scores is shown in Figure 11.2.

FIGURE 11.2 The Step-by-Step Process for Tallying Scores

---

1. Add the lesson's scores from all features.
2. Count the number of NAs, multiply by 4, and then subtract this number from 120.
3. Divide the number from step 2 into the number from step 1 (the adjusted possible score into the lesson's score).

In our research studies using the SIOP protocol for measuring level of implementation, we established the following guidelines:

High implementation—lessons that receive a score of 75% or higher

Low implementation—lessons that receive a score of 50% or lower

This indicates that a lesson (one day or several days) included all 30 features and each feature was rated as 0–4. Then the total score was calculated using the process in Figure 11.2.

Sample Lesson

In this section of the chapter, we will describe an entire science lesson conducted by a sixth-grade teacher and show how it was scored on the SIOP protocol. Ms. Clark received professional development training and has been using the SIOP for lesson planning and delivery for about 16 months. This lesson took place at the end of the first quarter of the school year. The class consisted of beginning ESL students from varying language backgrounds and countries of origin. The class has been studying a unit on minerals and visited a local natural history museum. The students have examined rocks in class as well. Ms. Clark provided us with a lesson plan before we conducted the observation.

In the classroom, the desks were arranged in three circular groups. Some students had to turn around to see the board and overhead screen at the front of the room. The class objectives and agenda were written on a whiteboard at the side. Two bulletin boards in the back of the room displayed the students' work for a language arts project and a science project. A Spanish-speaking bilingual aide assisted the teacher and also helped newly arrived Spanish-speaking students. The class period was 45 minutes long.

The teacher began the class by complimenting the students for their performance on a test they had taken on minerals and singled out one student who received the highest A grade in the class. She then asked the students to read the objectives and activities for the day silently while she read them aloud:

Content Objective: Today we will:

- create a semantic map by writing facts about volcanoes.
- identify the sequence of events that leads to volcano eruption.

Then she stated her plan for the day:

- First, I will demonstrate how rocks could move and what happens when they move.
- Second, you will use a semantic web worksheet to recall what you know about volcanoes.
- Third, I will use a model to show how a volcano erupts.
- Fourth, you will make predictions about the story *Pompeii . . . Buried Alive*, and then read pages 4 to 9 silently.

- Fifth, you will refer to information on page 6 in the book to write on a worksheet the steps that happen before a volcano erupts.
- Your homework is to draw a volcano and label the parts. The vocabulary words and terms for the day are: *melts, blast, mixture, rumbles, straw, pipe, shepherd, giant, peddler, crater, lava, magma, magma chamber.*

The teacher then demonstrated for the class what happens when rocks move against each other, using two stacks of books. After placing the stacks side by side on a desk, she pushed against one stack so the other stack slid off the desk and scattered onto the floor. She asked the students what happens when one set of rocks moves another set of rocks. The students responded that the rocks break.

The aide distributed semantic web worksheets to the students and asked them to write "Volcano" in the center circle. Then, in the other spaces, students were to write everything they already knew about volcanoes. While the students worked, the teacher and aide circulated to monitor the students' understanding of the task and to see how they were progressing.

After the students filled in their webs, the teacher led them in a discussion of what they had written and wrote some of their comments on the whiteboard:

- Lava melts and explodes
- When it erupts, all that force comes from the middle of the earth
- Volcanoes are formed deep inside the earth
- When a volcano is under water, the lava comes out and makes an island

The teacher repeated that she was going to make a model volcano and asked the class what a "model" is. One student answered that it is an example, not a real volcano. All of the students were watching as the teacher showed them a bottle and explained it would be like the magma chamber that is inside a volcano. She poured a cup of warm water inside the bottle. While it cooled slightly, she showed the class a diagram of the model for the experiment, with the corresponding volcano parts labeled. They discussed each part of the volcano and in doing so emphasized some of the key vocabulary words and terms: *crater, magma pipe, lava, magma, magma chamber, basin.*

The teacher returned to the model and placed a few drops of liquid dish detergent in the warm water. Next, she picked up an object and asked the students to identify it. One student said it was a measuring spoon. The teacher measured a teaspoon of baking soda and put it into the water and detergent mixture. She asked the students to identify where she was putting it. The students responded, "magma chamber." She put in a second teaspoon of baking soda and then held up the bottle for the students to observe, and then they reviewed the ingredients. To speed up the process, she added vinegar to the bottle. She asked them, "When was the last time we used vinegar?" The students said they had used it on the previous day. The "volcano" began to erupt, and the teacher displayed the bottle so that the students could see the foam overflowing.

The class reviewed the process and the ingredients for the model volcano. Individual students were called to the front to participate in a second volcano demonstration, each one completing one of the steps to produce another "eruption." The second "lava" flow was a bit larger than the first.

The teacher asked the whole class to think about "What causes a volcano to erupt?" and added, "We used warm water. What will happen to heat in a chamber?" One student answered, "Heat rises." The teacher explained that it was not just the heat that caused the eruption and asked them to think of the other ingredients and what happened when they were mixed. The teacher went on to explain, "The mixture of gases produces carbon monoxide," and wrote "carbon monoxide" and its chemical symbol on the board. She also asked them what they knew about plants and said, "They breathe in carbon monoxide. We breathe out carbon monoxide; we breathe in oxygen." [This part was an error, but the teacher did not realize her mistake in calling carbon dioxide (for plants and humans), carbon monoxide.]

One student wanted to know why rocks come out of volcanoes and another student offered an explanation, "The volcano is inside of a mountain of rocks." The teacher commented that whatever is inside the chamber when it erupts will come out with the lava, and if they had put small bits of material inside their model, those bits also would have come out when it erupted.

The teacher and aide handed out the storybook *Pompeii . . . Buried Alive* to the students, and they began prereading activities. The teacher focused their attention on the title and asked them to predict what they thought the book would be about. One student said, "Volcanoes erupting." The teacher asked, "Where do you think it takes place?" Students guessed various places: Nicaragua, Rome, Greece, England. The teacher commented on the togas in the cover's picture. She then directed their attention to the back cover and read the summary aloud, stating the story took place 2,000 years ago in Italy. She asked, "Is it a true story?" Some students guessed yes; others no. "How do you know it's true?" They discussed that the term "took place" and the use of a specific time in history meant that it was true. The teacher then asked for a student volunteer to point out Italy on the wall map, and the class discussed the location of Italy in southern Europe.

The teacher asked how many of the students came from countries with volcanoes. Students from Ethiopia, El Salvador, and Guatemala said they knew about volcanoes in their countries. One student asked if it had to be a hot country to have a volcano. The teacher asked if they knew where the most recent eruption had occurred. She told them it was Montserrat in the Caribbean and that volcanoes often occur in warm countries, but not all are in warm countries. She asked if they knew about a volcano in the United States and told them about Mt. St. Helens in Washington, a state that is cold in winter. She showed them Washington on the map. One student commented on the way precipitation forms and tried to compare it with what happens in the formation of a volcano.

The teacher directed the students to read pages 4 to 9 silently for two minutes. While they were reading, she distributed worksheets with a sequencing exercise to describe what happens before a volcano erupts. The instructions told students to put the sentences in order according to what they read on page 6. They could refer back to the reading.

The teacher began to read the passage aloud slowly about three minutes later, although some students indicated that they had not yet finished reading it silently.

As she read, she again displayed the transparency with the model volcano diagram on the overhead and referred to it and to the key vocabulary as she read. She also paused from time to time to ask comprehension questions. Students were able to answer questions orally, using the model and naming the parts of a volcano. They discussed unknown words in the reading, such as *peddler*, *rumbled*, and *shepherd*, as they went along.

As the period drew to a close, the teacher told the students they would complete the sequencing worksheet the next day. She reminded them of the homework—draw a volcano in their journal and label the parts. They were also told to place the webs they had completed in their journals. The teacher then led a brief wrap-up of the lesson, asking questions about a volcano, which students answered.

On the following pages (Figure 11.3), you will see how Ms. Clark was scored on the SIOP items and the Comments that provide evidence for her score.

Using SIOP® Scores and Comments

If lessons are rated, comments supporting the scores are essential. A completed protocol can be used as a starting point for a collaborative discussion between a teacher and a supervisor or coach, or among a group of teachers. We have found that videotaping a lesson, rating it (or writing comments without scores), and discussing it with the teacher provides an effective forum for professional growth. We also get valuable information from teachers explaining a student's behavior or why something may not have taken place despite the lesson plan that included it, for example. The discussion may take place between the teacher and the observer, or a group of teachers may meet on a regular basis to provide feedback to one another and assist in refining their teaching.

Scores can also be documented on a SIOP Lesson Rating Form over time to show growth (see Figure 11.4). Using percentages, teachers can see how their implementation of the SIOP features improves. This type of documentation is also useful for research purposes to document systematic implementation of the SIOP and fidelity of implementation.

Further, plotting scores on a graph, as seen in Figure 11.5, is an effective way to illustrate strong areas as well as areas that require attention, or areas teachers have highlighted as important for their own growth. If a lesson consistently shows low scores on certain features, this information provides the teacher with clear feedback for areas on which to focus. Staff developers and teacher educators may use the scores to determine areas for further discussion and practice in workshops and course sessions if several teachers are having difficulty with the same feature or component.

Finally, while the SIOP protocol is a useful tool for professional development, scores should be used with caution. Many variables affect the success or failure of a given lesson such as time of day, time of year, dynamics between students, and numerous other factors. Rather than just doing one observation and scoring of a lesson, several lessons should be rated over time for a more complete picture of the teacher's implementation of sheltered instruction.

FIGURE 11.3 The Sheltered Instruction on Observation Protocol (SIOP®)

The Sheltered Instruction Observation Protocol (SIOP®)
(Echevarria, Vogt, & Short, 2000; 2004; 2008)

Observer(s): J. Cruz
Date: 4/3
Grade: 6
ESL Level: 6

Teacher: Cloverleaf
School: Science
Class/Topic: Total
Lesson: Multiday Single-day (circle one)

Points Possible: 120 (Subtract 4 points for each NA given) 120

Total Points Earned: 94   Percentage Score: 78%

Directions: Circle the number that best reflects what you observe in a sheltered lesson. You may give a score from 0–4 (or NA on selected items).
Cite under "Comments" specific examples of the behaviors observed.

Lesson Preparation

(4)	3	2	1	0
1. **Content objectives** are clearly defined, displayed and reviewed with students		**Content objectives** for students implied		No clearly defined **content objectives** for students

Comments: Content objectives were written and stated at the beginning of the lesson.

4	3	(2)	1	0
2. **Language objectives** are clearly defined, displayed and reviewed with students		**Language objectives** for students implied		No clearly defined **language objectives** for students

Comments: No specific language objective was written or stated. Key vocabulary was listed, but the language skills to be targeted were listed and stated as activities and not written as objectives.

4	3	(2)	1	0
3. **Content concepts** appropriate for age and educational background level of students		**Content concepts** somewhat appropriate for age and educational background level of students		**Content concepts** inappropriate for age and educational background level of students

Comments: Students seemed to understand the concepts. However, several students mentioned that they studied volcanoes in earlier school years.
It is unclear why volcanoes were taught when these concepts had been introduced previously.

(continued)

FIGURE 11.3 The Sheltered Instruction Observation Protocol (SIOP®) (continued)

4	3	2	1	0	NA
4. **Supplementary materials** used to a high degree, making the lesson clear and meaningful (e.g., computer programs, graphs, models, visuals)		Some use of **supplementary materials**		No use of **supplementary materials**	

Comments: Good use of supplementary materials to enhance students' understanding of volcanoes such as copies of semantic maps, pull-down maps, a book, Pompeii . . . Buried Alive, a transparency indicating the parts of a volcano, stacks of books to demonstrate rocks pushing against each other, household items to illustrate a volcanic eruption.

4	3	2	1	0	NA
5. **Adaptation of content** (e.g., text, assignment) to all levels of student proficiency		Some **adaption of content** to all levels of student proficiency		No significant **adaption of content** to all levels of student proficiency	

Comments: All students were given the same text with which to work. There were no specific adaptations made to the text itself to address the varying levels of language proficiency. However, the teacher had prepared a sequencing activity for students to complete where she identified sentences that explained the process of a volcanic eruption and students were required to put the steps in order. In addition, she began reading the text aloud to the students and paused frequently to ask questions and to check for clarification.

4	3	2	1	0	NA
6. **Meaningful activities** that integrate lesson concepts (e.g., surveys, letter writing, simulations, models) with language practice opportunities for reading, writing, listening, and/or speaking		**Meaningful activities** that integrate lesson concepts but provide little opportunity for language practice with opportunities for reading, writing, listening, and/or speaking		No **meaningful activities** that integrate lesson concepts with language practice	

Comments: There were a lot of meaningful and interesting activities that provided students with language practice (e.g., participation in building the model volcano, discussing information from their semantic maps about volcanoes, and reading authentic text).

Building Background

4	3	2	1	0	NA
7. **Concepts explicitly linked** to students' background experiences		**Concepts loosely linked** to students' background experiences		**Concepts not explicitly linked** to students' background experiences	

Comments: The teacher tapped into students' understanding of volcanoes by asking them to complete a semantic mapping exercise writing everything they knew about volcanoes.

8. Links explicitly made between past learning and new concepts

4	3	②	1	0
Links explicitly made between past learning and new concepts		**Few links made** between past learning and new concepts		**No links made** between past learning and new concepts

Comments: There were few links made between past learning and its connection to new concepts. The teacher initiated the class by reminding the students of the visit to the Museum of Natural History and also reminded them of the rocks they had brought in. However, she did not explain how the visit or the collection of rocks related to that day's lesson about volcanoes.

9. Key vocabulary emphasized (e.g., introduced, written, repeated, and highlighted for students to see)

④	3	2	1	0
Key vocabulary emphasized (e.g., introduced, written, repeated, and highlighted for students to see)		**Key vocabulary** introduced, but not emphasized		**Key vocabulary** not introduced or emphasized

Comments: The key vocabulary words used for this lesson were written on the board, stated to the students at the beginning of the lesson, and reiterated throughout the lesson, particularly when the teacher and students constructed the model volcano.

Comprehensible Input

10. Speech appropriate for students' proficiency levels (e.g., slower rate, enunciation, and simple sentence structure for beginners)

④	3	2	1	0
Speech appropriate for students' proficiency levels (e.g., slower rate, enunciation, and simple sentence structure for beginners)		**Speech** sometimes inappropriate for students' proficiency levels		**Speech** inappropriate for students' proficiency levels

Comments: The teacher explained tasks well and modeled the demonstrations first before the students participated.

11. Clear explanation of academic tasks

④	3	2	1	0
Clear explanation of academic tasks		**Unclear explanation of** academic tasks		**No explanation** of academic tasks

Comments: The teacher explained tasks well and modeled the demonstrations first before the students participated.

(continued)

FIGURE 11.3 The Sheltered Instruction Observation Protocol (SIOP®) (continued)

4	3	2	1	0
12. A **variety of techniques** used to make content concepts clear (e.g., modeling, visuals, hands-on activities, demonstrations, gestures, body language) ④		Some **techniques** used to make content concepts clear		No **techniques** used to make content concepts clear

Comments: A variety of techniques were used in this lesson: the use of the overhead transparency with a diagram of a volcano and the labeled parts, brainstorming in the semantic mapping activity, demonstrating a model of a volcanic eruption, and reading about the topic after exploring it orally and visually. Used sequencing steps to check reading comprehension.

Strategies

4	3	2	1	0
13. Ample opportunities provided for students to use **learning strategies**	③	Inadequate opportunities provided for students to use **learning strategies**		No opportunity provided for students to use **learning strategies**

Comments: The teacher used various strategies with students such as accessing prior knowledge and having them make predictions. Students, however, used these strategies with the teacher, not with other students.

4	3	2	1	0
14. **Scaffolding techniques** consistently used, assisting and supporting student understanding (e.g., think-alouds) ④		**Scaffolding techniques** occasionally used		**Scaffolding techniques** not used

Comments: The teacher used various scaffolding techniques throughout the lesson to promote and assess students' comprehension of content concepts by means of questions, visuals, models, graphic organizers, prereading predictions, and demonstrations.

4	3	2	1	0
15. A **variety of questions or tasks that promote higher-order thinking skills** (e.g., literal, analytical, and interpretive questions)	③	Infrequent **questions or tasks that promote higher-order thinking skills**		No **questions or tasks that promote higher-order thinking skills**

Comments: Most of the questions for this beginning level consisted of more factual/identification questions. In some cases, more elaborated responses were required of students, for example, "What happens when one set of rocks moves against another?" "Can you think of other places in the world where eruptions have occurred?" "Tell me about volcanoes in your country?" "How do you know this is a true story?"

Interaction

16.

4	3	2	1	0
Frequent opportunities for **interaction** and discussion between teacher/student and among students, which encourage elaborated responses about lesson concepts	③	**Interaction** mostly teacher-dominated with some opportunities for students to talk about or question lesson concepts		**Interaction** teacher-dominated with no opportunities for students to discuss lesson concepts

Comments: The teacher engaged the students in discussions about volcanoes throughout the class period. The semantic mapping exercise, the demonstration, and the prereading activity were all means that facilitated student interaction. The majority of interactions were teacher-student.

17. Grouping configurations support language and content objectives of the lesson

4	3	2	1	0
Grouping configurations support language and content objectives of the lesson	3	**Grouping configurations** unevenly support the language and content objectives ②		**Grouping configurations** do not support the language and content objectives

Comments: Although students were seated in groups, there was little opportunity for them to interact to practice their language skills. The whole-class setting supported the demonstration about volcanic eruption.

18.

4	3	2	1	0
Sufficient **wait time for student responses** consistently provided ④	3	Sufficient **wait time for student responses** occasionally provided		Sufficient **wait time for student responses** not provided

Comments: At times there were students who wanted to respond but were overlooked, perhaps because the period was running out of time. For those students selected to respond, the teacher allowed them time to articulate their thoughts.

19.

4	3	2	1	0	NA
Ample opportunities for students to **clarify key concepts in L1** as needed with aide, peer, or L1 text	③	Some opportunities for students to **clarify key concepts in L1**		No opportunities for students to **clarify key concepts in L1**	NA

Comments: Only a few students could be identified as using their L1 during the lesson, and they were seated in the far left corner of the classroom where the bilingual aide assisted them. The other students in the classroom did not seem to need to use their L1 text.

Practice/Application

20.

4	3	2	1	0	NA
Hands-on materials and/or manipulatives provided for students to practice using new content knowledge	③	**Few hands-on materials and/or manipulatives** provided for students to practice using new content knowledge		**No hands-on materials and/or manipulatives** provided for students to practice using new content knowledge	NA

Comments: The lesson involved manipulatives. During the experiment/demonstration for the volcanic eruption, for example, the teacher used materials such as a bottle, liquid detergent, warm water, measuring spoons, baking soda, and vinegar. Only a few students, though, used these materials themselves.

(continued)

FIGURE 11.3 The Sheltered Instruction Observation Protocol (SIOP®) (continued)

4	3	2	1	0	NA
21. Activities provided for students to **apply content and language knowledge** in the classroom	③	Activities provided for students to **apply either content or language knowledge** in the classroom	1	No activities provided for students to **apply content or language knowledge** in the classroom	NA

Comments: For the most part, students applied content and language. More student-student interactions would have been beneficial and provided better opportunities for assessment.

4	3	2	1	0	NA
22. Activities integrate all **language skills** (i.e., reading, writing, listening, and speaking)	③	Activities integrate some **language skills**	1	Activities do not integrate **language skills**	

Comments: The lesson allowed students an opportunity to use all language skills (some more than others) such as listening, speaking, and reading. Writing was evident mostly in the semantic mapping activity. Some predicting and scanning for information was part of the reading skills practiced.

Lesson Delivery

4	3	2	1	0
23. **Content objectives** clearly supported by lesson delivery	③	**Content objectives** supported somewhat by lesson delivery	1	**Content objectives** not supported by lesson delivery

Comments: The demonstration and discussion along with the constant repetition of key vocabulary served to accomplish most of the content objectives for the lesson. While students seemed to indicate an understanding of what volcanoes are, it is not certain that they fully understand what causes them to erupt.

4	3	2	1	0
24. **Language objectives** clearly supported by lesson delivery	3	② **Language objectives** somewhat supported by lesson delivery	1	**Language objectives** not supported by lesson delivery

Comments: Most of the language objectives were supported by the delivery. Students did not have a chance to complete the sequencing activity based on the reading in order to assess their reading comprehension.

4	3	2	1	0
25. **Students engaged** approximately 90% to 100% of the period	③	**Students engaged** approximately 70% of the period	1	**Students engaged** less than 50% of the period

Comments: Students were on task throughout the lesson activity.

4   3   ②   1   0

4	3	2	1	0
26. **Pacing** of the lesson appropriate to students' ability levels		**Pacing** generally appropriate, but at times too fast or too slow		**Pacing** inappropriate to the students' ability levels

Comments: The pacing seemed fine, but was a little rushed at times, which prevented students from completing some activities such as the individual silent reading and sequencing activity.

Review/Assessment

④	3	2	1	0
27. **Comprehensive review of key vocabulary**		Uneven **review of key vocabulary**		No **review of key vocabulary**

Comments: Teacher reviewed key vocabulary at the beginning of the lesson and reinforced it throughout. No final review took place at the end of the lesson.

4	3	②	1	0
28. **Comprehensive review of key content concepts**		Uneven **review of key content concepts**		No **review of key content concepts**

Comments: The key content concepts were reviewed throughout the lesson, but there was no comprehensive review to wrap up the lesson, other than the final question posed to students at the end of the class, "What is a volcano?"

4	3	②	1	0
29. Regular **feedback** provided to students on their output (e.g., language, content, work)		Inconsistent **feedback** provided to students on their output		No **feedback** provided to students on their output

Comments: The teacher gave positive feedback to students' responses in most cases. In some instances, when time was short, she did not always respond to students whose hands were raised. She guided the brainstorming and prereading discussions.

4	③	2	1	0
30. **Assessment of student comprehension and learning** of all lesson objectives (e.g., spot checking, group response) throughout the lesson		**Assessment of student comprehension and learning** of some lesson objectives		No **assessment of student comprehension and learning** of lesson objectives

Comments: Throughout the lesson, the teacher checked students' understanding of some concepts and of the instructional tasks. She monitored the classroom to answer questions and to provide assistance. During the reading activity, however, students were not allotted sufficient time to read individually, and the sequencing activity was moved to the following day. Therefore, it is unclear how she was able to assess individual student comprehension before she began reading the text to students.

FIGURE 11.4 SIOP® Lesson Rating Form

Teacher	Observation 1	Observation 2	Observation 3

FIGURE 11.5 Ms. Clark's Scores

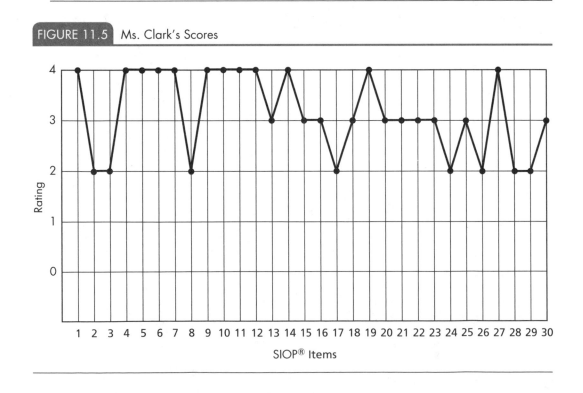

SIOP® Items

Reliability and Validity of the SIOP®

After several years of field testing and refining the SIOP, a study was conducted (Guarino, Echevarria, Short, Schick, Forbes, & Rueda, 2001) to establish the validity and reliability of the instrument. The findings of the study indicated that the SIOP is a highly reliable and valid measure of sheltered instruction (see Appendix C for a discussion of the study).

Summary

This book has been developed for teachers, supervisors, instructional coaches, administrators, teacher education faculty, professional developers, and researchers as a resource for increasing the effectiveness of instruction for elementary English learners. We have presented a research-based, professional development model of sheltered instruction, the SIOP Model, whose protocol may be used as an observation instrument, as well as a lesson planning guide.

The SIOP Model and protocol provide concrete examples of the features of effective instruction for English learners, and the book has been written as a way to illustrate and elucidate those features by describing how real teachers might actually teach SIOP lessons in grades K–6. The use of vignettes allows readers to "see" what each feature might look like in a classroom setting. The features of the SIOP Model represent best practice for teaching English learners and have been shown to benefit English-speaking students as well.

Discussion Questions

1. The SIOP has a number of uses by different constituencies (e.g., teachers, supervisors, administrators, and researchers). How can you begin using the SIOP? What additional uses might it have for you or other constituencies?

2. Reread the sample lesson on pages 265–268. Would you score this lesson differently from the sample SIOP scores? On what items would you differ? What was the basis of your disagreement?

3. Look at the sample SIOP protocol and change any two scores to 1. What would be the total score and percentage score on the revised and recalculated SIOP?

4. Imagine that you and a supervisor or an instructional coach have just watched a videotape of your SIOP lesson. You are discussing the SIOP rating sheet that each of you scored independently. What would be the most collaborative way to approach the discussion of your teaching? What would yield the most useful information for improving your teaching?

CHAPTER 12

Frequently Asked Questions: Getting Started with the SIOP® Model

After reading, discussing, and engaging in activities related to this chapter, you will be able to meet the following content and language objectives.

Content Objectives

Plan initial steps to get started with SIOP implementation in the classroom and school.

Identify a variety of uses for the SIOP protocol.

Language Objectives

Discuss with colleagues the most frequently asked questions and responses about the SIOP Model for those who are beginning "SIOPers."

Generate questions of your own and possible answers about the SIOP Model.

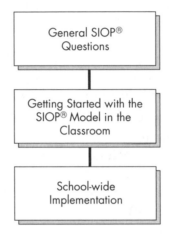

General SIOP® Questions

Getting Started with the SIOP® Model in the Classroom

School-wide Implementation

The purpose of this final chapter is to provide you with information and suggestions for beginning your work with the SIOP Model. Over the years, we have worked with thousands of teachers and administrators who are becoming "SIOPers." Frequently, we are asked about how to effectively implement the SIOP Model in classrooms, schools, and districts. From many conversations, we have culled some of the most common questions and we provide answers to those questions in this chapter.

For a comprehensive guide to implementing the SIOP Model, with profiles of 17 SIOP districts, information about funding sources, suggestions for creating a SIOP implementation plan, SIOP coaching, SIOP professional development, data collection, and more, see *Implementing the SIOP® Model through Effective Professional Development and Coaching* (Echevarría, Short, & Vogt, 2008).

General SIOP® Questions

PD TOOLKIT™ for SIOP®

Click on Videos, then search for "Getting Started With SIOP" to hear a 5th grade teacher share how she implements the SIOP Model in her diverse classroom.

1. Who can implement the SIOP Model?

   - Pre-K, elementary, and secondary subject area teachers, reading/language arts and English teachers, resource teachers, coaches, specialists, special educators, community college, and university professors can and do implement the SIOP Model. The Model can be used in a variety of educational program designs (Duff, 2005; Echevarría & Short, 2010; Genesee, 1999). In fact, any teacher who has students learning content through a nonnative language can use the SIOP Model effectively. It may be part of a general education program, an ESL program, a late-exit bilingual program, a dual language/two-way bilingual immersion program, a newcomer program, a sheltered program, or a foreign language immersion program. In order to implement the Model well, we recommend teachers participate in professional development for at least one year.

2. Is the SIOP Model only for English learners?

   - No. The SIOP Model has been validated also with native English speaking students, both general education and special education students, and former English learners. When teachers implement the 30 features consistently, all subgroups of students, including students receiving special education services, demonstrate academic gains.

PD **TOOLKIT™ for SIOP®**

Click on Videos, then search for "Isn't the SIOP Model just good instruction?" to see Dr. MaryEllen Vogt talk about this question.

3. Isn't the SIOP Model just good instruction?

- Certainly the SIOP Model is excellent instruction with research-based features that have been proven effective with English learners and other learners. What distinguishes it is the systematic, consistent, and simultaneous teaching of both content concepts and academic language through its 30 features.

- What also distinguishes SIOP is that, as of the time of this writing, it is the only empirically validated model of sheltered instruction for English learners that exists.

4. What is the relationship between the SIOP Model and Culturally Responsive Teaching?

- Almost by definition, when teachers implement the SIOP Model to a high degree, they're engaging in culturally responsive teaching. For example, SIOP respects students' home languages and cultures by incorporating students' background knowledge and experiences into lessons.

- Effective SIOP teachers create groups where students work together on relevant activities, making sure that English learners are equal participants.

- With the SIOP Model, teachers hold high expectations for all students, and adjust instruction and materials to provide access to the grade-level curriculum. Compare the tenets of culturally responsive teaching and the features of the SIOP Model and you will see that they intersect naturally, and thus are not separate or competing instructional approaches.

5. What if there are only a few English learners in my classroom?

- First, we now have empirical evidence that all students benefit academically when teachers implement the SIOP Model to a high degree. Therefore, all teachers who have English learners in their classrooms should become SIOP teachers, regardless of the number. SIOP isn't something that teachers "turn on" and "turn off," depending on the makeup of their classes. Rather, it becomes the way they teach from period to period, subject to subject, throughout the day.

6. What is the most important thing I should keep in mind (whether a teacher, coach, or administrator)?

- Recognize that learning to implement the SIOP Model is a process. Not all features will be observed to a high degree in the beginning stages. Reflect on your lessons after class and use the SIOP protocol to assess your planning and delivery. Work through the SIOP Model systematically to ensure it will become internalized and part of your regular classroom practice.

Questions about Getting Started with the SIOP® Model in the Classroom

1. How do I get started using the SIOP Model in my classroom?

- Assess your areas of strength and your areas for needed improvement with the SIOP protocol.

- Begin with one component at a time, gradually adding the others over time.
- As you attain proficiency in one component of the SIOP Model, add other components of the Model to your teaching repertoire.

2. Do I have to implement the eight components in the order they're presented in the book?

- No. There's no intended hierarchy or order of the components, with the exception, perhaps, of Lesson Preparation. However, teachers may choose to begin with another component first, if that's more comfortable. We recommend that Lesson Preparation not be delayed beyond the second or third component because of the necessity of including content and language objectives in lessons.

3. Do I have to incorporate all 30 SIOP features in every lesson?

- Eventually, yes. We recommend that elementary teachers begin implementing one component at a time in one subject area, until all components are implemented in that subject area. The ultimate goal is to add other subjects until all are "SIOPized." Secondary teachers are encouraged to begin with one class period, gradually adding the other periods until all are "SIOPized." However, there might be occasional lessons where not all features are present, such as in a review lesson at the end of a unit. If you're able to speed up this process (adding new components and subject areas or periods), so much the better!

- Keep in mind that the definition of "a lesson" varies somewhat depending on the age of students you're teaching, and the way the classroom day is organized. For example, pre-K, kindergarten, and first-grade teachers present many lessons in 15- to 20-minute (or less) blocks of time, while upper grade (4–6) lessons may be 30–45 minutes. A rule of thumb is: What can you teach, provide practice and application for, and assess in a given period of time? That's what constitutes a "lesson" with the SIOP Model.

4. What if I have students who can't speak any English? Will the SIOP Model help?

- It will certainly help, but it's not enough. Beginning speakers, or newcomers, need intensive English instruction provided by an ESL or ELD teacher, in addition to effective SIOP instruction the rest of the day. If newcomer programs are not available, SIOP instruction provides students with the best opportunity to comprehend lessons.

5. How long will it take for me to become an effective SIOP teacher?

- It depends on the support you receive. Our research has shown teachers can become effective SIOP teachers in one year with coaching, observations, workshops, and planning time. Realistically, we generally say it takes 2–3 years with consistent focus on the eight components and 30 features to become a high implementer of the Model. And, of course, follow-up professional development, observations, and coaching certainly help.

PD **TOOLKIT**™ **for SIOP®**

Click on Videos, then search for "Using the Protocol" to hear about uses of the SIOP protocol.

6. How should I use the SIOP protocol?

- Use it as a lesson plan checklist and self-assessment tool. You may wish to videotape yourself teaching and use the protocol to check the degree to which you are implementing particular features.

- Once you are familiar with the features in the individual components, use the protocol as a tool for post-teaching reflection. One resource that may be helpful while planning lessons is a book that offers a multitude of teaching ideas and activities for enhancing SIOP components in your lessons (Vogt & Echevarría, 2008). (At the time of this writing, volume 2 of the teaching ideas book is in press with additional teaching techniques for implementing the SIOP Model.)

- Observe a peer and use the protocol as a checklist to determine if the SIOP features are present or absent in the lesson you watch.

7. Now that I've read the book and tried out some components, how do I deepen my SIOP knowledge?

- Collaborate with and observe other educators who are committed to excellent SIOP teaching.

- Observe other SIOP classrooms and frankly discuss what is working and what is problematic, and what a teacher can do to overcome any problems.

- Read the other SIOP books that are cited in this text. Also there are a number of research articles written about the SIOP Model. Form a cohort of "SIOPers" and have a study group with these resources.

- Take advantage of the classroom video clips and other resources that are included in the SIOP PDToolkit (see inside back cover for information on how to access this electronic resource).

- Connect with other SIOP schools and districts. See Appendix D for contact information.

Questions about Schoolwide Implementation of the SIOP® Model

1. How should we get started in our school implementation?

- It's critically important that you have a plan in place, including who will receive professional development, who will provide it, where the funding will come from, and so forth. See Echevarría, Short, and Vogt, 2008, for details about how to create a plan, and how other schools and districts have rolled out their plan once it was created.

- Get your school administrator on board with the SIOP Model as a schoolwide initiative. See Echevarría, Short, and Vogt, 2008 for ideas.

- Pearson Professional Development can also assist you with your planning. See www.pearsonpd.com for more information.

2. Who should receive professional development with the SIOP Model?

- Anyone who will be working with English learners, including teachers, support personnel, instructional assistants, and administrators.

- In addition, an overview of the SIOP Model is beneficial for School Board members and district-level administrators so everyone is starting on the "same page," with the same ultimate goal.

3. What should SIOP professional development look like?

- Ideally, a combination of workshops, coaching, observations and conferences, book groups with this text, and follow-up workshops focusing on individual SIOP components. (See Echevarría, Short, and Vogt, 2008 for more specific information and profiles of large and small districts that have implemented the SIOP Model.)

4. How should the SIOP protocol be used?

- As a source of conversation about best practices for teaching English learners.

- As an informal observation instrument for peers, mentors, coaches, and administrators.

- As a tool for observing growth in implementation of separate SIOP features, over time.

- As a research observation tool for fidelity of model implementation.

- Please do not use the protocol for teacher evaluation, especially while the teachers are learning the Model. In order to change their regular lesson planning style to the SIOP Model, teachers must take some risks. Because the process takes time and is challenging, lessons should not be scored during the process.

- The protocol is also an excellent tool for targeted and productive discussions among preservice student teachers, master teachers, and university supervisors, and between a teacher and coach.

PD **TOOLKIT™ for SIOP®**

Click on Videos, then search for "Professional Development" to hear a principal talk about teacher buy-in and change in teacher practice.

5. What should we do about resistant or reluctant teachers?

- Don't begin with them; instead, begin professional development with those who want to improve their instruction for English learners and other students.

- That said, if these teachers have English learners in their classrooms, they need to receive and be held accountable for SIOP professional development. From our experience, when resistant teachers hear their colleagues talk about SIOP successes, they come around and want to be part of the story, particularly if their English learners are not experiencing academic success but those students of SIOP teachers are.

PD **TOOLKIT™ for SIOP®**

Click on Videos, then search for "Coaching" to hear how coaching helps refine and focus teaching for English learners.

6. With whom should we collaborate during SIOP implementation?

- Collaborate with anyone who works with English learners, including the classroom teacher, ESL teacher, SIOP coaches, special educators, paraprofessionals, and administrators.

- Use a collaborative approach with teachers, including conferencing about observations, setting goals for implementing other features of the Model, reflecting on progress in using the SIOP Model, and so forth.

7. What does it mean to be a high-implementing SIOP teacher?

- The SIOP protocol measures teachers' level of implementation of the SIOP Model with the protocol.

- From our research, and that of others, we have learned that fidelity (level of implementation) to the SIOP Model really makes a difference in student performance. High implementers are those teachers who score 75% or higher on the SIOP protocol as measured during classroom observations. (See Chapter 11 for more information.)

8. Is the SIOP Model compatible with the Common Core State Standards?

- Yes. The Common Core State Standards can be used to guide content and language objectives in English language arts and mathematics. The fact that the Common Core State Standards include listening and speaking standards, when a number of state English language arts standards do not, is beneficial to teachers working with English learners.

- Since the CCSS do not directly address *how* English learners (and struggling learners) are to attain the standards, the SIOP Model provides just the assistance teachers need to help their students be successful in a Common Core classroom.

9. The SIOP Model is a lesson planning and delivery system for teachers, but what about student outcomes?

- Our research has focused almost exclusively on the impact of the SIOP Model on student achievement (see Appendices C and D). In the classroom, the features of the SIOP Model translate directly into student outcomes when implemented well. (See Figure 12.1 for ways that the features benefit students.) At

---

FIGURE 12.1 Learner Outcomes

High Quality SIOP Lessons: Checking Learner Outcomes

Learners...
- demonstrated that they understood the purpose and objectives of the lesson.
- used the differentiated materials available and participated in meaningful activities.
- were actively encouraged to make links between their own background and the lesson's concepts and activities.
- had multiple opportunities to use new vocabulary in meaningful ways.
- responded to the teacher's modified speech and comprehensible input techniques.
- used learning strategies in completing tasks and assignments.
- were supported while completing tasks and assignments at their level of academic and language proficiency.
- were able to respond to a variety of questions including higher-order questions.
- demonstrated that they could work both independently and collaboratively, using academic English.
- participated in a variety of grouping configurations that facilitate interaction and discussion.
- used their home language as needed to clarify key concepts.
- contributed to the lesson by using hands-on materials and/or manipulatives to practice and apply content knowledge.
- were engaged and working at their potential throughout the lesson.
- followed the pace of the lesson.
- demonstrated understanding of the lesson's key vocabulary and content concepts.
- received appropriate and regular feedback on their output (e.g., language, content, work).
- were aware of their progress through assessment of the lesson's objectives.

---

the conclusion of an effective SIOP lesson, students should be able to demonstrate the outcomes as shown in Figure 12.1. This checklist may be used as a spot check to gauge the effectiveness of SIOP lessons.

10. As an administrator, where can I get some assistance?

- Additional considerations about school-level implementation of the SIOP Model from an administrator's perspective can be found in *The SIOP® Model for Administrators* (Short, Vogt, & Echevarría, 2008).

- Become familiar with the additional SIOP resources that support lesson planning and delivery. Books of lesson techniques, SIOP lessons and units for English-language arts, mathematics, history/social studies, and science, and of the Model's use in Response to Intervention programs are available. (See Appendix D for resources, including links to downloadable research briefs.)

- Other versions of this text, *Making Content Comprehensible for English Learners: The SIOP® Model*, have been written specifically for K–12 students (Echevarría, Vogt, & Short, 2013).

- Pearson Education offers a variety of professional development options on the SIOP Model, including training for administrators. See www.pearsonpd.com for more information.

11. How can the SIOP protocol be used by researchers and program evaluators to measure teachers' level of implementation of the SIOP Model with the protocol?

- Because it is the only empirically validated, instructional approach for English learners at the time of this writing, the protocol can help determine if a school's or district's investment in the SIOP Model staff development is returning dividends.

- Analyze student performance in conjunction with teachers' level of implementation.

As we conclude this second edition of *Making Content Comprehensible for Elementary English Learners*, we thank you for your interest in the SIOP Model and hope that you find that the effort to become a high-implementing SIOP teacher (or effective coach or administrator) is well worth the journey. From our work, we have learned that the benefits of this effort include:

- teachers empowered to meet their students' needs
- improved academic achievement for English learners and other students
- gains in English language proficiency
- students who are active, engaged participants in their classrooms

The English learners in our schools deserve our best efforts because they and their native English-speaking peers are our future. Welcome aboard!

PD TOOLKIT™ for SIOP®

Click on Videos, then search for "The SIOP Model: Marcy Granillo" to learn about SIOP® implementation schoolwide.

PD TOOLKIT™ for SIOP®

Click on Videos, then search for "Why SIOP?" to hear a principal's description of how the SIOP Model was initially implemented in her school.

PD TOOLKIT™ for SIOP®

Click on Videos, then search "Administrative Support" to hear how administrative support can lead to excellence.

Observer(s): _____   Teacher: _____

Date: _____   School: _____

Grade: _____   Class/Topic: _____

ESL Level: _____   Lesson: Multi-day   Single-day   (*circle one*)

Total Points Possible: 120 (Subtract 4 points for each NA given: _____)

Total Points Earned: _____   Percentage Score: _____

Directions: Circle the number that best reflects what you observe in a sheltered lesson. You may give a score from 0–4 (or NA on selected items). Cite under "Comments" specific examples of the behaviors observed.

Lesson Preparation

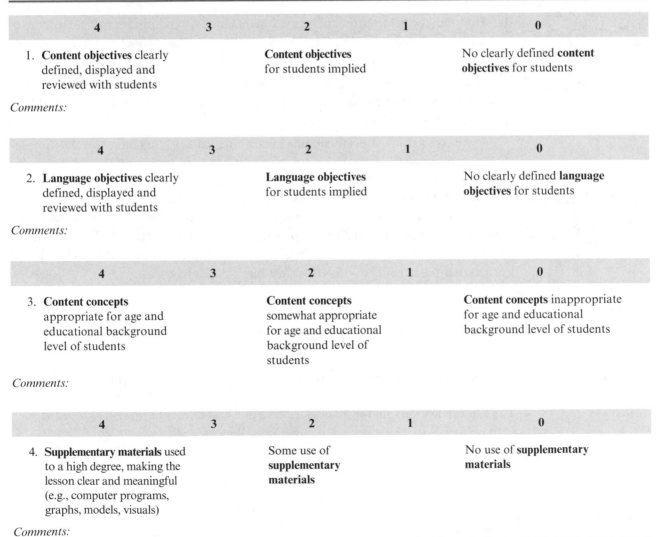

4	3	2	1	0
1. **Content objectives** clearly defined, displayed and reviewed with students		**Content objectives** for students implied		No clearly defined **content objectives** for students

Comments:

4	3	2	1	0
2. **Language objectives** clearly defined, displayed and reviewed with students		**Language objectives** for students implied		No clearly defined **language objectives** for students

Comments:

4	3	2	1	0
3. **Content concepts** appropriate for age and educational background level of students		**Content concepts** somewhat appropriate for age and educational background level of students		**Content concepts** inappropriate for age and educational background level of students

Comments:

4	3	2	1	0
4. **Supplementary materials** used to a high degree, making the lesson clear and meaningful (e.g., computer programs, graphs, models, visuals)		Some use of **supplementary materials**		No use of **supplementary materials**

Comments:

(Echevarria, Vogt, & Short, 2000, 2004, 2008, 2013)

4	3	2	1	0	NA

5. **Adaptation of content** (e.g., text, assignment) to all levels of student proficiency

Some **adaptation of content** to all levels of student proficiency

No significant **adaptation of content** to all levels of student proficiency

Comments:

4	3	2	1	0

6. **Meaningful activities** that integrate lesson concepts (e.g., interviews, letter writing, simulations, models) with language practice opportunities for reading, writing, listening, and/or speaking

Meaningful activities that integrate lesson concepts but provide few language practice opportunities for reading, writing, listening, and/or speaking

No **meaningful activities** that integrate lesson concepts with language practice

Comments:

Building Background

4	3	2	1	0	NA

7. **Concepts explicitly linked** to students' background experiences

Concepts loosely linked to students' background experiences

Concepts not explicitly linked to students' background experiences

Comments:

4	3	2	1	0

8. **Links explicitly made** between past learning and new concepts

Few links made between past learning and new concepts

No links made between past learning and new concepts

Comments:

4	3	2	1	0

9. **Key vocabulary** emphasized (e.g., introduced, written, repeated, and highlighted for students to see)

Key vocabulary introduced, but not emphasized

Key vocabulary not introduced or emphasized

Comments:

Comprehensible Input

4	3	2	1	0

10. **Speech** appropriate for students' proficiency levels (e.g., slower rate, enunciation, and simple sentence structure for beginners)

      (2) **Speech** sometimes inappropriate for students' proficiency levels

      (0) **Speech** inappropriate for students' proficiency levels

Comments:

4	3	2	1	0

11. **Clear explanation** of academic tasks

      (2) **Unclear explanation** of academic tasks

      (0) **No explanation** of academic tasks

Comments:

4	3	2	1	0

12. **A variety of techniques** used to make content concepts clear (e.g., modeling, visuals, hands-on activities, demonstrations, gestures, body language)

      (2) **Some techniques** used to make content concepts clear

      (0) **No techniques** used to make concepts clear

Comments:

Strategies

4	3	2	1	0

13. Ample opportunities provided for students to use **learning strategies**

      (2) Inadequate opportunities provided for students to use **learning strategies**

      (0) No opportunity provided for students to use **learning strategies**

Comments:

4	3	2	1	0

14. **Scaffolding techniques** consistently used, assisting and supporting student understanding (e.g., think-alouds)

      (2) **Scaffolding techniques** occasionally used

      (0) **Scaffolding techniques** not used

Comments:

4	3	2	1	0

15. A variety of **questions or tasks that promote higher-order thinking skills** (e.g., literal, analytical, and interpretive questions) | | Infrequent **questions or tasks that promote higher-order thinking skills** | | No **questions or tasks that promote higher-order thinking skills** |

Comments:

Interaction

4	3	2	1	0

16. Frequent opportunities for **interaction** and discussion between teacher/student and among students, which encourage elaborated responses about lesson concepts | | **Interaction** mostly teacher-dominated with some opportunities for students to talk about or question lesson concepts | | **Interaction** teacher-dominated with no opportunities for students to discuss lesson concepts |

Comments:

4	3	2	1	0

17. **Grouping configurations** support language and content objectives of the lesson | | **Grouping configurations** unevenly support the language and content objectives | | **Grouping configurations** do not support the language and content objectives |

Comments:

4	3	2	1	0

18. Sufficient **wait time for student responses** consistently provided | | Sufficient **wait time for student responses** occasionally provided | | Sufficient **wait time for student responses** not provided |

Comments:

4	3	2	1	0	NA

19. Ample opportunities for students to **clarify key concepts in L1** as needed with aide, peer, or L1 text | | Some opportunities for students to **clarify key concepts in L1** | | No opportunities for students to **clarify key concepts in L1** |

Comments:

Practice & Application

4	3	2	1	0	NA
20. **Hands-on materials and/or manipulatives** provided for students to practice using new content knowledge		Few **hands-on materials and/or manipulatives** provided for students to practice using new content knowledge		No **hands-on materials and/or manipulatives** provided for students to practice using new content knowledge	

Comments:

4	3	2	1	0	NA
21. Activities provided for students to **apply content and language knowledge** in the classroom		Activities provided for students to **apply** either **content or language knowledge** in the classroom		No activities provided for students to **apply content and language knowledge** in the classroom	

Comments:

4	3	2	1	0
22. Activities integrate all **language skills** (i.e., reading, writing, listening, and speaking)		Activities integrate some **language skills**		Activities do not integrate **language skills**

Comments:

Lesson Delivery

4	3	2	1	0
23. **Content objectives** clearly supported by lesson delivery		**Content objectives** somewhat supported by lesson delivery		**Content objectives** not supported by lesson delivery

Comments:

4	3	2	1	0
24. **Language objectives** clearly supported by lesson delivery		**Language objectives** somewhat supported by lesson delivery		**Language objectives** not supported by lesson delivery

Comments:

4	3	2	1	0
25. **Students engaged** approximately 90% to 100% of the period		**Students engaged** approximately 70% of the period		**Students engaged** less than 50% of the period

Comments:

4	3	2	1	0
26. **Pacing** of the lesson appropriate to students' ability levels		**Pacing** generally appropriate, but at times too fast or too slow		**Pacing** inappropriate to students' ability levels

Comments:

Review & Assessment

4	3	2	1	0
27. Comprehensive **review of key vocabulary**		Uneven **review of key vocabulary**		No **review of key vocabulary**

Comments:

4	3	2	1	0
28. Comprehensive **review of key content concepts**		Uneven **review of key content concepts**		No **review of key content concepts**

Comments:

4	3	2	1	0
29. Regular **feedback** provided to students on their output (e.g., language, content, work)		Inconsistent **feedback** provided to students on their output		No **feedback** provided to students on their output

Comments:

4	3	2	1	0
30. **Assessment of student comprehension and learning** of all lesson objectives (e.g., spot checking, group response) throughout the lesson		**Assessment of student comprehension and learning** of some lesson objectives		No **assessment of student comprehension and learning** of lesson objectives

Comments:

**The Sheltered Instruction
Observation Protocol (SIOP®)**
(Echevarria, Vogt, & Short, 2000, 2004, 2008,
2013)

Observer(s): _____ School: _____
Date: _____ Teacher: _____
Grade: _____ Class/Topic: _____
ESL Level: _____ Lesson: Multi-day Single-day *(circle one)*

Total Points Possible: 120 (Subtract 4 points for each NA given) _____
Total Points Earned: _____ Percentage Score: _____

Directions: Circle the number that best reflects what you observe in a sheltered lesson. You may give a score from 0–4 (or NA on selected items). Cite under "Comments" specific examples of the behaviors observed.

	Highly Evident	Somewhat Evident		Not Evident	
Preparation	4	3	2	1	0
1. **Content objectives** clearly defined, displayed, and reviewed with students	❑	❑	❑	❑	❑
2. **Language objectives** clearly defined, displayed, and reviewed with students	❑	❑	❑	❑	❑
3. **Content concepts** appropriate for age and educational background level of students	❑	❑	❑	❑	❑
4. **Supplementary materials** used to a high degree, making the lesson clear and meaningful (e.g., computer programs, graphs, models, visuals)	❑	❑	❑	❑	❑	
5. **Adaptation of content** (e.g., text, assignment) to all levels of student proficiency [NA above col 0]	❑	❑	❑	❑	❑	❑ NA
6. **Meaningful activities** that integrate lesson concepts (e.g., surveys, letter writing, simulations, constructing models) with language practice opportunities for reading, writing, listening, and/or speaking [NA above col 1]	❑	❑	❑	❑ NA	❑

Comments:

Building Background	4	3	2	1	0	NA
7. **Concepts explicitly linked** to students' background experiences	❑	❑	❑	❑	❑	❑
8. **Links explicitly made** between past learning and new concepts	❑	❑	❑	❑	❑	
9. **Key vocabulary** emphasized (e.g., introduced, written, repeated, and highlighted for students to see)	❑	❑	❑	❑	❑	

Comments:

Comprehensible Input	4	3	2	1	0
10. **Speech** appropriate for students' proficiency level (e.g., slower rate, enunciation, and simple sentence structure for beginners)	❑	❑	❑	❑	❑
11. **Clear explanation** of academic tasks	❑	❑	❑	❑	❑
12. **A variety of techniques** used to make content concepts clear (e.g., modeling, visuals, hands-on activities, demonstrations, gestures, body language)	❑	❑	❑	❑	❑

Comments:

Strategies	4	3	2	1	0	
13. Ample opportunities provided for students to use **learning strategies**	❑	❑	❑	❑	❑	
14. **Scaffolding techniques** consistently used assisting and supporting student understanding (e.g., think-alouds)	❑	❑	❑	❑	❑	
15. A variety of **questions or tasks that promote higher-order thinking skills** (e.g., literal, analytical, and interpretive questions)	❑	❑	❑	❑	❑	

Comments:

Interaction	4	3	2	1	0	
16. Frequent opportunities for **interaction** and discussion between teacher/student and among students, which encourage elaborated responses about lesson concepts	❑	❑	❑	❑	❑	
17. **Grouping configurations** support language and content objectives of the lesson	❑	❑	❑	❑	❑	
18. Sufficient **wait time for student responses** consistently provided	❑	❑	❑	❑	❑	
19. Ample opportunities for students to **clarify key concepts in L1** as needed with aide, peer, or L1 text	❑	❑	❑	❑	❑	**NA** ❑

Comments:

Practice & Application	4	3	2	1	0	NA
20. **Hands-on materials and/or manipulatives** provided for students to practice using new content knowledge	❑	❑	❑	❑	❑	❑
21. Activities provided for students to **apply content and language knowledge** in the classroom	❑	❑	❑	❑	❑	**NA** ❑
22. Activities integrate all **language skills** (i.e., reading, writing, listening, and speaking)	❑	❑	❑	❑	❑	

Comments:

Lesson Delivery	4	3	2	1	0
23. **Content objectives** clearly supported by lesson delivery	❑	❑	❑	❑	❑
24. **Language objectives** clearly supported by lesson delivery	❑	❑	❑	❑	❑
25. **Students engaged** approximately 90% to 100% of the period	❑	❑	❑	❑	❑
26. **Pacing** of the lesson appropriate to students' ability level	❑	❑	❑	❑	❑

Comments:

Review & Assessment	4	3	2	1	0
27. Comprehensive **review of key vocabulary**	❑	❑	❑	❑	❑
28. Comprehensive **review of key content concepts**	❑	❑	❑	❑	❑
29. Regular **feedback** provided to students on their output (e.g., language, content, work)	❑	❑	❑	❑	❑
30. **Assessment of student comprehension and learning** of all lesson objectives (e.g., spot checking, group response) throughout the lesson	❑	❑	❑	❑	❑

Comments:

SIOP® Lesson Plan Template 1

Date: _____ Grade/Class/Subject: _____

Unit/Theme: _____ Standards: _____

Content Objective(s): _____

_____

Language Objective(s): _____

_____

Key Vocabulary	Supplementary Materials

SIOP® Features

Preparation
___ Adaptation of Content
___ Links to Background
___ Links to Past Learning
___ Strategies incorporated

Scaffolding
___ Modeling
___ Guided practice
___ Independent practice
___ Comprehensible input

Grouping Options
___ Whole class
___ Small groups
___ Partners
___ Independent

Integration of Processes
___ Reading
___ Writing
___ Speaking
___ Listening

Application
___ Hands-on
___ Meaningful
___ Linked to objectives
___ Promotes engagement

Assessment
___ Individual
___ Group
___ Written
___ Oral

Lesson Sequence

Reflections:

(Reproduction of this material is restricted to use with Echevarria, Vogt, and Short (2008), *Making Content Comprehensible for English Learners: The SIOP® Model.*)

SIOP® Lesson Plan Template 2

STANDARDS:

THEME:

LESSON TOPIC:

OBJECTIVES:
Language

Content

LEARNING STRATEGIES:

KEY VOCABULARY:

MATERIALS:

MOTIVATION:
(Building background)

PRESENTATION:
(Language and content objectives, comprehensible input, strategies, interaction, feedback)

PRACTICE/APPLICATION:
(Meaningful activities, interaction, strategies, practice/application, feedback)

REVIEW/ASSESSMENT:
(Review objectives and vocabulary, assess learning)

EXTENSION:

SIOP® Lesson Plan Template 3

Topic:	Class:	Date:

Content Objectives:

Language Objectives:

Key Vocabulary:

Materials (including supplementary and adapted):

Higher-Order Questions:

Time:	Activities
	Building Background
	Links to Experience:
	Links to Learning:
	Key Vocabulary:

(Continued on next page)

Time:	**Student Activities** (Check all that apply for activities throughout lesson):

Scaffolding: ❏ Modeling   ❏ Guided   ❏ Independent

Grouping: ❏ Whole Class   ❏ Small Group   ❏ Partners   ❏ Independent

Processes: ❏ Reading   ❏ Writing   ❏ Listening   ❏ Independent

Strategies: ❏ Hands-on   ❏ Meaningful   ❏ Links to Objectives

Review and Assessment (Check all that apply):

Individual ❏   Group ❏   Written ❏   Oral ❏

Review Key Vocabulary:

Review Key Content Concepts:

(Developed by John Seidlitz. Used with permission.)

SIOP® Lesson Plan Template 4

Key: SW = Students will; TW = Teacher will; SWBAT = Students will be able to . . . ; HOTS = Higher-Order Thinking Skills

SIOP® Lesson Grade:
Content Standards:

Key Vocabulary:

Visuals/Resources:

HOTS:

Connections: Prior Knowledge/Building Background/Prior Learning:

Content Objectives:

Meaningful Activities:

Review/Assessment:

(Continued on next page)

(Developed by Melissa Castillo & Nicole Teyechea. Used with permission.)

Language Objectives:

Wrap-up:

(Developed by Melissa Castillo & Nicole Teyechea. Used with permission.)

The SIOP Model has been developed and refined through more than 15 years of sustained research and development studies (Short, Echevarría, & Richards-Tutor, 2011). The following discussion highlights the investigations over time:

CREDE Research: Development of the SIOP Model, Protocol, and Professional Development Program

- The first version of the Sheltered Instruction Observation Protocol (SIOP®) began in the early 1990s as an observation tool to determine if observed teachers incorporated key sheltered techniques consistently in their lessons.

- The protocol evolved into a lesson planning and delivery approach, known as the SIOP Model (Echevarría, Vogt, & Short, 2000), through a 7-year, quasi-experimental research study, *The Effects of Sheltered Instruction on the Achievement of Limited English Proficient Students*, that was sponsored by the Center for Research on Education, Diversity & Excellence (CREDE) and funded by the U.S. Department of Education. It began in 1996.

  - The goals of the research project were to (1) develop an explicit model of sheltered instruction; (2) use that model to train teachers in effective sheltered strategies; and (3) conduct field experiments and collect data to evaluate teacher change and the effects of sheltered instruction on limited English proficient (LEP) students' English language development and content knowledge.

  - This original SIOP study involved collaborating middle school teachers in four large metropolitan school districts—two on the East Coast and two on the West Coast—who worked with researchers to identify key practices for sheltered instruction and develop a professional development model that would enable more teachers to use sheltered instruction effectively in their classrooms. Dr. Jana Echevarría of California State University, Long Beach, and Dr. Deborah Short of the Center for Applied Linguistics in Washington, DC, were co-project investigators.

  - Together, we reviewed the professional literature on best practices for English learners in the areas of ESL, bilingual education, reading, second language acquisition, discourse studies, special education, and classroom management and found many techniques that showed promise but hadn't been empirically investigated. We decided to test combinations of these techniques and thus built our initial model.

  - During four years of field testing, we analyzed teacher implementation and student effects as teachers tried out variations in their classrooms.

◆ In 2000, we finalized the format—30 features of instruction grouped into eight components essential for making content comprehensible for English learners—Lesson Preparation, Building Background, Comprehensible Input, Strategies, Interaction, Practice & Application, Lesson Delivery, and Review & Assessment (Echevarría, Vogt, & Short, 2000; Short & Echevarría, 1999). These components emphasize the instructional practices that are critical for second language learners as well as high-quality practices that benefit all students. The eight components are:

- The six features under *Lesson Preparation* initiate the lesson planning process, so teachers include content and language objectives, use supplementary materials, create meaningful activities, and more.

- *Building Background* focuses on making connections with students' background experiences and prior learning, and on developing their academic vocabulary.

- *Comprehensible Input* considers how teachers should adjust their speech, model academic tasks, and use multimodal techniques to enhance comprehension.

- The *Strategies* component emphasizes teaching learning strategies to students, scaffolding instruction, and promoting higher-order thinking skills.

- *Interaction* prompts teachers to encourage students to elaborate their speech and to group students appropriately for language and content development.

- *Practice & Application* provides activities to practice and extend language and content learning.

- *Lesson Delivery* ensures that teachers present a lesson that meets the planned objectives and promotes student engagement.

- The *Review & Assessment* component reminds teachers to review the key language and content concepts, assess student learning, and provide specific academic feedback to students on their output.

◆ We created a 5-point scale for each feature on the observation protocol so we could measure the level of implementation in any lesson (4—closest to recommended practice, 0—no evidence of the use of the practice). A separate study confirmed the SIOP protocol as a valid and highly reliable measure of sheltered instruction (Guarino et al., 2001). Experienced observers of classroom instruction (e.g., teacher education faculty who supervise student teachers) who were *not* specifically trained in the SIOP Model were able to use the protocol to distinguish between high and low implementers of the model. A statistical analysis revealed an interrater of correlation of 0.90 or higher.

◆ Because this CREDE study predated NCLB, most of the English learners in the research districts were exempted from the standardized testing process. To investigate whether the model yielded positive results in terms of student performance, we used pre- and post-measures of the Illinois Measurement of Annual Growth in English (IMAGE) writing test as an outcome measure of academic literacy. The IMAGE was the standardized assessment of reading and writing used by the state of Illinois to measure annual growth of these skills in their limited English proficient students in Grades 3–12. It was correlated to and a predictor of scores on the IGAP (the state standardized test of achievement) that was given to all students in Illinois, except those exempted for linguistic development reasons or learning disabilities. The IMAGE Writing Test provided separate scores for five features of writing: Language Production, Focus, Support/Elaboration, Organization, and Mechanics, as well as an overall score.

- ◆ Two distinct, but similar, cohorts of English learners in sheltered classes participated: students whose teachers were trained in implementing the SIOP Model (the treatment group), and students whose teachers had no exposure to the SIOP Model (the comparison group). The students in both groups were in Grades 6–8 in the same districts and represented mixed proficiency levels. We found that students who participated in classes taught by teachers trained in the SIOP Model improved their writing skills significantly more than students in classes with non–SIOP-trained teachers. They also made greater gains from the fall to spring administrations of the test. These findings were statistically significant (Echevarría, Short, & Powers, 2006).

- ◆ We found that this model can be applied in ESL classes as well as all content area classes because it offers a framework for instruction that incorporates best practices for teaching both language and content.

- ◆ From 1999 to 2002, we field-tested and refined the SIOP Model's professional development program, which incorporates key features of effective teacher development as recommended then by Darling-Hammond (1998) and still recommended today (Darling-Hammond & Richardson, 2009). The program includes professional development institutes (see www.siopinstitute.net), videotapes of exemplary SIOP teachers (Hudec & Short, 2002a, 2002b), facilitator's guides (Echevarría & Vogt, 2007; Short, Hudec, & Echevarría, 2002), and other training materials.

NJ SIOP Research: Improvement in English Language Proficiency

- ● From 2004–2007 we replicated and scaled up the SIOP research in a quasi-experimental study. *Academic Literacy through Sheltered Instruction for Secondary English Language Learners* was conducted by researchers at the Center for Applied Linguistics in two districts in New Jersey and funded by the Carnegie Corporation of New York and the Rockefeller Foundation from 2004–2007. The treatment and comparison districts each had one high school and two middle schools with ESL programs and had multilingual student populations.

- ◆ In the treatment site, math, science, social studies, language arts, ESL, and technology teachers participated in ongoing SIOP Model training: approximately 35 teachers for two years (Cohort 1) and an additional 25 for one (Cohort 2). The professional development program included summer institutes, follow-up workshops, and on-site coaching. The teachers in the comparison site did not receive any SIOP Model training.

- We collected teacher implementation data (two classroom observations each year, one in the fall, the other in the spring) using the SIOP protocol at both sites. We found that 56% of the treatment teachers in Cohort 1 became high implementers of the SIOP Model after one year and 71% were high implementers after two. Seventy-four percent of the Cohort 2 teachers, who joined the Cohort 1 teachers at their schools, reached the high implementation level in just one year. At the comparison site, fewer teachers implemented the SIOP features to a high level: 5% of the teachers in the first year; 17% by the second year (Short, Fidelman, & Louguit, 2012).

- We also collected student data from the state English language proficiency assessment at that time, the IPT (Idea Proficiency Test), for all English learners in Grades 6–12. Students with SIOP-trained teachers made statistically significant gains in their average mean scores for oral language, writing, and total proficiency on the state assessment of English language proficiency, compared to the comparison group of English learners (Short, Fidelman, & Louguit, 2012).

CREATE Research: Fidelity Matters and All Students Benefit—English Learners and English Speakers Alike

- From 2005–2012, researchers from California State University, Long Beach, and the Center for Applied Linguistics participated in the program of studies at the National Center for Research on the Educational Achievement and Teaching of English Language Learners (CREATE), funded by the U.S. Department of Education. The study, *The Impact of the SIOP® Model on Middle School Science and Language Learning*, first examined the SIOP Model in middle school science classrooms (Himmel, Short, Richards, & Echevarría, 2009) and later applied the SIOP Model as the professional development framework for a schoolwide intervention (Echevarría & Short, 2011).

  - A pilot study was conducted to develop SIOP science curriculum units, where local standards and curricula were enhanced with SIOP features, and to design and field-test science language assessments that would measure student scientific vocabulary, reading comprehension, and writing skills.

  - In 2006–2007, an experimental study was conducted in eight middle schools for one semester. Five received the treatment, which was SIOP professional development, classroom-based coaching, and four SIOP science units developed by researchers and teacher consultants. Three schools were control sites where teachers taught in their regular fashion with their own lessons. Treatment and control teachers were observed and their lessons were rated using the SIOP protocol.

  - Results showed that students in the treatment classes outperformed control students (Echevarría, Richards-Tutor, Canges, & Francis, 2011) and the higher the level of SIOP implementation, the better the students performed on assessments (Echevarría, Richards-Tutor, Chinn, & Ratleff, 2011). This result held true for English learners, former English learners, and native English speakers.

♦ During the 2009–2010 school year, another experimental study took place. This 2-year intervention focused schoolwide on Grade 7 and the SIOP Model was the overarching professional development framework (Echevarría, Short, Richards-Tutor, & Himmel, in progress). Other content-specific curriculum interventions tested through earlier years of the CREATE program were implemented as well. Eight schools were randomly assigned to treatment or control. The four treatment schools had SIOP professional development and classroom-based coaching for SIOP implementation, and, where applicable, for the content-specific curriculum intervention. The teachers in the four control schools delivered regular instruction without curriculum units or SIOP training. Their instruction was observed for research purposes but they did not receive feedback.

♦ In the 2010–2011 school year, teachers in three of the prior year's control schools became treatment teachers and received the SIOP professional development and curriculum interventions as well. A new treatment school joined the study that year, bringing the number of schools to four.

● Researchers collected data in the treatment and control sites during both years. Teacher implementation levels were measured with the SIOP protocol and other tools. Student performance was measured with standardized tests and curriculum-based assessments. Analyses show that this schoolwide intervention improved outcomes in content knowledge and academic English for both English learners and native English speakers in the treatment classes (Echevarria, Vaughn & Francis, in progress).

Program Evaluation Research

● School districts have conducted a number of program evaluations on their implementation of the SIOP Model that can be reviewed in *Implementing the SIOP® Model through Effective Professional Development and Coaching* (Echevarría, Short, & Vogt, 2008).

Uses of the SIOP Model and Protocol

Since the SIOP Model was first published in 2000, the following uses for the observation tool and professional development program have been realized:

● Teacher lesson plan checklist and self-reflection guide
● Classroom observation tool for administrators
● Supervision tool for faculty to observe student teachers
● Research observation tool for fidelity of model implementation
● Program of professional development
● Framework for development of sheltered curricula

Conclusion: SIOP Research to Date

When looking at these research studies as a whole, we can see that SIOP Model instruction is making a positive learning difference for English learners and for other students who are in the classrooms. No one is disadvantaged by SIOP instruction; rather, the focus on academic literacy and scaffolded instruction helps all students learn academic English and content curricula better.

Books

Core SIOP Texts:

Echevarría, J., Short, D., & Peterson, C. (2012). *Using the SIOP® Model with pre-K and kindergarten English learners.* Boston: Allyn & Bacon.

Echevarría, J., Vogt, M.E., & Short, D. (2013). *Making content comprehensible for English learners: The SIOP® Model,* Fourth Edition. Boston: Allyn & Bacon.

Echevarría, J., Vogt, M.E., & Short, D. (2014a). *Making content comprehensible for elementary English learners: The SIOP® Model.* Boston: Allyn & Bacon.

Echevarría, J., Vogt, M.E., & Short, D. (2014b). *Making content comprehensible for secondary English learners: The SIOP® Model.* Boston: Allyn & Bacon.

Additional SIOP Texts:

Echevarría, J., Short, D., & Vogt, M.E. (2008). *Implementing the SIOP® Model through effective professional development and coaching.* Boston: Allyn & Bacon.

Echevarría, J., Vogt, M.E., & Short, D. (2010). *The SIOP® Model for teaching mathematics to English learners.* Boston: Allyn & Bacon.

Short, D., & Echevarría, J. (in progress). *Developing academic language with the SIOP Model.* Boston: Allyn & Bacon.

Short, D., Echevarría, J., & Vogt, M.E. (2008). *The SIOP® Model for administrators.* Boston: Allyn & Bacon.

Short, D., Vogt, M.E., & Echevarría, J. (2011a). *The SIOP® Model for teaching history-social studies to English learners.* Boston: Allyn & Bacon.

Short, D., Vogt, M.E., & Echevarría, J. (2011b). *The SIOP® Model for teaching science to English learners.* Boston: Allyn & Bacon.

Vogt, M.E., & Echevarría, J. (2008). *99 ideas and activities for teaching English learners with the SIOP® Model.* Boston: Allyn & Bacon.

Vogt, M.E., Echevarría, J., & Short, D. (2010). *The SIOP® Model for teaching English-language arts to English learners.* Boston: Allyn & Bacon.

Teaching English Learners with Learning Challenges:

Echevarría, J., & Graves, A. (2010). *Sheltered content instruction: Teaching English learners with diverse abilities,* Fourth Edition. Boston: Allyn & Bacon.

Echevarría, J., & Vogt, M.E. (2011). *RTI and English learners: Making it happen.* Boston: Allyn & Bacon.

Journal Articles and Book Chapters

Echevarría, J., & Colburn, A. (2006). Designing lessons: Inquiry approach to science using the SIOP® Model. In A. Fathman & D. Crowther, (Eds.), *Science for English language learners* (pp. 95–108). Arlington, VA: National Science Teachers Association Press.

Echevarría, J., Richards-Tutor, C., Canges, R., & Francis, D. (2011). Using the SIOP Model to promote the acquisition of language and science concepts with English learners. *Bilingual Research Journal, 34*(3), 334–351.

Echevarría, J., Richards-Tutor, C., Chinn, V., & Ratleff, P. (2011). Did they get it? The role of fidelity in teaching English learners. *Journal of Adolescent and Adult Literacy, 54*(6), 425–434.

Echevarría, J., & Short, D. (2004). Using multiple perspectives in observations of diverse classrooms: The Sheltered Instruction Observation Protocol (SIOP). In H. Waxman, R. Tharp, & S. Hilberg (Eds.), *Observational research in U.S. classrooms: New approaches for understanding cultural and linguistic diversity*. Boston: Cambridge University Press.

Echevarría, J., & Short, D. (2010). Programs and practices for effective sheltered content instruction. In California Department of Education (Ed.), *Improving education for English learners: Research-based approaches* (pp. 250–321). Sacramento, CA: CDE Press.

Echevarría, J., Short, D., & Powers, K. (2006). School reform and standards-based education: An instructional model for English language learners. *Journal of Educational Research, 99*(4), 195–210.

Echevarría, J., Short, D., Richards-Tutor, C., & Himmel, J. (in progress). Using the SIOP Model as a professional development framework for comprehensive schoolwide intervention. In J. Echevarría, S. Vaughn, & D. Francis (Eds.), *English learners in content area classes: Teaching for achievement in the middle grades*. Boston: Allyn & Bacon.

Echevarría, J., & Vogt, M.E. (2010). Using the SIOP® Model to improve literacy for English learners. *New England Reading Association Journal (NERAJ), 46*(1) 8–15.

Guarino, A.J., Echevarría, J., Short, D., Schick, J.E., Forbes, S., & Rueda, R. (2001). The Sheltered Instruction Observation Protocol. *Journal of Research in Education, 11*(1), 138–140.

Short, D., & Echevarría, J. (2004/2005). Teacher skills to support English language learners. *Educational Leadership, 62*(4), 8–13.

Short, D., Echevarría, J., & Richards-Tutor, C. (2011). Research on academic literacy development in sheltered instruction classrooms. *Language Teaching Research, 15*(3), 363–380.

Short, D., Fidelman, C., & Louguit, M. (2012). Developing academic language in English language learners through sheltered instruction. *TESOL Quarterly, 46*(2), 333–360.

Vogt, M.E. (2012). English learners: Developing their literate lives. In R. M. Bean & A. S. Dagen (Eds.), *Best practice of literacy leaders: Keys to school improvement.* New York: The Guilford Press, 248–260.

Research Briefs (Downloadable)

Echevarría, J. (2012). *Effective practices for increasing the achievement of English learners.* Washington, DC: Center for Research on the Educational Achievement and Teaching of English Language Learners. Retrieved from www.cal.org/create/resources/pubs/

Echevarría, J., & Hasbrouck, J. (2009). *Response to intervention and English learners.* Washington, DC: Center for Research on the Educational Achievement and Teaching of English Language Learners. Retrieved from www.cal.org/create/resources/pubs/responsetointerv.html

Echevarría, J., & Short, D. (2011). *The SIOP® Model: A professional development framework for comprehensive school-wide intervention.* Washington, DC: Center for Research on the Educational Achievement and Teaching of English Language Learners. Retrieved from www.cal.org/create/resources/pubs/professional-development-framework.html

Himmel, J., Short, D.J., Richards, C., & Echevarría, J. (2009). *Using the SIOP® Model to improve middle school science instruction.* Washington, DC: Center for Research on the Educational Achievement and Teaching of English Language Learners. Retrieved from www.cal.org/create/resources/pubs/siopscience.htm

Glossary

Academic language: Language used in formal contexts for academic subjects. The aspect of language connected with literacy and academic achievement. This includes technical and academic terms (*see* Cognitive/Academic Language Proficiency–CALP) and reading, writing, listening, and speaking skills as used in school to acquire new knowledge and accomplish academic tasks.

Additive bilingualism: Rather than neglecting or rejecting students' language and culture, additive bilingualism promotes building on what the child brings to the classroom and adding to it. The goal is proficiency in both the native language and the new language.

Alignment: Match among the ESL and content standards, instruction, curriculum, and assessment.

Assessment: The orderly process of gathering, analyzing, interpreting, and reporting student performance, ideally from multiple sources over a period of time.

Basic Interpersonal Communicative Skills (BICS): Face-to-face conversational fluency, including mastery of pronunciation, vocabulary, and grammar. English learners typically acquire conversational language used in everyday activities before they develop more complex, conceptual, academic language proficiency. (*See* Social language.)

Bilingual instruction: School instruction using two languages, generally a native language of the student and a second language. The amount of time that each language is used depends on the type of bilingual program, its specific objectives, and students' level of language proficiency.

Cognitive Academic Language Learning Approach (CALLA): An instructional model developed by Chamot and O'Malley (1987, 2009) for content

and language learning that incorporates student development of learning strategies, specifically metacognitive, cognitive, and social/affective strategies.

Cognitive/Academic Language Proficiency (CALP): Language proficiency associated with schooling, and the abstract language abilities required for academic work. A more complex, conceptual, linguistic ability that includes analysis, synthesis, and evaluation. (*See* Academic language.)

Common Core State Standards (CCSS): A common set of Grades K–12 English language arts and mathematics standards, adopted by most states in the United States and the District of Columbia.

Communicative competence: The combination of grammatical, discourse, strategic, and sociolinguistic competence that allows the recognition and production of fluent and appropriate language in all communicative settings.

Content-based ESL: An instructional approach in which content topics are used as the vehicle for second language learning. A system of instruction in which teachers use a variety of instructional techniques as a way of developing second language, content knowledge, and cognitive and study skills. It is often delivered through thematic units.

Content objectives: Statements that identify what students should know and be able to do in a particular content area for a given lesson. They support school district and state content standards and learning outcomes, and they guide teaching and learning in the classroom.

Content standards: Definitions of what students are expected to know and be capable of doing for a given content area; the knowledge and skills that need to be taught in order for students to reach competency; what students are expected to learn and what schools are expected to teach. May be national, state, or district standards.

Cross-cultural competence: The ability to understand and follow the cultural rules and norms of more than one system. The ability to respond to the demands of a given situation in a culturally acceptable way.

Culturally responsive teaching: An approach to classroom instruction and communication that respects the different cultural characteristics of all students. The learning environment reflects high expectations for all. Class discussions are open to cultural viewpoints, student ways of knowing are elicited, collaboration is frequent, pedagogical materials are multicultural, and values are shared and affirmed. The goal is equitable access for all to high quality instruction. Also known as culturally relevant teaching.

Culture: The customs, lifestyle, traditions, behavior, attitudes, and artifacts of a given people. Culture also encompasses the ways people organize and interpret the world, and the way events are perceived based on established social norms. A system of standards for understanding the world.

Dialect: The form of a language distinctive to a specific region. Features a variation in vocabulary, grammar, and pronunciation.

Differentiated instruction: In order to create a learning environment that addresses the diversity of abilities and language proficiency levels represented in many classrooms, teachers adjust the pace, amount, level, or kind of instruction to meet the individual needs and abilities of each learner. Teachers may differentiate the texts being used, the tasks being required of students, or the grouping of the learners.

Engagement: When students are fully taking part in a lesson, they are said to be engaged. This is a holistic term that encompasses active listening, reading, writing, responding, and discussing.

The level of students' engagement during a lesson may be assessed to a greater or lesser degree. A low SIOP score for engagement would imply frequent chatting, daydreaming, nonattention, and other off-task behaviors.

English language development (ELD): Used in some regions to refer to programs and classes to teach students English as a second (additional) language. (*See* ESL.)

English language proficiency (ELP) standards: Definitions of what students are expected to know and be capable of doing in English; the knowledge and skills that need to be taught in order for students to reach competency; what students are expected to learn and what schools are expected to teach. May be national, state, or district standards. Each state is required by the federal government to have ELP standards and related assessments.

English learners (ELs): Children and adults who are learning English as a second or additional language. This term may apply to learners across various levels of proficiency in English. English learners may also be referred to as English language learners (ELLs), non–English speaking (NES) students, limited English proficient (LEP), and nonnative speakers (NNS).

English-only (EO): Used in some regions, English-only or EO refers to students whose native language is English.

ESL: English as a second language. Used to refer to programs and classes to teach students English as a second (additional) language. May refer to the language teaching specialists and their teaching certifications or endorsements.

ESOL: English speakers of other languages. Students whose first language is not English and who do not write, speak, and understand the language as well as their classmates. In some regions, this term also refers to the programs and classes for English learners.

Evaluation: Judgments about students' learning made by interpreting and analyzing assessment data; the process of judging achievement, growth, product, processes, or changes in these; judgments of education programs. The processes of assessment and evaluation can be viewed as progressive: first, assessment; then, evaluation.

Formative evaluation: Ongoing collection, analysis, and reporting of information about student performance or program effectiveness for purposes of instruction and learning.

Grouping: The assignment of students into groups or classes for instruction, such as by age, ability, or achievement; or within classes, such as by reading ability, proficiency, language background, or interests.

Home language: The language, or languages, spoken in the student's home by people who live there. Also referred to as first language (L1), primary language, or native language.

Informal assessment: Appraisal of student performance through unstructured observation; characterized as frequent, ongoing, continuous, and involving simple but important techniques such as verbal checks for understanding, teacher-created assessments, and other nonstandardized procedures. This type of assessment provides teachers with immediate feedback.

Instructional conversations (IC): An approach to teaching that is an interactive dialogue with an instructional intent. An IC approach encourages thoughtful discussion around a concept or idea with balanced participation between teacher and students.

Inter-rater reliability: Measure of the degree of agreement between two different raters on separate ratings of one assessment indicator using the same scale and criteria.

L1: First language. A widely used abbreviation for the primary, home, or native language.

Language competence: An individual's total language ability. The underlying language system as indicated by the individual's language performance.

Language minority: In the United States, a student whose native language is not English. The

individual student's ability to speak English will vary.

Language objectives: Statements that identify what students should know and be able to do while learning English (or another language) in a given lesson. They support students' language development, often focusing on vocabulary, functional language, language skills in reading, writing, listening and speaking, grammatical knowledge, and language learning strategies.

Language proficiency: An individual's competence in using a language for basic communication and for academic purposes. May be categorized as stages of language acquisition. (*See* Levels of language proficiency.)

Levels of language proficiency: Students learning language progress through stages. To date, the stages or levels have been labeled differently in a number of states. In seminal work in this area, Krashen and Terrell (1983) described the stages as the following: Preproduction, Early production, Speech emergence, Intermediate fluency, and Advanced fluency. At present, many states have levels similar to those in the WIDA (World-class Instructional Design and Assessment) English language proficiency standards (WIDA, 2007):

Entering (Level 1): Lowest level, essentially no English proficiency. Students are often newcomers and need extensive pictorial and non-linguistic support. They need to learn basic oral language and literacy skills in English.

Beginning (Level 2): Second lowest level. Students use phrases and short sentences and are introduced to general content vocabulary and lesson tasks.

Developing (Level 3): Next level of proficiency. Students can use general and specific language related to the content areas; they can speak and write sentences and paragraphs although with some errors, and they can read with instructional supports.

Expanding (Level 4): Akin to an intermediate level of proficiency. Students use general, academic, and specific language related to content areas. They have improved speaking and writing skills and stronger reading comprehension skills (compared to the Developing level).

Bridging (Level 5): Akin to advanced intermediate or advanced level of proficiency. Students use general academic and technical language of the content areas. They can read·and write with linguistic complexity. Students at this level have often exited the ESL or ELD program but their language and academic performance is still monitored.

Reaching (Level 6): At or close to grade-level proficiency. Students' oral and written communication skills are comparable to those of native English speakers at their grade level. Students at this level have exited the ESL or ELD program but their language and academic performance is still monitored.

Limited English proficient (LEP): A term used to refer to a student with restricted understanding or use of written and spoken English; a learner who is still developing competence in using English. The federal government continues to use the term *LEP*, while *EL* or *ELL* is more commonly used in schools.

Mnemonics: From the Greek *mnemon*, meaning "mindful." Mnemonics are devices to jog the memory. For example, steps of a learning strategy are often abbreviated to form an acronym or word that enables the learner to remember the steps.

Multilingualism: The ability to speak more than two languages; proficiency in more than two languages.

Native English speaker: An individual whose first language is English. (*See* English-only.)

Native language: An individual's primary, home, or first language (L1).

No Child Left Behind (NCLB) Act of 2001: A major school reform initiative developed and regulated by the federal government. It holds schools accountable for the success of all of their students and requires highly qualified teachers in core content areas. Each state has standards for mathematics, reading/language arts, English language development, and science, and all implement high-stakes tests based on these standards.

Non–English speaking (NES): Individuals who are in an English-speaking environment (such as U.S. schools) but who have not acquired any English proficiency.

Nonverbal communication: Paralinguistic messages such as intonation, stress, pauses, and rate of speech, and nonlinguistic messages such as gestures, facial expressions, and body language that can accompany speech or be conveyed without the aid of speech.

Performance assessment: A measure of educational achievement in which students produce a response, create a product, or apply knowledge in ways similar to tasks required in.the instructional or real-life environment. The performance measures are analyzed and interpreted according to preset criteria.

Portfolio assessment: A type of performance assessment that involves gathering multiple indicators of student progress to support course goals in a dynamic, ongoing process. Portfolios are purposeful collections of student performance that evince students' efforts, progress, and achievement over time.

Primary language: An individual's home, native, or first language (L1).

Pull-out instruction: Students are "pulled-out" from their regular classes for separate classes of ESL instruction, remediation, or acceleration. These are more commonly found in elementary programs.

Realia: Real-life objects and artifacts used to supplement teaching; can provide effective visual scaffolds for English learners.

Reliability: Statistical consistency in measurements and tests, such as the extent to which one assessment will repeatedly produce the same results given the same conditions and student population.

Response to Intervention (RTI): The intent of RTI is to identify at-risk learners early and, using a tiered system, provide effective instruction in general education first (typically called Tier 1) followed by targeted intervention (Tiers 2 and 3) as needed. This process is designed to reduce the number of students eligible for and in need of special education services. The focus is on finding ways to change instruction (or student behaviors) so the learner can be successful. RTI involves documenting a change in behavior or performance as a result of intervention and assessments.

Rubrics: Statements that describe indicators of performance, which include scoring criteria, on a continuum; may be described as "developmental" (e.g., emergent, beginning, developing, proficient) or "evaluative" (e.g., exceptional, thorough, adequate, inadequate).

Scaffolding: Adult (e.g., teacher) support for learning and student performance of the tasks through instruction, modeling, verbal prompts (e.g., questioning), feedback, graphic organizers, and more, across successive engagements. These supports are gradually withdrawn, thus transferring more and more autonomy to the child. Scaffolding activities provide support for learning that can be removed as learners are able to demonstrate strategic behaviors in their own learning activities.

SDAIE (Specially Designed Academic Instruction in English): A term for sheltered instruction used mostly in California and Nevada. It features strategies and techniques for making content understandable for English learners. Although some SDAIE techniques are research based, SDAIE itself has not been scientifically validated. (*See* Sheltered instruction.)

Self-contained ESL class: A class consisting solely of English speakers of other languages for the purpose of learning English; content may also be taught. An effective alternative to pull-out instruction.

Sheltered instruction: A means for making content comprehensible for English learners while they are developing academic English proficiency. The SIOP Model is an empirically validated model of sheltered instruction. Sheltered classrooms may include a mix of native English speakers and English learners or only English learners. Sheltered lessons integrate language and content learning and may include culturally responsive instruction as well. (*See* SDAIE and SIOP®.)

SIOP® (Sheltered Instruction Observation Protocol): An empirically validated model of sheltered instruction designed to make grade-level academic content understandable for English learners while at the same time developing their academic English language proficiency. The protocol and lesson planning guide ensure that teachers are consistently implementing practices known to be effective for English learners.

Social language: Basic language proficiency associated with fluency in day-to-day situations, including the classroom. Also referred to as conversational language. (*See* Basic Interpersonal Communicative Skills [BICS].)

Standard: *See* Content standards and Language standards.

Standard American English: "That variety of American English in which most educational texts, government, and media publications are written in the United States; English as it is spoken and written by those groups with social, economic, and political power in the United States. Standard American English is a relative concept, varying widely in pronunciation and in idiomatic use but maintaining a fairly uniform grammatical structure" (Harris & Hodges, 1995, p. 241).

Standards-based assessment: Assessment involving the planning, gathering, analyzing, and reporting of a student's performance according to the ESL and/or content standards.

Strategies: Mental processes and plans that people use to help them comprehend, learn, and retain new information. There are three types of strategies—cognitive, metacognitive, and social/affective—and these are consciously adapted and monitored during reading, writing, and learning.

Subtractive bilingualism: The learning of a new language at the expense of the native language. Learners often lose their native language and culture because they don't have opportunities to continue learning or using it, or they perceive that language to be of lower status.

Summative evaluation: The final collection, analysis, and reporting of information about student achievement or program effectiveness at the end of a given time frame.

Task: An activity that calls for a response to a question, issue, or problem; an instructional activity.

Validity: A statistical measure of an assessment's match between the information collected and its stated purpose; evidence that inferences from evaluation are trustworthy.

Abedi, J. (2002). Standardized achievement tests and English language learners: Psychometric issues. *Educational Assessment, 8*(3), 234–257.

Abedi, J., & Lord, C. (2001). The language factor in mathematics tests. *Applied Measurement in Education, 14*(3), 219–234.

Allen, J. (2007). *Inside words: Tools for teaching academic vocabulary, grades 4–12.* Portland, ME: Stenhouse Publishers.

Alliance for Excellent Education. (2010). *High school dropouts in America.* Fact Sheet. Washington, DC: Author. Retrieved from www.all4ed.org/files/HighSchoolDropouts.pdf

Alliance for Excellent Education. (2011a). *Engineering solutions to the national crisis in literacy: How to make good on the promise of the Common Core State Standards.* Policy Brief. Washington, DC: Author. Retrieved from www.all4ed.org/files/EngineeringSolutionsLiteracy.pdf

Alliance for Excellent Education. (2011b). *Digital learning and technology: Federal policy recommendations to seize the opportunity—and promising practices that inspire them.* Policy Brief. Washington, DC: Author. Retrieved from www.all4ed.org/files/DigitalLearning.pdf

Alvarez, M.C. (1990). *Knowledge activation and schema construction.* Paper presented at the Annual Meeting of the American Educational Research Association, Boston, MA, 1990. [ED 317 988].

Anderson, L.W., & Krathwohl, D.R. (Eds.). (2001). *Taxonomy for learning, teaching, and assessing: A revision of Bloom's Taxonomy of Educational Objectives.* Boston, MA: Longman.

Anderson, R.C. (1984). Role of the reader's schema in comprehension, learning, and memory. In R.C. Anderson, J. Osborn, & R.J. Tierney (Eds.), *Learning to read in American schools: Basal readers and content texts* (pp. 243–258). Hillsdale, NJ: Erlbaum.

Anderson, R.C. (1994). Role of the reader's schema in comprehension, learning, and memory. In R. Ruddell, M. Ruddell, & H. Singer (Eds.), *Theoretical models and processes of reading* (4th ed., pp. 469–482). Newark, DE: International Reading Association.

Anstrom, K., DiCerbo, P., Butler, F., Katz, A., Millet, J., & Rivera, C. (2010). *A review of the literature on Academic English: Implications for K–12 English language learners.* Arlington, VA: The George Washington University Center for Equity and Excellence in Education.

Aronson, E., Blaney, N.T., Stephan, C., Rosenfield, R., & Sikes, J. (1977). Interdependence in the classroom: A field study. *Journal of Educational Psychology, 69,* 121–128.

Artiles, A. (1998). Overrepresentation of minority students: The case for greater specificity or reconsideration of the variables examined. *The Journal of Special Education, 32*(1), 32–36.

Au, K., Garcia, G.G., Goldenberg, C., & Vogt, M.E. (2005). *Handbook for English language learners.* Boston, MA: Houghton Mifflin.

August, D.A. (2006). How does first language literacy development relate to second language literacy development? In E. Hamayan & R. Freeman (Eds.), *English language learners in school: Over 50 experts answer YOUR questions* (pp. 71–72). Philadelphia, PA: Caslon Publishing.

August, D., & Hakuta, K. (Eds.). (1997). *Improving schooling for language minority children: A research agenda.* Washington, DC: National Academy Press.

August, D., & Shanahan T. (Eds.). (2006). *Developing literacy in second-language learners: A report of the National Literacy Panel on Language-Minority Children and Youth.* Mahwah, NJ: Erlbaum.

August, D., & Shanahan, T. (2010). Effective English literacy instruction for English learners. In California Department of Education (Ed.), *Improving education for English learners: Research-based approaches.* Sacramento, CA: CDE Press.

Bailey, A. (Ed.). (2007). *The language demands of school: Putting academic English to the test.* New Haven, CT: Yale University Press.

Bailey, A., & Butler, F. (2007). A conceptual framework of academic English language for broad application to education. In A. Bailey (Ed.), *The language demands of school: Putting academic English to the test* (pp. 68–102). New Haven, CT: Yale University Press.

Baker, L. (2004). Reading comprehension and science inquiry: Metacognitive connections. In E.W. Saul (Ed.), *Crossing borders in literacy and science instruction: Perspectives on theory and practice* (pp. 239–257). Newark, DE: International Reading Association; Arlington, VA: National Science Teachers Association (NSTA) Press.

Baker, L. (2008). Metacognitive development in reading: Contributors and consequences. In K. Mokhtari & R. Sheorey (Eds.), *Reading strategies of first-and second-language learners: See how they read.* Norwood, MA: Christopher-Gordon Publishers, Inc.

Baker, L., & Brown, A.L. (1984). Metacognitive skills and reading. In P.D. Pearson (Ed.), *Handbook of reading research* (pp. 353–394). New York, NY: Longman.

Balfanz, R., McPartland, J.M., & Shaw, A. (2002). *Re-conceptualizing extra help for high school students in a high standards era.* Baltimore, MD: Center for Social Organization of Schools, Johns Hopkins University.

Ballantyne, K., Sanderman, A., & Levy, J. (2008). *Educating English language learners: Building teacher capacity.* Washington, DC: National Clearinghouse for English Language Acquisition. Retrieved from http://www.ncela.gwu.edu/files/uploads/3/EducatingELLsBuildingTeacherCapacity Vol1.pdf

Barnes, C., Mercer, G., & Shakespeare, T. (1999). *Exploring disability: A sociological introduction.* Cambridge, MA: Polity Press.

Barnhardt, S. (1997). Effective memory strategies. *NCLRC Language Resource, 1*(6).

Bartolome, L.I. (1994). Beyond the methods fetish: Toward a humanizing pedagogy. *Harvard Educational Review, 64*(2), 173–194.

Barton, M.L., Heidama, C., & Jordan, D. (2002). Teaching reading in mathematics and science. *Educational Leadership, 60*(3), 24–28.

Batalova, J., Fix, M., & Murray, J. (2007). *Measures of change: The demography and literacy of adolescent English learners.* Washington, DC: Migration Policy Institute.

Batt, E. (2010). Cognitive coaching: A critical phase in professional development to implement sheltered instruction. *Teaching and Teacher Education 26,* 997–1005.

Baumann, J., Jones, L., & Seifert-Kessell, N. (1993). Using think-alouds to enhance children's comprehension monitoring abilities. *The Reading Teacher, 47*(3), 184–193.

Baumann, J.F. (2005). Vocabulary-comprehension relationships. In B. Maloch, J.V. Hoffman, D.L. Schallert, C.M. Fairbanks, & J. Worthy (Eds.), *54th Yearbook of the National Reading Conference.* Oak Creek, WI: National Reading Conference, Inc.

Bean, T.W. (2000). Reading in the content areas: Social constructivist dimensions. In M.L. Kamil, P.B. Mosenthal, P.D. Pearson, & R. Barr (Eds.), *Handbook of reading research* (Vol. III, pp. 629–644). Mahwah, NJ: Erlbaum.

Bear, D.R., Helman, L., Invernizzi, M., Templeton, S., & Johnston, F. (2011). *Words their way with English learners: Word study for spelling, phonics, and vocabulary instruction* (2nd ed.). Boston, MA: Pearson.

Bear, D.R., Invernizzi, M., Templeton, S., & Johnston, F. (2011). *Words their way: Word study for phonics, vocabulary, and spelling instruction* (5th ed.). Boston, MA: Pearson.

Bear, D.R., Templeton, S., Helman, L.A., & Baren, T. (2003). Orthographic development and learning to read in different languages. In G. Garcia (Ed.), *English learners: Reaching the highest level of English literacy.* Newark, DE: International Reading Association.

Beck, I.L., & McKeown, M.G. (2002). Questioning the author: Making sense of social studies. *Educational Leadership, 60*(3), 44–47.

Beck, I.L., & McKeown, M.G. (2006). *Improving comprehension with Questioning the Author: A fresh and expanded view of a powerful approach.* New York, NY: Scholastic.

Beck, I.L., & McKeown, M.G. (2008). *Improving comprehension with Questioning the Author: A fresh and expanded view of a powerful approach.* New York, NY: Scholastic.

Beck, I.L, McKeown, M.G., & Kucan, L. (2002). *Bringing words to life: Robust vocabulary instruction.* New York, NY: Guilford Press.

Beck, I.L., Perfetti, C., & McKeown, M.G. (1982). Effects of long-term vocabulary instruction on lexical access and reading comprehension. *Journal of Educational Psychology, 74*, 506–521.

Berliner, D.C. (1984). The half-full glass: A review of research on teaching. In P.L. Hosford (Ed.), *Using what we know about teaching* (pp. 51–77). Alexandria, VA: Association for Supervision and Curriculum Development.

Biancarosa, G., & Snow, C. (2004). *Reading next: A vision for action and research in middle and high school literacy.* Report to the Carnegie Corporation of New York. Washington, DC: Alliance for Excellent Education.

Biemiller, A. (2004). Teaching vocabulary in the primary grades. In J.F. Baumann & J.E. Kame'enui (Eds.), *Vocabulary instruction: Research to practice.* New York, NY: Guilford Press.

Biemiller, A. (2005). Vocabulary development and instruction: A prerequisite for school learning. In D. Dickinson & S. Neuman (Eds.), *Handbook of early literacy research,* Vol. 2. New York, NY: Guilford Press.

Blachowicz, L.Z., & Fisher, P. (2000). Vocabulary instruction. In R.L. Kamil, P.B. Mosenthal, P.D. Pearson, & R. Barr (Eds.), *Handbook of reading research* (Vol. 3, pp. 503–523). Mahwah, NJ: Erlbaum.

Bloom, B., Engelhart, M., Furst, E., Hill, W., & Krathworl, D. (Eds.). (1956). *Taxonomy of educational objectives: The classification of educational goals. Handbook I: Cognitive domain.* New York, NY: David McKay Co.

Borko, H. (2004). Professional development and teacher learning: Mapping the terrain. *Educational Researcher, 33*(8), 3–15.

Bransford, J. (2004). Schema activation and schema acquisition: Comments on Richard C. Anderson's remarks. In R. Ruddell, M. Ruddell, & H. Singer (Eds.), *Theoretical models and processes of reading* (5th ed., pp. 607–619). Newark, DE: International Reading Association.

Brooks, K., & Thurston, L. (2010). English language learner academic engagement and instructional grouping configurations. *American Secondary Education, 39*(1), 45–60.

Brown, B, & Ryoo, K. (2008). Teaching science as a language: A "content-first" approach to science teaching. *Journal of Research in Science Teaching, 45*(5), 529–553.

Brown, R. (2008). The road not yet taken: A transactional strategies approach to comprehension instruction. *The Reading Teacher, 6*(7), 538–547.

Brozo, W. (2010). The role of content literacy in an effective RTI program. *The Reading Teacher, 64*(2), 147–150.

Bruner, J. (1983). *Child's talk: Learning to use language.* New York, NY: W.W. Norton.

Buck, B., Carr, S., & Robertson, J. (2008). Positive psychology and student engagement. *Journal of Cross-Disciplinary Perspectives in Education, 1*(1), 28–35.

Buehl, D. (2006). *Scaffolding.* Wisconsin Education Association Council. Retrieved from http://www.weac.org/news_and_publications/education_news/2005-2006/readingroomoct06.aspx

Buehl, D. (2009). *Classroom strategies for interactive learning* (3rd ed.). Newark, DE: International Reading Association.

Burke, J. (2002). The Internet reader. *Educational Leadership, 60*(3), 38–42.

Calderón, M., & Minaya-Rowe, L. (2011). *Preventing long-term ELs: Transforming schools to meet core standards.* Thousand Oaks, CA: Corwin.

California Department of Education. (2010). *Improving education for English learners: Research-based approaches.* Sacramento, CA: CDE Press. (See http://www.cde.ca.gov/re/pn for more information.)

Calkins, L., Ehrenworth, M., & Lehman, C. (2012). *Pathways to the Common Core: Accelerating achievement.* Portsmouth, NH: Heinemann.

Callahan, R.M. (2005). Tracking and high school English language learners: Limiting opportunity to learn. *American Educational Research Journal, 42*(2), 305–328.

Cañado, M.L.P. (2005). English and Spanish spelling: Are they really different? *The Reading Teacher, 58*(6), 522–530.

Carnegie Corporation of New York. (2010). *Advancing adolescent literacy: The cornerstone of school reform.* New York, NY: Author.

Carrell, P. (1987). Content and formal schemata in ESL reading. *TESOL Quarterly, 21*(3), 461–481.

Cazden, C. (2001). *Classroom discourse: The language of teaching and learning.* New York, NY: Heinemann.

Chamot, A.U. (2009). *The CALLA handbook* (2nd ed.). Boston, MA: Pearson Education, Inc.

Chamot, A.U., & O'Malley, J.M. (1987). The cognitive academic language learning approach: A bridge to the mainstream. *TESOL Quarterly, 21*(2), 227–249.

Chiesi, H., Spilich, G., & Voss, J. (1979). Acquisition of domain-related information in relation to high- and low-domain knowledge. *Journal of Verbal Learning and Verbal Behavior, 18*, 257–274.

Cloud, N., Genesee, F., & Hamayan, E. (2009). *Literacy instruction for English language learners.* Portsmouth, NH: Heinemann.

Cloud, N., Healey, K., Paul, M., Short, D., & Winiarski, P. (2010). *Preparing adolescents for the academic listening demands of secondary school classrooms.* In N. Ashcraft & A. Tran (Eds.), *Listening: TESOL classroom practice series* (pp. 151–167). Alexandria, VA: Teachers of English to Speakers of Other Languages.

Cohen, A.D., & Macaro, E. (Eds.). (2008). *Language learner strategies: 30 years of research and practice.* Oxford, UK: Oxford University Press.

Colburn, A., & Echevarría, J. (1999). Meaningful lessons. *The Science Teacher, 66*(2), 36–39.

Collier, V.P. (1987). Age and rate of acquisition of language for academic purposes. *TESOL Quarterly, 21*(4), 677.

Comer, J.P. (1984). Home-school relationships as they affect the academic success of children. *Education and Urban Society, 16*(3), 323–337.

Common Core State Standards. (2010). Retrieved from www.doe.in.gov/commoncore

Cooper, J.D., Pikulski, J.J., Au, K., Calderon, M., Comas, J., Lipson, M., Mims, S., Page, S., Valencia, S., & Vogt, M.E. (2003). *Invitations to literacy.* Boston, MA: Houghton Mifflin Company.

Cortiella, C. (2011). *The state of learning disabilities.* New York, NY: National.

Crane, E.W., Barrat, V.X., & Huang, M. (2011). *The relationship between English proficiency and content knowledge for English language learner students in grades 10 and 11 in Utah.* (REL 2011–No. 110). Washington, DC: U.S. Department of Education, Institute of Education Sciences, National Center for Education Evaluation and Regional Assistance, Regional Educational Laboratory West. Retrieved from http://ies.ed.gov/ncee/edlabs

Crossley, S., McCarthy, P., Louwerse, M., & McNamara, D. (2007). A linguistic analysis of simplified and authentic texts. *The Modern Language Journal, 19*(2), 15–30.

Cummins, J. (1984). *Bilingualism and special education: Issues in assessment and pedagogy.* Clevedon, England: Multilingual Matters.

Cummins, J. (2000). *Language, power and pedagogy.* Clevedon, England: Multilingual Matters.

Cunningham, P.M. (2004). *Phonics they use: Words for reading and writing* (4th ed.). New York, NY: Harper-Collins College Press.

Dale, E. (1965). Vocabulary measurement: Techniques and major findings. *Elementary English, 42,* 82–88.

Dale, E., & O'Rourke, J. (1981). *Living word vocabulary.* Chicago, IL: World Book/Childcraft International.

Dalton, B., & Grisham, D. (2011). eVoc strategies: 10 ways to use technology to build vocabulary. *The Reading Teacher, 64*(5), 306–317.

Darling-Hammond, L. (1998). Teacher learning that supports student learning. *Educational Leadership, 55*(5), 6–11.

Darling-Hammond, L., & Richardson, N. (2009). Teachers learning: What matters? *Educational Leadership,* 66(5), 46–53.

Davis, S.J., & Winek, J. (1989). Improving expository writing by increasing background knowledge. *Journal of Reading 33*(3), 178–181.

Davison, C. (2006). Collaboration between ESL and content teachers: How do we know when we are doing it right? *International Journal of Bilingual Education and Bilingualism, 9*(4), 454–475.

Day, R. (Ed.). (1986). *Talking to learn: Conversation in second language acquisition.* Cambridge, MA: Newbury House Publishers.

DeLeeuw, H. (2008). *English language learners in Washington State.* Executive Summary. Report to the Washington State Board of Education, Olympia, WA, January 10, 2008.

Deschenes, C., Ebeling, D., & Sprague, J. (1994). *Adapting curriculum and instruction in inclusive classrooms: A teacher's desk reference.* Bloomington, IN: Institute for the Study of Developmental Disabilities, Indiana University.

Deshler, D., & Schumaker, J. (2006). *Teaching adolescents with disabilities: Accessing the general education curriculum.* Thousand Oaks, CA: Corwin Press.

Diamond, L., & Gutlohn, L. (2006). *Vocabulary handbook.* Berkeley, CA: Core Literacy Library.

Dianda, M. (2008). *Preventing future high school dropouts: An advocacy and action guide for NEA state and local affiliates.* Washington, DC: National Education Association.

Dietz, S. (2010). *State high school tests: Exit exams and other assessments.* Washington, DC: Center on Education Policy.

Dockrell, J., Stewart, M., & King, D. (2010). Supporting early oral language skills for English language learners in inner city preschool provision. *British Journal of Educational Psychology, 80,* 497–515.

Dole, J., Duffy, G., Roehler, L., & Pearson, P.D. (1991). Moving from the old to the new: Research in reading comprehension instruction. *Review of Educational Research, 61,* 239–264.

Donnelly, W.B., & Roe, C.J. (2010). Using sentence frames to develop academic vocabulary for English learners. *The Reading Teacher, 64*(2), 131–136.

Dreher, M.J., & Gray, J.L. (2009). Compare, contrast, comprehend: Using compare-contrast text structures with ELLs in K–3 classrooms. *The Reading Teacher, 63*(2), 132–141.

Duff, P.A. (2005). ESL in secondary schools: Programs, problematics, and possibilities. *Annual Review of Applied Linguistics,* 45–63.

Duffy, G.G. (2002). The case for direct explanation of strategies. In C.C. Block & M. Pressley (Eds.), *Comprehension instruction: Research-based best practices* (pp. 28–41). New York, NY: Guilford Press.

Dunn, L. (1968). Special education for the mildly retarded: Is much of it justifiable? *Exceptional Children, 34,* 5–22.

Dutro, S., & Kinsella, K. (2010). English language development: Issues and implementation at grades 6 through 12. In California Department of

Education (Ed.), *Improving education for English learners: Research-based approaches* (pp. 151–207). Sacramento: CA Dept. of Education.

Dymock, S., & Nicholson, R. (2010). High 5! Strategies to enhance comprehension of expository text. *The Reading Teacher, 64*(3), 166–178.

Echevarría, J. (1995a). Sheltered instruction for students with learning disabilities who have limited English proficiency. *Intervention in School and Clinic, 30*(5), 302–305.

Echevarría, J. (1995b). Interactive reading instruction: A comparison of proximal and distal effects of instructional conversations. *Exceptional Children, 61*(6), 536–552.

Echevarría, J. (1998). *A model of sheltered instruction for English language learners.* Paper presented at the conference for the Division on Diversity of the Council for Exceptional Children, Washington, DC.

Echevarría, J., & Graves, A. (2007). *Sheltered content instruction: Teaching English language learners with diverse abilities* (3rd ed.). Boston, MA: Allyn & Bacon.

Echevarría, J., & Graves, A. (2010). *Sheltered content instruction: Teaching English learners with diverse abilities* (4th ed.). Boston, MA: Allyn & Bacon.

Echevarría, J., Greene, G., & Goldenberg, C. (1996). *A comparison of sheltered instruction and effective non-sheltered instruction on the achievement of LEP students.* Pilot study.

Echevarría, J., & Hasbrouck, J. (2009). *Response to intervention and English learners* (CREATE Brief). Washington, DC: Center for Research on the Educational Achievement and Teaching of English Language Learners. Retrieved from http://www.cal.org/create/resources/pubs/responsetointerv.html

Echevarría, J., Powers, K., & Elliott, J. (2004). Promising practices for curbing disproportionate representation of minority students in special education. *Issues in Teacher Education: Themed Issues on Special Needs Education, 13*(1), 19–34.

Echevarría, J., Richards-Tutor, C., Canges, R., & Francis, D. (2011). Using the SIOP Model to promote the acquisition of language and science concepts with English learners. *Bilingual Research Journal, 34*(3), 334–351.

Echevarría, J., Richards-Tutor, C., Chinn, V., & Ratleff, P. (2011). Did they get it? The role of fidelity in teaching English learners. *Journal of Adolescent and Adult Literacy, 54*(6), 425–434.

Echevarría, J., & Short, D. (2010). Programs and practices for effective sheltered content instruction. In California Department of Education (Ed.), *Improving education for English learners: Research-based approaches* (pp. 250–321). Sacramento, CA: CDE Press.

Echevarría, J., Short, D., & Peterson, C. (2012). *Using the SIOP Model with pre-K and kindergarten English learners.* Boston, MA: Allyn & Bacon.

Echevarría, J., Short, D., & Powers, K. (2006). School reform and standards-based education: An instructional model for English language learners. *Journal of Educational Research, 99*(4), 195–211.

Echevarría, J., Short, D., Richards-Tutor, C., & Himmel, J. (in press). Using the SIOP Model as a professional development framework for comprehensive schoolwide intervention. In J. Echevarría, S. Vaughn, & D. Francis (Eds.), *English learners in content area classes: Teaching for achievement in the middle grades* Boston, MA: Pearson.

Echevarría, J., Short, D., & Vogt, M.E. (2008). *Implementing the SIOP® Model through effective professional development and coaching.* Boston, MA: Pearson/Allyn & Bacon.

Echevarría, J., Vaughn, S., & Francis, D. (Eds.). (in press). *English learners in content area classes: Teaching for achievement in the middle grades.* Boston, MA: Pearson.

Echevarría, J., & Vogt, M. (2011). *RTI and English learners: Making it happen.* Boston, MA: Allyn & Bacon.

Echevarría, J., Vogt, M.E., & Short, D. (2000). *Making content comprehensible for English language* learners: *The SIOP® Model.* Needham Heights, MA: Allyn & Bacon.

Echevarría, J., Vogt, M.E., & Short, D. (2004). *Making content comprehensible for English learners: The SIOP® Model* (2nd ed.). Boston, MA: Pearson/Allyn & Bacon.

Echevarría, J., Vogt, M.E., & Short, D. (2008). *Making content comprehensible for English learners: The SIOP® Model* (3rd ed.). Boston, MA: Pearson/Allyn & Bacon.

Echevarría, J., Vogt, M.E., & Short, D. (2010a). *Making content comprehensible for elementary English learners: The SIOP® Model.* Boston, MA: Pearson/Allyn & Bacon.

Echevarría, J., Vogt, M.E., & Short, D. (2010b). *Making content comprehensible for secondary English learners: The SIOP® Model.* Boston, MA: Pearson/Allyn & Bacon.

Echevarría, J., Vogt, M.E., & Short, D. (2010c). *The SIOP® Model for teaching mathematics to English learners.* Boston, MA: Pearson/Allyn & Bacon.

Ellis, R. (2006). Current issues in the teaching of grammar: An SLA perspective. *TESOL Quarterly, 40*(1), 83–107.

Ellis, R. (2008). *Principles of instructed second language acquisition.* CAL Digest. Washington, DC: Center for Applied Linguistics.

Erickson, F., & Shultz, J. (1991). Students' experience of the curriculum. In P.W. Jackson (Ed.), *Handbook of research on curriculum.* New York, NY: Macmillan.

Fathman, A., & Crowther, D. (Eds.). (2006). *Science for English language learners: K–12 classroom strategies.* Arlington, VA: NSTA Press.

Fillmore, L.W., & Valadez, C. (1986). Teaching bilingual learners. In M.C. Wittrock (Ed.), *Handbook of research on teaching* (pp. 648–685). New York, NY: Macmillan.

Fisher, D., & Frey, N. (2008a). *Better learning through structured teaching.* Alexandria, VA: Association for Supervision and Curriculum Development.

Fisher, D., & Frey, N. (2008b). *Wordwise & content rich: Five essential steps to teaching academic vocabulary.* Portsmouth, NH: Heinemann.

Fisher, D., Frey, N., & Williams, D. (2002). Seven literacy strategies that work. *Educational Leadership, 60*(3), 70–73.

Fix, M., & McHugh, M. (2009). *A discussion guide: Education, diversity and the second generation.* Washington, DC: Migration Policy Institute.

Flood, J., Lapp, D., Flood, S., & Nagel, G. (1992). Am I allowed to group? Using flexible patterns for effective instruction. *The Reading Teacher, 45,* 608–616.

Flores, S.M., Batalova, J., & Fix, M. (2012). *The educational trajectories of English-language learners in Texas.* Washington, DC: Migration Policy Institute.

Fordham, D. (2006). Crafting questions that address comprehension strategies in content reading. *Journal of Adolescent & Adult Literacy, 49*(5), 391–396.

Freeman, Y., & Freeman, D. (2009). *Academic language for ELLs and struggling readers.* Portsmouth, NH: Heinemann.

Fuchs, D., Fuchs, L.S., & Bahr, M.W. (1990). Mainstream assistance teams: A scientific basis for the art of consultation. *Exceptional Children, 57,* 128–139.

Futrell, M., & Gomez, J. (2008). How tracking creates a poverty of learning. *Educational Leadership, 65*(8), 74–78.

Gall, M. (1984). Synthesis of research on teachers' questioning. *Educational Leadership,* 40–47.

Garcia, G.E., & Godina, H. (2004). Addressing the literacy needs of adolescent English language learners. In T. Jetton & J. Dole (Eds.), *Adolescent literacy: Research and practice* (pp. 304–320). New York, NY: The Guilford Press.

Gardner, H. (1993). *Multiple intelligences: The theory in practice.* New York, NY: Basic Books.

Genesee, F. (Ed.). (1999). *Program alternatives for linguistically diverse students.* Educational Practice Report No. 1. Santa Cruz, CA, and Washington, DC: Center for Research on Education, Diversity & Excellence.

Genesee, F., Lindholm-Leary, K., Saunders, W., & Christian, D. (2006). *Educating English language learners: A synthesis of research evidence.* New York, NY: Cambridge University Press.

Gersten, R., Baker, S., Shanahan, T., Linan-Thompson, S., Collins, P., & Scarcella, R. (2007). *Effective literacy and English language instruction for English learners in the elementary grades: A practice guide* (NCEE 2007-4011). Washington, DC: National Center for Education Evaluation and Regional Assistance, Institute of Education Sciences, U.S. Department of Education. Retrieved from http://ies.ed.gov/ncee

Geva, E. (2006). Second-language oral proficiency and second-language literacy. In D. August & T. Shanahan (Eds.), *Developing literacy in second-language learners: Report of the National Literacy Panel on Language Minority Children and Youth.* Mahwah, NJ: Erlbaum.

Gibbons, P. (2002). *Scaffolding language, scaffolding learning.* Portsmouth, NH: Heineman.

Gibbons, P. (2003). Mediating language learning: Teacher interactions with ESL students in a content-based classroom. *TESOL Quarterly, 37*(2), 247–273.

Gibson, V., & Hasbrouck, J. (2008). *Differentiated instruction: Grouping for success.* New York, NY: McGraw-Hill.

Glick, J.E., & White, M.J. (2004). Post-secondary school participation of immigrant and native youth: The role of familial resources and educational expectations. *Social Science Research, 33,* 272–299.

Goldenberg, C. (1992–93). Instructional conversations: Promoting comprehension through discussion. *The Reading Teacher, 46*(4), 316–326.

Goldenberg, C. (2006, July 26). Improving achievement for English-learners: What the research tells us. *Education Week, 25*(43), 34–36.

Goldenberg, C. (2008). Teaching English language learners: What research does—and does not say. *American Educator, 32*(2), 8–23, 42–44.

González, J.M., & Darling-Hammond, L. (1997). *New concepts for new challenges: Professional development for teachers of immigrant youth.* McHenry, IL: Delta Systems and CAL.

Goodlad, J. (1984). *A place called school: Prospects for the future.* New York, NY: McGraw-Hill.

Graff, G. (2003). *Clueless in academe.* New Haven, CT: Yale University Press.

Graham, S., & Perin, D. (2007). *Writing next: Effective strategies to improve writing of adolescents in middle and high schools. A report to Carnegie Corporation of New York.* Washington, DC: Alliance for Excellent Education.

Graves, A., Gersten, R., & Haager, D. (2004). Literacy instruction in multiple-language first-grade classrooms: Linking student outcomes to observed instructional practice. *Learning Disabilities Research & Practice, 19*(4), 262–272.

Graves, M.F. (2011). Ask the expert. *The Reading Teacher, 64*(7), 541.

Graves, M.F., & Fitzgerald, J. (2006). Effective vocabulary instruction for English-language learners. In C.C. Block & J.N. Mangieri (Eds.), *The vocabulary-enriched classroom: Practice for improving the reading performance of all students in grades 3 and up* (pp. 118–137). New York, NY: Scholastic.

Gray, W.S., & Leary, B.E. (1935). *What makes a book readable?* Chicago, IL: The University of Chicago Press.

Guarino, A.J., Echevarría, J., Short, D., Schick, J.E., Forbes, S., & Rueda, R. (2001). The Sheltered Instruction Observation Protocol. *Journal of Research in Education, 11*(1), 138–140.

Guthrie, J.T., & Ozgungor, S. (2002). Instructional contexts for reading engagement. In C.C. Block & M. Pressley (Eds.), *Comprehension instruction: Research-based best practices* (pp. 275–288). New York, NY: Guilford Press.

Gutiérrez, K.D. (2004). Literacy as laminated activity: Rethinking literacy for English learners. In C.M. Fairbanks, J. Worthy, B. Maloch, J.V. Hoffman, & D.L. Schallert (Eds.), *53rd Yearbook of the National Reading Conference.* Oak Creek, WI: National Reading Conference.

Hakuta, K., Butler, Y., & Witt, D. (2000). *How long does it take English learners to attain proficiency?* Policy Report 2000–1. Santa Barbara, CA: University of California, Linguistic Minority Research Institute.

Harris, T.L., & Hodges, R.E. (Eds.). (1995). *The literacy dictionary: The vocabulary of reading and writing.* Newark, DE: International Reading Association.

Harry, B. (1992). Restructuring the participation of African-American parents in special education. *Exceptional Children, 59*(2), 123–131.

Hart, B., & Risley, T.R. (2003). The early catastrophe: The 30 million word gap. *American Educator, 27,* 4–9.

Hawkin, L. (2005). Behavior programs for older students: What's helpful in secondary schools? *The Special Edge, 19*(1), 1–5.

Hayes, D.A., & Tierney, R.J. (1982). Developing readers' knowledge through analogy. *Reading Research Quarterly 17*(2), 256–280.

Helman, L., Bear, D., Templeton, S., & Invernizzi, M. (2011). *Words their way with English learners: Words study for phonics, vocabulary, and spelling* (2nd ed.). Boston, MA: Pearson.

Helman, M., & Buchanan, K. (1993, Fall). *Reforming mathematics instruction for ESL literacy students.* NCBE Program Information Guide Series, Number 15. Retrieved from www.ncela.gwu.edu/ncbepubs/pigs/pig15.htm

Henry, M.K. (1990). *TUTOR 3.* Los Gatos, CA: Lex Press.

Herrell, A., & Jordan, M. (2008). *Fifty strategies for teaching English language learners* (3rd ed.) Upper Saddle River, NJ: Pearson/Merrill Prentice Hall.

Hiebert, E.H. (1983). An examination of ability grouping for reading instruction. *Reading Research Quarterly, 18,* 231–255.

Himmel, J., Short, D.J., Richards, C., & Echevarría, J. (2009). *Using the SIOP Model to improve middle school science instruction* (CREATE Brief). Washington, DC: Center for Research on the Educational Achievement and Teaching of English Language Learners/CAL.

Hinkel, E. (2006). Current perspectives on teaching the four skills. *TESOL Quarterly, 40*(1), 109–131.

Honea, J.M. (1982, December). Wait-time as an instructional variable: An influence on teacher and student. *Clearinghouse, 56*(4), 167–170.

Hudec, J., & Short, D. (Prods.). (2002a). *Helping English learners succeed: An overview of the SIOP® Model.* (Video). Washington, DC: Center for Applied Linguistics.

Hudec, J., & Short, D. (Prods.) (2002b). *The SIOP® Model: Sheltered instruction for academic achievement.* (Video). Washington, DC: Center for Applied Linguistics.

Hunter, M. (1982). *Mastery teaching: Increasing instructional effectiveness in secondary schools, college, and universities.* El Segundo, CA: TIP Publications.

Jensen, E. (2005). *Teaching with the brain in mind* (2nd ed.). Alexandria, VA: Association for Supervision and Curriculum Development.

Jensen, E. (2008). *Brain-based learning* (2nd ed.). Thousand Oaks, CA: Corwin Press.

Jeon, H., Peterson, C., Wall, S., Carta, J., Luze, G., Eshbaugh, E., & Swanson, M. (2011). Predicting school readiness for low-income children with disability risks identified early. *Exceptional Children, 77*(4), 435–452.

Jiménez, R.T. (2004). More equitable literacy assessments for Latino students. *The Reading Teacher, 57*(6), 576–578.

Jiménez, R.T., Garcia, G.E., & Pearson, P.D. (1996). The reading strategies of bilingual Latina/o students who are successful English readers: Opportunities and obstacles. *Reading Research Quarterly, 31*(1), 90–112.

Kagan, S. (1994). *Cooperative learning.* San Clemente, CA: Kagan Publishing.

Kamil, M. (2003). *Adolescents and literacy: Reading for the 21st century.* Washington, DC: Alliance for Excellent Education.

Kea, C., & Utley, C. (1998). To teach me is to know me. *Journal of Special Education, 32*(1), 44–48.

Keene, E.O., & Zimmerman, S. (1997). *Mosaic of thought: Teaching comprehension in a reader's workshop.* Portsmouth, NH: Heinemann.

Kilgo, M. (no date). *Definitions of verbs in the Common Core State Standards for reading comprehension—grades K–5.* Handout.

Klingner, J., & Harry, B. (2006). The special education referral and decision-making process for English Language Learners: Child study team meetings and placement conferences. *Teachers College Record, 108*(11), 2247–2281.

Klingner, J.K., & Vaughn, S. (1999). Promoting reading comprehension, content learning, and English acquisition through collaborative strategic reading (CSR). *The Reading Teacher, 52,* 738–747.

Klingner, J.K., & Vaughn, S. (2000). The helping behaviors of fifth-graders while using collaborative strategic reading (CSR) during ESL content classes. *TESOL Quarterly, 34,* 69–98.

Klingner, J.K., Vaughn, S., Argüelles, M.E., Hughes, M.T., & Ahwee, S. (2004). Collaborative strategic reading: "Real world" lessons from classroom teachers. *Remedial and Special Education, 25,* 291–302.

Klingner, J.K., Vaughn, S., & Schumm, J.S. (1998). Collaborative strategic reading during social studies in heterogeneous fourth-grade classrooms. *Elementary School Journal, 99,* 3–21.

Kober, N., Zabala, D., Chudowsky, N., Chudowsky, V., Gayler, K., & McMurrer, J. (2006). *State high school exit exams: A challenging year.* Washington, DC: Center for Education Policy.

Konstantopoulos, S. (2011). Teacher effects in early grades: Evidence from a randomized study. *Teachers College Record, 113*(7). http://www.tcrecord.org. ID Number: 16099.

Krashen, S. (1985). *The input hypothesis: Issues and implications.* New York, NY: Longman.

Krashen, S. (2003). Three roles for reading for minority-language children. In G. Garcia (Ed.), *English learners: Reaching the highest level of English literacy* (pp. 55–70). Newark, DE: International Reading Association.

Krashen, S., & Terrell, T. (1983). *The natural approach: Language acquisition in the classroom.* Englewood Cliffs, NJ: Alemany/Prentice Hall.

Kretlow, A., & Blatz, S. (2011) The ABC's of evidence-based practice for teachers. *Teaching Exceptional Children, 43*(5), 8–19.

Kucan, L. (2012). What is most important to know about vocabulary? *The Reading Teacher, 65*(6), 360–366.

Kukic, S.J. (2002). *The complete school for all.* Keynote presentation at the 2nd Annual Pacific Northwest Behavior Symposium, Seattle, WA.

Lacina, J., Levine, L.N., & Sowa, P. (2006). *Helping English language learners succeed in preK–elementary schools.* Alexandria, VA: Teachers of English to Speakers of Other Languages, Inc.

Leafstedt, J., Richards, C., & Gerber, M. (2004). Effectiveness of explicit phonological-awareness instruction for at-risk English learners. *Learning Disabilities Research & Practice, 19*(4), 252–261.

Leinhardt, G., Bickel, W., & Pallay, A. (1982). Unlabeled but still entitled: Toward more effective remediation. *Teachers College Record, 84*(2), 391–422.

Lemke, C., & Coughlin, E. (2009). The change agents. *Educational Leadership, 67*(1), 54–59.

Lemke, J. (1988). Genres, semantics, and classroom education. *Linguistics and Education, 1,* 81–99.

Lenski, S.D., Ehlers-Zavala, F., Daniel, M.C., & Sun-Irminger, X. (2006). Assessing English-language learners in mainstream classrooms. *The Reading Teacher, 60*(1), 24–34.

Lenters, K. (2005). No half measures: Reading instruction for young second-language learners. *The Reading Teacher, 58*(4), 328–336.

Lesaux, N.K., & Geva, E. (2006). Synthesis: Development of literacy in language minority students. In D. August & T. Shanahan (Eds.), *Developing literacy in second language learners: Report of the National Literacy Panel on Language-Minority Children and Youth* (pp. 53–74). Mahwah, NJ: Erlbaum.

Lesaux, N.K., Kieffer, M.J., Faller, S.E., & Kelley, J.G. (2010). The effectiveness and ease of implementation of an academic vocabulary intervention for linguistically diverse students in urban middle schools. *Reading Research Quarterly, 45*(2), 196–228.

Limbos, M., & Geva, E. (2001). Accuracy of teacher assessments of second-language students at risk for reading disability. *Journal of Learning Disabilities, 34*, 136–151.

Lindholm-Leary, K., & Borsato, G. (2006). Academic achievement. In F. Genesee, K. Lindholm-Leary, W. Saunders, & D. Christian (Eds.), *Educating English language learners: A synthesis of research evidence* (pp. 176–221). New York, NY: Cambridge University Press.

Lipson, M., & Wixson, K. (2012). *Assessment of reading and writing difficulties: An interactive approach* (5th ed.). New York, NY: Longman.

Losen, D., & Orfield, G. (2002). *Racial inequity in special education.* Cambridge, MA: Harvard Education Publishing Company.

Lucas, S.R. (1999). *Tracking inequality: Stratification and mobility in American high schools.* New York, NY: Teachers College Press.

Lyman, F. (1981). The responsive classroom discussion. In Anderson, A.S. (Ed.), *Mainstreaming digest.* College Park, MD: University of Maryland College of Education.

Lynch, S. (2000). *Equity and science education reform.* Mahwah, NJ: Erlbaum.

MacMillan, D., & Reschly, D. (1998). Overrepresentation of minority students: The case for greater specificity or reconsideration of the variables examined. *Journal of Special Education, 32*(1), 15–20.

Macon, J., Buell, D., & Vogt, M.E. (1991). *Responses to literature: Grades K–8.* Newark, DE: International Reading Association.

Manyak, P.C. (2010). Vocabulary instruction for English learners: Lesson from MCVIP. *The Reading Teacher, 64*(2), 143–146.

Manzo, A.J., Manzo, U.C., & Thomas, M.T. (2005). *Content area literacy: Strategic thinking for strategic learning* (4th ed.). New York, NY: John Wiley & Sons, Inc.

Marcell, B., DeCleene, J., & Juettner, M.R. (2010). Caution! Hard Hat Area! Comprehension under construction: Cementing a foundation of comprehension strategy usage that carries over to independent practice. *The Reading Teacher, 63*(8), 687–691.

Marshall, J. (2000). Research on response to literature. In R.L. Kamil, P.B. Mosenthal, P.D. Son, & R. Barr (Eds.), *Handbook of reading research* (Vol. 3, pp. 381–402). Mahwah, NJ: Erlbaum.

Marzano, R., Pickering, D., & Pollock, J. (2001). *Classroom instruction that works.* Alexandria, VA: Association for Supervision and Curriculum Development.

Mathis, W.J. (2010). *The "common core" standards initiative: An effective reform tool?* Boulder, CO: Great Lakes Center for Education Research & Practice.

May, L.A. (2011). Situating strategies: An examination of comprehension strategy instruction in one upper elementary classroom oriented toward culturally relevant teaching. *Literacy Research and Instruction, 50*(1), 31–43.

McAndrews, S. (2008). *Diagnostic literacy assessments and instructional strategies: A literacy specialist's resource.* Newark, DE: International Reading Association.

McCormick, C.B., & Pressley, M. (1997). *Educational psychology: Learning, instruction, assessment.* New York, NY: Longman.

McGraner, K., & Saenz, L. (2009). *Preparing teachers of English language learners.* Washington DC: National Comprehensive Center for Teacher Quality.

McIntyre, E., Kyle, D., Chen, C., Muñoz, M., & Beldon, S. (2010). Teacher learning and ELL reading achievement in sheltered instruction classrooms: Linking professional development to student development. *Literacy Research and Instruction, 49*(4), 334–351.

McKeown, M.G., Beck, I.L., & Blake, R.G.K. (2009). Rethinking reading comprehension instruction: A comparison of instruction for strategies and content approaches. *Reading Research Quarterly, 44*(3), 218–253.

McLaughlin, M. (2010). *Content area reading: Teaching and learning in an age of multiple literacies.* Boston, MA: Pearson.

McLaughlin, M. (2012). Reading comprehension: What every teacher needs to know. *The Reading Teacher, 65* (7), 432–440.

McLaughlin, M., & Allen, M.B. (2009). *Guided comprehension: A teaching model* (2nd ed.). Newark, DE: International Reading Association.

McLaughlin, M., & Vogt, M.E. (2000). *Creativity and innovation in content area teaching: A resource for intermediate, middle, and high school teachers.* Norwood, MA: Christopher-Gordon Publishers.

McNeil, L.M., Coppola, E., Radigan, J., & Vasquez Heilig, J. (2008). Avoidable losses: High-stakes accountability and the dropout crisis. *Education Policy Analysis Archives, 16*(3). Retrieved from http://epaa.asu.edu/epaa/v16n3/

Menken, K. (2008). *English learners left behind: Standardized testing as language policy.* Clevedon, England: Multilingual Matters.

Menken, K., & Kleyn, T. (2010). The long-term impact of subtractive schooling in the educational experiences of secondary English language learners. *International Journal of Bilingual Education and Bilingualism, 13*(4), 399–417.

Migration Policy Institute. (2012). *Education PK–12.* Washington, DC: Author. Retrieved from www.migrationinformation.org/integration/education.cfm

Miholic, V. (1990). Constructing a semantic map for textbooks. *Journal of Reading, 33*(6), 464–465.

Mohan, B., Leung, C., & Davison, C. (Eds.). (2001). *English as a second language in the mainstream.* Harlow, England: Pearson.

Montelongo, J.A., Hernandez, A.C., Herter, R.J., & Cuello, J. (2011). Using cognates to scaffold context clue strategies for Latino ELs. *The Reading Teacher, 64*(6), 429–434.

Muth, K.D., & Alvermann, D.E. (1999). *Teaching and learning in the middle grades* (2nd ed.). Needham Heights, MA: Allyn & Bacon.

National Center for Education Statistics. (2012a). *The nation's report card: Mathematics 2011* (NCES 2012–455). Washington, DC: National Center for Education Statistics, Institute of Education Sciences, U.S. Department of Education.

National Center for Education Statistics (2012b). *The nation's report card: Reading 2011* (NCES 2012–458). Washington, DC: Institute of Education Sciences, U.S. Department of Education.

National Clearinghouse for English Language Acquisition (NCELA). (2011). *The growing numbers of English learner students.* Retrieved from www.ncela.gwu.edu/files/uploads/9/growing_EL_0910.pdf

National Comprehensive Center for Teacher Quality. (2009). *Certification and licensure of teachers of English language learners.* Washington DC: Author. Retrieved from www.tqsource.org/pdfs/CertificationandLicensureforTeachersofELLs.pdf

National Governors Association. Center for Best Practices and Council of Chief State School Officers. (2010a). *Common core state standards for English language arts and literacy in history/social studies, science, and technical subjects.* Washington, DC: Author.

National Governors Association. Center for Best Practices and Council of Chief State School Officers. (2010b). *Common core state standards for mathematics.* Washington, DC: Author.

National Institute of Child Health and Human Development (NICHD). (2000). *Report of the National Reading Panel. Teaching children to read: An evidence-based assessment of the scientific research literature on reading and its implications for reading instruction.* (NIH Publication No. 00–4769). Washington, DC: U.S. Department of Health and Human Services.

New York City Department of Education. (2004). *The class of 2000 final longitudinal report: A three year follow-up study.* New York, NY: New York City Department of Education, Division of Assessment and Accountability.

New York City Department of Education. (2011). *New York City Department of Education graduation results: 6-year outcome cohorts of 2001–2004*

New York State calculation method by English language proficiency. New York, NY: Author. Retrieved from http://schools.nyc.gov/Accountability/data/GraduationDropoutReports/default.htm

Nieto, S., & Bode, P. (2008). *Affirming diversity: The sociopolitical context of multicultural education* (5th ed.). Boston, MA: Allyn & Bacon.

No Child Left Behind Act of 2001. 107th Congress of the United States of America. Retrieved from www.ed.gov/legislation/ESEA02/107-110.pdf

O'Malley, J.M., & Pierce, L.V. (1996). *Authentic assessment for English language learners: Practical approaches for teachers.* Reading, MA: Addison-Wesley.

Oakes, J. (1985). *Keeping track: How schools structure inequality.* New Haven, CT: Yale University Press.

Oczkus, L.D. (2010). *Reciprocal teaching at work: Strategies for improving reading comprehension* (2nd ed.). Newark, DE: International Reading Association.

Ogle, D. (1986). K-W-L: A teaching model that develops active reading of expository text. *The Reading Teacher, 39,* 564–570.

Olsen, L. (2010). *Reparable harm: Fulfilling the unkept promise of educational opportunity for California's long term English learners.* Long Beach, CA: Californians Together. Retrieved from http://www.californianstogether.org/docs/download.aspx?fileId=12

Olson, C.B., Land, R., Anselmi, T., & AuBuchon, C. (2011). Teaching secondary English learners to understand, analyze, and write interpretive essays about theme. *Journal of Adolescent and Adult Literacy, 54*(4), 245–256.

Orfield, G., Losen, D., & Edley, Jr., C. (2001). *The Civil Rights Project,* Harvard University. Cambridge, MA: The Civil Rights Project at Harvard University.

Ortiz, A. (2002). Prevention of school failure and early intervention. In A. Artiles & A. Ortiz (Eds.), *English language learners with special education needs* (pp. 31–63). Washington, DC: Center for Applied Linguistics.

Palinscar, A.C., & Brown, A.L. (1984). Reciprocal teaching of comprehension-fostering and comprehension-monitoring activities. *Cognition and Instruction, 1,* 117–175.

Pandya, C., Batalova, J., & McHugh, M. (2011). *Limited English proficient individuals in the United States: Number, share, growth, and linguistic diversity.* Washington, DC: Migration Policy Institute.

Paris, S. (2001). Classroom applications of research on self-regulated learning. *Educational Psychologist, 36*(3), 89–102.

Paris, S.G., Lipson, M.Y., & Wixson, K. (1983). Becoming a strategic reader. *Contemporary Educational Psychology, 8,* 293–316.

Parish, T., Merikel, A., Perez, M., Linquanti, R., Socias, M., Spain, M., et al. (2006). *Effects of the implementation of Proposition 227 on the education of English learners, K–12: Findings from a five-year evaluation.* Palo Alto, CA: American Institutes for Research.

Pearson, P.D., & Gallagher, M. (1983). The instruction of reading comprehension. *Contemporary Educational Psychology, 8*(3), 317–344.

Peregoy, S.F., & Boyle, O.F. (2005). *Reading, writing, and learning in ESL: A resource book for K–12 teachers* (4th ed.). New York, NY: Longman.

Peterson, D.S., & Taylor, B.M. (2012). Using higher order questioning to accelerate students' growth in reading. *The Reading Teacher, 65*(5), 295–304.

Podell, D.M., & Soodak, L.C. (1993). Teacher efficacy and bias in special education referrals. *Journal of Educational Research, 86*(4), 247–253.

Poldrack, R., Clark, J., Pare-Blagoev, E., Shohamy, D., Creso Moyano, J., Myers, C., & Gluck, M. (2001). Interactive memory systems in the human brain. *Nature, 414,* 546–550.

Powers, K., (2001). Problem solving student support teams. *The California School Psychologist, 6,* 19–30.

Pressley, M. (2000). What should comprehension instruction be instruction of? In M.L. Kamil, P.B. Mosenthal, P.D. Pearson, & R. Barr (Eds.), *Handbook of reading research* (Vol. III, pp. 545–561). Mahwah, NJ: Erlbaum.

Pressley, M. (2002). Comprehension strategies instruction: A turn-of-the-century status report. In C.C. Block & M. Pressley (Eds.), *Comprehension instruction: Research-based best practices* (pp. 11–27). New York, NY: Guilford.

Pressley, M., & Woloshyn, V. (Eds.). (1995). *Cognitive strategy instruction that really improves children's academic performance.* Cambridge, MA: Brookline Books.

Professional learning in the learning profession: A status report on teacher development in the United States and abroad. Dallas, TX: National Staff Development Council.

Ramirez, J., Yuen, S., Ramey, D., & Pasta, D. (1991). *Executive summary: Final report: Longitudinal study of structured English immersion strategy, early-exit and late-exit transitional bilingual education programs for language-minority children.* (Contract No. 300087–0156). Submitted to the U.S. Department of Education. San Mateo, CA: Aguirre International.

Rance-Roney, J. (2010). Jump-starting language and schema for English-language learners: Teacher-composed digital jumpstarts for academic reading. *Journal of Adolescent and Adult Literacy, 53*(5), 386–395.

Raphael, T.E. (1984). Teaching learners about sources of information for answering comprehension questions. *Journal of Reading, 27*, 303–311.

Raphael, T.E., Highfield, K., & Au, K.H. (2006). *QAR now: A powerful and practical framework that develops comprehension and higher-level thinking skills.* New York, NY: Scholastic.

Rasinski, T., & Padak, N. (2004). *Effective reading strategies: Teaching children who find reading difficult.* Upper Saddle River, NJ: Pearson Merrill Prentice Hall.

Readence, J., Bean, T., & Baldwin, R.S. (2001). *Teaching reading in the content areas* (8th ed.). Dubuque, IA: Kendall Hunt.

Readence, J.E., Bean, T.W., & Baldwin, R.S. (2012). *Content area literacy: An integrated approach* (10th ed.). Dubuque, IA: Kendall/Hunt.

Reardon, S., & Galindo, C. (2009). The Hispanic-White achievement gap in math and reading in the elementary grades. *American Educational Research Journal, 46*(3), 853–891.

Reutebuch, C. (2010). *Effective social studies instruction to promote knowledge acquisition and vocabulary learning of English language learners in the middle grades.* Washington, DC: Center for Research on the Educational Achievement and Teaching of English Language Learners. Retrieved from http://www.cal.org/create/resources/pubs/effective-social-studies-instruction.html

Reutzel, D.R., & Morgan, B.C. (1990). Effects of prior knowledge, explicitness, and clause order on children's comprehension of causal relationships. *Reading Psychology, 11*(2), 93–109.

Richards, C., & Funk, L. (2009). *Writing of students with LD who are also English learners.* Paper presented at the Council for Exceptional Children Convention, Seattle.

Rinaldi, C., & Sampson, J. (2008). English language learners and response to intervention: Referral considerations. *Teaching Exceptional Children, 40*(5), 6–14.

Rothenberg, C., & Fisher, D. (2007). *Teaching English learners: A differentiated approach.* Boston, MA: Pearson/Merrill/Prentice Hall.

Rowe, M. (2003). Wait-time and rewards as instructional variables, their influence on language, logic and fate control: Part one—wait-time. *Journal of Research in Science Teaching*, Vol. 40, Supplement S19-S32.

Ruddell, M.R. (2007). *Teaching content reading and writing* (5th ed.). Hoboken, NJ: John Wiley & Sons, Inc.

Ruddell, M.R., & Shearer, B.A. (2002). "Extraordinary," "tremendous," "exhilarating," "magnificent": Middle school at-risk students become avid word learners with the Vocabulary Self-Collection Strategy (VSS). *Journal of Adolescent and Adult Literacy, 45*(4), 352–363.

Rumberger, R. (2007). Lagging behind: Linguistic minorities' educational progress during elementary school. *University of California Linguistic Minority Research Institute Newsletter, 16*(2), 1–3.

Rumberger, R. (2011). *Dropping out: Why students drop out of high school and what can be done about it.* Cambridge, MA: Harvard University Press.

Rumelhart, D.E. (1980). Schemata: The building blocks of cognition. In R.J. Spiro et al. (Eds.), *Theoretical issues in reading comprehension* (pp. 33–58). Hillsdale, NJ: Erlbaum.

Saunders, W., & Goldenberg, C. (1999). The effects of instructional conversations and literature logs on limited and fluent English proficient students' story comprehension and thematic understanding. *The Elementary School Journal, 99,* 277–301.

Saunders, W., & Goldenberg, C. (2007). Talking texts: How speech and writing interact in school learning. In R. Horowitz (Ed.), *The effects of an instructional conversation on English language learners' concepts of friendship and story comprehension* (pp. 221–252). Mahwah, NJ: Erlbaum.

Saunders, W., & Goldenberg, C. (2010). Research to guide English language development instruction. In California Department of Education (Ed.), *Improving education for English learners: Research-based approaches* (pp. 21–81). Sacramento, CA: CDE Press.

Saunders, W., & O'Brien, G. (2006). Oral language. In F. Genesee, K. Lindholm-Leary, W. Saunders, & D. Christian (Eds.), *Educating English language learners: A synthesis of research evidence* (pp. 14–63). New York, NY: Cambridge University Press.

Saville-Troike, M. (1984). What really matters in second language learning for academic achievement? *TESOL Quarterly, 18,* 117–131.

Schleppegrell, M. (2004). *The language of schooling: A functional linguistic perspective.* Mahwah, NJ: Erlbaum.

Schleppegrell, M., Achugar, M., & Orteíza, T. (2004). The grammar of history: Enhancing content-based instruction through a functional focus on language. *TESOL Quarterly, 38*(1), 67–93.

Schmoker, M. (2001). *The results fieldbook: Practical strategies from dramatically improved schools.* Alexandria, VA: Association for Supervision and Curriculum Development.

Schmoker, M. (2006). *Results now.* Alexandria, VA: Association for Supervision and Curriculum Development.

Schmoker, M. (2011). *Focus: Elevating the essential to radically improve student learning.* Alexandria, VA: Association of Supervision and Curriculum Development.

Seidlitz, J. (2008) *Navigating the ELPS: Using the new standards to improve instruction for English language learners.* San Antonio, TX: Canter Press.

Shearer, B.A., Ruddell, M.R., & Vogt, M.E. (2001). Successful middle school intervention: Negotiated strategies and individual choice. In T. Shanahan & F.V. Rodriguez (Eds.), *National Reading Conference Yearbook, 50* (pp. 558–571). National Reading Conference.

Short, D. (2002). Language learning in sheltered social studies classes. *TESOL Journal, 11*(1), 18–24.

Short, D. (2006). Language and content learning and teaching. In B. Spolsky (Ed.), *Encyclopedia of Language and Linguistics* (2nd ed.). Vol. 3 (pp. 101–105). Oxford, England: Elsevier.

Short, D., & Boyson, B. (2012). *Helping newcomer students succeed in secondary schools and beyond.* Washington, DC: Center for Applied Linguistics.

Short, D., Cloud, N., Morris, P. & Motta, J. (2012). Cross-district collaboration: Curriculum and professional development. *TESOL Journal, 3*(3), 402–424.

Short, D., & Echevarría, J. (1999). The sheltered instruction observation protocol: Teacher-researcher collaboration and professional development. *Educational Practice Report No. 3.* Santa Cruz, CA, and Washington, DC: Center for Research on Education, Diversity & Excellence.

Short, D., & Echevarría, J. (2004). Teacher skills to support English language learners. *Educational Leadership, 62*(4), 9–13.

Short, D., Echevarría, J., & Richards-Tutor, C. (2011). Research on academic literacy development in sheltered instruction classrooms. *Language Teaching Research, 15*(3), 363–380.

Short, D., Fidelman, C., & Louguit, M. (2012). Developing academic language in English language learners through sheltered instruction. *TESOL Quarterly, 46*(2), 333–360.

Short, D., & Fitzsimmons, S. (2007). *Double the work: Challenges and solutions to acquiring language and academic literacy for adolescent English language learners.* Report to Carnegie Corporation of New York. Washington, DC: Alliance for Excellent Education.

Short, D., Hudec, J., & Echevarría, J. (2002). *Using the SIOP® Model: Professional development manual for sheltered instruction.* Washington, DC: Center for Applied Linguistics.

Short, D., Vogt, M.E., & Echevarría, J. (2008). *The SIOP® Model for administrators.* Boston, MA: Pearson/Allyn & Bacon.

Short, D., Vogt, M.E., & Echevarría, J. (2011a). *The SIOP® Model for teaching history-social studies to English learners.* Boston, MA: Allyn & Bacon.

Short, D., Vogt, M.E., & Echevarría, J. (2011b). *The SIOP® Model for teaching science to English learners.* Boston, MA: Allyn & Bacon.

Silverstein, S. (1964). *The giving tree.* New York, NY: Harper Collins.

Sirotnik, K. (1983). What you see is what you get: Consistency, persistency, and mediocrity in classrooms. *Harvard Educational Review, 53*, 16–31.

Skiba, R., Simmons, A.B., Ritter, S., Gibb, A.C., Rausch, M., Cuadrado, J., & Chung, C-G. (2008). Achieving equity in special education: History, status and current challenges. *Exceptional Children, 72*, 264–288.

Slater, W.H., & Horstman, F.R. (2002). Teaching reading and writing to struggling middle school and high school students: The case for reciprocal teaching. *Preventing School Failure, 46*(4), 163–167.

Slavin, R.E., & Cheung, A. (2004). How do English language learners learn to read? *Educational Leadership, 61*(6), 52–57.

Slocum, T., Mason, L., Okeeffe, B., & Bedesem, P. (2011). Empirical research on ethnic minority students: 1995–2009. *Learning Disabilities Research & Practice, 26*(2), 84–93.

Smith, D. (2009). *Introduction to special-education: Making a difference* (9th ed.). Boston, MA: Allyn & Bacon.

Snow, C.E., Burns, S., Griffin, P. (Eds.). (1998). *Preventing reading difficulties in young children.* Washington, DC: National Academy Press.

Snow, C.E., Cancino, H., De Temple, J., & Schley, S. (1991). Giving formal definitions: A linguistic or metalinguistic skill? In E. Bialystok (Ed.), *Language processing and language awareness by bilingual children* (pp. 90–102). New York, NY: Cambridge University Press.

Snow, C.E., Griffin, P., & Burns, M.S. (Eds.). (2005). *Knowledge to support the teaching of reading: Preparing teachers for a changing world.* San Francisco, CA: Jossey-Bass.

Snow, M.A., & Katz, A. (2010). English language development: Issues and implementation at grades K through 5. In California Department of Education (Ed.), *Improving education for English learners: Research-based approaches* (pp. 83–148). Sacramento, CA: Department of Education.

Solano-Flores, G., & Trumbull, E. (2003). Examining language in context: The need for new research and practice paradigms in the testing of English language learners. *Educational Researcher, 32*(2), 3–13.

Sparks, S. (2010). *Giving students a say may spur engagement and achievement.* Retrieved from http://blogs.edweek.org/edweek/inide school-research/2010

Stahl, S., & Nagy, W. (2006). *Teaching word meanings.* Mahwah, NJ: Erlbaum.

Stanovich, K.E. (1986). Matthew effects in reading: Some consequences of individual differences in the acquisition of literacy. *Reading Research Quarterly, 21*, 360–406.

State of New Jersey Department of Education. (2006). *Preliminary analysis of former limited English proficient students' scores on the New Jersey language arts and literacy exam, 2005-2006.* Trenton, NJ: State of New Jersey Department of Education, New Jersey State Assessment Office of Title I.

Stauffer, R. (1969). *Teaching reading as a thinking process.* New York, NY: Harper & Row.

Stauffer, R. (1980). *The language-experience approach to the teaching of reading* (2nd ed.). New York, NY: Harper & Row.

Steinberg, A., & Almeida, C. (2004). *The dropout crisis: Promising approaches in prevention and recovery.* Boston, MA: Jobs for the Future.

Stenner, A.J., & Burdick, X. (1997). *The objective measurement of reading comprehension.* Durham, NC: Metametrics, Inc.

Stoller, F. (2004). Content-based instruction: Perspectives on curriculum planning. *Annual Review of Applied Linguistics, 24,* 261–283.

Sullivan, P., Yeager, M., O'Brien, E., Kober, N., Gayler, K., Chudowsky, N., Chudowsky, V., Wooden, J., Jennings, J., & Stark Rentner, D. (2005). *States try harder, but gaps persist: High school exit exams 2005.* Washington, DC: Center on Education Policy.

Swain, M. (1985). Communicative competence: Some roles of comprehensible input and output in its development. In S. Gass & C. Madden (Eds.), *Input in second language acquisition* (pp. 235–256). Rowley, MA: Newbury House.

Swift, J.N., & Gooding, C.T. (1983). Interaction of wait time feedback and questioning instruction on middle school science teaching. *Journal of Research in Science Teaching, 20,* 721–730.

Sylvester, R., & Greenidge, W. (2009). Digital storytelling: Extending the potential for struggling writers. *The Reading Teacher, 64*(4), 284–295.

Syvanen, C. (2000). Recycling. In K. Samway (Ed.), *Integrating ESL standards into classroom practice: Grades 3–5* (pp. 133–149). Alexandria, VA: Teachers of English to Speakers of Other Languages.

Taboada, A., & Guthrie, J.T. (2006). Contributions of student questioning and prior knowledge to construction of knowledge from reading information text. *Journal of Literacy Research, 38*(1), 1–35.

Tabors, P.O., & Snow, C.E. (2005). Young bilingual children and early literacy development. In R.B. Ruddell & N.J. Unrau (Eds.), *Theoretical models and processes of reading* (5th ed., pp. 240–267). Newark, DE: International Reading Association.

Tatum, A. (2008). Toward a more anatomically complete model of literacy instruction: A focus on African American males and texts. *Harvard Educational Review, 78*(1), 155–180.

Teachers of English to Speakers of Other Languages, Inc. (TESOL). (2006). *PreK–12 English language proficiency standards.* Alexandria, VA: Author.

Tharp, R., & Gallimore, R. (1988). *Rousing minds to life.* Cambridge, MA: Cambridge University Press.

Thomas, W.P., & Collier, V.P. (2002). *A national study of school effectiveness for language minority students' long-term academic achievement.* Santa Cruz, CA, and Washington, DC: Center on Research, Diversity & Excellence.

Tilly, D. (2006). Response to Intervention: An overview. *The Special Edge, 19*(2), 1–5.

Tobin, K. (1987). The role of wait time in higher cognitive level learning. *Review of Educational Research, 57,* 69–95.

Tolchinsky, L., & Teberosky, A. (1998). The development of word segmentation and writing in two scripts. *Cognitive Development, 13,* 1–24.

Tomlinson, C. (2005). *How to differentiate instruction in mixed-ability classrooms* (2nd ed.). Upper Saddle River, NJ: Pearson.

Tomlinson, C., & Imbeau, M. (2010). *Leading and managing a differentiated classroom.* Alexandria, VA: Association of Supervision and Curriculum Development.

Tompkins, G.E. (2006). *Literacy for the 21st century: A balanced approach* (4th ed.). Upper Saddle River, NJ: Merrill Prentice Hall.

Torgesen, J., Houston, D., Rissman, L., Decker, S., Roberts, G., Vaughn, S., Wexler, J., Francis, D., Rivera, M., & Lesaux, N. (2007). *Academic literacy instruction for adolescents.* Portsmouth, NH: RMC Research Corporation, Center on Instruction.

Trent, S.C., Kea, C.D., & Oh, K. (2008). Research on preparing preservice educators for cultural diversity: How far have we come? *Exceptional Children, 74,* 328–350.

Treptow, M.A., Burns, M.K., & McComas, J.J. (2007). Reading at the frustration, instructional, and independent levels: Effects on student time on task and comprehension. *School Psychology Review, 36,* 159–166.

Turner, J. (2007). Beyond cultural awareness: Prospective teachers' visions of culturally responsive teaching. *Action in Teacher Education, 29*(3), 12–24.

Uribe, M., & Nathenson-Mejía, S. (2008). *Literacy essentials for English language learners: Successful transitions.* New York, NY: Teacher's College Press.

U.S. Census Bureau. (2012). *American Community Survey, 2010.* Retrieved from www.census.gov

Vacca, R., Vacca, J.A., & Mraz, M. (2010). *Content area reading: Literacy and learning across the curriculum* (10th ed.). New York, NY: Longman.

Van de Pol, J., Volman, M., & Beishuizen, J. (2010). Scaffolding in teacher–student interaction: A decade of research. *Educational Psychology Review, 22,* 271–296.

Vasquez III, E., Lopez, A., Straub, C., Powell, S., McKinney, T., Walker, Z., Gonzalez, T., Slocum, T., Mason, L., Okeeffe, B., & Bedesem, P. (2011). Empirical research on ethnic minority students: 1995–2009. *Learning Disabilities Research & Practice, 26*(2), 84–93.

Vaughn, S., Linan-Thompson, S., Kouzekanani, K., Bryant, D.P., Dickson, S., & Blozis, S.A. (2003). Reading instruction grouping for students with reading difficulties. *Remedial and Special Education, 24*(5), 301–315.

Vaughn, S., & Ortiz, A. (2011). *Response to Intervention in Reading for English language learners.* Retrieved from http://www.rtinetwork.org/learn/diversity/englishlanguagelearners

Vogt, M.E. (1989). *A comparison of preservice and inservice teachers' attitudes and practices toward high and low achieving students.* Unpublished doctoral dissertation. University of California, Berkeley.

Vogt, M.E. (2000). Content learning for students needing modifications: An issue of access. In M. McLaughlin & M.E. Vogt (Eds.), *Creativity and innovation in content area teaching: A resource for intermediate, middle, and high school teachers.* Norwood, MA: Christopher Gordon Publishers.

Vogt, M.E. (2002). *SQP2RS: Increasing students' understandings of expository text through cognitive and metacognitive strategy application.* Paper presented at the 52nd Annual Meeting of the National Reading Conference.

Vogt, M.E. (2005). Improving achievement for ELLs through sheltered instruction. *Language Learner, 1*(1), 22, 25.

Vogt, M.E. (2009). Teachers of English learners: Issues of preparation and professional development. In F. Falk-Ross, S. Szabo, M.B. Sampson, & M.M. Foote (Eds.), *Literacy issues during changing times: A call to action* (pp. 23–36). The Thirtieth Yearbook of the College Reading Association (now Association of Literacy Educators and Researchers).

Vogt, M.E. (2012). English learners: Developing their literate lives. In R.M. Bean & A.S. Dagen (Eds.), *Best practice of literacy leaders: Keys to school improvement* (pp. 248–260). New York, NY: Guilford Press.

Vogt, M.E. (2014). Reading linguistically diverse students. In S. B. Wepner, D. S. Strickland, & D. Quatroche (Eds.), *The administration and supervision of reading programs,* 5th ed. New York, NY: Teachers College Press.

Vogt, M.E., & Echevarría, J. (2008). *99 ideas and activities for teaching English learners with the SIOP® Model.* Boston, MA: Allyn & Bacon.

Vogt, M.E., Echevarría, J., & Short, D. (2010). *Teaching English-language arts to English learners with the SIOP® Model.* Boston, MA: Pearson.

Vogt, M.E., & Nagano, P. (2003). *Turn it on with Light Bulb Reading! Sound-switching strategies for struggling readers, 57*(3), 214–221.

Vogt, M.E., & Shearer, B.A. (2007). *Reading specialists and literacy coaches in the real world* (2nd ed.). Boston, MA: Allyn & Bacon.

Vogt, M.E., & Shearer, B.A. (2011). *Reading specialists and literacy coaches in the real world* (3rd ed.). Boston, MA: Allyn & Bacon.

Vygotsky, L. (1978). *Mind and society: The development of higher psychological processes* (M. Cole, V. John-Steiner, S. Scribner, & E. Souberman, Eds. and trans.). Cambridge, MA: Harvard University Press.

Walqui, A. (2006). Scaffolding instruction for English language learners: A conceptual framework. *The International Journal of Bilingual Education and Bilingualism, 9*(2), 159–180.

Watson, K., & Young, B. (1986). Discourse for learning in the classroom. *Language Arts, 63*(2), 126–133.

Webb, N.L. (1997). Determining alignment of expectations and assessment in math and science education. *NISE Brief, 1*(1), 1–8. National Institute for Science Education, University of Wisconsin, Madison.

Webb, N.L. (2002). *Depth-of-knowledge levels for four content areas.* Unpublished paper, retrieved from www.facstaff.wcer.wisc.edu/normw/All % 20content % 20areas % 20 % 20DOK % 20levels % 20328702.doc

Wei, R.C., Darling-Hammond, L., Andree, A., Richardson, N., & Orphanos, S. (2009). *Professional learning in the learning profession: A status report on teacher development in the United States and abroad.* Dallas, TX: National Staff Development Council.

WIDA (World-class Instructional Design and Assessment) Consortium. (2005–2011). *Assessing Comprehension and Communication in English State-to-State for English Language Learners (ACCESS for ELLs®).* Madison, WI: The Board of Regents of the University of Wisconsin System.

WIDA Consortium. (2007). *English language proficiency standards and resource guide, 2007 edition, prekindergarten through grade 12.* Madison, WI: The Board of Regents of the University of Wisconsin System.

Wiggins, G., & McTighe, J. (2008). *Understanding by design.* Upper Saddle River, NJ: Prentice Hall.

Williams, J.A. (2010). Taking on the role of questioner: Revisiting reciprocal teaching. *The Reading Teacher, 64*(4), 278–281.

Wixson, K., & Valencia, S. (2011) Assessment in RTI: What teachers and specialists need to know. *The Reading Teacher, 64*(6), 466–469.

Wong-Fillmore, L., & Valadez, C. (1986). Teaching bilingual learners. In M.C. Wittrock (Ed.), *Handbook of research on teaching* (pp. 648–685). New York, NY: Macmillan.

Yoon, B. (2008). Uninvited guests: The influence of teachers' roles and pedagogies on the positioning of English language learners in the regular classroom. *American Educational Research Journal, 45*(2), 495–522.

Ysseldyke, J., & Marston, D. (1999). Origins of categorical special education services in schools and a rationale for changing them. In D. Reschly, W.D. Tilly III, & J. Grimes (Eds.), *Special education in transition: Functional assessment and noncategorical programming* (pp. 1–18). Longmont, CO: Sopris West.

Zike, D. (1994). *The big book of math—Elementary K–6.* San Antonio, TX: Dinah-Might Adventures.

Zike, D. (2004a). *The big book of science—Elementary K–6.* San Antonio, TX: Dinah-Might Adventures.

Zike, D. (2004b). *The big book of United States history for middle and high school.* San Antonio, TX: Dinah-Might Adventures.

Zwiers, J. (2008). *Building academic language: Essential practices for content classrooms.* San Francisco, CA: John Wiley & Sons, Inc.

Zwiers, J., & Crawford, M. (2009). How to start academic conversations. *Educational Leadership, 66*(7), 70–73.

Index

A

Ability grouping, 155–156. *See also* Grouping students
Academic language and literacy, 10–14
    components of, 69–76
    content-specific vs. general, 12
    defined, 10–11
    definition of, 10, 69–70
    L2 learning and, 11
    research on, 12–14
    role in schooling, 11–12
    teaching of, 12
Academic learning time, 194–195
Academic standards. *See* Common Core State Standards
Academic vocabulary, 69–76. *See also* Vocabulary
    comprehensive review of, 215–216
    content, 70–71
    contextualizing, 80
    controlled, 27–28
    cross-curricular terms in, 71
    general, 71
    instructional approaches for, 75–76
    language processes and functions in, 71
    objectives for, 33, 35–36
    state standards for, 70
    subject specific terms in, 70–71
    technical terms in, 70–71
    Tier One, Two, and Three Words in, 72, 74
    word lists for, 73–74, 215
    word parts in, 71–72
Academic Word List, 73–74
ACCESS for ELLs®, 12
Achievement tests. *See also* Assessment; Standardized tests
    performance gap on, 7–9
Adapted content, 27–28, 43–45, 241
Adapted texts, 27–28
Administrators, SIOP® Protocol use by, 261
Affixes, 71–72
Allocated time, 194
Analogies, 214
Anderson et al.'s (Revised Bloom's) Taxonomy, 124–125
Antonyms, 214
Assessment. *See also* Review & Assessment
    alternatives to testing in, 21–22
    authentic, 212
    vs. evaluation, 212
    formal, 213
    formative, 212, 213
    informal, 212–213
    multidimensional, 213
    multiple indicators in, 213
    on-the-spot, 221–222
    of reading proficiency, 241–244
    SIOP® Protocol in, 261–265
    summative, 212, 213
    testing in, 211–213. *See also* Standardized tests
Assistive technology, 255
Attention
    pacing and, 195–196, 197–198
    student engagement and, 193–195, 197
    students with special needs and, 255
Audio supported text, 48–49
Audiotape texts, 103
Authentic activities, 45–46
Authentic assessment, 212

B

Background experiences. *See also* Building Background
    differences in, 65–66
    instructional impact of, 68
    learning strategies and, 119
    prior knowledge and, 68
Best practices
    for SIOP® Model framework organization, 22
    in SIOP® Protocol use, 260–261
Bird-walking, 215
Birthday Party, 158
Bloom's Taxonomy, 124–125
    Revised Taxonomy, 124–125
Body language, as feedback, 217
Books. *See* Texts
Bruner, Jerome, 120
Building Background, 64–93
    background experiences and, 66–68
    lesson evaluation for, 90–93
    links between past learning and new concepts in, 68
    for multi-level classes, 84
    overview of, 65–66
    past learning and, 68
    sample lesson for, 84–85
    student background experiences, 40–41
    teaching ideas for, 76–83
    teaching scenarios for, 85–90
    vocabulary and, 69–76. *See also* Academic vocabulary

C

Cave, Hugh B. *See Two Were Left* (Cave)
Center for Intercultural and Multilingual Advocacy (CIMA), 223
Center for Research on the Educational Achievement and Teaching of English Language Learners (CREATE), 18
Chapter summaries, 43
Character diaries, 177
Chat rooms, 219
Chunk and Chew, 198
Classroom context
    Review & Assessment components and, 211–212
    student match vs. mismatch with, 211–212
Cloze sentences, 83, 178–179
Cognates, 99, 240
Cognitive learning strategies, 117–118
Collaborative learning, 196. *See also* Interaction
    motivation and, 244–245
Collaborative strategic reading, 255
Common Core State Standards, 9–10
    content objectives and, 29, 34
    language objectives and, 33
    learning strategies and, 119, 120
    for oral language development, 150–151
    for reading, writing, listening, and speaking, 244–245
    school reform and, 9–10
    for vocabulary development, 70
Common Word Roots, 73–74
Comprehensible Input, 95–113
    clarifying content concepts and, 101–104
    described, 96
    explanation of academic tasks and, 99–101
    lesson evaluation for, 110–113
    lesson preparation and, 104
    for multi-level classes, 104–105
    overview of, 97
    sample lesson for, 105–106
    speech appropriate for proficiency level and, 97–99
    teaching ideas for, 104
    teaching scenarios for, 106–109
Comprehension checks, varying, 199
Concept Definition Map, 81–82, 184
Conditional knowledge, 119
Consonant sounds, 242, 243
Content, adapted, 27–28, 43–45, 241
Content areas, prior knowledge of, 68. *See also* Background experiences
Content-based ESL/ELD instruction, 15–17
    goals of, 15
    objectives for, 30

Content concepts, 40–41, 42–43
  instructional techniques for, 101–104
  review of, 215–216
Content objectives, 28–30
  checklist for, 39
  evaluation of, 39
  and language objectives, 38–39
  Lesson Delivery and, 191–192,
    194–195
  observability, measurability, and
    assessibility of, 193
  posting of, 215–216
  self-assessment of, 46–47
  sources of, 29, 33–34
  verbs for writing, 39
  writing of, 33–39, 45
Content vocabulary, 70–71. See also
    Academic vocabulary
Contextual definitions, 122
Controlled vocabulary, 27–28
Conversational fluency, academic
    language acquisition and, 8
Conversations, instructional, 150–151.
    See also Interaction
Correcting errors, 175–176, 216
Criterion-referenced tests, 213
Critical thinking, promotion of, 124–125
Cross-curricular terms, 71
Cultural factors, in special education,
    249–250
Culturally and linguistically diverse students,
    in special education, 249–250
Culturally responsive teaching, 67, 211,
    249, 280
Curriculum, in special education, 256

D
Declarative knowledge, 119
Deep languages, 242, 244
Definitions
  contextual, 122
  dictionary, 215
Demonstrations, 42
Depth of Knowledge (DOK) model, 125
  question levels in, 125
Dialogue Journals, 158
Diaries, character, 177
Dictation, regular vs. cloze, 178–179
Dictionaries
  personal, 81
  picture, 76
Dictionary definitions, 215
Differentiated instruction
  Background Building in, 84–85
  Comprehensible Input in, 104–105
  Interaction in, 159–160
  Lesson Delivery in, 199–200
  Lesson Preparation in, 49–50, 104–105
  Practice & Application in, 171–172,
    177–179
  Review & Assessment in, 223–224
  scaffolding in, 129–130, 160
  Strategies in, 129–130

Differentiated sentence starters, 49–50
Differentiated signal words, 84
Digital jump-starts, 76
Digital storytelling, 126
Dinner Party, 158
Directed Reading-Thinking Activity
    (DR-TA), 126–127
Directions
  clear explanation of, 99–101
  recording of, 103
Discussion. See Interaction
Dry-erase response boards, 221

E
E-journals, 199
Educational objectives, taxonomy of,
    124–125
Elaboration, 98, 123
  encouraging, 151–152
Electronic devices, in Review &
    Assessment, 219
Electronic games, 176
Engaged time, 194
Engagement, 193–195, 197
English language proficiency standards,
    12
English learners, 3–9
  access to services for, 8–9. See also
    Special education
  achievement gap and, 7–9
  and Common Core State Standards
    for reading, writing, listening, and
    speaking, 244–245
  content-based instruction for, 15–17
  demographics of, 3–4
  diversity of, 4–7
  educational backgrounds of, 4–7
  grouping of, 153–156, 177
  long-term, 5, 6
  proficiency standards for, 12
  reading, RTI and special education
    for, 237–255
Error correction, 175–176, 216
Evaluation, vs. assessment, 212
Evidence-based practice, in special
    education, 255
Expectations, clear explanation of,
    99–101
Expert Stay & Stray, 158
Explanations, clear vs. unclear, examples
    of, 101

F
Facial expressions, as feedback, 217
FAST Math, 40
Feedback, effective, 216–218
Fiction, 42–43
50-50 technique, 158
First language literacy. See L1 (first
    language) literacy
Flip charts, 176
Fluency, conversational, academic
    language acquisition and, 8

Foldables, 176
Formal assessment, 213
Formative assessment, 212, 213
Four Corners Vocabulary Charts, 81
Frequently asked questions, 278–285
Front-loading. See Jump-start
    minilessons
Frustration-level reading, 241
Frustration levels, in students with special
    needs, 256

G
Games
  electronic, 176
  hands-on, 176
  in Review & Assessment, 220
  vocabulary, 83
GIST (Generating Interactions between
    Schemata and Texts), 127–128
The Giving Tree (Silverstein), 34
Gradual release of responsibility model,
    120–121
Graphic organizers, 47–48
  completion of, 100
  effective use of, 103
  instructions for, 99–101
  learning strategies and, 128
Grouping students, 153–156. See also
    Differentiated instruction
  by ability, 155–156
  for Practice & Application, 177
  varying configurations in, 153–156
Guided practice, 172–173

H
Handheld devices, in Review &
    Assessment, 219
Hands-on materials, 42, 172–173, 176
Headline writing, 199
Hi-lo readers, 43
High-stakes testing, 213
Higher-order thinking skills, promotion
    of, 124–125
Highlighted text, 50
Homographs, 75
Hunter, Madeline, 215

I
Idioms, 98
Images. See Visual materials
Inclusion, in special education, 250–251
Independent-level reading, 241
Individualized educational plan (IEP),
    254–255
Informal assessment, 212–213
Information gap activities, 179
Instructional conversations, 150–151
Instructional-level reading, 241
Instructional scaffolding, 123. See also
    Scaffolding
Instructions
  clear explanation of, 99–101
  recording of, 104

Interaction, 143–167
  balanced approach to, 152–153
  barriers to, 145, 146–147
  benefits of, 145–146
  clarifying concepts in L1 and, 157
  described, 144
  in giving feedback, 217–218
  grouping and, 153–156
  lesson evaluation for, 164–167
  in multi-level classes, 159–160
  opportunities for, 149–153
  overview of, 145–149
  sample lesson for, 160
  teaching ideas for, 157–158
  teaching scenarios for, 161–164
  in traditional vs. SIOP® Model lesson,
    146–149
  wait time in, 156–157, 160, 256
Interdisciplinary projects, 196. *See also*
    Interaction

J
Jigsaw text reading, 47
Journals
  dialogue, 158
  electronic, 199
  vocabulary, 219–220
Jump-start minilessons, 41
  digital, 76

K
Knowledge
  conditional, 119
  declarative, 119
  prior, 68. *See also* Background
    experiences
  procedural, 119

L
L1 (first language) literacy
  clarifying concepts and, 157
  interaction and, 157, 160
  supports for, 13, 44
L2 (second language) literacy, 13
Language differences, language learning
  disabilities vs., 253
Language errors, correction of, 175–176,
  216
Language Experience Approach (LEA),
  239
Language learning strategies, 118
Language objectives, 30–39, 175
  for academic vocabulary, 33, 35–36, 37
  activities for language practice vs.,
    45–46
  checklist for, 39
  and content objectives, 38–39
  evaluation of, 39
  examples of, 37
  for language learning strategies,
    36, 37
  for language skills and functions,
    36, 37

for language structures or grammar,
    36, 37
  Lesson Delivery and, 192–193
  observability, measurability, and
    assessibility of, 193
  posting of, 215–216
  sources of, 33
  verbs for writing, 39
  writing of, 33–39
Language processes and functions
  in academic vocabulary, 71
  integration of, 175
Language skills, receptive vs. productive,
  31
Language transparency, 242
Learner outcomes, using SIOP® Protocol,
  284
Learning
  collaborative, 196, 244–245. *See also*
    Interaction
  linking past and new, 68. *See also*
    Background experiences
  self-directed, 244–245
  self-regulated, 117–120
Learning disabilities, 6–7, 252–255. *See
    also* Special education
  causes of, 252
  identification of, 245–246, 252–254
  language differences vs., 253
  site-based intervention teams for,
    254–255
Learning strategies. *See* Strategies
Lesson Delivery, 190–207
  content objectives and, 191–192,
    192–193
  language objectives and, 192–193
  lesson evaluation for, 203–207
  Lesson Preparation and, 191, 197–198
  for multi-level classes, 199–200
  overview of, 191
  pacing and, 195–196, 197–198
  sample lesson for, 200
  student engagement and, 193–195, 197
  teaching ideas for, 198–199
  teaching scenarios for, 200–203
  wrap-up techniques for, 216
Lesson evaluation
  for Building Background, 90–93
  for Comprehensible Input, 110–113
  for Interaction, 164–167
  for Lesson Delivery, 203–207
  for Lesson Preparation, 57–62
  for Practice & Application, 185–187
  for Review & Assessment, 231–234
  for Strategies, 137–141
Lesson plan sample (fourth grade social
    studies), 59
Lesson plan templates, 294–299
Lesson Preparation, 26–62
  adapted content in, 43–45
  content concepts in, 40–41
  content objectives in, 28–30, 33–39.
    See also Content objectives

example of, 52–57. *See also* Sample
    lesson
  language objectives in, 30–39. *See also*
    Language objectives
  Lesson Delivery and, 191, 197–198
  lesson evaluation in, 57–62
  meaningful activities in, 45–46
  for multi-level classes, 49–50, 104–105
  overview of, 27–28
  planning process in, 34–35
  rating with SIOP® Protocol, 51
  sample lesson for, 51–52
  supplementary materials in, 41–43
  teaching ideas for, 46–49
  teaching scenarios for, 52–57
  written objectives and, 33–39
Leveled questions, 49, 50, 178
Leveled study guides, 50
Levels of Word Knowledge, 83
Lexile levels, 27
Listening development, 244–245
Literacy. *See* Academic language and
    literacy; Reading; Writing
Literature, related, 42–43, 238–245
Long-term English learners, 5, 6

M
Manipulatives, 42, 172–173, 176
Meaningful activities, 45–46
Metacognitive learning strategies, 118
Minilessons (jump-starts), 41
  digital, 76
Mismatched schemata, 66, 67
Mistakes, correction of, 175–176, 216
Modeling
  of appropriate speech, 98
  for content concepts, 102
  as feedback, 217
Motivation, 177, 194–195
  collaboration and, 244–245
Movement
  importance of, 156
  manipulatives and, 172–173, 176
Multi-level classes. *See* Differentiated
    instruction
Multidimensional assessment, 213
Multimedia, 102
Multimedia resources, 42

N
National Assessment for Educational
    Progress (NAEP) exams, 7
National Center for Research on
    Education, Diversity & Excellence
    (CREDE), 13, 17, 18
National Literacy Panel on Language-
    Minority Children and Youth
    (NLP), 12–13, 149, 239
Native language literacy. *See* L1 (first
    language) literacy
No Child Left Behind Act, 8, 9, 191
Non-print review, in Review &
    Assessment, 220

Nonfiction, 42–43
    reading development and, 244–245
Nonverbal feedback, 217
Norm-referenced tests, 213
Not applicable (NA) category, in scoring, 263
Number 1, 2, 3 for Self-Assessment of Objectives, 46–47
Number wheels, 220–221
Numbered Heads Together, 177
Numbers 3, 2, 1 for self-assessment, 221

O
On-the-spot assessment, 221–222
Opaque languages, 242, 243
Oral language development, 244–245.
    See also Speech; Vocabulary
    consonant sounds and, 242, 243
    interaction in, 149–153. *See also*
      Interaction
    reading development and, 149–153, 242–245
    standards for, 244–245
    vowel sounds and, 242, 243
    writing development and, 149–153, 244–245
Orthographies, 242, 244
Outcome sentences, 216
Outlines, scaffolded, 48

P
Pacing, 195–196, 197–198
Paraphrasing, 98, 122
    as feedback, 217
    in vocabulary review, 214–215
Partner Share, 158
Peer coaching, 260
Performance-oriented verbs, 32
Personal dictionaries, 81
Phone a friend technique, 158
Phonics, 242
Picture dictionaries, 76
Picture walks, 239
Pictures. *See* Visual materials
Plot Chart, 76–77
Podcasts, 198
Practice, guided, 172–173
Practice & Application, 169–187
    applying content and language knowledge in, 173–174
    hands-on materials and manipulatives in, 172–173, 176
    integrating language skills and, 174–176
    lesson evaluation for, 185–187
    in multi-level classes, 171–172, 177–179
    overview of, 170–172
    sample lesson for, 179
    teaching ideas for, 176–177
    teaching scenarios for, 179–185
Pragmatics, 214
Pre-questioning, 129
Prefixes, 71–72
Pretest with a Partner, 77

Prior knowledge, 68. *See also* Background experiences
Procedural knowledge, 119
Procedural scaffolding, 123. *See also* Scaffolding
Process-oriented verbs, 32
Professional development. *See also* SIOP® Professional Development
    SIOP® Protocol in, 261, 282–283
Progress monitoring process questions, 211–212
Progress monitoring questions, 213
Progress scores, 200
Projects, 199
    interdisciplinary, 196
Pronunciation, in verbal scaffolding, 122–123

Q
Question-answer relationships, 128–129
Questioning the Author (QtA), 129
Question(s)
    about nonfiction reading, 244–245
    encouraging elaborated responses to, 151–152
    leveled, 49, 50, 178
    levels in DOK model, 125
    in progress monitoring process, 211–212, 213
    promoting critical thinking, 124–125
    wait time and, 156–157, 256

R
Radio Advice Line, 199
Readability formulae, 27
Reader's Theater, 177
Reading
    collaborative strategic, 255
    frustration level, 241
    independent level, 241
    instructional level, 241
    jigsaw text, 47
Reading aloud, 76
    of nonfiction texts, 244–245
Reading development, 238–247
    assessment and, 241–244
    oral language development and, 149–153, 242–244
    phonics and, 242
    reading levels in, 241–242
    RTI and, 238, 246–248
    standards for, 244–245
    teaching ideas for, 239
    text selection for, 242
Reading problems
    identification of, 245–246
    instructional approaches for, 246–248.
      See also Response to Intervention;
      Special education
    referral for, 240, 249–251
Realia, 42
Reciprocal teaching, 128
Recursive teaching, 121

Related literature, 42–43
Repetition, 98
    in special education, 255
Research
    on academic language and literacy, 12–14
    on SIOP® Model, 14
    SIOP® Protocol for, 265
Response boards, 221
Response to Intervention (RTI), 238, 246–248
    general education (Tier 1) component of, 247–248
    intensive intervention (Tier 3) in, 248
    online community for, 219
    targeted intervention (Tier 2) in, 248
Response to Intervention (RTI), progress monitoring questions in, 211–212, 213
Review & Assessment, 209–234. *See also* Assessment
    of content concepts, 215–216
    key vocabulary review in, 213–215
    lesson evaluation for, 231–234
    for multi-level classes, 223–224
    overview of, 210–213
    regular feedback in, 216–218
    sample lesson for, 224–225
    teaching ideas for, 219–223
    teaching scenarios for, 225–231
    throughout the lesson, 218–219
Roam and Review, 198
Role plays, 177
Roots, 71–72
    Common Word Roots, 73–74
Rubrics, in Review & Assessment, 220

S
Sample lesson(s)
    analysis of, 57–62
    for Building Background, 84–85
    for Comprehensible Input, 105–106
    content of, 51–52
    for Interaction, 160
    for Lesson Delivery, 200
    for Lesson Preparation, 51–52
    for Practice & Application, 179
    for Review & Assessment, 224–225
    SIOP® Protocol and, 265–268
    for Strategies, 130–131
    teaching scenarios for, 52–57
Scaffolded outlines, 48
Scaffolding, 120–123
    cloze sentences and, 178–179
    definition of, 120
    in differentiated instruction, 129–130, 160
    gradual increase of student independence, 121–122
    gradual release of responsibility model and, 120–121
    grouping students and, 154
    instructional, 123

interaction and, 160
in Lesson Delivery, 199
procedural, 123
in special education, 256
for student independence, 122
verbal, 121–123
Zone of Proximal Development and, 120–121
Scale, student mastery, 200
Schemata, 116
definition of, 66
mismatched, 66, 67
School reform, 9–10
Scores, progress, 200
Scoring, in SIOP® Protocol, 261–265, 270–275
assigning scores, 262–263
calculating/tallying scores, 264–265
Scoring system, in SIOP® Protocol, 286–293
Second language (L2) literacy, 13
Self-assessment
of content objectives, 46–47
levels of word knowledge, 83
3, 2, 1 for, 221
Self-directed learning, 244–245
Self-reflection guide, SIOP® Protocol as, 260
Self-regulated learning, 117–120. See also Strategies
Semitransparent languages, 242
Sentence starters, 50, 129–130
Sentence strips, 104
Sentence structure, simplification of, 99
Sentence(s)
cloze, 83, 178–179
outcome, 216
Sheltered content instruction, 15–17
goals of, 15
Sheltered Instruction Observation Protocol. See under SIOP® entries
Signal words, differentiated, 84
SIOP® Model, 14–23
Building Background in, 64–93
components of, 17–18
Comprehensible Input in, 95–113
CREDE research on, 300–305
described, 1–23
effective instruction using, 19–22
framework for, best practices for organizing, 22
frequently asked questions about, 278–285
general questions about, 279–280
getting started with, 280–282
implementation of, 23, 262
Interaction in, 143–167
learning disabilities and, 245–246
Lesson Delivery in, 190–207
Lesson Preparation in, 26–62
overview of, 14–15
Practice & Application in, 169–187

professional development resources for, 306–308
research and development of, 17–19
research studies on, 14
Review & Assessment in, 209–234
school-wide implementation of, 261, 282–285
in special education, 255
Strategies in, 115–141
supplementary materials for, 21
technology and, 21
terminology of, 19
SIOP® Professional Development
CREDE research on, 300–305
resources for, 306–308
SIOP® Protocol, 259–277. See also SIOP® Professional Development
best practices for, 260–261
CREDE research on, 300–305
example of, 268–275
learner outcomes and, 284
lesson plan templates for, 294–299
overview of, 260–261
in professional development, 261, 282–283
rating forms for, 276
rating lessons with, 51
reliability of, 277
sample lesson using, 265–268
scoring and interpretation of, 261–267, 268–275
scoring sheets for, 286–293
validity of, 277
Site-based intervention teams, 254–255
Small group minilessons, 41
Social-affective learning strategies, 118–119
Socioeconomic status, 6
special education and, 250
Special education, 6–7, 240, 248–256
culturally and linguistically diverse students in, 249–250
curriculum and, 256
evidence-based practice in, 255
IEPs in, 254–255
inclusion and, 250
overrepresented/underrepresented populations in, 249–250, 252–253
placement in, 254–255
referral for, 240, 249–251, 253–255
SIOP® Model in, 255
site-based intervention teams and, 254–255
teaching ideas for, 255–256
training in, 250
underachievement/Socioeconomic status and, 250
Speech. See also Comprehensible Input; Oral language development; Vocabulary
appropriate for proficiency level, 97–99
monitoring of, 98–99

oral language development and, 244–245
Spelling, 242, 244
SQP2RS (Squeepers), 127
for Math, 128
Standardized tests, 213. See also Assessment; Common Core State Standards
achievement gap and, 7–9
criterion-referenced, 213
high-stakes, 213
norm-referenced, 213
school reform and, 9–10
Standards-based school reform, 9–10
State standards. See Common Core State Standards
Stock Market, 222–223
Storytelling, digital, 126
Strategic Sentence Starters, 129–130
Strategies, 115–141
cognitive, 117–118
explicit instruction in, 117–120
higher-order thinking skills and, 124–125
importance of, 117
language, 118
lesson evaluation for, 137–141
metacognitive, 118
for multi-level classes, 129–130
overview of, 116
promoting critical thinking and, 124–125
sample lesson for, 130–131
scaffolding and, 120–123
self-regulated learning and, 117–120
social-affective, 118–119
teaching ideas for, 126–129
teaching scenarios for, 131–137
Student engagement, 193–195, 197
Student errors, correction of, 175–176, 216
Student independence, scaffolding for, 122
Student mastery scales, 200
Student-teacher interaction. See Interaction
Study guides, leveled, 50
Suffixes, 71–72
Summative assessment, 212, 213
Supplementary materials, 41–43
Synonyms, 214

T
Talking. See Speech
Targeted output, 170–171. See also Practice & Application
Task, pro-rating of, 199
Taxonomies of educational objectives, 124–125
Teacher-student interaction. See Interaction

Teachers
 classroom dominance by, 146–147
 culturally responsive, 251
 training for special education, 250
Teaching
 reciprocal, 128
 recursive, 121
Teaching ideas
 for Building Background, 76–83
 for Comprehensible Input, 104
 for Interaction, 157–158
 for Lesson Delivery, 198–199
 for Lesson Preparation, 46–49
 for Practice & Application, 176–177
 for reading development, 239
 for Review & Assessment, 219–223
 for special education, 255–256
 for Strategies, 126–129
Teaching scenarios
 for Building Background, 85–90
 for Comprehensible Input, 106–109
 for Interaction, 161–164
 for Lesson Delivery, 200–203
 for Lesson Preparation, 52–57
 for Practice & Application, 179–185
 for Review & Assessment, 225–231
 for sample lessons, 52–57
 for Strategies, 131–137
Technology, instructional, 21
Television talk show, 198
Templates, lesson plan, 294–299
Testing, 211–213. *See also* Assessment;
 Standardized tests
 alternative assessment measures, 21–22
Texts
 adapted, 27–28, 43–45, 241
 reading level and, 242
Thematic sets, 43
Think-alouds, 122
Think-Pair-Share, 198
Think-Pair-Square-Share, 198

Thinking skills, higher-order, 124–125
3, 2, 1 for self-assessment, 221
Thumbs up/thumbs down, 220
Tier One, Two, Three Words, 72, 74
Time
 academic learning, 194–195
 allocated, 194
 engaged, 194
Time management, 194, 196
 bird-walking and, 215–216
 pacing and, 195–196
Transparent languages, 242
Two Were Left (Cave), 84–85
 teaching scenarios for, 85–90
 word cloud example from, 89

V
Verbal scaffolding, 121–123. *See also*
 Scaffolding
Verbs
 process- and performance-oriented,
 32
 for writing content and language
 objectives, 39
Visual materials, 42. *See also* Graphic
 organizers
 for comprehensible input, 102, 103,
 104
 for content concepts, 102
 in picture dictionaries, 76
 in Review & Assessment, 220
 in special education, 255
Vocabulary. *See also under* Language;
 Word
 academic. *See* Academic vocabulary
 in Building Background, 69–76
 in Comprehensive Input, 97–99
 comprehensive review of, 215–216
 contextualizing, 80
 controlled, 27–28
 instructional approaches for, 75–76

 in Review & Assessment, 213–215
 self-assessment of, 83
Vocabulary-controlled texts, 27–28
Vocabulary games, 83
Vocabulary Journal, 219–220
Vocabulary Self-Collection Strategy, 80
Vowel sounds, 242, 243
Vygotsky, Lev, 120

W
Wait time, 156–157, 160, 256
Washam, Amy, lesson preparation
 techniques of, 34–35
WIDA standards, 12, 33
 language proficiency levels and, 98
Wiki entries, 199
Word clouds, 77–78
Word consciousness, 74–75
Word generation, 83
Word knowledge, levels of, 83
Word lists, 73–74, 215
Word parts, 71–72
Word searches, 83
Word Sorts, 78–80
Word Study Books, 83, 219
Word tiers, 72, 74
Word walls, 80–81
Wordplay, 74–75
Words, signal, 84
Wrap-up techniques, 216
Writing
 of content objectives, 33–39, 45
 of headlines, 199
 of language objectives, 33–39
Writing development, oral language
 development and, 149–153
 standards for, 244–245

Z
Zone of Proximal Development, 120–121.
 See also Scaffolding